individuality *in clothing selection and personal appearance*

individuality

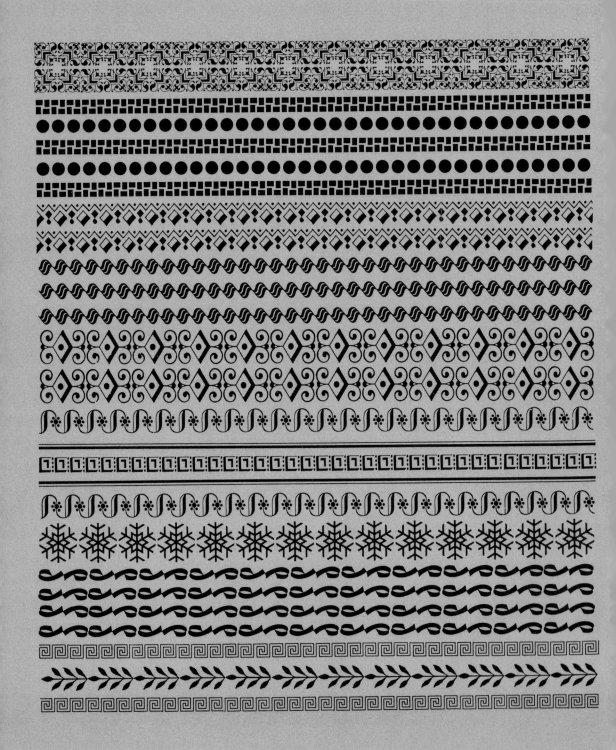

in clothing selection and personal appearance

a guide for the consumer

Mary Kefgen

California State College, Long Beach, California

Phyllis Touchie-Specht

Mt. San Antonio College, Walnut, California

THE MACMILLAN COMPANY, NEW YORK

COLLIER-MACMILLAN LIMITED, LONDON

The Macmillan Company
866 Third Avenue, New York, New York 10022

Collier-Macmillan Canada, Ltd., Toronto, Ontario

Library of Congress catalog card number: 73–121677

First Printing

to our families
and friends
for their interest,
support,
and encouragement
and
to our students,
who have taught us
so very much

preface

---

his book is designed to be used in a beginning study of clothing selection. It was developed with the concept that one must begin to understand himself before he can begin to understand those around him. The psychological, sociological, and political significance of clothing has emerged as an important area of clothing study. This text is offered as an introduction to such studies. It is believed that the student who develops an awareness of his own individuality in clothing selection and personal appearance can better appraise the importance of the clothing factor in other settings.

Special efforts have been made to make this text of use to both men and women from all ethnic backgrounds. In a society such as ours, the importance of self-presentation cannot be overlooked. In a time when traditional customs of dress are being challenged and changed, analysis of the individual's attitudes toward dress is indeed relevant. It is felt that this text will be of value to all students and therefore will be of merit in any course that considers clothing selection and personal appearance. The authors recognize that there is no one correct way to dress that must be used for everyone. This text encourages each student to evaluate his unique situation and to evolve a clothing philosophy to meet those individual needs.

A divergent and original approach has been taken regarding the traditional art principles as they apply to dress. Some of these principles no longer appear to be significant in modern clothing selection and therefore have been replaced by functional and aesthetic guidelines which current fashion expresses. These have been called guidelines rather than principles, as the latter signifies unbreakable laws and rigidity which the authors wish to avoid.

The simplified study of color is presented which relates to individual preference and personal coloring. It incorporates the use of the Color Key System and color charts. This approach will help the student gain an understanding of color so that he can learn immediately which colors to select and which to reject. This color system is supported by research from California State Polytechnic College and most other existing color systems. Most important, it applies to all races and ages.

The consumer is made aware of the economic influences of current fashion, the techniques of advertising and selling, and the pressures of an affluent society for unplanned spending. Consumer guides for planning and purchasing the wardrobe plus clothing maintenance and care are covered in a manner that relates them to the individual.

Numerous ideas have been included for enrichment assignments or activities as they relate to the subject matter in the various chapters. Suggested readings are included at the end of each chapter.

The book is not intended to be one of a scholarly nature. Rather it was the authors' intention to present a unique approach to the subject from a readable, appealing, and contemporary point of view, in order to stimulate the student to an appreciation and understanding of the importance of individuality in clothing selection and personal appearance. A complete study of the sociological, psychological, and economic aspects of dress is not within the scope of this book. These areas are included only where they have immediate application.

Each of the authors has spent many years in the classroom, developing both the materials and the philosophy presented in this text. Both authors are currently teaching in this area. Their constant contact with students in clothing selection classes has proven the merit of the subject matter included and the dire need for such a text.

The authors wish to acknowledge Mr. Sam Akers, Tournament of Roses, and Mr. Robert Dorr, Ameritone Color Key Corporation, for their most gracious cooperation. We are indebted to Mr. Chester Specht for his artistic contributions and continuous counsel. We appreciate the efforts of Noelle Jackson, Mary Lou Voight, and Christina Moran in preparation of the manuscript. We are most grateful to the many firms who granted permission to use copyrighted material and donated pictures for use in this book. We wish to extend special thanks to our many friends and colleagues who contributed ideas and suggestions that have been incorporated.

M. K.
P. T.-S

contents

xi

Contents

individuality *in clothing selection and personal appearance*

1

first impressions

*W*hen you looked at this book for the first time, you recorded an impression. The design and color of the cover, the type of print, the quality of the illustrations, the style of writing, the price—all were rapidly judged in the formation of the first impression. You might have decided the merit of the course based on this first impression. It is well known that more than one student has dropped a class simply because he did not like the first impression of the text. What was your first impression of this book?

As you read this introduction, what impressions are *you* giving to others? As you become aware that others might be judging you at this moment, what are your reactions? Are you self-conscious or full of confidence? Have you improved your posture? Are you becoming more aware of your clothing? How about your grooming? Are you as well-kempt as you would like to be? Would you like to go home and start all over again?

We are continually judged by others. The first impression is always a final impression, if there is no second encounter. What impression are you making at this moment?

importance of first impressions

First impressions are a vital form of communication in an urbanized society. Numerous first impressions are received, categorized, and acted upon. The rapidity and the completeness of the first impression are astonishing. The accuracy of first impressions is not reliable in most cases, yet lives are profoundly affected by them. In perceiving others, personal judgments and measuring devices are used. Each individual receives a unique impression based on a personal frame of reference. (See Figure 1–1.)

The importance of the first impression cannot be overemphasized. In many situations the first impression may become the last impression if a negative perception was made. An important example of this is the job interview. We are a society that moves geographically. First impressions in a new community, new school, new club, new job are significant. (See Figure 1–2.) Success in social settings is often dependent on the first impression—especially in dating! Estab-

1–1 First impressions are continually being made. What first impression are you giving now? What is your first impression of the individuals in this group? (Courtesy Australian Consulate)

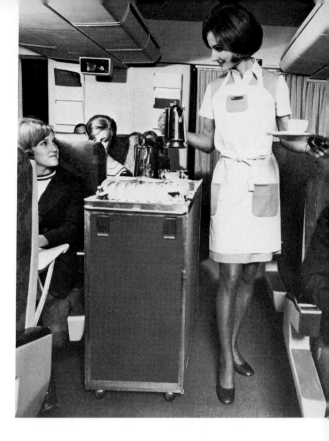

1–2   The first impression differentiates the stewardess from the rest of the passengers. The wearing of special garments for special tasks helps to distinguish persons and identifies their roles. (Courtesy Pan American World Airways)

lishing rapport in a teaching or speaking situation is often based on the initial impression. You can probably think of many other situations which would illustrate the importance of the first impression. Actually, it is hard to visualize a situation in this sophisticated society in which the individual is not continually involved in receiving and giving first impressions.

Analyze your own thinking. When you meet a person for the first time, what do you see? What messages are communicated? What judgments are made? How important is this impression? What kind of relationships will follow? Now consider the kind of first impression you made.

speed of first impressions

Allport has summarized the astonishing rapidity and completeness of the first impression:

> *With but the briefest visual perception, a complex mental process is aroused, resulting within a very short time, thirty seconds perhaps, in judgments of the sex, size, nationality, profession, and social caste of the stranger, together with some estimate of his temperament, his past suffering, his "hardness," his ascendance, friendliness, neatness, and even his trustworthiness and*

3

integrity. With further acquaintance many of the impressions would no doubt prove to be erroneous, but the exercise serves to call attention to the swift "totalizing" nature of our judgments.[1]

How does such a process come about? When we meet someone for the very first time, the effort put into the first impression is directly related to the importance we assign to the role this person is to play. For example, a person in the role of store clerk is identified; following performance of his service, the impression may be dismissed. After a lapse of time, it is often difficult to know which clerk had waited on us. However, when meeting the same clerk in a social situation, as in the home of a friend, we assign a great deal more importance to his role and appraise him much more completely. This latter type of impression is much stronger than the first type and lasts much longer. Therefore, it may be stated that the strength of the first impression is related to the importance we assign to the person we are meeting.

Let us analyze Allport's statement to determine how individual impressions are made. Judgments are made from a personal frame of reference which has been developed from both societal and psychological backgrounds. Our country, community, family, friends, education, and experiences all affect the kinds of judgments made. We judge sex by what we have learned to expect men and women to look like. Some periods of dress, particularly the recent costumed look of the hippy garb, can confuse appraisal of gender (Figure 1–3). Generally, each culture differentiates sexual accouterments. Age is judged by what we have been conditioned to expect; often age is equated to self, that is, older, younger, or about the same. Size is measured as being relative to something, often self. Nationality is rather more complex to observe, but race can be identified by even the most naive. Accurate impressions of professional and social caste are areas of great error because the beholder will identify stereotyped clues which are easily maneuverable. Emotional make-up is usually judged by facial attitudes and body movements that are identified to be indices of temperament. Grooming and cleanliness are values that carry strong connotations in the United States and are, therefore, heavily weighted in impressions. Honesty and integrity are characteristics many perceive as being visual, usually in the form of facial clues.

Judgments made in first impressions are always based on personal experiences and environmental and cultural influences. While individual impressions vary, research has shown that there are certain predictable patterns of perception among groups of population.

The complete analysis of the first impression is beyond the scope of this text. What is important is the role of clothing and personal appearance in first impressions. By developing an understanding of this facet of first impressions,

---

[1] Gordon W. Allport, *Personality—A Psychological Interpretation* (New York: Holt, 1937), p. 500.

1–3 Confusion of sexes. A variety of hair styles—short, long, and shoulder length—are displayed by three students receiving degrees at Carnegie-Mellon University, Pittsburgh, Penn. At left is a miss; the other two are men. (Courtesy United Press International)

we can employ it as a tool both in understanding others and in presenting ourselves to others.

clothing's effect on first impressions

Douty related personal perception to clothing by explaining that the way one person reacts to another on first meeting depends on the first person's impression of the role and the personality of the second person. Many reactions to people occur on a preconscious level of awareness, the effect of which can be as strong as though it were a conscious inventory. Since the person is located within the clothing, his clothing almost certainly influences another's first impression of him. Significant differences in social status and personality rating were found in this study to be associated with changes in clothing. Douty concluded that clothing did have a strong influence on the impressions one person makes of another.[2]

[2] Helen I. Douty, "Influence of Clothing on Perceptions of Persons," *Journal of Home Economics,* **55:**197–202 (March 1963).

6

Flugel believed that apart from face and hands, which are the most expressive parts of the body, what we actually see and react to are not the bodies but the clothes of those about us. From clothes we get a first impression. The study of facial features requires close inspection. Clothes, presenting as they do a much larger surface, can be clearly distinguished at a distance. It is the indirect expression of an individual through his garments and the movement of the limbs within the garments that identifies an acquaintance and further tells moods, such as friendly, angry, frightened, curious, hurried, or relaxed. In the case of the individual being met for the first time, the clothes tell at once sex, occupation, nationality, and social standing.[3]

Fitzsimmons suggested that people particularly tend to evaluate others at first meeting by their clothing, since it is the one thing about a person that can be seen by everyone. She cautioned that we are influenced by our own personal likes and dislikes in our evaluation of others. We see only what the person has on at that moment and know nothing about the influencing factors that might have affected his choice of garb. Traits such as pride and self-confidence are indicated in the care taken of personal appearance.[4]

CLOTHING CUES IN MAKING JUDGMENTS ABOUT A PERSON

Rosencranz attempted to measure the symbolic meanings attached to clothing through the use of a projective technique. A thematic apperception test was modified to examine this purpose. A series of seven drawings depicting incongruities between clothing and other aspects of the characters in the illustrations was used. Subjects were asked to tell a story about each picture. Tabulated results indicated a very strong influence of clothing cues in judgments made about the person. Rosencranz summarized that clothing is an important cue in the formation of impressions of other persons, and this is particularly significant when contact situations are limited.[5]

first impressions of classmates

Jacobson was able to draw a most interesting conclusion from a study conducted to measure the first impressions of classmates. The first impressions of 258 classmates, all Ohio University freshman women, were studied. Impres-

[3] John Carl Flugel, *The Psychology of Clothes* (London: Hogarth Press, 1930), p. 310.
[4] Cleo Fitzsimmons, *Consumer Buying for Better Living* (New York: Wiley, 1961), p. 302.
[5] Mary Lou Rosencranz, "Clothing Symbolism," *Journal of Home Economics,* **54**:18–22 (1962).

sions were classified in five categories: (1) physical characteristics; (2) intelligence; (3) clothing; (4) grooming; (5) psychological characteristics, such as traits, attitudes, and temperament. The students rated each other.

Of the five categories, responses of a psychological nature were most frequent, with grooming second, physical characteristics third, clothing fourth, and intelligence fifth. Some of the students had a slight acquaintanceship. It was found that the degree of acquaintanceship had little effect on the percentage of responses of a physical or clothing nature.

Characteristics of a physical nature, especially the face and the features, were commented on more frequently than other factors. On the whole, the students were very considerate when nothing could be done to correct the defect. They were especially critical when grooming was concerned.

There seemed to be no significant correlation between students' own personality adjustment or intelligence in the responses. They seemed to be independent of each other, except in the case of clothing, where there appeared to be a slight tendency for the more intelligent girl to comment about clothes.

Responses showed students vary greatly in their taste in dress, standards of grooming, and in their interpretation of traits, attitudes, and criteria for "good looks." Clothing and grooming showed the greatest percentages of responses.[6]

first impressions of an instructor on students

Lones did a study relating clothing to first impressions of an instructor. The study was conducted in a clothing selection class. Undergraduate college men and women, from varying major fields, participated in this classroom experiment. Seeing the instructor for the first time, they were asked to evaluate her. Instructions were given in written form. The instructor, new in the college, simply stood in front of the class. Evaluations were written anonymously.

Tabulation of the responses revealed the following:

11.4 per cent of the students mentioned the color of the costume worn by the instructor.

25.7 per cent did not mention clothing or grooming.

2.8 per cent who did not mention clothing drew conclusions not possible if clothing were not taken into consideration.

[6] Eilma E. Jacobson, "First Impressions of Classmates," *Journal of Applied Psychology,* **29**:148–55 (1945).

This poses a question, then, whether to consider 25.7 per cent or 28.5 per cent of the students as not being clothes-conscious, since they did not mention clothing.

A total of 68.8 per cent indicated that their faith in the instructor's ability to teach clothing selection was influenced by her own clothing and grooming. Eighty per cent of those who did not mention clothing discussed the instructor's ability to teach and/or to discipline. And 90.9 per cent of the students related their opinion of her ability to teach to the way she looked.

Lones concluded that this result lends some support to the belief that the way one dresses is very important and might even result in "success" or "failure" in one's particular field. Especially for the teacher, first impressions are vitally important.[7]

The authors, in an attempt to make this research more current, followed the pattern of the Lones study in several clothing selection classes. Women students in a junior college, from varying major academic fields, participated in this classroom survey. The instructor had been on the staff for several years but was known to very few of the students participating in the study.

The instructor entered the classroom ten minutes after the class was scheduled to meet. She greeted the class with a smile and said, "Good morning." She then asked the students to fill out the paper she distributed while she moved around the room. The paper stated:

Apparel Analysis 15
Mt. San Antonio College

First impressions are an important part of interpersonal relationships. This will be our first topic. For the purpose of further study, WRITE YOUR FIRST IMPRESSION OF THE INSTRUCTOR. Do not sign this paper.

The results of this questionnaire showed that all students commented on the personal appearance and manner of the instructor. Many assessed her knowledge of the subject and her teaching ability. Several projected guesses as to the type of class this would be as presented by this instructor. The following list shows the kinds of comments that were made in the various areas.

Appearance

Hair style attractive, suitable, fashionable	Lovely eyes
Make-up well done, makes the most of self	Fashionable
Takes care of self	Not faddy
Up-to-date	Well dressed
Has an eye for fashion	Presents best self

[7] Lelia Lillian Lones, "Clothing and First Impressions," *Journal of Home Economics,* **45:**740–42 (Dec. 1953).

Manner

Nice	Friendly	Pleasing
Poised	Easy to like	Flexible
Kind	Nice personality	Late
Self-confident	Bright	Tardy
Sincere	Creates happy atmosphere	Takes life as it comes
Warm	Good humor	

Class Projection

Will be easy to work with   Brightly colored dress helps classroom atmosphere

Fun to get to know   Fits this type of class

Ability to Teach

Could learn from her	Knows fashion
Will make this class worthwhile	Knows good clothing
Practices what she teaches	Shows she knows her subject

summary of research

While the research exploring the influence of clothing and personal appearance in the formation of first impressions is extremely limited, that which is available is significant. All studies show strong evidence that clothing and personal appearance are vital factors in the formation of first impressions.

Clothing, because it covers such a large part of the body and because it is familiar to all, is used as an index in making judgments. There is some evidence of a relationship between intelligence and a sensitivity to clothing.

First impressions are deeply affected by the frame of reference of the observer. Interpretations of the apparel being observed are very personal. A variety of people will have a variety of impressions.

Physical handicaps are not as significant in a first impression as clothing and grooming. A physical handicap, particularly one that cannot be corrected, is often overlooked and always forgiven. Untidy appearance and poorly selected clothing are rarely ignored.

Many of the studies related ability with presentation of self and clothing selection. In the various areas of education, and particularly in home economics, this is a most significant finding. Students often decide what type of course will be conducted, the skills, and the knowledge of the instructor by their first impression. This finding has important application in all fields of business and industry where personal contact is used. The salesman, the designer, the banker, and the lawyer all make an initial impression on which depends the "success" or "failure" of a particular enterprise.

A first impression is always a final impression if no further impression is made. In the complex and competitive society in which we live, there are many occasions where there is no second opportunity. Understanding the significance of clothing and personal appearance presents an effective tool which the student can employ in the presentation of himself and in judging others.

nonverbal communication of clothing

Clothing transmits a message. It is seen before the voice is heard. Sensitivity to the message depends on a number of variables such as setting, task acquaintanceship, cultural background, experience, and awareness. Certain

1–4 Nonverbal communication of clothing. The traditional wedding gown transmits a message which can be understood by all. Specific behavior of the wearer is anticipated when this ensemble is seen. (Courtesy Du Pont Company)

1–5 *Left,* nonverbal communication of the theater costume. *Right,* these costumes from a Noel Harrison television special depict period of history, role of the player, and mood of the sketch. (Courtesy Celanese Corporation)

types of clothing are always related to specific behavior. The perceiver automatically associates the action with the dress. Cultural and geographical differences sometimes indicate certain unfamiliar costumes, but once the regional differences are understood the clothing-behavior association is made. Some examples of nonverbal communication of clothing in our society are traditional wedding gowns, sports uniforms, occupational garb, and fraternal costumes (Figure 1–4).

THEATER COSTUME

One of the most exciting places to observe the impact of nonverbal communication of clothing is in the theater. The costume is founded upon a definite and psychological basis. It is the visible sign and symbol of its wearer. The script usually indicates the historic period, the environment, and the relationship of the characters with each other. The costumer translates these facts into visible signs. The costume must, in the first few minutes on stage, nonverbally communicate the period of history, the social status, and the environment, along with the relationship of the character with those on stage and those yet to be seen (Figure 1–5).

11

It has been said that clothing does not make the man, but it does much to explain him. By use of drape, fit, fabric, and color a costume is designed to quickly reveal the various performers. The silent communication of the garb sets the mood, historical period, and environment, makes introductions, and gives clues to expected behavior, thus saving pages of dialogue. What covers the body reveals the character.

SUBDIVISIONS OF NONVERBAL COMMUNICATION OF CLOTHING

What clothing communicates, nonverbally, can be subdivided into three dimensions: emotion, behavior, and differentiation. While there is overlapping or blurring of the message at times, distinctions can be made. Social psychology, in its many phases, is currently doing exciting research in each of these facets of clothing communication. Results of some of the findings of this research are being incorporated into programs in many social institutions, particularly those dealing with mental health and penal rehabilitation.

Emotion

The posture of the skeletal frame and the movement of the body within clothing, combined with the selection of raiment, communicate strong emotional messages. Vivid examples of this are found in the Bible where many references are made to the use of clothing to convey emotional feelings. The wearing of sackcloth expresses grief or agony; the rending of garments shows indignation or despair; Joseph's coat of many colors communicates joy.

Clothes express feelings of individual happiness which are communicated to others as indicated by the colloquial term, "glad rags." Festive or party clothes differ from everyday work clothes and allow the wearers to experience a freedom and gaiety which is transmitted to others (Figure 1–6). "Sunday clothes," while perhaps not too different from party or workday clothes, transmit a unique message in keeping with the wearer's religious beliefs.

Anthropologists have noted that for countless generations special clothes have been worn by people the world over as symbols of mourning. The length of time the special clothes are worn depends on the customs of the culture and the rank of the one being mourned. Color indicating mourning varies greatly from one area to another. (See Figure 7.) "Widow's weeds," a special black ensemble, was designed to symbolize the wife's grief. "Widow's weeds," when worn long enough, begin to communicate a different message—that the widow-lady is available for another husband!

The wedding pageant we are accustomed to in the United States illustrates emotional communication of clothing. The bride, marrying for the first time, wears a white gown, which symbolizes purity and virginity. If she marries for a second, third, fourth, or fifth time, the absence of the white gown tells the guests what

1–6 Happiness and pride are communicated by the party clothes worn by the child on the right. The everyday garb of the other children is irrelevant in their flirtation. (Courtesy Celanese Corporation)

1–7 An Australian aborigine of Arnhem Land, Northern Territory, painted for a Pukamuni or funeral ceremony. (Courtesy Qantas)

1–8 Traditional dress. Filipino girls in national costume. (Courtesy Qantas)

they already know. The bridal veil, which is used quite universally, originated as protection from evil eyes or evil spirits. The flowers used in the ceremony, particularly orange blossoms, symbolize love and fertility. The bridesmaids' array, while adding to the beauty of the ceremony, also communicates that the girls are available for marriage. The bridegroom seldom wears white in the United States but is often dressed in the same black suit associated with funerals!

Clothing has been used to arouse mass emotions such as patriotism and nationalism. Positive examples of this are the beautiful traditional costumes of each area of the world. Other examples of this are the devastating results of the "brown shirts" of the Nazis; the peasant garb of Red China; and the Green Beret. (See Figures 1–8 and 1–9.)

Most women have experienced at some time the wonderful emotional elation of a new garment or hair style. For many females, the quickest way to "lose the blues" is a shopping spree or an afternoon at the beauty salon.

Other illustrations of clothing conveying emotional messages may be de-

14

veloped. The desire to advertise emotions represented by various kinds of cloth- 15
ing motivates the choice of garb. Use of clothing to communicate emotion is
universal.

Behavior

We have established as part of our civilization rules for social behavior.
Conformity to these rules is generally expected, and deviation from these rules

1–9 Apprentice Geisha girls in Kyoto, Japan, model traditional Japanese
make-up and dress. (Courtesy Pan American World Airways)

is disapproved. There is a close relationship between clothing and behavior. Special kinds of behavior can be produced by the wearing of special kinds of clothing. This behavior can be socially acceptable or not. Illustrations of the relationships between clothing and behavior are found in various segments of society.

Children will show marked changes in behavior when tubbed, scrubbed, and "dressed up." While the puberty rite of boys donning their first long pants and girls putting up their hair and lengthening their skirts has long been relegated to ancient Americana, some types of clothing still have a maturing effect on children. The little boy dressed in his first Cub Scout uniform seems to grow in stature and acquire brusque military airs. For the young girl, the wearing of a "training bra" and sheer nylons marks the transformation into *femme fatale.*

Marked changes in behavior may be observed when women wear pants, even though fashion has made them socially acceptable. These changes may be observed in the behavior of both the women wearing the pants and the reactions of the men around her. Most women become more casual in their posture and less refined in their actions. Most men react accordingly, extending fewer courtesies to the pant-clad female. Compare the extremes in social graces between a bowling date in slacks and a prom in formal attire.

Hiding behind costumes and masks, Mardi Gras celebrants carry on their activities. Hell's Angels find courage in motorcycle garb. This apparel imparts a courage to its wearer that is part of the behavior pattern assumed with the choice of clothing. The soldier feels braver, the policeman more courageous, the Boy Scout more adventuresome, when they sally forth in their uniforms.

The clothes of the very poor, and the feelings of inadequacy or inferiority experienced by those wearing them, strongly affect behavior. A vital part of the Women's Job Corps training program is counseling in clothing selection and a clothing allowance to purchase new apparel.

Differentiation

Clothing can be used to show differentiation among peoples. Many of the theorists believe this is one of its primary purposes. The differentiation may be one of several types, showing differences from one society to another or differences within the society.

The recent hippy movement illustrates the use of clothing to express differentiation. Although hippies exhibit a wide variation in personal adornment, the clothing selected is identified with the cult.

Stereotyped societal uniforms are often attached to various cultures as means of differentiation. Generally, these stereotypes are completely antiquated, yet many people cling to such stereotypes, as Eskimos exclusively in parkas; Mexicans only in sombreros and serapes; Hawaiians always in grass skirts (Figure 1–10); Africans never in anything but skin! Such typing contributes also to harmful and completely unnecessary prejudices.

1–10 Stereotyped societal uniforms such as these grass skirts are often associated with people of the South Seas. Here Tahitian dancers greet tourists at an air terminal, thus promoting such typing. (Courtesy Qantas)

Differentiation on a clothing basis is to be found everywhere. Obvious uniforms are those of the clergyman, the military, the police. Many schools and clubs have special dress (Figures 1–11 and 1–12). Service people such as clerks, maids, and waitresses often have a hierarchy of dress that differentiates them from those they serve. Subgrouping of these orders is continued by the use of insignia, color, cut, or fit of the uniform. Less obvious differentiation is found in

17

1–11 Women love a uniform! The eight-year-old cub scout maintains proper military aloofness amongst his admirers. (UPI Photo)

1–12 Japanese school girls wear uniforms that differentiate them from others. (Courtesy Consulate General of Japan)

18

1–13 A high school fad is exhibited by these young ladies of Union, New Jersey. Compare this illustration with the Australian aborigine in mourning (Figure 1–7). (Courtesy United Press International)

social groupings such as women's clubs, schools, and fraternal organizations which do not have a specific uniform yet tend to have a certain style of dress. Often these groups have some badge that indicates stratification among members.

High school students frequently create clothing fads to differentiate among themselves. Some of these fads, such as abstract paintings on jeans and tennis shoes, are unique to a small group; while others, like the varsity sweater, are passed from one generation to another. (See Figure 1–13.)

Differentiation in dress serves as a device to identify a stranger and quickly determine social attitudes to be used toward him. Errors in judgment are possible, of course, but in a society where brief social contacts are numerous clothing becomes an important index to behavior and status.

conclusions

Personal accouterments assist the individual in presenting an image and in expressing himself. He can manipulate his appearance to fit his interpretation of a specific role, adjusting to the variety of situations in which he finds himself.

As a man presents himself, so he is perceived. The first impression is made with great rapidity. Clothing and personal appearance are perceived as an important part of the first judgment. Clothing is a form of nonverbal communication that conveys emotion, behavior, differentiation. As the body is located within the garments, it is the clothing or the movement of the clothing that creates the impact of the first impression. The perceiver interprets clothing in his own personal frame of reference.

As new methods of research become available, especially in the areas of home economics and social sciences, more valuable studies can be conducted to measure the influence of clothing and appearance on man. Understandings gained will cast light on the total picture of human behavior.

The student of clothing selection is in an excellent position to experiment with the effect of clothing and personal appearance on both himself and those around him. Understanding the role of clothing in first impressions and other interpersonal relations will give the student an effective tool to employ in life situations. The student is further challenged to analyze himself from all aspects so that he may understand better the role of clothing and personal appearance in his life and utilize this information in his daily living.

suggested readings

Coleman, J. S. *Adolescent Society.* New York: The Free Press, 1961.

Douty, Helen I. "Influence of Clothing on Perceptions of Persons." *Journal of Home Economics,* **55** (March 1963), 197–202.

Fitzsimmons, Cleo. *Consumer Buying for Better Living.* New York: John Wiley & Sons, Inc., 1961.

Flugel, John Carl. *The Psychology of Clothing.* London: The Hogarth Press, Ltd., 1930.

Goffman, E. *Behavior in Public Places.* New York: The Free Press, 1963.

Langner, Lawrence. *The Importance of Wearing Clothing.* New York: Hastings House Publishers, Inc., 1959.

Morton, Grace. *The Arts of Costume and Personal Appearance.* New York: John Wiley & Sons, Inc., 1964.

Proceedings of the Eleventh Conference of College Teachers of Clothing, Textiles, and Related Arts. Western Region. Logan, Utah: Utah State University, Oct. 1964. P. 23.

Ruesh, Jurgen, and Weldon Kees. *Nonverbal Communications: Notes on the Visual Perception of Human Relations.* Berkeley: University of California Press, 1956.

Ryan, Mary Shaw. *Clothing: A Study in Human Behavior.* New York: Holt, Rinehart & Winston, Inc., 1966.

Walkup, Fairfax Proudfit. *Dressing the Part.* New York: Appleton-Century-Crofts, Inc., 1950.

2

developing objectivity

One of the most difficult observations to make is to see ourselves as we really are. Close your eyes and try to visualize your own face. Now try to see the face of a close friend. Which comes in most clearly? Probably it is the face of the friend! It is extremely difficult, and impossible for some, to clearly visualize the self-image. Yet, seeing ourselves in an objective manner is vital to applying the principles and theory of a clothing selection study to oneself. Objectivity is one of the most complex areas of learning; it requires analytical thinking, insight, and maturity. The failure on the part of too many individuals to view themselves with complete objectivity is obvious by the way they adorn themselves. It also explains why too many excellent students of clothing construction appear frumpy. They have not learned to be objective about themselves. They select garments that exhibit all the techniques of construction they do so well; yet the end result shows that they do not have an understanding of clothing with application to themselves.

The old Chinese proverb, "We see ourselves with what is behind our eyes," beautifully explains why objectivity about oneself is so difficult to achieve. Because of the phenomenal complexity of each human being, the factors influencing who we are and what we think we are produce a kind of "mirror myopia," which allows us to see only what we want to see.

To develop an accurate image of oneself, several types of study are required. You must analyze your physical self—your body, your limbs, hands, feet, your face, your features, your coloring, your hair. You must analyze the image you wish to project; what you think of yourself and what you want others to think of you. You must evaluate the kind of life you lead and the kind of life you expect to lead five to ten years in the future. You need to decide the kind of clothing you like and feel comfortable in. You need to understand yourself, the influences that control your life and direct your choices. When you have carefully and honestly completed this thorough self-analysis, you will have a much more accurate picture of yourself. You still may not have a crisp visual image of you, but you will have a mental image that will do just as well.

It is the purpose of this text to assist you to develop self-analysis; to present theory, guidelines, ideas, and information that will help you to develop a clothing philosophy that will represent you as you wish to be presented to the world. In essence, this is a laboratory course, and you are the subject to be dissected. You will find that as you become involved in the subject matter the study of clothing selection and personal appearance requires constant attention. Every place you go and everyone you meet presents new subject matter. This area of study is most dynamic and exciting!

To those who have never considered the importance and impact of clothing on their lives and the lives of those around them, the study of clothing selection and personal appearance may seem frivolous. As a home economics student, you have probably been teased about enrolling in such a "cinch course." In answer to this taunt, we would challenge both you and your teasers to name another area of study that draws on more root subjects for theory and research or has a stronger relationship and influence on daily life.

The study of clothing selection and personal appearance can challenge all intellects. It involves problems of engineering (fit and construction), chemistry (textiles and cosmetics), physiology (anatomy and physical fitness), art (color and design), psychology (self-concept, interpersonal relationships), sociology (societal concepts), anthropology (cultural aspects), history (historical foundations), and economics (expenditure per capita, industrial contribution). It is the assemblage and application of this variety of interdisciplinary knowledge that delineates the scope of this course. The material can be highly academic, presenting subject matter for research in doctoral studies; or it can be simplified for presentation to Girl Scouts and Blue Birds. That this discipline of study is of great importance cannot be denied. As illustrated in the first chapter, individual success or failure can be attributed to dressing habits. In the economy of the United States, expenditures on clothing and cosmetics represent approximately thirty-seven billion dollars annually. The sad fact that there are so many atrociously dressed men and women, in all strata of the population, emphasizes the need for study, research, and understanding in this area.

We hope you will accept the intellectual challenge of this text. Try to apply what you are learning to yourself and to everyone you see. Study with an open mind, for this is a prime requisite in developing objectivity. When you encounter personal prejudices, which you will, examine them and understand them (you may keep them but know why). This class can be a tool to help you understand yourself and your fellow being. Use it. We think you will have fun, too!

what influences the choice of clothing?

To develop objectivity about oneself and one's selection of personal adornment, a broad study of the influences in selection of clothing is necessary. By understanding the importance of the variety of factors influencing personal adornment, we can better interpret individual choices.

What are our reasons for wearing clothing? The answers to this question can be categorized in three areas: protection, modesty, and decoration. Langner called attention to many primitive societies where the decorative feature has long preceded the need for protection. He dismissed modesty by quoting an anonymous writer who said, "Modesty is a feeling merely of acute self-consciousness due to appearing unusual and is the result of wearing clothing rather than the cause." [1] Langer ascribed to clothing an exceedingly important place in the development of civilized societies. He noted that man from earliest times has worn clothes to overcome his feelings of inferiority and to achieve a conviction of his superiority to the rest of creation. Clothing is worn to win admiration and assure man that he "belongs." [2]

If the three basic reasons for wearing clothing are analyzed in a modern setting, they continue to hold true. Technology of the twentieth century has made possible the complete insulation of the individual from the elements. The pattern of our lives requires very little exposure to the weather; this exposure is generally a choice rather than a necessity. Therefore, clothing for protection is absolutely necessary only for brief periods of time. (See Figures 2–1 and 2–2.)

Wearing clothing for modesty is well explained by Langner. If no one wore clothing, there could be no feelings of modesty. Folkways and customs are probably most responsible for the habits of clothing (Figure 2–3). In our society we are clothed from birth to burial. Our clothing becomes a second skin, and we

---

[1] Lawrence Langner, *The Importance of Wearing Clothing* (New York: Hastings House, 1959), p. 72.
[2] *Ibid.,* p. 12.

2–1 Clothing worn for protection. The native garb of Morocco has evolved to protect its inhabitants from the wind, heat, or cold of the area. The headdress may be arranged to protect the face completely if so desired. (Courtesy Pan American World Airways)

2–2 These children of northern Japan live in a district of abundant snowfall. From October to March the people are virtually buried under snow. Children of the area wear this type of clothing for protection. Colorful hoods and scarves denote the school district of the children. (Courtesy Consulate General of Japan)

2–3 These women of Ovambo, Southwest Africa, do not consider their attire immodest as it is the accepted dress of their area. Folkways and customs are probably most responsible for clothing habits. (Courtesy South African Consulate General)

are uncomfortable without it. While feelings toward bodily exposure have changed radically in recent years, public nudity is rarely acceptable in our society. We must wear clothing, and it is the clothing habit that makes us modest.

The last reason listed for wearing clothing, for personal adornment, remains the most significant. This is the principal reason people continue to wear clothing. Most people select clothing to make themselves more attractive. Personal differences are responsible for the wide variety of individual choices of adornment, but each choice is made in the belief that it enhances the appearance of the wearer. (See Figure 2–4.)

2–4 Clothing worn for self-adornment. A Balinese child prays before a statue of a god. (Courtesy Qantas)

2–5 The culture or society to which one belongs determines how one will dress. These festively dressed children are from West Highland, New Guinea. (Courtesy Qantas)

WHY DO WE WEAR A CERTAIN TYPE OF CLOTHING?

One of the primary influences on the type of clothing worn is the cultural or societal group to which we belong (Figure 2–5). Although mass media and modern transportation have broken down some of the cultural differences and there seems to be a general trend toward westernization of dress, firm cultural patterns of dress do remain in many parts of the world. In the United States, women have a broad choice of skirts and pants: in Africa, in the Sahara, nomadic tribeswomen are covered by the *burnoose* (hooded cloak); in Pakistan women select the *shalwar* (trouser) and *kmeez* (long shirt) or the *sari* (draped fabric) and *choi* (blouse); and in Java women wear the *batik sarong* and *kebaya* (blouse).

Climate, geography, and the era influence cultural choices of clothing. As mankind has adapted his life to survive in a fantastic variety of habitats, clothing has been created to meet the needs of the locales. Hence, we have the sarong of the South Seas, the parka of the Far North, the loincloth of the tropics, the spacesuit for interplanetary exploration (Figure 2–6). In technical societies, the

2–6 Man has always adapted his clothing to his habitat. The latest example of this is found in the spacesuit worn in interplanetary travel. (Courtesy NASA)

evolution of fashion is closely related to industrialization, whereas in nontechnical societies styles remain more static. In the United States, which is rated among the most industrial societies, fashions have always been an important part of the culture. Since the founding of the nation up to the present, fashions have changed with inventions and technological improvements. Fashion also represents an important part of the American economy. In India, which is among the least industrial societies, the *sari* for women and the *doti* for men have been worn for centuries. Although subtle changes in the fabric design and drape of the *sari* are found, fashion is not an important part of the Indian economy.

The polity and ideals of a society are reflected in the dress of the nation. In a totalitarian state clothing is regulated by the state. In a democratic state choices are made by the individual. Many religions have some influence on the clothing of its followers: the Jews wear the *yarmulke* (skullcap); the Moslem women wear the *burkah* so no man can see them uncovered; the Amish disdain modern dress and ornamentation; and the Catholics, who in the United States traditionally have women cover their heads, in Europe have them cover their arms and in Asia have them cover neither head nor arms.

Attitudes toward women and their degree of emancipation are reflected in the freedom of clothing selection. In a society where women are shielded or protected from outside contact, their clothing choices are also restricted. Study of the history of the active sportswear of women in the United States will reveal changes in attitudes toward women (Figures 2–7 and 2–8), as will clothing needs of the working woman.

Attitudes toward children are also reflected in dress (Figure 2–9). In a society that pampers and cherishes its children, the clothing of the young meets the needs of children. The bell anklets of the Indonesian children are a delightful example of this. Children are always carried by an adult until long past walking stage. At a symbolic ceremony the bell anklets are placed on the child. This ceremony commemorates a stage in the child's life and also provides a protective device to warn the family if the child should meet with danger or wander too far.

Customs and folkways are maintained which influence dress. The wearing of gloves to protect the hands from soil is still expected, even though modern cleanliness makes this unnecessary in many cases. We like the finishing touch of gloves, so we continue to wear them. Custom decrees that the later in the day the occasion, the more formal the attire. Clothing selected for breakfasts, brunches, or luncheons is always less formal than that chosen for dinner. The

2–7 Attitudes toward women and their degree of emancipation are reflected in their clothing. Changes of attitudes toward women are shown in these tennis dresses. On the left Molly Bjursted and Eleanor Sears dress for tennis in 1918. (Courtesy United Press International and Simplicity Pattern Company)

2–8 The body-revealing swimsuits of the 1970s contrast sharply with those of yesteryear. The suits are not only brief, but figure-clinging as well. (Courtesy Catalina) At left, Actress Gloria Swanson models a swimsuit of the twenties. (Courtesy United Press International)

later in the day the wedding, the more formal the attire. Dress for matinee performances in the theater or symphony is more casual than for evening performances.

Current events have a very strong influence on clothing choices. Interest in regional attire, such as Afghanistan, Mexican, or Argentine, may be stimulated by political happenings in those areas. (See Figures 2–10 and 2–11.) Popular movies and television series create fashion inspiration. Wars, recessions, prosperity, and affluence all are reflected in apparel. The revolution in dress introduced by the Beatles broke down some very firmly entrenched male clothing habits on all socioeconomic levels by bringing back the costume look, complete with jewelry, beards, and long hair.[3]

In the United States ethnic backgrounds can make a difference in clothing

[3] Thomas Thompson, "A Peer with Unlordly Ambitions," *Life*, **65**:35–41 (July 26, 1968).

selection. Research studies in this area are quite superficial and findings, to date, not too decisive. Racial influence is most likely to be strongest when the ties to the countries of origin are the strongest. For this reason the Indian exchange student may cling to her *sari,* while she is in school; if she marries and continues to live in the United States, she may eventually adopt Western dress. Older generations, which remain close to the land of their origin, may influence younger generations. The Mexican grandmother may urge black clothing on her granddaughter; the Chinese grandfather may delight in seeing his granddaughter in the *ch'i pao.* Asians or Africans, even though they are third- or fourth-generation Americans, may elect to wear native costumes on certain occasions because they are proud of their cultural heritage. Displays of national or regional costumes may be found at festivals of the Swiss, Mexican, Scotch, Austrian, and American Indian for the same reason.

Economic status probably has more influence on clothing choices than race. Often members of a lower economic level will spend proportionally more of their income for clothing. Several reasons may be responsible for this: (1) their total income is less, so a larger percentage of it is required just to cover them; (2) the types of clothing available in their price range, or shopping centers, may not have lasting qualities; (3) clothing can be a common denominator: when one leaves home and family to go out to school or business, clothing can be a passport to a different existence.

The size of the community in which one lives has been noted to influence selection of clothing. Studies show that the smaller the community, the less emphasis there is on clothing. Perhaps an explanation of this lies in the hominess

2–9 Attitudes toward children are reflected in dress. These charming, leaf-clad children steal the scene at a Polynesian feast in the Pacific Kingdom of Tonga, southeast coast of Fiji. (Courtesy Qantas)

2–10 Regional interest inspires fashion design. This Tunisian-style tunic of unbleached cotton is worn as a man's beach cover-up. (Courtesy National Cotton Council)

2–11 Japanese-style kimonos are translated into rich cotton terry robes. On the left is a screen-printed butterfly design, on the right a bold black and white motif that says "I Love You" in Japanese. (Courtesy National Cotton Council)

of the rural area. In a small town everyone usually knows a great deal about everyone else; a change in dress is not going to impress anyone. However, with mass media and rapid transportation, the "rural rube" has disappeared. Clothing choices are much less limited in rural areas than in years past. If the small town does not have the types of stores a woman desires, she has the means to go to the cities that do. Today's farm wife may be just as chic and sophisticated as the corporation wife—and that goes for the farmer's daughter, too!

roles in society

Each complex society assigns to its citizens cultural roles. The individual assumes a number of these roles in the activities of his life. Each sex, age, socio-economic, occupational, and regional group has certain characteristics assigned to it by the culture. The individuals within these groups tend to follow the patterns expected by the society. Clothing is used as a means of defining the role presently being enacted. For example, a middle-aged woman may be a wife, mother, daughter, teacher, and golfer in suburban California. Her wardrobe would include a variety of garments ranging from sophisticated to very casual. Some of the clothing could do double duty and be appropriate for wear in her roles at home, in the classroom, and in the community. Her very sophisticated party dresses would not be acceptable in the classroom nor would her casual golf garb.

In our culture clothing does not distinguish age or marital status. It is generally assumed that as men and women mature, they will adopt a more reserved state of dress. This is not always true. Americans are both severely criticized and greatly admired for their clothing choices. What is suitable, appropriate, and in good taste for one is not always acceptable for another.

The pressures of our society are not the only forces which influence clothing selection and behavior. Just as groups vary greatly in their thinking toward apparel and appearance, so do individuals. Because clothing is such an intimate part of ourselves, derogatory remarks made about clothing become personal insults. They cast aspersions not only on our appearance but on our personal tastes and preferences as well. William James, the psychologist, summarized it in this manner:

> *The old saying that the human person is composed of three parts—soul, body, and clothes—is more than a joke. We so appropriate our clothes and identify ourselves with them that there are few of us who, if asked to choose between having a beautiful body clad in raiment perpetually shabby and unclean, and having an ugly and blemished form always spotless attired, would not hesitate a moment before making a decisive reply.*[4]

[4] William James, *Philosophy of William James* (New York: Modern Library [n.d.]), p. 126.

In dressing we should strive to express our individuality. While young people enjoy dressing alike, no mature woman wants to dress exactly like another. When two grown women wear exactly the same gown to a social function, everyone is embarrassed, as much so if they had planned this as when it is coincidence.

Clothing is considered to be an expression of self. Therefore, it is imperative that each individual develop enough self-confidence to dress as he pleases and not as another dictates. When one finds himself dressing as another suggests (be it father, mother, friend, wife, or husband), he is relinquishing part of his self-identity and is usually unhappy about it. This is why a study of clothing selection must include analysis and understanding of the self. Once this understanding has been developed, the individual can choose self adornment with much greater confidence and assurance. (See Chapter 4 for further discussion of roles.)

the changing of taste by habituation

Important to the development of objectivity is the understanding of the phenomena of habituation. Taste is a subjective judgment which results in a decision to like or dislike. Our tastes are affected by our values, attitudes, and interests. The approval and enjoyment of much around us conform to a cultural pattern. Tastes are also influenced by training, experience, sensitivity, and the socioeconomic class to which we belong.

Our tastes can be changed and expanded by a process called habituation (Figure 2–12). As "likings" are expanded, our tastes change. We have all experienced this phenomenon in some manner or another. Perhaps in meeting people, tasting new foods, in appreciation of new music forms, or getting accustomed to new clothing styles, our original "dislikes" have changed into "likes."

Pepper gave the example of people who "learn" to like cheese. He said that there is a uniformity in the sequence of liking cheeses from the mild to the strong flavors. A person begins with a mild cream cheese and works up to the medium flavors such as Edam and then on to the strong Roquefort. As long as any one of the new tastes is not too unique, a change in "likes" takes place.[5]

The chief characteristic of habituation is that the new element which was changed from "dislike" to "like" becomes the most liked in the sequence; the former elements in the sequence seem tame or neutralized in our "likes." Sometimes the first item in the sequence which was "liked" becomes "disliked." The fashion cycles discussed in Chapter 3 showing gradual changes could be explained as a result of habituation.

[5] Stephen Pepper, *Principles of Art Appreciation* (New York: Harcourt, 1949), p. 28.

2–12 Our tastes in fashion change by habituation. Airline stewardesses have led the career-girl fashion parade for the past several decades. Their hemlines always have been at a fashionable height. At top (left to right), the uniforms represent the years 1930, 1935, 1940, 1945, and 1950. The contemporary stewardess ensembles shown in bottom photo were designed by Jean Louis of Hollywood. (Courtesy United Airlines)

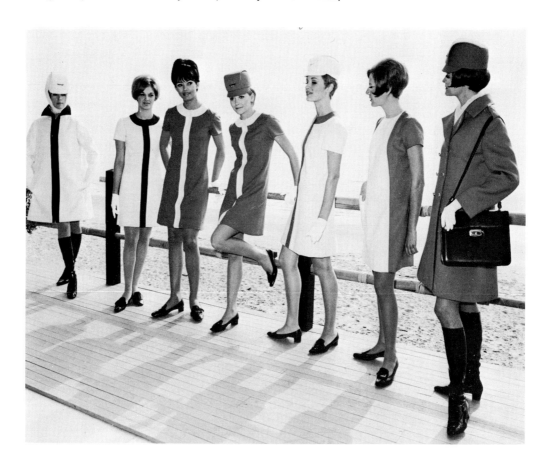

Some people do not go through the process of habituation in a sequence of "dislikes" to "likes," but can accept something extreme at once. These are the avant-garde. They are the ones who embrace that which is new and make it popular.

Habituation is not the same as habit. Habit makes us do things unconsciously, and we generally have neutral feelings about it. The growth that takes place by habituation makes us learn to like the item. The evidence that our tastes can be changed from "dislike" to "like" can broaden our aesthetic horizons in music, food, art, and fashion. Getting used to new experiences through sequential steps is rather painless; simply expose yourself to things just beyond what you now know. Changing our tastes can enrich and expand our lives by adding new and exciting interests and enjoyment. Those who refuse this process limit their lives.

techniques for developing objectivity

The clothing students must develop a sensitivity to personal appearance if they are to become objective. In addition to the personal inventory recommended at the beginning of this chapter, other techniques for developing objectivity must be employed. The purpose is to become aware of the total self and personal patterns of dress and appearance. By developing this objectivity, one can begin to manipulate one's appearance to present the image one wishes to project.

Objectivity takes much practice and effort. It is not easy. To see oneself clearly and accurately requires analytical thinking, introspection, and maturity. As Chanel cautioned: "Beware of mirrors. They reflect only the image we have of ourselves." [6]

PEOPLE WATCHING

As a student of clothing it is important that you develop the technique of people watching. Wherever you go, look at the people and the clothing they are wearing. When you arrive early for class, watch the others pass in; when you wait for a friend in the coffee shop, check the garb of those around you; as you move from campus to town, be aware of the habiliments of others. Public transportation depots are wonderful people-watching centers; here you can observe geographical differences in clothing selection. The library, the theater, the snack bar, every place people gather, you can watch them. Working, playing, studying, shopping—watch the people and analyze their clothing.

[6] Gabrielle Chanel, "Collections by Chanel," *McCall's* (June 1968), p. 38.

As you develop your skill at people watching, learn to consider each component of the total image. Mentally run through this check list.

1. Attractiveness   Consider the total image. Is it attractive or not? If so, why? If not, why?

2. Appropriateness   Is it appropriate for the location?
Is it appropriate for the occasion?

3. Suitability   Is it suitable for the figure?
Is it suitable for the coloring?
Is it suitable for the age?
Is it suitable for the personality projected?

4. Unity   Does it go together?
Does it go with the wearer?
Does it go with the surroundings?

5. Relationships   Are the divisions within the costume attractive for the physical shape of the wearer?
Are the accessories—hat, bag, shoes—in pleasing relationship to the wearer?
Are the textures and design sizes in pleasing relationship to the wearer?
Is the hair shape in pleasing relationship to the figure, the head, the face?

As you develop an awareness of clothing and grooming of others, you will find it easier to be objective about your own appearance. By detecting misinterpretation of dress in others, you will become more sensitive to your own detailing of costume. Studying the blunders of others can assist you in avoiding this misuse of adornment. This continual analysis will better your understanding of the guidelines and theory presented in this text. Application of knowledge in everyday life is true learning. "People watching" can be a never-ending adventure in expanding your awareness, sensitivity, and objectivity.

POINT COUNT FOR WOMEN

There are many variations of point count in dress. It is much the same idea as point count in the game of bridge. It is a tool to help you evaluate the costume and accessories you have selected. The system must be somewhat flexible to allow for fashion changes which over a period of time fluctuate from a very understated look to its extreme. The point count presented here will help you locate the eye-arresting areas of your ensemble. It will help you establish the relationships of dominance and subordination. It will give you a key to understanding accessories and use of color and texture in a costume.

2–13 The point count total for this ensemble is as follows:

Shoes	2
Stockings	1
Dress	3
Scarf	3
	9 point total

A handbag, wrap, and jewelry would increase total. (Courtesy Simplicity Pattern Company)

The point count system which seems to be the most usable and versatile is the simplest. It can be used in evaluating dress for any occasion and for any individual. The point count is

One point for each change in color.

One point for each change in texture.

If the item is particularly eye arresting, such as some prints, you may add bonus points.

Elaborate make-up and hair styles should also be given bonus points.

Point count totals will vary with the fashion period. Ten or eleven points would be considered underdressed; twelve to sixteen points, well dressed; above twenty points, quite flamboyant.

Total looks should be evaluated, that is, the complete ensemble as you will present yourself, including handbag. Evaluate points with coat on and with coat off.

Evening wear point counts are higher than daytime.

To determine your point count now, start with your feet and work up. Add one point for each change of texture and color. (See Figure 2–13.)

Point Count Details

Shoes. Shoes are often very eye arresting. Add one point for each change in color and texture, including cut-out areas.

Hosiery. If the hosiery is neutral in color, it counts one point. If it is colored or textured, it becomes eye arresting and rates bonus points. Add one point for color and one for texture; the more pattern, the more points.

Dresses. A solid color, one-piece, untextured dress is one point. If the dress is a print, add one point for each hue represented. If the dress is two pieces, add a point for each section, just as you would for matching skirt and blouse.

Skirts. A solid skirt is one point; a patterned skirt is totaled by the number of colors of importance and the texture. A corduroy skirt would be one point for color, one point for texture. Jackets and sweaters are rated in the same manner.

Accessories. Evaluate each color and texture presented. These often cost a lot of points.

Jewelry. Jewelry is worn because it is eye arresting. It will cost you many points. If you feel the point count is getting too high, best to take off some of the jewelry. A plain gold watch with a black band would be four points: one for the gold case, one for crystal, one for band, one for buckle. A gold ring with a diamond and ruby would be three points. Wedding and engagement rings are counted as a unit and given only one point unless very elaborate. Bracelets, pins, earrings, eyeglasses, hair ornaments, necklaces—all are evaluated counting each color and texture.

Coats. The same rules apply: fur coats and colors should be given bonus points, determined by color and uniqueness of the fur.

Décolleté necklines are always eye arresting and should be awarded bonus points.

closet comments

Discovery of our individuality may be approached by studying an extension of ourselves, that is, our clothing. An objective analysis of your wardrobe is an exercise that may help you to discover what impressions your clothes give to others and what your clothes may say about the kind of person you are. You must be as objective as possible while doing this analysis; if that is not possible, ask someone to do it for you. Open your closet as though you were seeing the wardrobe for the first time. Imagine that it belongs to someone you have never seen. You want to learn as much as possible about this individual, and the only cues that you have to the personality are the garments before you.

First, take a look at the arrangement of the clothes, shoes, and garments hanging on hooks. Do they reveal a person who is average in neatness and orderliness, extremely fastidious, sloppy and unorganized, or one who does not seem to think about the care of clothes? Are all the clothes in a state of readiness, or do they need pressing, repairing, mending, or discarding?

Next, look at the garments. Do they express a person who is fashion conscious, a fashion leader, a follower, or one who would blend in with the crowd? Is there any hint of creativity? What do the skirt lengths or pant styles reveal, the shapes of the shoe toes and heels? Does the clothing show thought, planning, coordination, or impulse buying?

Are the fabric designs exciting or unusual, classic or traditional, or are they drab and uninteresting? Do colors give you a picture of the individual's personal coloring? Do they characterize self-confidence or lack of personal confidence?

What activities do the clothes suggest? Active sports, parties, employment, student? What roles does the individual play? Do textures, colors, and styles reiterate a mood or feeling that suggests some personality traits? How would you describe the image this person has of himself? What values are represented by the clothing?

If thoughtfully considered, this assignment may be informative to you. You may find that you are fairly accurate and consistent in revealing a true image of yourself. If you do not like the image that your clothes show, you have an opportunity to change it with each new garment you add in the future. Whatever your results reveal, they are the cues which many others may use to understand how you feel about yourself and to understand the person that you are.

summary

To fully understand your individual requirements of dress, it is fundamental to see yourself objectively. Understanding why we wear clothes, the influences of our society on our clothing choices, and how our tastes evolve is only part of the information needed for objectivity. A most candid personal analysis is the other element required. As there are many facets to each individual, many approaches to objectivity are necessary. Several techniques have been suggested to sharpen your sensitivity to yourself. More ideas will follow in other chapters. Total awareness of the self is the first step of objectivity.

suggested readings

Anspach, Karlyne. *The Why of Fashion.* Ames, Iowa: Iowa State University Press, 1967.

Ellis, A. *The American Sexual Tragedy.* New York: Grove Press, Inc., 1962.

Garland, M. *Fashion.* Baltimore: Penguin Books, Inc., 1962.

Lang, K. and G. *Collective Dynamics.* New York: Thomas Y. Crowell Company, 1961.

Langner, Lawrence. *The Importance of Wearing Clothes.* New York: Hastings House Publishers, Inc., 1959.

Pepper, Stephen. *Principles of Art Appreciation.* New York: Harcourt, Brace & World, Inc., 1949.

Roach, Mary Ellen, and Joanne B. Eicher. *Dress, Adornment, and the Social Order.* New York: John Wiley & Sons, Inc., 1965.

Ryan, Mary Shaw. *Clothing: A Study in Human Behavior.* Holt, Rinehart & Winston, Inc., 1966.

3

fashion

 large segment of society is greatly affected by fashion, whether they are aware of this phenomenon or not. Huge expenditures of time and money are involved in the pursuit of fashion.

Fashion is dynamic yet evolves slowly, and we subconsciously change with it. This occurrence is demonstrated by the subtle rejection of certain garments; we begin to push them back in the closet, wear them infrequently, and finally ignore them. Sometimes women feel a sudden need to alter a hem, add a belt, take off a sleeve in a garment that has become dowdy. Men may have lapels or cuffs restyled or add a new color shirt or tie to update their wardrobe. As new styles are introduced, we slowly find them more appealing, and as we become more familiar with them, we choose certain ones to make fashionable. Personal acceptance of fashion for many occurs through habituation. To cater to this whim, a worldwide industry has developed. Fashion is a tremendous factor in our personal lives and also in world economy.

fashion leadership of france

Since the middle of the seventeenth century, when the court of Louis XIV were the tastemakers, France has been in a position of fashion leadership. Why has this phenomenon been true? France, and particularly Paris, has maintained the reputation of "Fashion Capital of the World" because of the continued fostering of a climate and atmosphere that encourages creativity and inspiration. Paris has continued to be a meeting ground for all of the arts. It is the city where the world's aspiring musicians, writers, and artists are attracted by the magnetism of the creative climate which abounds for all of the arts. The architecture, parks, monuments, and the very layout of the city present unequaled expressions of beauty along the winding river Seine.

Fashion is regarded as a national industry in France, and as such it is fostered, protected, and financed. The artists of fashion design find inspiration in the priceless collections of art found in the hundreds of museums. The Institute of Documentation of Costume located in Paris is sponsored by the French government to assist in the research of costume. Here are found historical records of price, swatches, and the amounts of fabric used by each designer on individual garments, along with a complete costume library and costume and textile collection. Dressmaking is a most honorable profession in France; legions of well-trained seamstresses are available to execute a designer's work. A great spirit of cooperation exists among the allied trades; for example, buttonmakers will provide just the exact fastener that the designer requests or needs. Entire cities such as Alençon, Chantilly, Valenciennes, and Calais exist to support the fashion industry with their products of exquisite laces and trims.

The various French textile manufacturers cooperate by providing fabrics to the designer free of charge for the first model. The silk and textiles industry has been given financial assistance by the French government since the fifteenth century. Because of this subsidy production continues, and the beautiful cottons, lovely silks, and fine wools of France are known and treasured throughout the world. *Toile de Jouy,* the printed fabric made in the town of Jouy, was developed by an engraver-designer named Oberkampf during the time of Napoleon. Oberkampf was awarded the French Legion of Honor for his contribution to the French fashion industry.

The trade association, *Chambre Syndicale de la Couture Parisienne,* founded in 1868, has protected the French designer ever since. The general function of this organization is to serve its membership in all branches of fashion. The *Chambre Syndicale* acts as advisor and counselor in such matters as interpretation of laws and taxes, employment relationships, and business management.

It coordinates the dates for showing each designer's collection and offers protection from "idea pirates." A series of identifying photographs of each design is registered with the *Chambre Syndicale,* so that any pirating of designs can be prosecuted. The *Chambre Syndicale* also conducts a school to train personnel for the needle trades, thus assuring a continued supply of these vital workers.

The emphasis placed on clothing by French women has also had an impact on the fashion industry. Historically, Madame de Pompadour and Madame du Barry, both mistresses of Louis XV, are credited with setting the pace for court attire by arraying themselves in magnificent clothes. Marie Antoinette symbolized the epitome of fashion impact in her day. She spent most of her time and the fortunes of the king on her personal adornment and introduced many innovations which became fashion. So powerful was Marie Antoinette and so strong was her interest in clothing that she made her dressmaker, Madame Bertin, Minister of Fashion.

The first haute couture salon was opened in Paris in 1860 by an Englishman, Charles Worth. He designed show pieces for his wife and then escorted her to the most important social functions. In this manner he attracted the attention of Empress Eugénie, wife of Napoleon III, and became her dressmaker. This relationship with the Empress secured his position as the "father of the couture." (A House of Worth has been in continued existence to this date; its importance in fashion has been very minor in recent times.)

Soon other houses were established, and royalty both supported and encouraged them. Most memorable of the early couturiers were Madame Cheruit and Redfern in 1881, Jeanne Lanvin in 1890, and the House of Callot Soeurs in 1895. As the status of royalty changed with political events, the clientele of the couture of necessity expanded to include the very wealthy, the international set, actresses of the stage, and later the films, and finally society women and wives of political and business leaders. Magazine and newspaper coverage given to these famous women in their various activities helped to spread the favored styles. Fashion magazines were created with the specific purpose of spreading the fashion news to even a wider public. Fashions were copied by "little dressmakers" or home seamstresses everywhere. This in turn gave rise to an entirely new facet of fashion, the pattern industry.

A new concept in fashion was initiated when Paul Poiret, who had worked in the House of Worth, opened his own salon. Poiret designed gowns that for the first time released women from the constricting corsets and allowed them to breathe! Walking was free and easy in this new style, so Poiret innovated his scandalous culottes and walking skirt, the *trotteur.* Paul Poiret became an "ambassador of fashion" by traveling around the world with his mannequins advertising French fashion. He was the first couturier to create a perfume. In 1914 Poiret sadly closed his house and went to serve his country in World War I. He reopened his salon after the war but was not able to regain his former fame. In the war years fashion had changed, and Poiret seemed unable to understand or appreciate the new trends. Paul Poiret who had contributed so much to the world of fashion died in poverty in 1944.

In 1914 Madeleine Vionnet opened her house only to be closed by World War I. She bravely reopened in 1919 and made tremendous contributions to fashion. Vionnet was art nouveau before there was such a period! Her sketches and designs are collectors' items of this intriguing art form. She was the first to design asymmetrical necklines, skirts with handkerchief points, and costumes with the coat lining and dress fabric the same. Her greatest innovation was the use of bias. If you can imagine, no one had used the bias cut before Vionnet.

In 1918 Gabrielle "Coco" Chanel established her house. This designer may well be regarded as one of the "wonders of the world" as she has been a dynamic force in fashion ever since. Her designs are as popular today as they have ever been. She continues to set trends and produce popular designs. Her designs and innovations have become classics. It is really safe to say that the wardrobes of all women in the Western world have felt the impact of Chanel.

In 1919 Chanel shocked the fashion world by using wool knits in suits and coats. Until this time this fabric had been used only for underwear. The popularity of wool knits today illustrates Chanel's farsighted approach to fashion. The chemise dress featured in the 1924 collection became fashionable at all social levels, so much so that it could be regarded as the "uniform of the day." Chanel has always shown a great understanding of fabric and fit. Her garments seem so simple in design, yet they use fabric to its best advantage. A Chanel design is reputed to be the most comfortable of all clothes to wear. The "Chanel Suit" is a common fashion term used to describe any suit with a collarless, cardigan jacket. Her perfume, Chanel No. 5, is probably the one best known throughout the world. It was named for her favorite number.

Because of her pleasure in jewelry, a whole new concept of jewelry has evolved. Chanel has always loved extravagant ropes of pearls; large, bright pins and bracelets; colorful earrings. Until she featured this costume jewelry in her 1920 collection, it was not socially accepted. The only kind of jewelry regarded as proper was made of precious metals and stones. Think of how limited your jewelry collection would be if this were true today! Chanel's penchant for jewelry gave us the wide variety of costume jewelry we all enjoy today.

Chanel closed her house in 1939; both the coming of World War II and a certain indifference to fashion prompted this. In 1954 she made a triumphant return and continues today. She is small in stature, quick of wit and tongue. Although she has never married, her life has been filled with romance and color. A Broadway show "Coco" is based on her life's story.

Some of Chanel's quotations:

To dress young, you must feel young. That means being free and easy and unpretentious in your clothes, being able to breathe and move and sit without being conscious of what you have on. Some teen-agers are the oldest women I know.

Youth must be replaced by mystery, prettiness by beauty. To be called pretty at 40 is no compliment.

. . . .

If a woman is out of fashion because she dresses to be beautiful and not a freak, then there is only one comment to make: Too bad for fashion.[1]

Elsa Schiaparelli entered the fashion world because of economic necessity. She had many wealthy, socialite friends to whom she sold her latest designs. Her first effort was a trimmed cardigan sweater which we now regard as a classic. Her feeling for design in some ways is comparable to Chanel's, in that she stressed comfort and movement in her clothing. Among her contributions to fashion were shoulder emphasis, accessorizing with scarves, use of synthetic fabrics, chic tailored evening dresses, and *shocking pink,* the fashion color. She is also credited with removing class distinction from clothing through simplicity of designs that were suitable for mass production.

Many other designers, too numerous to mention here, left their impact on fashion during these times. Each made a romantic and important contribution to haute couture. The student is urged to pursue an interest in this historical costume period in other references.

american designers

During World War II France was occupied by Nazi Germany. From 1940 to 1945 French fashions were paralyzed. Many of the great houses closed rather than serve the conqueror. Designers became national heroes and vital Paris underground workers rather than submit to a plan of Hitler's to move the Paris couture to Germany. Hitler knew how strong the economic force of fashion was and felt it should be a part of postwar Germany.

It was during this time that American designers moved into prominence. Among these early designers were Norman Norell, Claire McCardle, Mainbocher, Howard Greer, and Charles James. The man who probably had the most influence has never received adequate recognition. This was Gilbert Adrian, who designed for the movies when Hollywood was at its zenith and the neighborhood theater of every town and hamlet was the social and cultural mecca. Sadly, very little of Adrian's work has been preserved.

Listing American designers is indeed difficult, as they have not had the recognition of the European designer. (See Figure 3–1.) Often American designers work for large manufacturers rather than the small houses and thus their reputations are overshadowed. Some of the important American designers are inde-

[1] Gabrielle Chanel, "Collections by Chanel," *McCall's* (June 1968), p. 38.

3–1 A silver see-through bodice panel, sprinkled with chunky stones, contrasts sharply with the demure long-sleeved, full-skirted styling by American designer Dominic Rompollo for Teal Traina. (Courtesy Du Pont Company)

pendent and have patterned their business operations after those in Paris. (See Figure 3–2.) Among the best known are James Galanos, Pauline Trigere, Bonnie Cashin, Ben Zuckerman, Sidney Wragge, Rudi Gernreich, Oleg Cassini, Anne Fogarty, Bill Blass, Geoffrey Beene. Probably the greatest contributions of Americans have been in the areas of sportswear, particularly swim wear. Standardization of size and engineering of design of American foundation garments have no equals in the world. American textile research and production too have made possible whole new concepts for the designer. Lastly, American mass production has made fashion a commodity available to all, and its innovation of planned obsolescence keeps fashion vital, alive, and on the move.

3–2 American designer Sarmi presents an elegantly modern gown in black double-woven satin. The high waistline falling from a discreetly plunged neckline expresses an exciting fashion message for evening wear. (Courtesy Du Pont Company)

3–3 Christian Dior's New Look. Presented immediately after World War II it is rated the fashion coup of all time. (Courtesy Christian Dior)

french fashion post-world war II

After World War II Christian Dior created the fashion coup of all time by introducing the *New Look*. Skirts plunged toward the ankles; the natural shoulder and the nipped-in waist displayed feminine curves in a manner that delighted both sexes (Figure 3–3). The lifting of rationing and wartime restrictions plus the mood of the times made this phenomenon of fashion possible. It is doubtful if any other designer will ever be able to duplicate this feat. Within four years the New Look had completely swept the fashion world. Every woman with the ability and means to do so had completely replaced her wardrobe, if not with Paris originals, with mass-produced copies or homemade creations. The New Look pumped new blood into French fashion and was instrumental in revitalizing the couture. The houses of Balenciaga, Givenchy, La Roche, and Chanel flourished. New darlings arrived, including Fath, Cardin, Balmain, St. Laurent, Courreges, Bohan, Valentino, and Ungaro.

50

3–4 A current creation from Christian Dior Boutique, Avenue Montaigne, Paris. (Courtesy Christian Dior)

3–5 A glamorous lounge ensemble from Christian Dior Boutique presented in Fall Collection, 1969–70. (Courtesy Christian Dior)

3–6 From the French *pret à porter* collections. On the left, a bare black jersey dress that clings with know-how by Patou. On the right, Lanvin's long pullover of the same jersey is shown with a white scarf casually flung over the shoulder and trailing to the floor. (Courtesy Celanese Corporation)

3–8 Patou presents a jumper-jacket combination in modern no-wrinkle fabric. (Courtesy Celanese Corporation)

3–7 Designed by Guy La Roche in pale oatmeal jersey of Fortrel polyester, mohair, and wool. (Courtesy Celanese Corporation)

3–9 Lanvin's signature scarf, a status accessory, is gently looped through portholes in this exciting design. (Courtesy Celanese Corporation)

But times have changed. To most, French couture seems like a relic of the opulent past. Economic pressures and the change in the mode of living, the rise of a large and influential middle class, the mass of youth—all have affected French couture. It is reported that the steady clientele of the couture numbers only around 3,000. Many of the houses have been forced to close. Others have had to diversify their interests. Cosmetics, accessories, and perfumes bearing the names of the famous houses verify this. The boutique has become a very profitable addition to most couture establishments. Most "name" boutiques are on the street floor of the salon and are open to the general public. They feature accessories and ready-to-wear items bearing the famous label of the house (Figures 3–4 and 3–5). Boutique prices are much lower than is customary for couture. Some designers, such as Yves St. Laurent, have turned to boutique trade only and operate on a worldwide basis. Interestingly, the boutique is not a new innovation; in 1929 Patou, Chanel, and Lelong all had this type of shop. (See Figures 3–6, 3–7, 3–8, and 3–9.)

Givenchy stated as he prepared for his 1970 collection:

> *It's folly to try and continue the couture like I do it. For me, everything has to be just right . . . the right color hat to go with the right coat . . . the threads just the exact match . . . the buttons. Here in Paris, there are still the possibilities to create like this . . . there are still people around who make it possible for us. But. . . .*[2]

international designers

Fashion has become international. Designers from all over the world now contribute inspiration to the fashion picture. Many governments have encouraged and subsidized designers because of the important economic benefits for their country. In England Mary Quant created the "mod look" (Figure 3–10). For this she was recognized by Queen Elizabeth and presented with the Order of the British Empire for her contribution to the stimulation of the English fashion industry and its monetary benefits to the country. Sybil Connolly, of Ireland, has revived a fashion interest in Irish tweeds and linens through her designs. For this, she has been granted official recognition and financial support by her government.

Italy now enjoys a reputation for both creative couture and quality ready-to-wear. It is the biggest European exporter of wearing apparel. American buyers converge on Rome and Florence for their showings. Fontana and Simonetta are famous for high-fashion gowns. Pucci has created a worldwide cult of followers

[2] *Women's Wear Daily*, July 14, 1969, p. 119.

for his exciting prints, playclothes, and ski apparel. The leather work of Italy is also a fashion leader. Gucci handbags and Ferragamo shoes are coveted on a universal basis.

"Design Thai" is a lovely line of dresses and loungewear from Thailand. The clothes are unique in design and executed in the exciting fabrics of the country, silks and cottons.

Hong Kong probably has the world's largest export business. The clothing originating there has found its way everywhere. The workmanship of the Hong Kong product is exquisite. The seam finish that adorns every possible garment is now known as the Hong Kong finish.

The list could go on and on of international fashion design and contributions. (See Figures 3–12, 3–13, and 3–14.) A stroll through any American department store will reveal how very international our tastes have become. For fashion this can only be a romantic adventure forward. As each designer makes his unique contribution from his corner of the world, inspiration is excited in another land. Thus, we have the Tyrolean-inspired embroidery gracing a Japanese fabric, the mandarin neckline on a Mexican peasant shirt, Javanese batik print on an African burnoose for American loungewear. The desire of women and men for something different, unique, and exciting creates the impetus for the international market of fashion.

3–10 Fashion designer Mary Quant displays her O.B.E. (Order of the British Empire) award after receiving it from Queen Elizabeth. Famous for introducing the world to mod fashions and the mini skirt, Miss Quant joins such luminaries as the Beatles in receiving the award. (Courtesy United Press International)

3–11 Medieval grandeur in an intricately compact tapestry weave. The long evening coat is by Carossa of Italy. (Courtesy Penny Baker, Inc., Dow Badische)

3–12 Christel Anne of Lisbon created this flapper-inspired dress of hand-crocheted ribbon. (Courtesy Penny Baker, Inc., Dow Badische)

3–13 Modern-day romantica by Jon Higgins blends artfully with the ruins of a Roman theater of the third century B.C. found on the island of Sardinia. (Courtesy Celanese Corporation)

3–14 Framed against the Sea of Sardinia and Punic-Roman ruins of the island is a white Arnel triacetate and nylon outfit by Glenora. The full-sleeved Hamlet-type overblouse tops an easy moving pleated skirt. (Courtesy Celanese Corporation)

the designer—creator of fashion inspiration

The creators of new fashion ideas are the designers who initiate the styles that the buying public accepts or rejects. Designers must continually provide innovations in style because of the demands of their clientele. Designers often develop classic designs which are the backbone of their collections. Chanel has done this with her suits, Balenciaga with the little black dress, Givenchy with his coats, Balmain with fabulous ball gowns. These are their specialties, yet to remain competitive they must continually devise variations of these staples as well as create fresh designs.

Designers often show a similar trend each season, and it is commonly thought that they work together to form a conspiracy that will direct the public acceptance of their work. This is not true. Designers work independently. Actually, they are most jealous of their collections and work in utmost secrecy. Seamstresses, mannequins, custodians, and other personnel who have access to workrooms and designs are carefully policed so that they will not pass "trade secrets." Many designers do not complete a garment until moments before the mannequin presents it for the first time.

The successful designers must be in constant touch with the times. They must understand the people for whom they design, their interests, attitudes and values of dress, modes of living, and occupations. Designers must also be aware of political affairs. In the Fall 1968 opening collections, which followed closely the violent student revolution that paralyzed Paris, many designers featured the color red. As Coco Chanel proclaimed, "I love red this season, I too am revolutionary." [3]

Popular newspapers and magazines, books, plays, television, motion pictures, and music all have a direct influence on fashion. (See Figure 3–15.) The current interests of celebrities are often translated into designs that gain instant acceptance. When the Beatles retreated to India to study under a guru, other celebrities followed, and the Nehru coat and meditation shirt became fashionable. A designer must be sensitive to such influences and be able to translate into fabric the feeling of the times. Style of clothing, as much as any other criteria, represents the era. As the famous French philosopher Anatole France observed when noting what literature he would choose as an index to a culture a hundred years after his death:

I would simply take, my friend, a fashion paper to see how women dressed a century after my decease. Their ribbons and bibbons would tell me more about future humanity than all the philosophers, novelists, preachers and men of science.[4]

Brockman qualified this thinking and applied it more directly to the modern designer by stating: "The trend setter is the designer who expresses the essence of an era with the greatest fashion awareness." [5]

This explains why designers tend to show similar trends each year. They are each affected by the same influences, which in turn make fashion. They read the same magazines and newspapers, see the same films, plays, television shows, react to the same triumphs and tragedies of mankind. (See Figure 3–16.) When the current events focus on a particular person or place, designers translate these happenings into clothing styles.

---

[3] "Coco's Own Thing," *Women's Wear Daily*, July 2, 1968, p. 4.

[4] Jean Brousson, *Anatole France Himself*, trans. J. Pollock (Philadelphia: Lippincott, 1925), p. 106.

[5] Helen L. Brockman, *The Theory of Fashion Design* (New York: Wiley, 1965), p. 74.

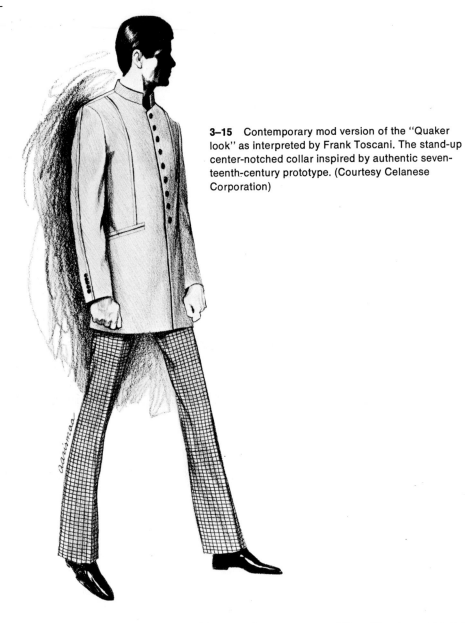

3–15 Contemporary mod version of the "Quaker look" as interpreted by Frank Toscani. The stand-up center-notched collar inspired by authentic seventeenth-century prototype. (Courtesy Celanese Corporation)

Yet the real makers of fashion are the consumers. The ultimate success of any design is dependent on the response of the buying public. A design cannot be considered a fashion until it has been accepted by a large segment of the population for a period of time. Many factors have direct bearing upon approval of a given style. Acceptance is rarely immediate. The avant-garde, those who are more courageous and adventuresome, accept the novel more readily. After it becomes familiar the followers adopt the style. Therefore, the movers of fashion are the followers; they take time to get acquainted with a style before they

3–16 Florentine artistry is revealed in this stunning evening pantaloon designed by Cesare Guidi. Renaissance richness and the look of precious

accept it and wear it awhile before they reject it. Mass media have made this group very knowledgeable. Affluency has also contributed to fashion making as more money is available to spend on clothing. Attitudes that have changed from frugality to obsolescence have also contributed to fashion success. It has been stated that only the very poor and the very very rich ever wear out their clothes.[6] The designer has capitalized on the feminine desire for change and freshness in style.

In reality fashions evolve. What is right for the mood of the time becomes fashion. Other designs fail. The role of the designer is to create enough designs (usually 250 per collection) that a selection is possible. If one design of the entire collection becomes fashionable in a season, it is considered a successful season.

Women's Wear Daily reported:

> *For years the couture, brainwashed by the myth of the sudden new look— which happened once since the war with Dior, and once with Courreges—has been obsessed with the idea of reinventing fashion every six months.*
>
> *The idea was an illusive light that led the courturiers through all sorts of costumery. It falsified their goals, made them favor the new gimmick over the real dress. The press, more interested in circus than bread, egged the whole routine on. But fashion won't change profoundly more frequently than people change profoundly. People don't change profoundly every six months.*
>
> *What seems to count is a continual refreshment, a style that develops but keeps its own signature. Courreges will be the first to tell you that now. Ungaro would rather keep renewing his collection little by little all year round than to do two collections. Cardin doesn't want to do more than one collection a year.*
>
> *Chanel told them that a long time ago. You may reproach her for being all the same, far too static. Her answer is that her stock in trade is nuance.[7]*

paris shows

While French couture is fighting for survival, it still has an important fashion function. Twice each year, in January and July, buyers, fashion editors, and selected clientele converge on Paris for the openings of the designer collections. The mass media carry the fashion news of each collection, often picking up the most bizarre and extreme designs for exploitation. Buyers for wholesale and retail establishments are required to either purchase a number of models or pay a "caution fee" (about $3,200). This is to discourage pirating of designs (the French government does its utmost to protect the industry).

[6] Vance Packard, *The Wastemakers* (New York: McKay, 1960), p. 61.
[7] "Coco's Own Thing," *op. cit.*

In every collection buyers look for the one or two models that may become trend setters. Often originals may vary only slightly from last year's, but a subtle change in sleeve fullness, neckline cut, or waist placement may be just what the makers of fashion desire. Buyers purchase those garments which show new trends and those which can be adapted for American ready-to-wear.

Models cost from $600 up. Buyers can purchase models for copy purposes only. The originals may not be resold but must be returned by a specified date. Replicas of the original are sold. These gowns are limited in number, and expensive models called *toiles* may also be purchased. These are made of muslin, and full direction for making them are included. These become the designs for ready-to-wear. Often adaptations must be made so that the garment may be manufactured in certain price ranges. If a *toile* is reproduced without variation, it carries a higher price.

Many large retailers, including Montgomery Ward, Sears Roebuck, and J. C. Penney, have French couturier designers creating styles for them exclusively. Often these same designers will launch the line with a series of fashion shows and personal appearances. Pattern companies feature name couturier original designs and also adapt variations of these designs into their own patterns.

As fashion becomes more international, the role of the Paris couturier will continue to be challenged. Whether as a group they can continue to influence press and buyer remains to be seen. Pierre Cardin has acknowledged that there is creative fashion talent all over the world and not just in Paris. In his recent collections he has made a start toward a dream he has always had. He has always believed that expecting a designer to turn out two major fashion collections a year, with new ideas demanded, is sheer madness. No designer should be forced to face such a challenge, Cardin concluded, and, besides, fashion ought not to change that fast.[8]

fashion promotion—from designer to closet

Before a new style becomes fashion, a feeling of familiarity must be established. The first of a long line of publicity begins when a new collection is presented by the designer. As each model is presented at the showing, it is labeled with a name such as "babydoll," "fluid look," "space age." This helps to establish the mood the designer is developing in his line.

As buyers make their selections, fashion writers and editors appraise the collection and send stories and sketches to their newspapers and magazines.

[8] "Cardin Molds Dresses for Mass Production," *Los Angeles Times,* August 1, 1968, Pt. 4, p. 4.

Established or prestige customers attend the openings also. Their individual purchases are noted and revealed to the general public by the fashion writers. The first news releases appear in the women's section of the daily newspapers and therefore quickly reach the public. Often the fashion reporter selects the most extreme and bizarre models, as these make good copy. Magazine writers select the models of the collection that they feel will appeal to their particular reading audience. *Women's Wear Daily* is *the* publication of the garment industry. It is closely read by those interested and involved in fashion, both in and out of the trade. While it does sometimes get a bit frivolous in its gossip, it continually reflects the fashion action. To maintain the position of leadership on the fashion scene, it maintains a resident staff in all the major cities in the United States and abroad.

Women's fashion magazines carry the collection news about two months after the opening presentations. They cater to all ages, purses, and tastes and do much to promote trends. Editors in this medium have the power to make or break either a design or a designer. These editors can and do exert much influence in the fashion world. Some magazines have the policy of promoting their advertisers through their editorial sections. This type of cooperative promotion is highly desirable and thus very profitable to the magazine.[9]

A single advertisement in a magazine is very costly. Actual rates vary with the circulation of the magazine. Examples of these costs are: *Life* or *Look*—$60,000 for full-page color; lady's magazine—$35,000 for full-page color.

High-fashion magazines currently in popularity are *Vogue* and *Harper's Bazaar.* European high-fashion magazines such as *L'Officiel* from Paris and *Linea Italiana* from Italy reflect a slightly different approach and are interesting to compare with the American magazines. Fashion magazines directed toward the college or career girls are *Mademoiselle* and *Glamour.* Both of these publications present youthful, avant-garde fashions. *Seventeen* presents less sophisticated styles for a 17 to 24 age group. Combined, these publications exert tremendous influence on fashion and fashion trends.

A child once commented that high-fashion magazines were in reality comic books for ladies; there are many that would agree with this astute observation. Yet once the purpose of the high-fashion magazine is understood, it becomes an important reference for fashionable women. By picturing the latest work of the designers, high-fashion magazines present to a wide audience the new ideas that will become fashion. The astute woman can learn to discern fashion trends from these magazines.

Fashion illustrations capture the essence of the new style image. Fashion photography is an art form that has become a multimillion dollar business. It uses as its setting every geographical location from the outposts of the Sahara to the deltas of the Ganges to publicize high fashion. Mannequins used are more

---

[9] P. Levine, *The Wheels of Fashion* (Garden City, N.Y.: Doubleday, 1965), pp. 92–93.

representative of the fashion figure than the average female figure. That is, they have long, drawn out, slender figures, often with very few womanly curves. The poses used in fashion illustrations are often-times grotesque. The purpose of this generally is to create an art image, pique the interest of the reader, or show the mood of the garment. It should always be remembered that fashion illustrations should never be copied exactly as they are too bizarre and exotic for everyday living.

Advertising by textile mills and clothing manufacturers formerly directed to the trade has lately been going more directly to the consumer by national media —newspapers, magazines, and television. The high cost of this advertising is often shared when related manufacturers join forces. A textile mill and a garment manufacturer may cooperate to publicize both companies and often extend this type of advertising further to tie in local merchants throughout the country.

At the community level, stores feature new designs in their advertising. Individual designers or lines are promoted in fashion shows throughout the local stores and restaurants. Flyers, enclosed with the monthly statements, reach the patron directly.

fashion leadership

Early each year the press presents featured picture stories on resort-wear fashions. These are the designs that promoters feel will be big sellers later in the season. The purpose of the emphasis on resort-wear fashions at this time is to feel out the market and get some indication of how the later spring and summer sales will go. Resort-wear fashions are made available in January for wear in the southern playgrounds such as the Mediterranean, the Greek Islands, the Bahamas, Florida, and Southern California. These testing grounds have been proven to give an indication of the success or failure of a new style. The growing popularity of skiing has somewhat lessened the impact of resort wear.

As the new designs become available, who are the first to pick them up? Generally, this avant-garde group is comprised of the wealthy, the socially prominent, actresses, wives of political and business leaders, and other women who are widely recognized and publicized. These women must have money and the opportunities to display their wardrobes. They must have the self-confidence to wear and show their new creations to advantage. They must have a strong desire to be identified with high fashion and the courage to dress differently than the masses.

Fashion leadership can be found at all social strata. The women who innovate new styles in their own local social groups can thus be categorized. Excellent examples of fashion leadership are to be found on college campuses and among career girls. Each social group seems to have a member or two that lead the way in new styles of dress. These also are fashion leaders. Jarnow pointed out:

> *Today, however, fashion is not a matter of imitating any particular social or economic class. Fashions seem to emerge spontaneously; if style offerings are appropriate and acceptable, they need not wait for the approval of an elite in order to become the fashion. . . .*[10]

After the fashion leaders introduce the new style, the followers take it up. Followers are basically imitative and need to become familiar with the new style to feel confident in it. Followers also need the assurance that the new style has gained the approval of a number of fashion leaders.

The duration of popularity of any fashion varies. The fad is the shortest lived. When people tire of a fashion, they discard it. As soon as the fashion has been accepted by the masses, the fashion leaders tire of it and experiment to find the next trend. This pattern appears to be followed by all but the very highest and the very lowest.

Understanding this movement of fashion is important to the expenditure of the clothing budget. Buying clothing on the outgoing phase of its popularity is more expensive than buying new fashion as it comes in, because the old will be discarded more quickly. This caution should be particularly applied to sale merchandise, as most of it is already obsolete or soon will be.

historical relationships to fashion movement

Fascination with the transition of fashion has long existed among students of clothing. Silhouette recurrence, the life expectancy of a fashion, and evolvement of design details have been the subject of much research and discussion. These studies have attempted to establish whether or not a predictable pattern occurs in fashion movement. If researchers could learn to predict an established pattern of style change and the duration of popularity of the style, it would greatly simplify the clothing industry. The designers, manufacturers, and consumers could eliminate all guessing in the predicting of the success or failure of a new style.

The questions researchers have tried to answer are as follows.

1. Is there a predictable pattern to the recurrence of the three basic silhouettes?

[10] Jeannette Jarnow and Beatrice Judelle, *Inside the Fashion Business* (New York: Wiley, 1966), p. 6.

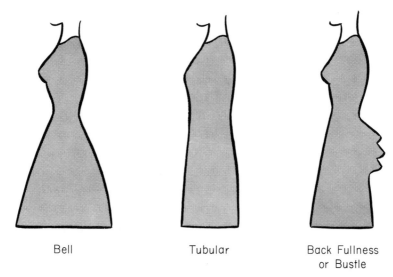

Bell   Tubular   Back Fullness
                                or Bustle

3–17 Throughout history there have been only three basic silhouettes: the bell, the tubular, and the back fullness, or bustle. They recur, but not in predictable cycles. The bell and tubular silhouettes, because they follow the contour of the body, are more predominant in fashion.

2. What is the length of time a fashion is popular?

3. Can the acceptance of a new fashion be predicted?

4. Is there a predictable pattern in the evolvement of fashion?

THE CYCLE OF SILHOUETTE CHANGE

Throughout fashion history there have been only three basic silhouettes: the bell, the tubular, and the back fullness, or bustle, silhouettes (Figure 3–17). Young made a study of typical daytime dress silhouettes for the period 1760 to 1931. This study revealed a recurrence of the shapes bell, back fullness, tubular, in that order, every 30 to 36 years. The full cycle of the three silhouettes took 100 years to complete.[11] Had the study continued beyond 1937, it would have revealed that the tubular shape which was revived in 1900 lasted until 1947. This was a span of 47 years. Explanation of this long span may be found in the fact that World War II occurred and necessitated a stop in fashion movement. The postwar "New Look" which was introduced in 1947 had the bell shape. According to the previous cycle pattern, this silhouette could be predicted to last until about 1977. However, it was replaced by the tubular silhouette by the end of the 1950s.

[11] Agatha Brooks Young, *Recurring Cycles of Fashion* (New York: Harper & Row, 1937), p. 214.

Thus, Young's theory of silhouette change is no longer valid. The silhouettes are not following the pattern of bell, back fullness, tubular, and they are not remaining fashionable for 30 to 36 years. Since the middle of the 1950s more than one silhouette has been simultaneously fashionable. Many new styles have reached their full peak without displacing former styles.[12]

CYCLE OF ACCEPTANCE AND POPULARITY OF FASHION

Ryan believes that there is a pattern in the movement of a new fashion and its acceptance.[13] At its introduction, a few of the avant-garde adopt the style. This is followed by a gradual rise in acceptance so that the style becomes a fashion popular with many. A period of decline follows, then sudden death. There is a variation in the speed of the rise and fall of various styles. In times past it took two years for a Paris fashion to be seen commonly on the streets of New York City and another two years to be popular in California. Today, acceptance occurs much faster, and there is very little difference between the East and West coasts of the United States in manner of dress. Mass media have made exposure of styles immediate to all. Mass production has dropped prices into ranges that are afforded by the vast middle class of America. What does remain, however, is the cyclical nature of the recognition of a style by a few innovators; the acceptance of the style by many, which makes it a fashion; and the decline, which makes it passé. It must be noted here that if a style has a certain quality that makes it good design, it will remain in the fashion picture and be called a classic. Examples of classics are the shirtmaker dress, the cardigan sweater, the middy blouse, the Chanel jacket.

CYCLICAL NATURE OF THE EVOLVEMENT OF NEW FASHIONS BY GRADUAL CHANGES

There appears to be another cycle evident in fashion change. It is the gradual change whereby a new fashion is built on an existing one. That is, some of the prevailing ideas of the style are retained and new innovations are added to them. For example, skirt lengths go up by degrees until they reach an extreme; then the gradual lengthening of hems takes over until another extreme is accomplished. More examples of this phenomenon can be found in sleeve fullness and neckline placement. The only recent interruptions to this type of gradual change occurred with the New Look when hems plunged to the ankles. The fashionless war years could explain this; perhaps skirts were just catching up to where they would have been if not interrupted!

---

[12] Jarnow and Judelle, *op. cit.,* p. 5.
[13] Mary Shaw Ryan, *Clothing: A Study in Human Behavior* (New York: Holt, 1966), p. 73.

Small changes in fashion seem to occur very quickly as compared to basic changes in the silhouette which take place over a period of years. It would appear that small changes in fashion are affected by fashion leadership, whereas the major changes are affected by political, economic, and cultural factors.[14]

summary

Fashion changes do occur in a somewhat rhythmical manner. Styles are accepted by the leadership and become fashion as they are accepted by the masses, fashion reaches an absorption point, and then declines or goes out of fashion. Some styles remain to become classics. The speed of a fashion cycle varies and is influenced by many factors. Fashion changes occur by gradual additions to existing styles; once extremes are reached, the trend reverses itself.

fashion terms

In order to be able to communicate effectively, it is necessary to understand the vocabulary of the technical area and the connotation of the terms applied. This is especially true in the field of clothing. Textbook authors and fashion reporters often attach personal meaning to the words used which may result in confusion in the mind of the reader. The following definitions and explanations are made to clarify the terms used in this text and should serve as a point of reference when reading the various chapters.

Couture. Couture is the French word for sewing. Popular connotation includes an establishment devoted to the creation of fashion where the designer, rather than working to meet the requirements of the individual customer, develops his own ideas.

Couturier. Couturier is the French term for dressmaker or designer.

High Fashion—Haute Couture. High fashion refers to new styles. Because high fashion is created to inspire fashion change, it has several identifiable characteristics. It is very expensive because of the specialness of the design, the quality of the fabric, and the excellence of workmanship. It is extreme sometimes to the point of being startling. This piques interest in the design and the designer but limits the appeal of the garment to those who can and will wear it. Some high-fashion designs may be too impractical to meet the needs of the

[14] Jarnow and Judelle, *op. cit.,* p. 15.

varied life of the modern woman. High fashion remains high fashion only until the newness wears off. If a high fashion gains acceptance and is mass produced, it then becomes fashion. High fashion is important because it is a source of fashion inspiration.

Fashion. Fashion is a style accepted by a large group of people at a particular time. As applied to dress, it is a style popular among a large group of people at a specific time. Antebellum fashion describes the bouffant style that was worn by women of the South before the Civil War. *Empire* fashions describe the clinging, draped, high-waisted gowns worn in Europe during the reign of Napoleon. *Mod* labels the fashions springing from England in the wake of the Beatles.

Horn stated:

> *If we define fashion in terms of its normative aspects, that is, its prevalence or acceptance within any given social aggregate, we observe another dimension which is not often recognized by critics of the fashion scene. Fashion is dependent upon the willingness of the majority to conform to it.... The crucial elements, then, in defining what is fashionable are the rate of change and the particular groups who effect the change, not the particular style features or the design aspect of the garment.*[15]

Fashion then includes style but expresses the acceptance of the style at a given time.

Style. Style is a distinctive characteristic or way of expression. There are styles of houses, styles of cars, styles of refrigerators, styles of life, and styles of speaking. Style in dress describes the lines that distinguish one form or shape from another. (See Figure 3–18.) Style creates an impression that reflects the outlook of the times. The pleated skirt, the A-line skirt, and the straight skirt are styles because they have characteristic shapes and lines. The mood or feeling created by particular styles is an emotional quality which reflects the outlook of a person or a group of persons during a certain period of time. The shirtmaker style is distinguished by its "no nonsense" look much like an extended man's shirt. It is simple and practical in design and reflects the needs and activities of the busy modern American woman (Figure 3–19).

Many styles are "rediscovered," modified, and enjoy new popularity in the fashion world (Figure 3–20). This is because of the limitations imposed by textiles and the human form. Designers of fashion seek inspiration from every source and very often from historical fashion.

A style remains a style whether it is fashionable or not. A middy blouse is always a middy blouse; a shift, a shift; a sheath, a sheath; a shirtmaker, a shirtmaker; a cardigan, a cardigan.

We often hear the expressions, "Phyllis has style" or "Joan dresses in a

[15] Marilyn J. Horn, *The Second Skin* (Boston: Houghton Mifflin, 1968), pp. 13–14.

stylish manner." This is a misuse of the term. Every person is clothed in a style because of the distinguishing characteristics of the garments worn. Style should not be equated with the words taste, chic, or elegance. Style is a general term used to describe the details of a garment.

Classics. Classics are styles that endure. They continue to be accepted by a large segment of the buying public because of their timeless quality. The cardigan sweater is a classic; it may go through minor variations such as the addition of sequins, fur, or embroidery but the style remains basic. Classic hat styles are the Breton, the pillbox, and the beret. Tailored shirts, Bermuda shorts, shirtwaist dresses, and pleated skirts are classic. A key to understanding what is classic is simplicity of design and suitability to the clothing needs of a large group. If the design of the article is good, it is always pleasing and therefore timeless or classic. (See Figures 3–21 and 3–22.)

3–18 The distinctive characteristics of this coat make it a recognizable style. (Courtesy National Cotton Council)

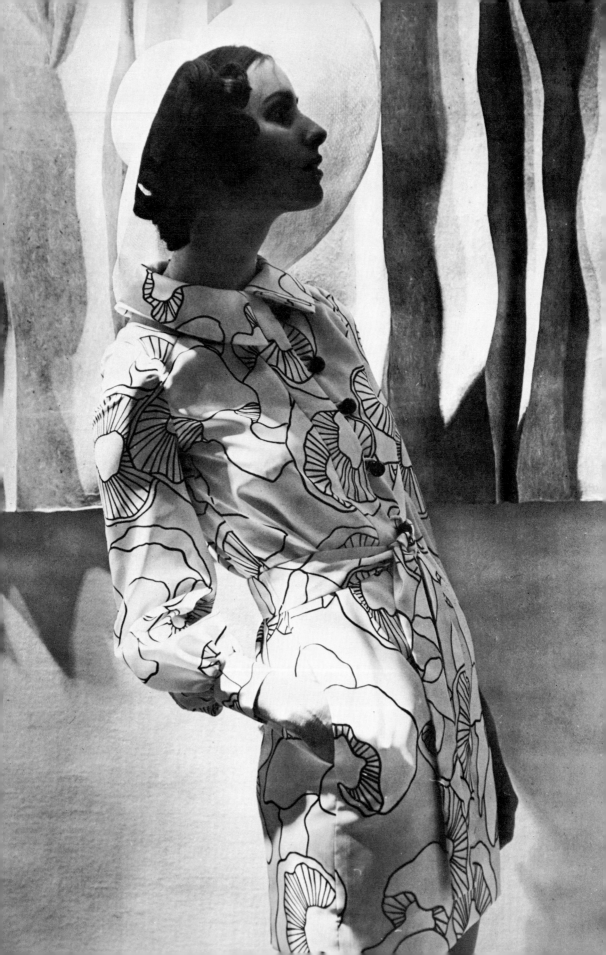

3–20 The beret, the shirt, the vest, and the pleated skirt are all styles that are often "rediscovered." (Courtesy Celanese Corporation)

3–19 The shirtmaker dress is a distinctive style that is rarely out of fashion. (Courtesy Celanese Corporation)

Fad. Fad is a fashion which is short lived. Fads usually have quick acceptance by a relatively small group of people. An interesting phenomenon of fads is their speed. They leave the scene with almost the same speed with which they arrive. When a clothing fad is passé, it is dead, and those who continue to wear it appear foolish.

Some clothing fads of recent years are crinoline petticoats, granny gowns, pedal pushers, bell-bottom trousers, chain belts, see-through blouses, and oversized and odd-shaped sunglasses. Accessory fads often occur in jewelry, purses, shoes, and gloves. Analyzing fads to determine why they are so short lived reveals that they are too flashy, poorly designed, easily available, and inexpensive.

Fads may be confined to a particular locale or sweep the country, as the hula hoop once did. A fad may appeal to a certain group or subgroup. Teen-age magazines often promote fads because young people are more accepting than adults. Fads may be bizarre or flamboyant and noticed by all, or extremely subtle and only known by an in-group.

3-21 The classic styles of the blazer, the turtleneck sweater, and plaid are enduring favorites. (Courtesy Simplicity Pattern Company)

3–22 Trench coats are classics that are popular with both men and women. (Courtesy Men's Fashion Association of America, Inc.)

Fads may become fashions. This occurs when many people accept the fad and it proves its usefulness. Examples of this are color in hosiery and loafers, which when first accepted were considered fads.

Elegance. Elegance is the harmony that results when all accouterments and actions are in tune with the physical being. It resembles beauty but is not a gift from nature; it is acquired. The word itself comes from the Latin root *eligere,* which means "to select." A truly elegant woman is elegant in every phase of the art of living, voice, manners, actions, and tastes. Elegance belongs only to the mature. Chanel commented, "Elegance is not the prerogative of those who have just escaped adolescence, but of those who have already taken possession of their future." [16]

[16] Chanel, *op. cit.*

75

Elegance differs from chic in that it is more a development of the habits of civilized culture. It is more studied than chic and requires maturity.

Examples of elegant women are Queen Sirikit of Thailand, Queen Farah of Iran, Eva Gabor, Diahann Carroll, Greer Garson, and Margaret Chase Smith. There are many other women out of public life who are also elegant; can you think of some among your acquaintances?

Chic (pronounced "sheek"). Chic is a smartness of style and manner. It is the essence of casual refinement, a special quality of some individuals. Beauty and wealth are not prerequisites for acquiring chic. No one is born chic—it is a quality that may also be acquired. A factory worker as well as a society matron can be chic. The chic woman selects only what suits her best and rejects what is not right for her.

Gloria Guinness defined chic as "a well studied attitude, an attitude that becomes natural by sheer self-confidence and a passionate enthusiasm for expressing oneself with beauty and balance, or with oddity and anger." [17] A woman who is chic is chic in every way. Her gestures, voice, and posture are as important as her thoughtfully selected wardrobe. She is recognizable immediately, although she is not flashy, loud, or flamboyant.

Taste. Taste is a subjective judgment of what we think is appropriate or beautiful. Because of the individualness of this judgment, standards of taste are not universal. What one person considers to be "good taste," another does not. Our taste is a result of (1) how we see things aesthetically; (2) the scope of our experience, both educationally and culturally; and (3) our own values and attitudes. As we mature, our tastes grow more varied and often broaden. Taste makes us reject certain styles and accept others. Rejection may evolve into acceptance as we become more familiar with the style.

Sophisticated. Sophisticated means worldly, educated, familiar with customs of the world. It implies confidence. It is not naive.

Silhouette. Silhouette is the outline of contours seen against a contrasting background; it is what is first seen from a distance. It is of significance in fashion because it determines the first impression of the style and defines the shape. The silhouette is determined by the physical contours of the body and the clothing covering the body. It also reveals height and breadth, hair shaping, neck length, sleeve lineation, waist placement, and skirt conformation.

Camouflage. Camouflage is changing appearance by concealing or disguising. Undesirable contours can be camouflaged by skillful use of line, texture, and color. The art of camouflage can create illusions of more desirable proportions of face and figure.

Total Look. Total look is the complete picture of the individual and all accouterments, which include all garments, accessories, make-up, and hair style. When a designer presents his collection, each ensemble is presented as a com-

[17] Gloria Guinness, *Gloria Guinness Anthology* (New York: Hearst Corporation, 1966), p. 22.

plete unit. Gloves, shoes, stockings, hats, handbags, foundations, jewelry, make-up, coiffure, and mannequin are carefully selected to reinforce the impression of the design.

Total look differs from chic in that chic includes voice, gestures, and personal qualities. It is possible for each person to acquire the unity of the total look. Raquel Welch presents a total look of the sex queen; Mrs. Richard Nixon presents a total look of ladylike refinement.

The unity of the total look is weakened when an error in the selection of any one element of the ensemble is made. This error is most often made by women accessorizing a costume with what is available in their closets and ignoring the entire idea presented by the designer. Through careful observation of fashion shows and illustrations, a better understanding of the total look can be developed.

Ensemble (Costume). Ensemble, or costume, is the term used to include the principal garment plus all the accessories worn with it. It differs from total look in that the latter term includes make-up and hair style.

Custom. Custom means made for the individual. The garment is cut and fitted on the figure so that correction may be made to fit body contours. The custom market today is very limited because of high labor costs and the availability of a large variety of ready-to-wear in all price ranges.

Basic Garments and Accessories. Basic garments and accessories are those that are adaptable to many uses. They are basic because they are not exciting, unusual, or eye arresting; rather, they show simplicity and restraint. Basic garments are often thought of as garments that form the foundation of the wardrobe.

Basic Color (Staple Color). Basic or staple colors are those that may be worn with a wide variety of other colors. Basic colors are black, black-brown, navy blue, beige, and white.

Individuality. Individuality is the personification of characteristics that make us unique. In dress our individuality is revealed by our clothing. The kind of clothing we select gives clues as to our role, personality, and tastes. The wearing of uniforms was devised to lessen individuality and promote group conformity. Mass production of apparel makes it more difficult to reveal individuality in dress. In its extreme sense, individuality would be nonconformity or rebellion to accepted standards.

tournament of roses pictorial review

Figures 3–23, A–W, show the Tournament of Roses queens and courts of the past seventy years. Study the pictures for details of fashion such as garment design, fabrics, and accessories. Note the changes in standards of beauty as emphasized by make-up, hair style, and grooming. Compare the total look presented in each era for recurring fashion trends.

The Tournament of Roses selects seven girls each year to reign during the New Year's festivities and throughout the year. These finalists are chosen from several hundred senior high and junior college students in the Pasadena, California, area. From the time the first announcement of the finalists is made until their first official appearance, the girls are groomed for their public. Wardrobes are selected for them that represent the newest trends in fashion. The girls are taught correct make-up techniques and their hair is coiffed. (Longer than shoulder-length hair is cut.) The Tournament of Roses queen and her court represent the latest look of the coeds for the year that they reign.

3–23 Tournament of Roses pictorial review shows changes in standards of beauty and fashion since 1901. (Courtesy Pasadena Tournament of Roses Association)

Here comes the parade! First Rose Parade, Pasadena, California, January 1, 1901. Note street-length skirts, bell or bustle silhouettes, hats, and hair styles.

Hallie Woods was selected the first
Tournament of Roses Queen in 1905. Hat,
hair style, and lacy blouse represent
period.

In 1906, the Rose Queen has a large court. The dresses represent the
period and are not costumes. Long, upswept hair was a fashion that
denoted maturity. Hairdos of this period were revived in late 1969 and
early 1970.

79

Style influx in 1930 as shown by the variety of hemlines in this Tournament of Roses Court. Bobbed hair, short skirts, and the flapper style reign.

A close-up of the Rose Queen of 1930 reveals marcelled hair, plucked eyebrows, and cupid-bow mouth.

In 1932 short hair and obvious make-up are the new rage. The crown of this Rose Queen is much like the millinery of the time.

In 1933 the Rose Queen posed in this understated gown. Hair style and make-up are more natural than in previous years.

A face portrait of the 1939 Rose Queen reveals the natural all-American look. Note brows and emphasized mouth. Longer hair is popular. The elaborate sleeve treatment is typical of the period.

The 1939 Rose Queen and her Court display a tailored look. Compare details of dress with pictures of other courts.

Gowns representing the latest 1940 fashions are modeled by this
Tournament of Roses Court. The shapelessness of bodice is not due to lack
of feminine curves, the uplift bra had not been invented.

1944—wide shoulders, elaborate detail of dress design, and open-toed shoes are the fashion news of this Rose Court. Hair styles are representative of the time.

1942—America is just entering World War II. The luxurious satin gowns with square shoulders, long sleeves, and peplums are the ultimate in fashion. A fresh scrubbed face, framed by casually styled hair, is the collegiate look of the day.

1946—a tailored look prevails, each college woman builds her wardrobe around a suit. Shortages of stockings make the "bobby sox" a favorite.

Rose Parade Marshall Bob Hope consults with the Rose Queen in 1947. The veiled hat and shortie coat are most popular. Mr. Hope's classic tweed sports coat features wide lapels and shoulders, as emphasized by a carefully folded handkerchief.

1947—emphasis at the shoulder line is exaggerated, as shown by this Rose Court. Long curly hair styles are made popular by the introduction of the home permanent.

1948—the natural look typifies this Rose Court. Note suit details. Make-up emphasis is at the mouth.

Nylon tulle came to the Tournament of Roses in 1954. This new textile
made possible many new effects in clothing. The strapless formal was
almost a uniform for most coeds.

1959—dressmaker suits with natural shoulders and long slender skirts accessorized with the pearl choker represent the fashion of this period. Note new spike-heeled pump.

The influence of Dior's New Look is shown by the skirt lengths in this 1957 Rose Court.

The Rose Bowl Game, 1968. Hair is teased away from head. Skirts are shorter. Shoes are chunkier. The striped coat is very new this year.

The Rose Queen and her Court, 1969. The classic skirt and sweater are updated to present this nautical look. Hair is styled closer to the face, make-up emphasizes eyes. Shoe heels are getting higher.

Rose Court 1959 holds a tenth reunion.

Compare the changes in fashion and the appearance of each woman.
The styles of the late sixties reflect a definite emphasis on youth.

suggested readings

Anspach, Karlyne. *The Why of Fashion*. Ames, Iowa: Iowa State University Press, 1967.

Bell, Quentin. *On Human Finery*. London: The Hogarth Press, Ltd., 1947.

Brockman, Helen L. *The Theory of Fashion Design*. New York: John Wiley & Sons, Inc., 1965.

Contini, Eila. *Fashion from Ancient Egypt to the Present Day*. New York: The Odyssey Press, Inc., 1965.

Dariaux, Geneviève Antoine. *Elegance*. Garden City, N.Y.: Doubleday & Company, Inc., 1964.

Fairchild, John. *The Fashionable Savages*. Garden City, N.Y.: Doubleday Company, Inc., 1965.

Garland, Madge. *Fashion*. Baltimore: Penguin Books, Inc., 1962.

Guinness, Gloria. *Gloria Guinness Anthology*. New York: The Hearst Corporation, 1966.

Horn, Marilyn J. *The Second Skin*. Boston: Houghton Mifflin Company, 1968.

Jarnow, Jeannette A., and Beatrice Judelle. *Inside the Fashion Business*. New York: John Wiley & Sons, Inc., 1966.

Levine, P. *The Wheels of Fashion*. Garden City, N.Y.: Doubleday & Company, Inc., 1965.

Packard, Vance. *The Wastemakers*. New York: David McKay Company, Inc., 1960.

Pickens, Mary Brooks, and Dora Loues Miller. *Dressmakers of France*. New York: Harper and Row, Publishers, Inc., 1956.

Roach, Mary Ellen, and Joanne B. Eicher. *Dress, Adornment, and the Social Order*. New York: John Wiley & Sons, Inc., 1965.

Roscho, Bernard. *The Rag Race*. Garden City, N.Y.: Doubleday & Company, Inc., 1965.

4

individuality

each human being is a unique individual. This individuality is our most precious possession. It is what sets us apart and makes us what we are. As we progress through childhood to adulthood, we go through stages where peer group identification is extremely important. This need is particularly strong in grade school where each child wants to be part of the gang; to be ostracized, for any reason, is most painful. This strong desire to be part of the group usually extends into the teen years when the uncertainties of adolescence are often coped with by group membership. One of the most overt symbols of this type of socialization is dress. Each generation has produced a "teen look" to identify themselves. Look through high school and college annuals that date back ten, fifteen, twenty, or thirty years, and you will see this dress fad in action. As each man and woman leaves this adolescent period of development for mature adulthood, the importance of peer group identification should lessen and more emphasis should be placed on individuality.

Of course, there are degrees of individual self-expression (Figure 4–1). Careful understanding of oneself is vital to the expression of individuality. One must strive to develop this self-

understanding so that the individual is the real you and not someone you think you should be. This is an important part of maturity. Understanding of oneself is indeed difficult and takes much thought and analysis. If, in your lifetime, anyone is to understand you, shouldn't it be you?

personality, roles, and individuality

Closely related to developing objectivity about oneself is the understanding of one's personality, roles, and individuality. Each person is the result of heredity, family environment, educational and emotional experiences. Because each person reacts to all the factors of life in a personal way, each one is a very exclusive human being.

The search for understanding of oneself is a very time-consuming and involved process. Therapeutic analysis, of course, requires the skills of a well-trained psychiatrist and is not the purpose of this text; greater personal awareness is. In order to understand the image that one projects through the selection of personal accouterments, a study of the elements that compose the self is necessary.

Simply thinking about the kind of person you are and the kind of person you want others to think you are is one step toward personal awareness. A very revealing exercise is to develop a list of adjectives you would use to describe yourself. From a long list of words reduce the list to five adjectives that you feel express the real you. Keep your own list a secret, but ask family, friends, and classmates to describe you in five adjectives. This is not only fun to do but gives you an understanding of what others think of you. In this type of exercise remarks of those who know you least can often be most revealing.

Think about what you admire most in others. Why have you selected the friends you have? What kind of people are your friends? What is your relationship to your parents, brothers, sisters, husband, and children? How do you relate to your family? How has this family shaped you and your thinking? What do you challenge about your family's philosophy? Are there things about your life you would like to change? Are you satisfied with the person you are? Do you really like yourself? Where are you going? What kind of "senior citizen" are you going to be? Add to this list. Introspection of this type helps you to know and understand yourself. Try to analyze yourself as carefully as you can; be honest. If there are things about you you do not like, start to change them. The biblical statement "Love thy neighbor as thy self" is prudent advice yet often misinterpreted. We are to love each other as we love ourselves. This means that we must develop ourselves into the kind of person we like and admire. We must be our own best friend for we spend a lifetime with ourselves.

4–1 The desire for individual self-expression brings some buyers to second-hand stores featuring old uniforms. (Courtesy United Press International)

This concept of self-love is vital to the presentation of oneself to the world. It must be the basis of self-confidence and poise.

Each individual is composed of many parts. The physical composition of the individual is observable and can be most adequately measured and described. Later chapters will deal at length with the physical self. The nonphysical properties of the individual are much more difficult to assess as they are not observable and may only be discussed. Each individual interprets these nonphysical qualities in his own frame of reference. The sum of the physical and nonphysical qualities reveals a unique human being—one of a kind. It is the purpose of this chapter to help you understand the nonphysical qualities that are so great a part of the real you.

Certain terms, such as personality, self-concept, values, and attitudes, are used to describe the nonphysical qualities of the individual. Discussion of each of these should help you in considering various facets of yourself.

personality

The term personality is frequently used to describe the individual. We often hear: "Steve has a great personality." "Marcia is just blah, no personality." "Tracy has an outgoing personality." "Jeff has the right personality for leadership." Exactly what is meant by these descriptions? The dictionary supplies a number of definitions of personality for the layman, yet research shows that few professionals agree on an exact definition. Variation of interpretation for the term comes from the theoretical preference of the person making the definition. The psychologist, physician, sociologist, biologist, and philosopher all use the term in their own way. It becomes obvious that "personality" covers a multitude of definitions.

For our purpose a simple definition is best. We are concerned with a relationship between personality and clothing and personal appearance. Therefore, we shall define personality as the distinctive individual qualities of a person. We perceive another's personality from the visible aspects of his character.

Each person is an embodiment of a collection of qualities. Personality is influenced by abilities, temperament, talents, physical structure, emotional tendencies, ideas, ideals, skills, motives, memories, goals, values, moods, attitudes, feelings, beliefs, habits, and behavior. These qualities, all of which are highly individualized, make up personality. The influences of heredity, social and cultural contacts, learning, and experience also contribute.

Many attempts have been made to classify personalities into types in an effort to assist people to express their individual characteristics. This is par-

4–2 A study of fashion pictures illustrates that garments can communicate a variety of feelings. This jumper dress creates a mood of zingy effervescence. (Courtesy National Cotton Council)

ticularly true in the traditional clothing selection text. These classifications have labeled such personality types as romantic, athletic, ingenue, dramatic, and others. This typing is based on components that include physical build, coloring, voice, mannerism, temperament, and behavior. These types were devised by collecting composites of various personalities; they were not individuals but groups of many people. Personality types are artificial classifications.

This theory of personality typing assumes that individuals will fit into rigid groupings. Certainly it is possible to type people in some respects, but the many facets that make up our individuality cannot be pigeonholed into a simple classification that fits a large number of the population. Allport stated, "... each is of a type only with respect to some one segment of his nature. ... in reality types are valid only for a limited characteristic; they embrace a segment of individuality, but never the total individual. " [1]

Personality is sometimes described by trait names. A trait is the term used to describe a consistent manner of behavior, and the individual possesses a

[1] G. W. Allport, *Personality, A Psychological Interpretation* (New York: Holt, 1937), p. 15.

composite of many and varied traits. When we describe a person as being aggressive, friendly, artistic, or austere, we are describing qualities of behavior that are frequently observed in him. Again, personality traits do not fall into easily categorized types. It is impossible to put a variety of people into a filing system and expect results that will give an accurate definite type.

Your personality is your very own. To describe it or any other personality, groups of descriptive words must be used. Each individual will interpret your personality in his own frame of reference. Therefore, your personality becomes many faceted as it continually changes as you mature and evolve and as it is comprehended by others. Your personality is a vital expression of your individuality.

Many people make personal judgments on the basis of appearance. Hair styles, make-up, and clothing have a particularly strong influence on these judgments. Further cues are presented by the way we walk, talk, and move both face and body. The manner in which we present ourselves certainly does reflect how we feel about ourselves and others. It reflects the values placed on dress and appearance and expresses a personal philosophy.

In spite of the difficulty to do so, we should attempt to express our personality in dress. By striving for better understanding of ourselves, we can discover who we are and delimit the image we wish to present to others. The study of clothing and fashion will expand our knowledge of the symbolism of dress. By combining our self-understanding with the knowledge of clothing, we can present the image we desire.

HOW PERSONALITY IS EXPRESSED IN DRESS

If we use our definition of personality, we can make it applicable to dress. Clothes and combinations of garments present visible characteristics that give them personality. A study of fashion pictures will show that different garments communicate a variety of feelings (Figure 4–2); they also suggest where and when they are best worn. Some clothing may be classified as formal, casual, sophisticated, businesslike, feminine, masculine, dramatic, and so on (Figure 4–3). The degree of expressiveness that clothing possesses, of course, varies with the person making the observation. The student of clothing is far more sensitive to this expressiveness than others. The personality of clothing makes some garments unsuitable for particular persons, places, and events. A very soft, womanly type looks and may be uncomfortable in severely tailored tweeds. A very casual ensemble is suitable for lounging in the dorm but not for campus wear. A "teeny weeny" bikini looks terrific on the beach but not in the supermarket. A ball gown may be exquisite at a formal opening but not at the local matinee.

4-3 Charming and demure is the message of this Venet formal. The use of soft fabric contributes to the expression of the gown. (Courtesy Celanese Corporation)

In Chapter 15 "personality" clothing is discussed in more detail. The importance of mentioning it here is that the student becomes aware of the impact of matching clothing characteristics to personality qualities. A shy, reserved girl is overwhelmed by bold-colored and figure-revealing clothing. An effervescent gamine looks marvelous in gay, kooky clothing. A sophisticated man of the world is miserable when dressed to fade into the crowd. The personality of your clothing should complement your own personality.

self-concept—self-image

Self-concept is the general notion that each person has of himself. The term as used here encompasses the idea we have of ourselves both as a physical person and as a psychological person. We each have a mental concept of how we look and how we behave. For many, this self-image may be a very incorrect assessment of either the physical or the psychological self, or both. This is a kind of mental "myopia" which allows us to see ourselves only as we wish to be seen. What we want others to see may differ from what we conceive of ourselves.[2]

Our clothing choices reflect our self-concept. The examples of clothing easiest to understand in relationship to self-image seem to be negative ones. You have seen a chubby girl poured into stretch pants that outline her every bulge. You have probably wondered how she could appear in public in such unbecoming garb. One reason for her clothing selection may be her self-image. She does not see herself as overweight! She has an image that lets her believe she appears slim and trim and attractive in her pants.

We all have favorite articles of clothing, ones that are extremely comfortable and pleasing to us. These garments offer something more than physical comfort. They give us a psychological comfort because they are so closely related to our personal characteristics. These favored garments express our self-image. Psychological comfort or lack of comfort in clothing may be closely related to how well the garments express the self-image we each have.

We all have reasons for not wearing certain garments. Some are out of fashion, others fit poorly or are the wrong color. Still others may be difficult to maintain or are not in keeping with our style of life. Yet, there are some garments that are continually pushed to the back of the closet for no apparent reason. It is possible that we choose not to wear these garments because the image that the garment reflects is incompatible with the image we wish to project.

Many people have a variety of types of clothing, which is representative of various images. As each individual is a complex personality and engages in many activities, clothing for differing moods and occasions is almost a necessity. Clothes for school are representative of local campus customs. Clothing for employment will be determined by the job and the philosophy of the employer. Clothing for dating and social life will be characterized by the occasion. The degree to which clothing expresses these purposes will be related to the individual's self-image.

[2] Camilla M. Anderson, "The Self-Image, A Theory of the Dynamics of Behavior," *Mental Hygiene*, **36**: 227–44 (1952).

At this time, it is impossible to accurately prescribe clothing that will express individual psychological traits. At best, one can only survey the opinions of various persons and compile a composite of their interpretations of the communication particular garments suggest. However, as individuals progress toward maturity, they develop a more definite direction of clothing choices. The well-selected wardrobe of the mature person expresses a definite theme. Less diversity in clothing choices is the result of earlier experimentation plus a focused self-image. Research done supports this statement. Ditty reported that individuals who rated high in social maturity were more consistent in their clothing choices than were those rated socially immature.[3]

Some people purposely adopt clothing that does not reflect their self-image. They also attempt to behave in a manner that does not represent themselves. Exactly why they do this could betermined only by the individual; most often it is to gain social acceptance. Unless the person is a skillful actor, it is most difficult to effectively carry out such a program. It is too easy to slip out of character, to give oneself away by verbal expressions, actions, and mannerisms. It is too hard to be someone we are not, and it's a foolish project at best. There is much more satisfaction in developing oneself. Our uniqueness is ours alone, and we should capitalize on our own individuality.

values, attitudes, and interests

Values, attitudes, and interests all affect personality. We reflect our individuality by the values we esteem, the attitudes we express, and the interests that intrigue us. Basic values are derived from attitudes and interests; yet values are broader and more basic in concept.

We each learn values from our culture, environment, family, associates, and individual experiences. Mass media, especially television and advertising, have influenced value patterns. Some values are commonly held by members of a specific culture. There may be a wide variation in the application of cultural values. An example of this is the value of education in the United States. As a culture we value free education for the young; the amount of education deemed necessary by different segments of the population may vary from the basic reading and writing skills to advanced degrees. Individual experience is responsible for such a range in application of this value.

Values are a directive or motivating force in behavior and decision making. Research has established that values that direct other choices also will direct clothing choices. If one holds aesthetic values highest, then clothing will be

[3] Mary Shaw Ryan, *Clothing: A Study of Human Behavior* (New York: Holt, 1966), p. 94.

selected for its attractiveness of line, beauty of fabric, or personal satisfaction of being well dressed. If economic values are highest, clothing purchased may reveal the utility, quality, and price as most important; or the clothing selected may make a statement about financial status (high or low).

Creekmore developed the following relationships between clothing behavior and values rated high.[4]

Clothing Behavior	*Value Rated High*
Management of clothing	Economic
Experimenting in clothing	Exploratory
Status symbol	Political
Appearance	Aesthetic
Conformity	Social
Fashion	Political
Modesty	Religious

Understanding the influences of values on clothing choices is not always easy. Often values conflict, and there is a compromise on the part of the wearer. For example, a girl with a modest income may value conformity with her peer group, but if the family budget will not allow this, she must make some kind of value compromise. Often a conflict of values leads to serious altercation between parents and children. Amount of cosmetics, length of skirts, closeness of fit, décolleté of neckline have all been debated in many families. This happens when the values of the parents conflict with those of their offspring.

Horn found that "the importance of clothing as a means of achieving approval and acceptance is paramount in the value configuration of the adolescent, but this value appears to decrease in favor of aesthetic or economic considerations for those with greater maturity and/or self-confidence." [5] This may explain the wide variety of clothing found on the cosmopolitan college campus as contrasted to the small town high school. As we mature, we are able to express more individuality in our clothing selection.

Over a period of time values may change. Group value change becomes a cultural change. This is particularly true in a technical society. The individual must change with the times. An economic value that has changed drastically is the method most of us use to pay for our clothing. The charge account with all of its ease and temptation is in diametric opposition to the Puritanical belief that indebtedness is sinful. Several social values have changed as the result of understanding the need for physical fitness in men, women, and children. As science

[4] *Ibid.*, p. 103.
[5] Marilyn J. Horn, *The Second Skin* (Boston: Houghton Mifflin, 1968), p. 81.

made discoveries concerning nutrition and physiology, ideas about diet and exercise changed. The clothing requirements demanded by active sports resulted in value changes in how much body exposure was socially acceptable.

Spranger's six ideal types can be used as theoretical guides to aid in understanding people. These ideal types are value directed. Spranger believed that men are best known through a study of subjective values. In daily life a person meets with many situations that call for such evaluative judgments.[6]

Even though these types are isolated, Spranger concluded that one type would not exist in one man but that every value attitude can be found in all personalities in varying degrees.[7] Spranger believed that every person is best characterized by the things he considers of highest value.[8] These values reveal themselves in personalities in the areas that the individual considers to be of greatest importance.

Spranger's value profile is used for testing in the Allport, Vernon, Lindzey *Study of Values* to indicate major areas of endeavor most important to the individual.[9] This test, along with others using Spranger's values, is often used to relate personal values to clothing.

The following table is an adaptation of Spranger's values as applied to clothing. The authors have based the brief descriptions of value upon suggestions from Allport [10] and Hartmann.[11] The relationship of these values to clothing has been made by the authors.

Spranger Type	Description of Value	Relationship to Clothing
Theoretical	Discovery of truth, facts, and information; judgments regarding beauty and utility are not regarded.	Honest use of materials; wears only real jewelry, furs, and leather rather than simulated material; clothing probably of little importance; would look for label.
Economic	Usefulness important; practical; accumulation of wealth; luxury often confused with beauty; commercial.	Comfort, easy to maintain and use; examines carefully to get true dollar value for purchase; comparative shopper; gets best for least cost; abhors waste.

---

[6] P. E. Vernon and G. W. Allport, "A Test for Personal Values," *Journal of Abnormal and Social Psychology,* **26:**231 (1961).

[7] *Ibid.,* p. 236.

[8] George W. Hartmann, *Educational Psychology* (New York: American, 1941), p. 25.

[9] G. W. Allport, P. E. Vernon G. Lindzey, *Study of Values* (Boston: Houghton Mifflin, 1960).

[10] G. W. Allport, *Personality, A Psychological Interpretation,* p. 278.

[11] George W. Hartmann, "Clothing: Personal Problem and Social Issue," *Journal of Home Economics,* **41:**297–98 (1949).

Spranger Type	Description of Value	Relationship to Clothing
Aesthetic	Design; fit beauty; harmony; individualism; mass production a threat to him; expressiveness; creativeness.	Clothing must be attractive, well designed; fit must be perfect, texture and colors pleasing; individuality; hates uniforms; favors hand-woven, hand-wrought jewelry.
Social	Concern for welfare of people; kind; unselfish (concern for providing clothing that would better all people).	Dresses appropriately; would not offend others by wearing what would make them feel uncomfortable; dresses like those in his group; wishes to feel confident in-order to make others comfortable; would not try to dress better than others.
Political	Power; leadership; dominating people (masculinity); vanity; enhancement of self; esteem; wants admiration.	Dresses to impress others and to show he is better than others; would wear status clothing, lodge and fraternity buttons, school rings.
Religious	Mystical, relates himself to entire universe as a complete and orderly system; sees the divine in every event.	Appreciation of God-given gifts of fibers; simplicity is the ideal; no definite texture, no elegance; possesses modesty; uniforms acceptable.

Evaluative judgment of a bathing suit by six different women is given in the following example. One woman may look at a bathing suit and would evaluate its fiber content of polyester (*theoretical* value); another woman would evaluate its colors and design (*aesthetic*); a third woman would consider the care needed for the garment (*economic*); a fourth person might judge if it would be similar, suitable, and approved by other people (*social*); a fifth woman would evaluate it by its new and different lines which would impress people (*political*); and the sixth woman might consider it as being highly immodest (*religious*). (See Figure 4–4.)

A study made by Lapitsky confirmed that there is a positive relationship between clothing values and corresponding general values. This study used the same general values as given by Spranger, but she added a second social value, that of being accepted by others. The Spranger social value was based upon concern for others. She dropped the theoretical and religious values because it was her belief that they are not related to clothing interest.[12]

12 Ryan, *op. cit.*, p. 117.

4–4 Evaluative judgments of a garment will bring varied responses depending on individual attitudes and personal values. (Courtesy Celanese Corporation)

attitudes in relation to personality

Attitudes are individualistic. They are often inherited from parents or family. As we mature, we tend to mold our attitudes based on societal, familial, and educational experiences. Individual attitudes are closely associated with value patterns. A person who has strong aesthetic values will choose clothing for its beauty of design, excitement of texture, and interest of color. A person who has strong social values will select clothing acceptable to her social group (this type of motivation often leads to choices that are fashionable but not becoming to the individual). A person who has strong economic values may display more interest in construction, durability, and maintenance requirements than in the style of the garment. Individual application of values may be thought of as attitude.

The concept of attitude has been divided into three components. The *affective component* refers to the feelings or emotions associated with a given object or entity. Clothing choices can create a wide variety of feelings or emotions.[13] Examples of this are sexuality (by wearing a slinky, décolleté gown), femininity (by wearing a demure, lacy pastel dress), masculinity (by donning a severely tailored pants suit), youthfulness (by selecting a frilly babydoll dress), maturity (by trying a conservative black ensemble), superiority (by wearing very fashionable and expensive clothing), inferiority (by wearing very sleazy, inappropriate garments).

The *cognitive aspect* of attitudes concerns the ideas held about clothing. A man may believe that clothing is unimportant, that it is just a nuisance to be tolerated because of the dictates of his society. A woman may feel that clothing is the key to social status and that by acquiring a large and flamboyant wardrobe she will gain status and recognition.

The *behavioral component* of attitude is inferred from what the person actually does. A girl may stay home from a party because she does not have the right dress. A man may hide behind a voluminous coat because he is fat. Another girl may be an exhibitionist, flaunting propriety with her nudity.

Attitudes explain how we feel, what we think, and how we behave. In relation to clothing, attitudes are expressed in the clothing selected and the behavior while wearing that clothing. Attitudes are personal expressions or interpretations of the values we hold important.

interests in relation to personality

Interest is appeal, concern, or intrigue as opposed to indifference or dislike. One may be interested in a class of things such as rocks, animals, or flowers or interested in a field of study such as astronomy, anthropology, or mathematics. The stronger the interest in a subject, the more the effort put into the study of the area.

Most women are interested in clothing. Clothing is always a good topic of conversation when "small talking" with the girls. Even those who announce no interest in clothing have several opinions to state. The degree of interest in clothing is related to age. Studies report that the age of highest interest in

[13] Horn, *op. cit.,* p. 77.

clothing is late adolescence.[14] This is the age group with the largest wardrobe and the strongest needs to conform and be accepted by a peer group. As a woman matures, her interest in clothing becomes less emphatic, probably because so many other facets of her life develop. The clothing interest of the older woman emphasizes the aesthetic or the economic. She often expresses more individuality by choosing clothing that pleases her and also more concern for price, lasting qualities, and maintenance problems. Although the interest in clothing may be dormant at times in a woman's life, it is usually revived by a special invitation—and the female query: "What shall I wear?"

Men and women display varying degrees of interest in clothing through their attitudes toward clothing and the values they assign to clothing. These variations are due to societal, familial, educational, occupational, and environmental background. The values, attitudes, and interests expressed in clothing are related to other areas of living. The individuality of these values, attitudes, and interests is revealed in clothing selection.

role identification

The modern citizen functions in various capacities in daily living. He performs as a family member, income provider, community participant, friend, and neighbor. These diverse responsibilities are termed roles. A role is defined as the function or part one takes in a particular situation. People are identified by others as they carry out these roles. Part of the nonverbal communication of role identification is the clothing worn (Figure 4–5).

Clothing plays an important part in the life cycle of each individual. At each stage of development clothing functions in a role-identifying capacity. In our society rites of baptism, first communion, bar mitzvah, graduation, marriage, and mourning have certain dress requirements for each participant which identify their roles. Parallels of these examples can be found in even the most primitive societies. Clothing is used in all cultures to identify roles. Every man, woman, and child fulfills a variety of roles within a lifetime. For the purposes of this text we shall elaborate on the roles of women and the relationship of clothing to them.

A contemporary woman in her middle years generally has the primary role of wife. She also functions as mother, housekeeper, cook, hostess, nurse, chauffeur, business, and club woman. She may be employed outside her home and have the additional roles of employee, supervisor, and commuter. You, as a collegian, may have the primary role of a student, but your other functions may

---

[14] Ryan, *op. cit.,* p. 114.

include those of family member, boyfriend or girlfriend, and employee. As life progresses from childhood to old age, the major roles change, usually evolving slowly from one stage to another. Role changes can occur abruptly also—for example, from college student to employee when either funds or grades fail. Roles can and most often do overlap, such as those of student, spouse, and parent.

These diverse roles are expressed in part by clothing changes which a person deems appropriate for the situation. Clothing is used to identify or interpret the role for the observer (Figure 4–6). The waitress is identified by her dress, the hotel doorman is known by his uniform, the theater usher by his costume. This special kind of dress helps to avoid mistaken identity which may cause some embarrassment and also makes performance of tasks easier.

The clothing that one person selects for a specific role may not be expressive of that function to the perceiver. Confusion of roles can result from misinterpretation of clothing cues. When shopping in a department store, has a customer come to you for help, mistaking you for a saleswoman? Evidently the clothing that you donned in the role of shopper resembled the dress of the store personnel. A friend traveling in France purchased a beret so that he would feel dressed more in the manner of the natives. To his pure delight American tourists

4–5 Role identification is communicated by clothing. Pan American stewardesses model their uniforms for use on the 747 Superjet. (Courtesy Pan American World Airways)

4–6 Clothing identifies or interprets a role. The missionary sisters of the Immaculate Heart of Mary model the traditional garb worn by the sisters for sixty-seven years and the new garb with a shortened skirt and modified coif. (Courtesy United Press International)

mistook him for a Parisian and asked him for directions. He happily answered them in his best high school French, which no one could understand! This is an excellent example of clothing misinterpretation.

A serious problem of confusion of role identity from clothing selection results when the observer has preconceived standards of acceptable dress which differ from those of the person wearing the clothes. The student who selects, for classroom wear, an outfit that the instructor feels does not meet the standards of expected dress may set up an adverse reaction. The teacher may immediately equate the student who does not adhere to his dress code with poor scholars, troublemakers, or subversives. This negative impression created by clothing has been responsible for many erroneous judgments, yet people constantly use clothing to identify people.

Young people are probably the most harshly judged for their habiliments.

Older generations expect certain standards of dress. When young people fail to conform to them, they may be stereotyped as being no good. As an example, two attractive college girls experimented with dress on a shopping trip to an exclusive shopping area in Beverly Hills, California. They entered several stores neatly coiffed and groomed but wearing Levi's; they were refused service. They changed the pants for miniskirts and were welcomed into each of the stores. A recent story in the news told of several Cal Tech (brains only) students who were refused service in a restaurant. The boys, all sporting shoulder-length hair, had gone to the café with the mother of one of the students. The waitress observed them and reacted to the hair with the comment, "We do not serve your kind of people here."

The job interview is a situation where appropriate clothing selection is crucial. When applying for a position, one must understand the standards of dress expected. The interviewer will base a great part of his evaluation on the appearance of the applicant, especially clothing cues. Clothing requirements vary with the type of position and with the philosophy of the company. The wise applicant will learn what dress is expected before being interviewed for the job.

Society expects certain kinds of dress, but standards do change as attitudes change. These changes come slowly, however. People who initiate deviations of dress or attire themselves in defiance of the local customs will get more adverse reaction than those who follow later when changes have evolved. The bikini bathing suit was a real shocker when first introduced in the United States in the early 1960s; now it is well accepted. Girls who wore the first mini skirts were considered absolutely immoral by some of the same ladies who picked up the fashion several years after it had become established. A perusal of historical costume will reveal that all parts of the male and female anatomy have, at one time or another, been emphasized by fashion. Each innovation has caused excited disapproval which gradually calmed down into acceptance. To be a fashion innovator takes courage and flamboyance which all do not possess.

As the individual's roles change, wardrobe requirements also change. The more major the changes, the more demands for different kinds of clothing. As role change is anticipated, careful wardrobe plans should be made. The college graduate, ready for a career role, will find college clothing inadequate unless he has anticipated this change. The bride's extensive trousseau may soon be unsuitable when her role becomes that of mother. The position of a new career man may demand business attire which was absent from the collegiate wardrobe. The clothing purchases of the final school years should really be made with postschool roles in mind.

Consider your present roles. Make a list. Are you student, employee, date, sports enthusiast, club member? For each of your roles, what is considered appropriate dress? Can some of your clothing be used for several roles? What part of your wardrobe is limited to specific uses? How does your present wardrobe fit the many roles of your life?

what kind of person are you?

A person can never reach full potential unless he likes himself and those around him. This is a very important combination and is the basis of all interpersonal relationships.

One must like oneself to feel worthy of friendships and social intercourse. Liking oneself is closely related to how interesting a person you are. Continually expanding one's knowledge and experiences, learning tolerance and flexibility, developing sympathy and compassion are all attributes of the mature. Being both interested and interesting; learning to be generous with oneself and one's time; giving love, friendship, and support to those you hold dear; being the kind of friend to others that you expect in your own friendships—these attributes are the ones that put a glow in the plainest face. These are the unpurchasable accessories that complete every man and woman.

THE PERSON YOU ARE

What kind of person are you? Good looks, brains, and clothes aside, what do you possess in unpurchasable accessories? These are the traits, qualities, and attitudes that make up the person you are. They cannot be bought, but one can strive toward them. Do you make long and lasting friendships, or do people tend to shy away from you? Do you antagonize your friends and family, or do they seek you out? Is your attitude a cloud of gloom or one of brightness? Do you possess the personal qualities necessary to compete in the employment market? Everyone knows that appearance and skills are important, but employment counselors tell us that the most common reason for releasing employees is their inability to get along with others. Interpersonal relationships rate high in determining a person's success or failure in all phases of living.

Most every person is keenly interested in being sought after, admired by friends, and respected. Why do some people appear to have attained this goal, while others seem to be loners and ignored by all but a few? Take time to analyze those whom you admire. What makes them a success? What traits and qualities do they possess that give them this envied position? Close scrutiny of a person who has been successful in interpersonal relationships will undoubtedly reveal that it was not natural beauty or good looks or an expensive wardrobe. Those accouterments do not make friendships or success. They will attract momentary attention, but they will not sustain interest on the part of others unless something deeper becomes apparent rather quickly.

A person who has made deep and lasting friendships and who gets along well with others will be one whom others consider sincere, loyal, warm, and tactful. He expresses true interest in others, both older and younger. He will be himself in a truly individual manner and not try to be what he is not. Because he is himself, he is natural and unaffected and sincere. He makes friends not to benefit from them but because his interest in them is genuinely sincere. Psychologist Hoff said of a psychologically healthy person,

He treats others as ends in themselves rather than a means to his own ends. He values human relationships not for what they can bring him but for what they in themselves mean. He doesn't use people as things. He enjoys them as persons.[15]

True friendship means acceptance of others' shortcomings as well as acceptance of their positive virtues. Lasting friendships are built upon confidence and loyalty. One must stand by friends loyally and defend them when necessary. One must be trusted when confidences are given.

The quality of warmth is difficult to define, but it is readily felt. Warmth is the result of a feeling of sincerity on the part of the giver; friendly people are warm in their interactions with others. This quality is accompanied by a smile, direct eye contact, a firm handshake, and a genuine interest in other people.

Tact is defined as saying or doing the right thing without offending others. It does not mean that a person is always agreeable or insincere. A tactful person gets the point across without offending and always considers the feelings of others.

Attitude rates high in importance as an unpurchasable accessory. It is used here to describe disposition or temperament. Some people frame themselves with a frown and spread perpetual gloom. They most often see the dark side of every situation and are most willing to disapprove, criticize, and cast a curtain of despair and discouragement. These individuals are a trial to be around. Each person has his own share of discouraging and difficult problems without having the burden weighted by poor attitudes of others. Attitude is as contagious as the common cold. A cheerful and enthusiastic disposition evokes a positive reaction from others. It is also a people attractor. A pleasant attitude is signaled by a smile and a happy countenance. Of course, a bad day now and then happens to most everyone, but habitual grouchiness is too much for anyone to tolerate.

As you the kind of person who can be counted on to accept responsibility? When someone gives you something to do, can you be relied upon to get it done? Accepting responsibility involves meeting and solving problems as they arise and carrying out projects to completion. Many begin reading a book but never get to the end, never quite finish an assignment on time, continually drop

---

[15] George Hoff, "The Psychologically Healthy Person," *The South Coast Daily Pilot Newspaper,* February 25, 1967, p. 17.

courses, and forget to attend meetings. Accepting responsibility also means accepting the consequences of our actions, which is a sign of maturity. Placing the blame on someone else may help to protect the ego, but this is a distortion of reality.

Another valuable but unpurchasable accessory that some people have is the art of conversation. This is fast becoming a lost skill for those who have substituted TV, the radio, films, and games to fill in the moments that formerly were spent conversing with others. Many people are puzzled by what to talk about, and they are uncertain of how to begin a conversation. The transfer of ideas among people is a most satisfying experience. It requires being a good listener as well as developing the ability to verbally express oneself. It has been said that there are four levels of conversation. The highest level is the discussion of ideas, next is conversation about events and things that happen, followed by conversation about other people. The bottom level is talking about oneself. People do enjoy talking about themselves and their particular interests. Conversations can be easily initiated by asking others questions related to their interests. The top level of conversation requires a background of knowledge, reading, comparing, and thinking. This type of interchange is a rare phenomenon in most of our daily conversation. When talking to others, look at them directly; it shows your undivided interest in them.

These are but a few of the unpurchasable accessories that can help to make you the kind of person you may wish to be. They are qualities that are worth the time and effort it takes to make them a functioning part of our being and they are more valuable than anything we can buy.

conclusion

Understanding of oneself is the important element in individuality in clothing selection and personal appearance. The manner in which we present ourselves reflects how we feel about ourselves and others. In order to project ourselves in an accurate manner, it is necessary to undertake a study of our individuality so that we can determine the unique qualities that separate us from others. We must analyze our personality traits and develop an accurate self-concept. We need to become aware of our values, attitudes, and interests. We need to assess our roles and relationships to others. We must know who and what we are, and we must work to become a person we like and enjoy.

All of this is a difficult task for any person because it requires complete honesty and objectivity. It is especially difficult for young adults because their personalities are still forming. Learning, growing, and discovering are all part of the long road to maturity and should never stop. Along the way to adulthood many young people try different roles and forms of expression; for many this trial-and-error process is an important part of maturation. The important idea to remember is to continually seek better personal understanding. Years of growing, living, and experiencing are necessary to achieve self-knowledge. The teen and twenty years are needed for this; the thirties should be the time self-knowledge becomes a reality. The following years should be confident ones with continuous achievement, understanding, and compassion for others.

selected readings

Allport, G. W. *Becoming—Basic Considerations for a Psychology of Personality.* New Haven, Conn.: Yale University Press, 1968.

———. *Personality, a Psychological Interpretation.* New York: Holt, Rinehart & Winston, Inc., 1937.

Hall, Calvin S., and Gardner Lindzey. *Theories of Personality.* New York: John Wiley & Sons, Inc., 1962. Ch. 1.

Hartmann, George W. "Clothing: Personal Problem and Social Issue," *Journal of Home Economics,* **41** (1949), 297–98.

Horn, Marilyn J. *The Second Skin.* Boston: Houghton Mifflin Company, 1968.

Jersild, Arthur T. *Child Psychology.* Englewood Cliffs, N.J.: Prentice-Hall, Inc., 1968.

Ryan, Mary Shaw. *Clothing: A Study of Human Behavior.* New York: Holt, Rinehart & Winston, Inc., 1966.

Vernon, P. E., and G. W. Allport. "A Test for Personal Values," *Journal of Abnormal and Social Psychology,* **26** (1961), 231.

5

figure analysis, control, and camouflage

*P*eople come in an infinite variety of forms. Humans vary in height, weight, shape, posture, carriage, and bearing. The basic factors responsible for such variety are heredity, nutrition, and environment.

One of the most individual features about you is your figure or body structure. Unless yours was a multiple birth that resulted in identical siblings, you are the only one with your body design. The bone structure that you have inherited has been influenced by your racial background and your ancestral heritage. This frame is one thing you cannot change (there are some rare exceptions). If you are tall or short, small boned or large boned, accept it. This is you. This is part of your individuality.

Your nutritional status in early years has had a tremendous influence on your body development. Malnutrition in infancy and childhood, whatever its cause, affects the conformation of the body. Some evidences of nutritional deficiencies are stunted growth, misshapen limbs, emotional instability, dental caries, and obesity. Nutrition of the mature individual is a personal responsibility. If in the past you have had nutritional problems, make a concerted effort to correct them now.

5–1 The self-concept may not be realistic.

Environment and culture influence growth patterns. In the United States Westerners are generally larger than Easterners. Sunshine and exercise could be largely responsible for this. Cultural ideas of beauty have a tremendous influence on figure development. In a culture where bosoms are admired, women strive to develop the bust. In a culture where wide hips are a beauty symbol, hiplines are emphasized. Fashion also influences the figure. The beauties of the hourglass figure had the same standard equipment as those of the flapper age. This distortion of the body was dictated by fashion.

Another element closely related to the presentation of the figure is individual self-confidence. The man who has a positive attitude toward himself and life in general relates this in the manner in which he carries his body. The person who is less sure of himself often makes this statement in his carriage. Oftentimes his posture is slumped and slovenly, almost as though he were apologizing for taking up floor space.

Analyze your body as objectively as you can. List the assets and the liabilities. If you can make a correction, decide to do so. If you cannot make a change, decide to accept this as part of your uniqueness. It helps to keep in mind that no one is absolutely perfect, and it is the imperfections that give one individuality.

self-concept of physical self

As discussed in Chapter 4, we each have our own self-concept of our physical self. It is a mental image of ourself. This self-concept may be a distortion of reality (Figure 5–1). We often see people wearing clothing that tends to exaggerate the figure flaws we would imagine they would prefer to hide. Those people probably perceive themselves much differently from the observer seeing them. For example, the thin girl wearing clothing that exaggerates her boniness may not perceive herself as being skinny. The plump woman with broad hips and thighs who selects skin-tight stretch pants may not visualize herself as heavy in the derrière.

To have a true concept of one's physical self requires complete objectivity. An honest figure analysis must be made with the mind as well as the eye. Once the figure is realistically observed, clothing decisions can be made that will enhance the figure assets and camouflage the figure liabilities.

figure control

Physical fitness is imperative to good health. Most children and teen-agers exercise strenuously as part of their daily lives. As we mature, our daily activities usually grow less strenuous, and although we experience tiredness it is usually induced by boredom or mental fatigue rather than by strenuous exercise.

The body needs strenuous exercise to maintain tonus and strength, burn off food intake, and help in the functioning of the vital organs such as the heart, lungs, and circulatory system. Physical exertion, if incorporated into a lifelong plan, will also slow down the aging process and add grace to your movements. There are various kinds of exercises. Each kind of exercise produces a certain type of result.

ISOMETRICS (Literally, "Equal Measure")

Isometric exercises contract one set of muscles without producing movement or demanding large amounts of oxygen. They tense one set of muscles against another or against an immovable object. Examples of isometric exercises are pushing against opposite sides of a door jamb or pushing toes hard against the floor. Isometric exercises date back to the 1920s but have gained a great deal of popularity recently. Isometrics are capable of increasing the size and strength of individual skeletal muscles. They can firm and tone these muscles, and this is what they should be used to do. Let no claim of "physical fitness in only sixty seconds a day" mislead you. This is truly impossible. While isometrics are great for developing muscles, they have little significant effect on overall health, especially on the pulmonary and cardiovascular systems.

ISOTONICS (Literally, "Equal Tension")

Isotonic exercises contract muscles and produce movement. Popular isotonics are calisthenics and weight lifting and some games like shuffleboard, archery, and horseshoes. As a form of exercise, isotonics are preferable to isometrics because they exercise muscles over a range of motion. Isotonics also develop the skeletal muscles. They have very little effect on the pulmonary and cardiovascular systems because this type of exercise is not sustained over a long enough period of time. These exercises are fine for firming and toning the body. The biggest problem with them is maintaining vigor and enthusiasm while doing them. For some zealots this is great exercise, but for most it is just too much.

AEROBICS (Literally, "With Oxygen")

These are the exercises that demand oxygen and can be continued over a long period of time. The best exercises in this category are running, jogging, swimming, cycling, walking, and stationary running, in that order; also participant sports like golf, tennis, and volleyball. These exercises are the ones that should be the basis of any fitness program. The physical effects produced by aerobics are roughly these: your lungs begin processing more air and with less effort; your heart grows stronger, pumping more blood with fewer strokes; the blood supply to the muscles improves; and your total blood volume increases. In short, you are improving your body's capacity to bring in oxygen and deliver it to the tissue cells, where it combines with food to produce energy.

If you are interested in firming and reshaping the figure, a combination of all three types of exercises could be used in a crash program to speed results. For a lifetime of physical fitness one of the aerobic exercises should be incorporated into your pattern of living. Choose the things you really like to do. If you feel self-conscious, find a friend to do them with you. Walking the dog is a most compatible aerobic exercise and one that can be enjoyed completely by both parties.

height-weight distribution

In figure analysis the most important factor to consider is the distribution of weight on the frame. It is not your actual weight that is important, for this can vary widely among persons appearing to be the same size (Figure 5–2). Study of average weight charts is not particularly helpful either. These charts simply present the arithmetic average weight of a group of various sizes and ages of people. What matters most is how you carry your weight on your frame.

Pleasing distribution of flesh over the frame is the desirable. Too plump or too gaunt figures should be corrected. These figure faults are most obvious and most difficult to correct. Obesity is considered a leading nutritional disease in the United States. Its causes may be many, but in most all cases obesity can be corrected. Extreme overweight is probably the most difficult of all figure problems to live with. It is much like being locked in a jail of fat—and very often it is a solitary confinement. For at the very time the obese need attention and compatibility, they are most often rejected. The obese person should always seek competent professional help to plan and supervise a weight reduction plan. Many people have suffered serious consequences to their health because of "do-it-yourself" diets (see Chapter 6).

To the overweight, the underweight person's plight seems a delight. The underweight are generally healthier and usually live longer with fewer serious ailments. While fashion mannequins represent the ultimate in underweight, what woman really wants to be that bony in real life? It is the boniness that is really difficult to dress. An underweight woman must wear very concealing clothing or her bones show. Pant garments are at their very worst on the extremely thin woman. Décolleté necklines, sleeveless outfits, and figure-revealing garments are all impossible for the too thin.

A weight-gaining regime should follow the suggestions made in Chapter 6 on nutrition. It takes effort and patience. A reputable medical authority should be consulted. One nice thing about chronic underweight is that it usually disappears by middle age!

A very common figure fault is the deposits of avoirdupois tissue in certain areas such as the thigh, hip, or midriff. A person may have a very good distribution of weight on the frame except in these specific areas. It is common for family members to inherit this tendency of fat deposits. The remedy for this figure fault is exercise and physical fitness. The problem may never be completely remedied, but (excuse the pun) it will certainly be reduced.

A most important form of figure control is the development of strong muscles to support the body. Although foundation garments have a definite role in

5–2   Weight distribution varies with the individual.

the wardrobe, they should never be depended upon entirely for body support.
If you have depended on a girdle for support, decide now to make the effort
to develop your abdominal and back muscles. This is really vital to your
general health.

FIGURE CAMOUFLAGE FOR WOMEN

In several areas of this text we discuss the art of camouflage in dress. The
line, design, color, and texture of a garment all contribute to fashionable
camouflage. Eye-arresting elements can divert the eye of the beholder from
figure problem areas. A neat hair style and immaculate grooming also stream-
line. There is yet another set of tricks which can be incorporated by any woman
to create the illusion of a more perfect figure. These tricks are not magic at all—
but very basic. They all revolve around learning to use your body gracefully.

Instant Slimness

Most every woman dreams of instant slimness, and it really is simple to
achieve. With some concentration it can be yours always. Fundamental to instant
slimness is correct posture. Stand up and pull in the tummy and lift up the rib
cage—instantly your waist is smaller, perhaps an inch or two. Walk around as if
you were trying to see just over the head of someone walking in front of you.
Perhaps you would rather hold your head high by pretending you were being
lifted by the ears. Practice this posture. Avoid too stiff a look and do remember
to breathe!

The second part of instant slimness is the stance or standing position. Check
this one in the mirror and you will be delighted. Face the mirror with your new
posture and then turn slightly so you present your body on an angle. The forward foot should point straight ahead, the back foot placed at a 45-degree angle
just behind the front foot (Figure 5–3). The weight should be divided equally on

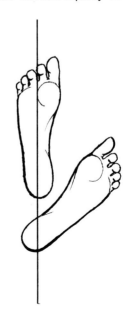

5–3 The foot position for the single-leg line.

both feet; this is important so that the back hip does not protrude. To maintain this position for long periods of time, keep the knees slightly flexed.

The foot position described above is called a single-leg line. This should be presented as often as possible. It gives a more flattering line to the legs and aids in camouflaging less-than-perfect leg contours. Examine your legs in the mirror. Compare the double-leg line with the single-leg line—instant slimness again!

Walking

This is one of the most important body movements to make you appear graceful. The walk you have acts as an introduction to you in a great number of situations. A walk should be easy and graceful. The length of your stride should be in proportion to your figure type. The tall woman walking with a mincing step is as silly looking as the petite girl who has the stride of a burly athlete.

When you walk, the feet should move parallel to each other; do not toe in (pigeon-toed) or toe out (duck walk). With each step, lead with the thigh (as though a string were pulling the thigh before the rest of the body). The knees should be slightly flexed so that they act as shock absorbers. The shoulders should be relaxed, the arms swinging easily. The palm of the hand is directed toward the skirt. The fingertips, slightly curved, should just brush the side of the skirt.

Accessories are an important part of "instant slimness" and should be considered briefly. A simple, uncluttered pump with fashionable heel height is most flattering to the leg. If the stocking and shoe color blend, the length of the leg will appear to be greater. Eye-arresting interest in the "personality area" emphasizes the upper part of the figure. Small handbags of the "clutch" variety held above the waistline lend themselves best to the illusion of slimness. The large dangling handbag adds width at the hipline or appears to drag the figure down when it is carried below the hemline.

Stairs

Maneuvering stairs gracefully is a challenge to anyone. The degree of skill in this feat is directly related to the strength in the thigh as are many graceful movements. Posture retains its importance in going up and down stairs. The back should be kept straight and the head up. View the stairs before you get there. A glance down as you begin the climb is permissible, but the stairs will not move, so intense staring is not necessary. Resting the hand easily on the banister is both a good safety habit and a graceful gesture.

Going up the stairs, place the entire foot on each step, push and lift with the thigh muscles. Going down the stairs, glance at each step as you approach it. Place the entire foot on the stair. Keep the weight on the back leg until the other foot is firmly placed on the step below.

If at all possible, practice stair climbing and descending in front of a mirror. Work to achieve a single-leg line here, too. Fashion models can be observed for

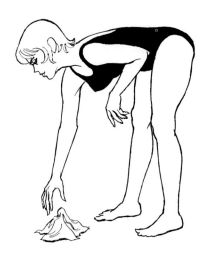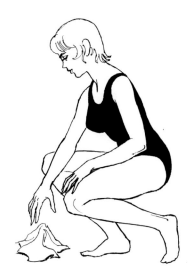

5–4   Depend on leg muscles rather than back muscles for bending and
lifting.

additional techniques. Most department stores feature fashion shows along with
their luncheon menu. As the mannequins parade, you can watch instant slimness
in action.

Picking Things Up

Methods of picking up objects from the floor should always use the strong
leg muscles which lower and push the body rather than the weaker back muscles (Figure 5–4). This holds true no matter how bulky the object. The correct
lifting technique also presents the prettiest picture.

Approach the object so that you are standing beside it; one hand should be
directly over the object, one foot slightly ahead of the other for balance. As you
pick up the object, bend deeply at the knees, with the buttocks tucked under
and the back straight. Return to standing positon.

Hand Grace

Hands can easily spoil the graceful illusion. When you have nothing to do
with your hands, let them do nothing! Study the effect of some of these hand
positions and use them. For a time they may seem a bit strained, but with practice they will quickly become a part of your movements.

Let one hand rest easily on a chair arm; let the other rest in your lap, palm
up, fingers slightly curled. Avoid both elbows on chair arms; this adds body
width and is not graceful.

Clasp hands slightly and let them both rest quietly in your lap. Do not twist
and fidget with them. Place one hand over the other and hold them slightly to one
side, resting palms down, on the upper thigh. The hand appears most graceful in

124   profile. Learn to keep your hands at a slight angle with the body. Hold the index finger slightly extended, the other fingers curled and the thumb curled just into the palm. When you must point, use this hand positon. When walking with a man, hold his arm, tucking your hand into the bend of his elbow. Do not allow him to hold your arm or propel you along by the elbow.

Arm Grace

When standing or walking, hold the elbows down and slightly out from the body so that the waist outline will be distinct. The arms in this position appear more graceful and the figure slimmer. When you are standing, your arms may be gracefully folded or clasped behind you. If the arms are hanging at the side of the body, always keep them behind the side seamline of the skirt. This position does not increase the width of the figure.

see yourself as you really are

Developing objectivity requires several approaches. While developing an understanding of the psyche, it is also important to learn about the physical self. Body proportions are based on the head length as the unit of measurement. For accuracy, have another person take your measurements.

Direction for Analysis of the Body Proportions
1. To measure the head length:
   a. Using two tailor's squares placed together as shown in Figure 5–5, measure from the top of the head to the chin. Make certain that the squares are level at the top of the head and the bottom of the chin. This can be marked

5–5

on a chalk board. (If necessary, rulers may be substituted for tailor's squares.)

b. Using this measurement of the head length, cut a piece of paper to the exact measurement.

c. Fold the paper in halfs, fourths, eights, and sixteenths along the head length measurement. Mark these divisions and label. Use this measurement exactly as you would use a ruler.

2. To measure the body length
   a. Use the head-length paper to measure your body lengths from top of head to the following points:
      (1) base of neck
      (2) shoulder
      (3) point of bust or chest
      (4) waist
      (5) fullest part of hip
      (6) center of knee cap
      (7) ankle
      (8) floor
   b. Record these on the chart.

3. To measure body widths
   a. Use the head length to measure body widths. (This is more accurately done by first using the two tailor's squares in the same manner as it was used to determine head length and later converting the measure into head lengths.) Measure the width of the following:
      (1) shoulder
      (2) waist
      (3) largest part of hip
      (4) knees (together, across center)
      (5) ankles (together, across bone)
   b. Record these on the chart.

4. Plot your proportions
   a. Using the scale of one head length to one inch, plot your body lengths and widths as shown in the fashion figure and the average figure.
   b. Fold the drawing of your figure crosswise in halfs and fourths.
      ½ of the figure—hip placement
      ¼ of the figure—underarm placement
      ¼ of the figure—knee placement
      ½ of the area between the underarm and the hip—waist placement

5. Compare your body proportions with the average figure and the fashion figure (Figures 5–6 and 5–7). The average figure is a compilation of many individuals' measurements. The fashion figure is an elongated artist's representation of the human body. The fashion figure is 8 to 8½ head-length's tall, while

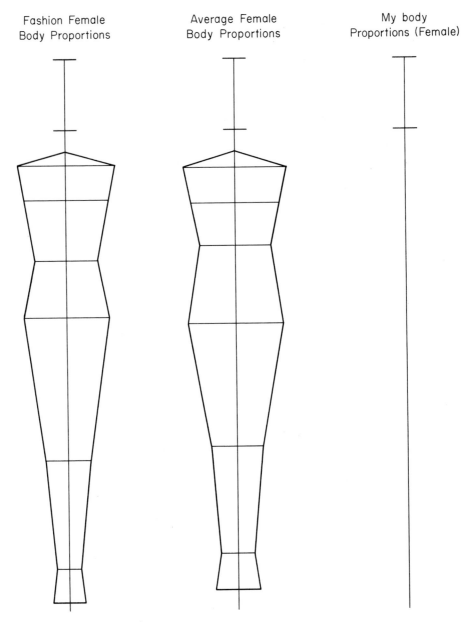

Fashion Female
Body Proportions

Average Female
Body Proportions

My body
Proportions (Female)

Scale ¾" = I head length

5–6

Average Male
Body Proportions

My Body
Proportions (Male)

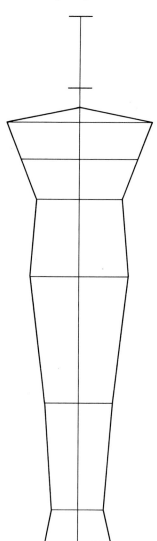

5–7

the average figure is 7½ head lengths. This may explain why clothing looks so very different when taken from the artist's sketch and placed on your figure.

Use this schematic drawing of your figure to compare with the fashion figure and average figure. Study the variations of the three body types. Use this comparison to decide how you wish to project your individual image. Application of the guidelines presented in further chapters will assist you in this project.

One of the most effective tools to employ to see yourself as you really are is a series of full-length photographs taken in a figure-revealing costume, such as a leotard. These pictures should be taken with the weight equally distributed on each foot; the hands and arms should not interfere with the body silhouette. Two pictures, front and profile, are necessary; if possible, a full back view is also helpful. These pictures should be studied carefully and every variation noted. Remember, it is the distribution of weight on the frame that is important. Body alignment can be checked by drawing a line from earlobe to anklebone on the profile. Compare sides of the line. On the front and/or back view draw a line from center head through ankles. Compare sides. Draw a line across shoulders, chest or bust, waist, hips, knees. Analyze your body carefully as shown in Figures 5–6 and 5–7—remember, this is how you look. Work with this figure now. If you "shape up" and add or lose weight, start over with new pictures. If you are going to learn to be objective with yourself, you must accept this picture as the truth and the starting point.

A third method for measuring body proportions is to trace the body against a large sheet of paper fixed to the wall. Outline of front and side view are drawn. Comparisons to average and fashion figures can then be made.

COMPARISON OF BODY PROPORTIONS BASED ON HEAD MEASUREMENT

Length	Female Fashion Figure	Young Female	Self	Male
Top of head to				
Chin	1	1	1	1
Base of neck	1⅓	1⅓		1⅓
Shoulder	1½	1½		1½
Bust–chest	2	2		2
Waist	2⅚	2⅔		2⅔
Full hip	4	3¾		3¾
Knee	6	5½		5½
Ankle	7½	7		7
Floor	8	7½		7½
Width				
Shoulder	1½	1½		2
Waist	1	¾		1¼
Full hip	1⅔	1¼		1½
Knee	¾	⅔		1
Ankle	½	⅓		¾

summary figure control

The skeletal frame of the body is a unique possession that has been determined by heredity. The distribution of flesh on this frame has certain family characteristics, but to a large extent it is determined by diet and activity. Good nutritional status is a vital part of figure control. Exercise in a variety of forms is necessary throughout the life span. Proper diet and exercise are both basic to good health and longevity.

The use of the body can create the illusion of grace and vitality. Correct posture while walking, standing, and sitting is important. Movement of the limbs should be done in a fluid manner. Hand, foot, arm, and leg positions should be studied so that they are graceful in motion or in repose.

suggested readings

Brockman, Helen L. *The Theory of Fashion Design.* New York: John Wiley & Sons, Inc., 1965.

Cooper, Kenneth H. *Aerobics.* New York: Bantam Books, 1968.

Morton, Grace. *The Arts of Costume and Personal Appearance.* New York: John Wiley & Sons, Inc., 1964.

Powers, John Robert. *How to Have Model Beauty, Poise, and Personality.* Englewood Cliffs, N.J.: Princeton-Hall, Inc., 1964.

President's Council on Physical Fitness. *Adult Physical Fitness.* Washington, D.C.: U.S. Government Printing Office. 1963.

Szekely, Edmond B. *Golden Door Book of Beauty and Health.* Rev. ed. Los Angeles: Ward Ritchie Press, 1967.

Tolman, Ruth. *Charm and Poise for Getting Ahead.* New York: Milady Publishing Corporation, 1968.

6

nutrition and health

no one, no matter what age, can ever reach his health potential without a well-balanced diet. We are what we eat! Hair, skin, nails, teeth, plus good health and emotional stability, all reflect the food habits of the individual. Each age of development, from embryo to elderly, has special nutrient needs. Understanding these nutritional needs for growth, development, and maintenance is essential for anyone who desires a lifetime of attractiveness, optimum health, and emotional stability.

Food patterns vary from one culture to another just as they do from one family to another. Before World War II the Japanese were of very small stature. Nutritional improvements since the end of World War II have helped many Japanese to reach their growth potential, which corresponds to that of the North Americans. Food habits of families are often obvious and are exhibited by overweight or underweight tendencies of family members.

An abundance of food does not necessarily mean that the nutritional needs of the individual will be met. For the individual makes the food choices, and these selections may not supply adequate nutrition. Many factors influence food patterns or choices. A discussion of these will help you analyze and understand your own diet pattern.

131

basic influences of eating habits

Basic influences on eating habits may be grouped as follows:

Food Supply. This refers to the amount and variety of food available, which vary tremendously from one area of the world to another. People who depend on their own resources to raise and provide their own food often have very limited supplies. Others who live in cosmopolitan centers have a great variety and volume of foodstuffs from which to choose.

Economic Status. Economic status is the ability of the individual or family to afford the foods that are available. However, recent studies have revealed that those with the most limited resources often make the poorest utilization of their food money; that is, they often buy high-cost items of low nutritional benefit.

Family Eating Habits. Family meal patterns may be deeply rooted in racial, religious, national, or regional customs. Family food habits are also developed over generations. Individual food habits are derived from these family practices.

Social Customs. Attitudes and practices of sharing food with friends and strangers may be based on ancient rites. Peer group practices further influence food choices.

Emotional Associations. Situations that generate emotions such as pleasure, annoyance, or frustration may result in strong attitudes, either positive or negative, toward individual foods or eating in general. Often, there is a strong carryover from childhood in these emotional associations. The practice of some families of forcing the child to always "clean up his plate" has been responsible for adult aversion to many foods. Candy or dessert given as a reward to a child has created a strong association between good behavior and sweets.

Sensory Reactions. The individual's response to the smell, flavor, appearance, and/or texture of various foods may result in acceptance or rejection of it.

Educational Influences. The understanding and application of the principles of basic nutrition can act as a guide to the selection and preparation of foods. Through education many food prejudices may be broken down. By understanding the basic concepts of nutrition, the individual can establish the patterns of eating to meet the daily requirements of the body for optimum health.

Relate these influences to your own dietary habits. Try to analyze why you eat as you are eating. Do you have food prejudices? What are they? Do they affect your nutritional status? What part does food play in your life—is it very important or not so important? If, by the end of this chapter, you find fault in your eating habits, are you going to be willing to change them? Do you use food in a capacity other than for nourishment; that is, as a reward or emotional release? How does your appearance reflect your nutritional status?

basic four

During World War II it was discovered that large numbers of draftees were unfit for military service because of nutritional deformities or diseases. Yes, this happened in the United States in the early 1940s. Because of this appalling situation President Roosevelt appointed a commission to develop a national guide to eating a nutritionally adequate diet. The result of this commission was the Basic Seven Food Plan, which has now been modified to the Basic Four (Figure 6–1). This is a guide to meal planning for all ages and a tool to use to measure each day's menu. Because of its simplicity, it should be committed to memory and used daily.

BASIC FOUR MEAL PATTERN

Many students being introduced to the Basic Four Meal Pattern for the first time react strongly. Some claim that if they ate all that food each day, they would become "elephantinas"; others claim that they could not possibly eat all that food in one week, let alone in one day! Yet, this is how we should eat. Listed below are several kinds of diets all following the Basic Four Meal Pattern. Study them closely and see which one meets your needs. Then try it for a period of time. Remember, this is the food pattern you should follow for optimum health, vitality, and emotional stability. Learn to make substitutions so that your favorite foods are fitted into the meal patterns. This should become a lifetime pattern for your own eating and also for family meal planning.

food nutrients and functions

In addition to the Basic Four, which is only a guide to meal planning, a knowledge of the six classes of essential nutrients will assist in forming a better understanding of the importance of the inclusion of each in the daily diet. There is some overlapping in the role of the various nutrients, but they may be classified as follows:

1. Body building, maintenance, and repair
   Proteins   Minerals
   Vitamins   Water

A Guide to Good Eating

Use Daily:

Milk Group

3 or more glasses milk — Children
smaller glasses for some children under **8**

4 or more glasses — Teen-agers

2 or more glasses — Adults

Cheese, ice cream and other milk-made foods can supply part of the milk

Meat Group

2 or more servings

Meats, fish, poultry, eggs, or cheese—with dry beans, peas, nuts as alternates

Vegetables and Fruits

4 or more servings

Include dark green or yellow vegetables; citrus fruit or tomatoes

Breads and Cereals

4 or more servings

Enriched or whole grain Added milk improves nutritional values

This is the foundation for a good diet. Use more of these and other foods as needed for growth, for activity, and for desirable weight.

The nutritional statements made in this leaflet have been reviewed by the Council on Foods and Nutrition of the American Medical Association and found consistent with current authoritative medical opinion.

6–1 Basic Four food groups. (Courtesy National Dairy Council)

2. Body fuel for energy and heat
    Carbohydrates (sugars and starches)
    Proteins
    Fats
3. Regulation of body processes
    Vitamins
    Minerals
    Water

BASIC MEAL PATTERN

Meal	For Weight Gain	Basic Meal Pattern	For Weight Loss
Breakfast	Have cereal and egg Increase butter Add jam Increase milk	Fruit Cereal or egg Toast Milk	Use nonfat milk

Lunch	Add soup, preferably
	  creamed
		Protein food: meat, fish,
		  chicken, cheese,
		  egg, peanut butter,
		  dried beans or peas
		Cooked vegetable
		Raw vegetable or fruit	

	Add extra slice of bread	Bread and butter	Omit bread and butter
	Choose puddings, cus- tards, or ice cream	Dessert	Choose fruit
	Increase milk	Milk	Use nonfat milk

Packed
  lunch
	Have two sandwiches	Sandwiches (using
		  meat, cheese, egg,
		  fish or peanut butter)
		Vegetable (carrot or
		  celery sticks)
		Fruit
			Only one sandwich

	Increase milk	Milk Dessert (cookies, cupcakes)	Use nonfat milk Omit dessert

Dinner	Add gravies
	Use extra butter
		Main dish (meat, fish,
		  poultry, or alternate)
		Potatoes
			Omit gravies and fried
			  foods
			Choose either potato
			  or bread

	Creamed vegetables Use oil dressing	Cooked vegetable Raw salad (fruit or vegetable) Bread and butter	

	Increase milk	Milk
		Dessert (puddings,
		  cake, cookies, pies,
		  ice cream)
			Use nonfat milk
			Omit dessert

PROTEINS

Proteins are essential to the building and maintenance of body tissues. Meat, eggs, legumes, cheese, milk, nuts, grain, and fish are sources of protein.

Proteins are part of every living cell, and life without them is not possible. The body wears out cells every second. These cells, blood, bone, muscle, nerve, and connective tissue must be rebuilt and repaired through protein-bearing foods. Protein will also be burned as fuel if the diet supplies too little of the carbohydrates and fats to meet the energy needs.

Proteins, through the process of digestion, are converted into building units called *amino acids.* Some proteins contain all the essential amino acids and are called "complete" proteins; others contain only a few amino acids and are referred to as "incomplete." The incomplete proteins need to be supplemented by other protein-bearing foods in order for the body to obtain the necessary amino acids. In general, proteins of animal origin are complete proteins, whereas vegetable proteins are usually incomplete or partially complete.

Protein is not stored in the body, so a daily supply is needed. One pint of milk, or milk substitute (cheese, ice cream), and two servings of protein food, of which one should be another complete protein, are recommended daily for upkeep of the adult body. In cooking, proteins are hardened and toughened by high temperatures. Proteins are most tender and readily digested when cooked at low temperatures.

MINERALS

The body contains many minerals which must be replaced daily by foods containing them. Minerals are essential for normal growth, body maintenance, and body-regulating processes. Minerals are constituents of bones, teeth, and soft tissues, and they give elasticity to muscle and nerves. In the American diet the minerals most often supplied in insufficient amounts are calcium, iodine, and iron. Interestingly, when these three minerals are adequately supplied, it generally is found that the other minerals are in sufficient amount.

Some minerals are water soluble, which means that they are absorbed from foods by liquids. In cooking very little water should be used. If liquid is left after food is removed, it should be utilized in soups or sauces, since discarding this liquid means a loss of minerals.

The role of each mineral is continually being investigated and better understood. Minerals in adequate supply are vital to life itself.

VITAMINS

Vitamins are compounds that occur in minute quantities in foods. They are necessary for normal growth and development of the body and for the maintenance of health. All vitamins are found in food sources, and some are synthesized or produced in the body.

Nutritional-deficiency diseases such as pellagra, beriberi, scurvy, and rickets may be eliminated by incorporation of vitamins in the diet. These diseases are thought by many to be relegated to history, yet it is not terribly uncommon to find symptoms of them in modern society, not only among the indigent who lack food resources but also among the legions of do-it-yourself dieters.

Vitamin potency is diminished in storage and often oxidized by exposure to air. Much vitamin value may be lost in food preparation (including the thawing of frozen foods).

Vitamins can be made synthetically, as is done in pills and food additives. The use of vitamin pills should be discussed with a personal physician.

Foods are the natural sources of vitamins. Very few foods contain all the known vitamins. Foods that come directly from nature to the table unprocessed are the highest in vitamin content. Dairy products, lean meats, whole grains, fruits, and vegetables are the chief sources of vitamins. A daily diet containing a sufficient supply of all vitamins is needed for optimum health and beauty.

CARBOHYDRATES

Carbohydrates, along with proteins and fats, are responsible for body heat and energy. They are not body builders but are necessary for body functioning. There are two large groups of carbohydrates, namely, sugars and starches. The sugar groups include cane and beet sugars and sugar products; candies, desserts, frostings; preserves, jams, jellies. The starch groups include bread, crackers, pasta, cereals. Fruits and vegetables are also carbohydrates and fit in both sugars and starches classifications, depending on the variety and age of the fruit or vegetable.

When digested, all carbohydrates are broken down into single sugars. Thus, a diet high in starches is really high in sugars. Sugars are necessary for heat and energy and should not be eliminated from the diet. Excessive carbohydrates in the diet are easily converted to fats and stored in the body.

While sugars and starches are necessary for body heat and energy, they must not be eaten in such large amounts that they replace the body-building foods. Too much of the carbohydrate foods not only lowers the intake of proteins, minerals, and vitamins but also promotes dental caries.

FATS

Fats also supply body heat and energy. In addition, they serve as carriers of the fat-soluble vitamins. Some unsaturated fatty acids are necessary for healthy skin.

Fats do not conduct heat, but the layer of fat beneath the skin helps conserve the body heat. Fats are stored in the body. Excessive fat stored on the body may be injurious to health. Fats supply a little over twice as many calories per gram as carbohydrates.

WATER

Most college students are negligent in the amounts of water they drink. Eight glasses of water a day, which is often recommended, sounds like a tremendous amount, particularly if consumed all at once. Half a glass every hour during the active day seems much more acceptable—a drink every time you pass by a fountain, even easier. Soups and beverages also contribute to the amount of water consumed.

calories

When food is consumed, digested, and utilized in the body, energy is released. Heat is a by-product of energy. While the body is definitely not a machine, it is sometimes easier to grasp the relationship between food and body when it is associated with fuel and the engine. Food ingested produces, among other things, the energy needed to allow the body to function.

The term "calorie" is the name given to the unit of measurement used to describe the amount of heat generated when food is burned by the body. The scientific definition of calorie is the unit of heat that will raise the temperature of one kilogram of water one degree centigrade. A calorie is not a nutrient. It serves simply as a convenient measurement of the yield of energy from nutrients—proteins, fats, carbohydrates. The energy or caloric measurements of separate nutrients of many foods and food combinations have been determined by special tests devised for this purpose. The objective of this work has been to determine the calorie values of foods as potential sources of energy for the body. The results of this work are presented in calorie charts.

The use of a calorie chart is simply another kind of tool to use in food planning. In studying the calorie values of various foods, it is easy to see that foods high in fat are high in calories. Actually, one gram of fat yields more than twice as many calories as one gram of either protein or carbohydrates. Removal of fat lowers the caloric count of a food. Nonfat milk has about half the number of calories as whole milk. Lean steak with the fat trimmed away is dramatically lower in calories than the untrimmed, well-marbled meat.

Calorie values of food vary greatly, and fat content is one of the prime reasons for this variation. But calories themselves do not vary in value; the unit of measurement always remains the same. Therefore, no food can be more "fattening" than any other food. Calories merely count up faster in concentrated foods that are high in fat.

The use of calories in weight control simplifies the task. Food intake becomes simple arithmetic. To gain, increase the intake; to lose, decrease the intake; to maintain, keep the same intake. Various favorite foods, even though high in calorie count, may be enjoyed if the daily totals are observed.

Study a table of nutritive values of foods and understand the contribution each food makes to your diet. Learn which foods fall into the category of "empty calories," that is, those that are high in calorie count but low in food value. Food is too essential to our well being not to be fully understood. Start getting full nutritional value for calorie value.

Keep track of your total food intake for three days, then evaluate it. Analyze your dietary weaknesses. Compare these with your figure, skin, hair, teeth, vitality, and emotional stability. If you see need for improvement, begin with a new food plan. Set a goal for summer, for Christmas, and eat your way toward it!

fad diets

Food quackery is big business in the United States today. Many people are being exploited by unscrupulous merchants in the business of selling health in food form. As an educated person, one should be alert to nutritional misinformation in whatever form it is dispersed. When material of questionable validity becomes available to you, it is important that you consider it carefully before accepting it. When in doubt, there are a number of reliable sources which will help you validate nutritional information. Among those offering accurate information are

1. Nutritionist connected with city, county, and state health offices or with social welfare offices
2. Teachers in the health and home economics fields on the high school and college level—including extension agents
3. The Federal Food and Drug Administration regarding labeling and practices related to food
4. The Federal Trade Commission for questions about advertising or doubtful statements made on mass media
5. Food editors of well-known newspapers or magazines
6. Your family physician

With the current fashion and scientific emphasis on weight control, many "fat doctors" and fad diets are popular. Before trusting your health to any of these, a thorough investigation of their merit should be made. The doctor's credentials and qualifications can be checked through your local health offices or medical associations. Your family doctor can also investigate this for you.

A fad diet should never be embarked upon without medical supervision. Common sense should always prevail whenever diets are planned. Compare any fad diet to the Basic Four and be aware of the nutritional discrepancies. Medical histories are written about persons who have ruined their health by do-it-yourself diets. Skeletons are skinny, but one has yet to win a beauty contest!

nutritional variations during the life cycle

Each age has it nutritional needs. The baby and child are growing and developing rapidly and, therefore, demand a balanced diet. The teen-ager has the same needs, but because this period of growth is intensified his food intake should be at a lifetime high. The late teens and early twenties are especially significant for women. Not only is the body completing the growth and development era, it is also preparing for, or actually engaged in, pregnancy. For the girl who has not built up sufficient nutritional reserves, the period of pregnancy and lactation is especially demanding. Some cases of physical and mental handicaps in infants have been attributed to poor nutrition of the mother both before and during pregnancy. After twenty-five the body needs are less, and, most often, so are the physical activities of many women. This is the period when eating habits must be carefully analyzed or the pounds begin to creep on. If a bride adds only a pound a year, she will be fifty pounds overweight when she celebrates her golden wedding anniversary! Nutritional needs should be based on the Basic Four for a lifetime; however, the amounts should be limited as the birthdays increase. Notice that the previous statement emphasizes that the amount of food eaten should decrease as one grows older. But the variety of food consumed remains important for the entire life cycle. Many of the problems, both physical and mental, of the elderly stem from malnutrition.

EATING PATTERNS

Once you understand the importance of the various foods and nutrients to the diet, you can make personal adjustments to established eating patterns. If you have a dislike for certain foods, learn to make appropriate nutritional substitutions. Many people have a strong dislike for milk. Appropriate substitutes for milk in the diet are the great variety of cheeses, creamed soups and vegetables, and milk desserts, such as puddings and ice cream. When making such substitutions, be certain that the amounts substituted equal the nutritional requirements. For example, three times the volume of tomato juice is required to equal the vitamin C content of orange juice. This information can be found in various food charts in nutrition publications or cookbooks.

Another eating pattern that may be varied to suit the individual preference is the accepted foods eaten for specific meals. We have traditional breakfast menus built around cereal, eggs, juice, toast, or quick breads. If you personally dislike such foods, there is absolutely no reason not to substitute other foods such as soup and sandwiches for breakfast—it's really up to you! Just be certain to include foods of nutritional value.

The intake of food should be spaced around the clock for best health. This is the reason infants are fed in the middle of the night. As we mature, we can go longer without nourishment, but the digestive system can function more efficiently when moderate amounts of food are supplied at various intervals.

One of the most often skipped meals is breakfast. The reasons for skipping this meal usually are sleeping late or weight watching. A recent study conducted among college students at the University of Iowa reported the following sad results among breakfast skippers and skimpers.

1. Poor performance in the classroom and in athletics
2. Dislike for school
3. A real work sag, particularly before noon
4. Lack of endurance for jobs that require strength
5. High-calorie nibbling all day

The ideal breakfast supplies about one-fourth of the day's calories. A breakfast of this size actually is a way of controlling weight because the body is more satisfied and less snacking occurs.

Good nutrition is possible without set meal patterns, as has been pointed out, but it is not likely without set times for meals. Eating routines should be an established pattern in your daily life. The time schedule should fit your activities and habits.

Your dedication to adequate nutrition rests on its importance to you. Your heredity plus the food you eat, your motivation, and your physical activity equal you! You cannot control your heredity, but you can control all the other factors in this equation. Whether you do or not is your choice. Your decision is advertised by how well you fulfill your beauty potential.

suggested readings

Bogert, L. Jean, George M. Briggs, and Doris H. Calloway. *Nutrition and Physical Fitness.* Philadelphia: W. B. Saunders Company, 1966.

Martin, Ethel A. *Nutrition in Action.* New York: Holt, Rinehart & Winston, Inc., 1963.

Meyer, Jean. *Overweight Causes, Cost and Control.* Englewood Cliffs, N.J.: Prentice-Hall, Inc., 1968.

"Nutritional Guidelines for Teenagers," *Nutrition Today* (March 1967), p. 2.

Robinson, Corinne H. *Fundamentals of Normal Nutrition.* New York: The Macmillan Company, 1968.

Wilson, Eva D., Katherine H. Fisher, and Mary E. Fuqua. *Principles of Nutrition.* New York: John Wiley & Sons, Inc., 1967.

7

---

skin care and cosmetics

everyone is concerned with the health and appearance of his skin. A "good skin" or a beautiful complexion is coveted by both men and women, young and old alike. Many would give much to recover the healthy skin of their childhood, and indeed they do. Each year huge sums of money are spent in search of skin beauty. Some seek the magic cure for skin blemishes associated with adolescence, which in reality last a lifetime; others fight the wrinkles, bags, and sags of age.

The skin is another unique possession. The way your skin reacts and functions will differ from all other skins. This is really hard to understand and accept, especially for the person who is suffering from a difficult skin problem. In the United States we often tend to limit our thinking of skin problems to those that are associated with adolescence. This, of course, is not valid. Skin problems come in tremendous variety and range over the complete life span. Allergies and rashes can, and do, appear at any time from infancy through old age. One may be unfortunate and have a lifetime of serious skin problems, or fortunate and be completely free of them. The care of the skin differs with each age and each problem that the skin presents.

Basic to skin beauty are good health and good health habits. Often the skin works as a weathervane to signal that all is not right within the body. Skin abnormalities are symptoms that can be used to diagnose serious health problems. Very often these health problems are nutritional in nature. In Chapter 6, food requirements were discussed. By following the Basic Four, you can actually eat your way to a prettier skin. Dermatologists (skin specialists) agree to this fact. They even have a list of certain foods that they recommend be limited or eliminated from the diet when skin problems erupt. This list may vary from one doctor to another but generally contains high-cholesterol foods such as chocolate, coconut, butterfat (whole milk, butter, cheese, yogurt, whipped cream, ice cream), fat meats, gravies, and pastries.

Cleanliness is also of vital importance to skin beauty. Bacteria on the skin which are not properly removed may cause problems. Methods of cleansing the face are widely varied and are discussed later in this chapter. It is important to consider the changes in skin as one matures and to alter the skin-care program as needed. The often harsh regime of high school skin care can cause aging if continued into the college years.

Products used on the face should be evaluated. Many women have drawers full of all kinds of cosmetic products. Oftentimes these boxes and jars have approached the grubby stage. Are you carefully cleaning your face and then using dirty pencils, brushes, or puffs for your art work? Self-defeating, isn't it? Volumes of cosmetics are sold because each jar offers hope—advertisements of cosmetics are based on promises of beauty. Analyze your cosmetic supply, and, if necessary, clean house—a little hope is wonderful, a drawerful, too much!

Fresh air and exercise stimulate the circulation, causing the blood to surge through the system. This physiological fact aids the facial skin. Another way of saying this is that girls who blush have pretty skins. If you must, give nature a hand and create a flush through exercise. Proper elimination will carry off body wastes which might otherwise clog pores. Sufficient rest allows for both the relaxation of the facial muscles and the revitalization of energy. Adequate rest also reduces the incidence of frowning and squinting which results in wrinkles, aging, or unhappy expressions.

skin types

Skin types can be divided into several broad classifications. Study your own skin carefully and try to decide which type you have. Remember that skin types can change with the years, so that it is important to note the condition of your skin from time to time.

Normal Skin Normal skin is soft, supple, smooth. It is neither oily nor dry in appearance. The texture is soft and fine. The color is clear and softly glowing.

Dry Skin Dry skin is rough and scaly. It looks and feels tight and drawn. It has lines or wrinkles at the mouth and corners of the eyes.

Oily Skin Oily skin has an oily appearance. It has a predisposition to blackheads, pimples, and enlarged pores.

Combination Skin This may be a combination of any or all of the listed types of skins. Often oily skin is found in the forehead, nose-chin area, whereas very dry skin may be found around the eyes and mouth. The cheek area may be normal, dry, or oily. Each type of skin should be cared for as each type indicates.

Problem Skin Problem skin requires the care of a doctor. A problem skin cannot be covered up and ignored. Allergies, rashes, acne, or unhealed blemishes, if not cared for, can result in very serious problems for both the skin and the mental health of the individual. An expensive medical treatment can be greatly reduced if the problem is treated promptly, before it is well established.

cleansing the skin

There are two schools of thought on facial cleansing: the soap-and-water advocates and the cleansing cream, or lotion, champions. The best method for you is the one that produces the best result for you and your skin. It really is that simple.

SOAP AND WATER

If you choose soap and water, you should be aware of the fact that it is drying to the skin. A young skin is often an oily skin, and the use of soap helps in drying the oiliness. However, harsh soap may stimulate the oiliness and thus defeat your original purpose. As the skin ages, and this may become noticeable around twenty years of age, it generally becomes less oily. If the harsh soap scrubbing of childhood is continued, it may produce early wrinkling and aging of the skin.

If you select the soap-and-water method of face cleansing, select a mild soap. Apply it gently, using upward and outward motions. The neck and chest should be washed in the same manner. This entire area should be treated gently to avoid stretching delicate muscles. Rinsing, rinsing, rinsing, and rinsing some more is most important when using soap for cleansing. It must be completely removed from the skin to avoid drying irritation.

CLEANSING CREAMS OR LOTIONS

There is a tremendous variety of cleansing cosmetics from which to select the ones you prefer. When making this choice, it is wisest to use the complete cleansing program developed by the cosmetic company. That is, use the cleansing products and the follow-up potions and lotions which balance the cleansing product. This way, you are taking advantage of the research of the cosmetic firm and using products developed to work together to produce the skin-care programs you need.

The application of cleansing creams or lotions is generally about the same for all varieties of the product, but you should always read the instructions carefully. This guide is part of what you paid for, so use it! The cleansing cream is dabbed on the face and worked into the skin, using gentle, upward and outward motions. Some cleansing lotions are water-based, so water is added as the final step.

Removal of the cleansing preparation must be gently done. It may be blotted off with a tissue. Never scrub with a tissue, as it is a fine abrasive. Many enjoy splashing the creamed face with warm water. For the extra special clean feeling, repeat this process before proceeding.

BALANCING THE SKIN

The second step in cleansing the face is balancing the pH of the skin. The products used for this are generally classified as astringents or fresheners. Astringents are harsh and are generally used for oily skin. Fresheners are used on other types of skins and are gentler. These two products are applied in the same manner: a small amount is sprinkled on a cotton pad and then spread over the face. Gentle upward and outward motions are again used. This is an excellent product to use around the hairline and ears, as it will not affect the hair style and will cleanse these areas.

MOISTURIZING

The third step in cleansing the face is moisturizing. This is a process designed to maintain skin moisture and protect the face from weather, dirt, and grime. It is essential to skin beauty. Climate and environment affect the moisture of the skin. If you live in a large, grimy city or in a dry, warm climate, the use of a moisturizer is even more crucial. This product would be applied as the instructions suggest.

SUMMARY

You may elect to cleanse your face with soap and water or with a cosmetic preparation. Whatever method you select for the initial step, it should be followed by a balancing potion and a moisturizer. Using the same brand cosmetic is important in the cleansing process, as they are developed to complement each other. Daily cleansing is vital to a pretty skin. It should be an important part of your morning and evening routine. A clean face is a necessary basis for any make-up and a clean face is necessary at bedtime, so that the skin may be revitalized during the sleep period.

facial cosmetics

The use of facial cosmetics is almost as old as man himself. As soon as civilization progressed past the point of survival, self-adornment became important. This holds true today. A study of the various cultures shows that, although the standards of beauty vary tremendously, facial make-up plays an important part in the lives of most females the world over.

Use of cosmetics in the United States has had a varied history. Their acceptance and popularity have been related to both social and religious beliefs. The majority of today's population accepts their use and enjoys their benefits.

Often a girl will reject cosmetics, saying that the men in her life prefer the natural look. The wiser girl will acknowledge this and use her cosmetics to enhance her beauty and still look natural. For this is what it is all about. In our culture and in today's fashion, cosmetics are designed to improve on nature without distorting the original. Properly applied cosmetics are never obvious. The misuse of the beauty products distracts from natural beauty. Extreme misuse of cosmetics can even cause health problems.

A wise woman learns to use the cosmetics that are best for her. She knows her facial assets and problems. She uses cosmetics to accent her best features and to camouflage the less than best. She studies the fashion trends of cosmetics in the current magazines and changes her routines to stay abreast of the time. She is also willing to practice to learn a new technique, so that when she presents herself, she is at her best.

This same wise woman has made a commitment to herself and to those around her. She will take the time and the effort always to appear well made up. It is a vital part of her grooming. It is as important to her private life as it is to her public life. She may sometimes vary the routine from a formal make-up suitable for glamorous evenings to a very casual make-up ready for sports and picnicking, but, nonetheless, she is made up.

The commitment means that she will always manage to have the time to properly cleanse and make up her face, comb her hair, and dress before making her appearance. This means that she can never be a "slug-a-bed," snoozing the last second away, because she must allow time for herself to prepare to face the world. Look around your early morning classes; check the early morning lady chauffeurs. It is obvious which women have enough self pride to present themselves to this early audience at their best.

A phenomenon very much involved with the female psyche is that the women who are faithful to their early morning beauty routine report that they actually get more accomplished than they did before starting. Housework goes faster, studying becomes more effective, and emergencies are easier to cope with. This same woman is never embarrassed by her appearance, for she is prepared to receive whoever knocks on her door, whether it be her best beau or fussy Aunt Minnie.

Properly applying make-up takes time. It begins with completely cleaning the face, balancing, and moisturizing. The art work follows. The popular magazines and newspapers are full of interviews with models and actresses who claim to take only ten minutes to make up. This cannot be true. If a picture accompanies the next article, analyze all the make-up she has on. Chances are she spent about six times that ten minutes on her face! Of course, it depends on what you are doing and your skill at applying make-up. But a much more honest time allotment would be thirty minutes for most days, sixty minutes for a special occasion.

The best way to learn about make-up is from a personal consultation with a cosmetologist. Most cosmetic firms train their representatives to help patrons learn to use their line. Many of these firms advertise free personal demonstrations. These ads are located in the advertising section of the telephone book, in the newspaper, and in magazines. They are not only fun to take advantage of, but most informative. Of course, the demonstrators are selling their products, but you need never buy more than you actually wish. And you can always think about it for a while. Stores that carry cosmetics also have specially trained people to help you, and often these people have free samples for you to try over a period of time.

Fashions in make-up change as quickly as fashions in clothing. Many magazines feature beauty columns and often do picture stories on new make-up techniques. Study these and apply what is good to yourself.

There are some fundamentals in make-up techniques and products, and we will discuss them. It is difficult in a text such as this not to make everything so general that it applies to no one, or to recommend what is in fashion at the writing of the book but what is antiquated by the date of publication.

To guide your make-up decisions, you must have a complete understanding of your face. Decide which features are your best, which you wish to camouflage.

Study your face carefully. Understand your personal coloring and undertones. Select cosmetics that will harmonize with your color scheme.

The cosmetic industry has recently exploded with new products for both men and women. There is a multitude from which to choose. Each company names its products differently. The following are products which are fundamental to the industry. We will discuss the purpose of each and the technique of application.

FOUNDATION

A foundation treatment may be obtained in cream or liquid form. It must be carefully matched to the color of the skin. It is applied as directed, usually with the fingertips or a sponge. It should be worked carefully over the face and down below the jawline (to avoid a masklike appearance). It smooths and blends the colors of the face evenly and also protects the face from dirt, grime, and weather. A foundation is just that—the vital first step upon which the rest of the make-up is dependent.

ROUGE

Rouge comes in liquid, cream, or dry form. Its purpose is to add color to the cheek area and sparkle the eye color. It must be selected in a color tone that complements the skin. It is applied as directed with the fingers or a brush. Rouge is placed high on the face in the "apple" of the cheek and above. (To find the "apple" of the cheek, smile broadly; the round area of the cheek is called the "apple.")

EYE SHADOW

Eye shadow comes in cream or powder form. It should be selected in a complementary shade. Colored shadow comes and goes in fashion, so be sensitive to this. Bright colors seem better after dark. Brown-toned shadow will make the flesh around the eye seem to recede. White-toned shadow will make the same area advance. These two tones may be used most effectively to recontour the area of the eye.

POWDER

The best buy in powder is the loose, translucent powder. It adapts itself to your skin tones, so only one powder is needed. Loose powder is a *must* in proper make-up routine. It should be puffed on all over the face in generous amounts after the foundation and other make-up steps are applied. The powder is then brushed off in downward strokes. All finishing steps should be in a downward direction, as this is the way the facial hair grows. Powder sets the make-up and protects it from smearing. Some women obtain a dewy look by blotting the entire face with a moistened sea sponge. This same powder used on the eyebrows both stays the pencils work and softens the color. It should be puffed on and then gently swept off.

If a good quality of make-up is used, touch-ups during the day are often not too necessary. However, if you wish, carry a compact of compressed, translucent powder for this purpose.

EYEBROW PENCIL

Almost everyone should use an eyebrow pencil to fill in the brow line. It must be sharp to be applied properly. For this reason the fine-line mechanical pencils are the best to use. Choose your brow pencil color to match your coloring. Avoid black if possible, as this is too harsh for most people and gives a hard, brittle look to the face. Always finish eyebrows by puffing on powder and brushing off the excess. This sets pencil and softens color.

EYELINER

The purpose of an eyeliner is to define the eye and add to the apparent length of the lashes. It usually requires a bit of practice to develop the technique, but it is worth it. Fashion changes rapidly in eye designs, so be alert. Eyeliner is best used on the upper lid at the base of the lashes. It should be used sparingly, if at all, on the lower lid. Never completely enclose the eye with liner, as it makes the eye smaller and the wearer look like something left over from Halloween. If you wish to use liner below the eye, try a series of dots or "twiggies." Keep these toward the outer edge of the eye to avoid making the eye look smaller. Eyeliner color should be coordinated with the other eye make-up. Avoid black for the reasons stated above.

MASCARA

Mascara comes in cream or cake form with a variety of applicators. Its purpose is to add color fullness to the lashes. It may be applied several times for increased effect. The lashes should be combed and separated when the mascara is dry for a more natural look.

FALSE EYELASHES

False eyelashes are here to stay. They may be improved upon and re-designed, but their popularity will continue. They add glamorous emphasis to the eyes and can change the appearance of the entire profile. They are a real must for the true blond who cannot achieve enough color with mascara. Besides, they are fun.

Eyelashes vary greatly in price. The inexpensive ones are just as satisfactory as the higher priced ones and are especially recommended for beginning experiments. The color, shape, and thickness are a matter of personal choice. Some choose them for impact, while others wish only to assist nature slightly. If the latter is your intent, choose lashes close in color to your own and in a believable length and thickness. Measure your eye as the upper lashes grow from inner to outer edge. Snip off the extra lashes. It is easier to fit a too short pair, so do not worry about this in your first attempts. Measure both eyes as they often differ.

Surgical glue purchased at the drugstore is the best adhesive. It is chemically pure; it dries quickly; and it is inexpensive and lasts a long time. Spread the glue carefully along the back of the false lash, allow about 30 seconds for glue to set, then place the lash against the base of your own lashes. Use a blunt pusher such as the back of a hairpin or eyebrow tweezer to reinforce the sticking. You will probably have white glue showing, but it dries transparently, so give it time.

The false lashes should be comfortable. If they are not, they may be glued incorrectly or you need to trim them some more. They will seem heavy at first, but you will adjust to this feeling before long. Clumps of lashes are sometimes used on the bottom lashes. These may be glued on separately or purchased as transparent strips. They are applied under your own bottom lashes. Practice should perfect this technique.

False lashes may be cleaned with rubbing alcohol. Just pop them in a small container and shake. Dry them on a tissue. They should last for about six weeks of daily wear.

LIPSTICK

The purpose of lipstick is to protect the delicate area of the mouth while emphasizing its beauty. Hues of lipstick are subject to fashion change. Wearing a brightly colored lipstick in a fashion period of pastel mouths is quite dating. Lipstick application done skillfully can correct a faulty lipline. The ideally shaped mouth is centered in the face. The upper lip has an evenly shaped "cupid's bow," and the lower lip is slightly fuller than the upper. Lipstick is an important part of face make-up because it balances the bottom part of the face with the eye area. If a lipstick is not used, the mouth is unprotected and the face may appear chinless.

MISCELLANEOUS COSMETICS

The industry is constantly introducing new cosmetics to the public. Most of them are variations of listed products. Some may seem essential to you, while others remain frivolous. Many women delight in experimenting with new products. Your attitude toward these should remain flexible. It is not necessary to try every new innovation—certainly, few could afford it!—but do not reject them simply because they are not familiar.

MEDICATED COSMETICS

Medicated cosmetics are big business. They are directed to each age group but especially to the teen-agers. Self-medication is almost an American tradition. The cosmetic industry has taken advantage of this and in reality has pushed into the province of patent medicine. Products ranging from baby powder to after-shave lotions boast of "special medicated ingredients." The teen-ager plagued with acne at a time when social acceptance is most important is a natural consumer of such products, especially when the cosmetic industry has directed its advertising and packaging specifically toward him. Medicated cosmetic products are most often the selected preference of this group because of a conditioned response developed by the ad men.

What advertising-heavy, research-light cosmetic companies seldom broadcast is the biological truth. The intact human skin has a phenomenal, built-in defense system against infectious bacteria. Constant degerming and chemical interfering with this natural restorative process of the skin can and often does lead to more, not less, trouble. If the skin is broken, simple cleansing with mild soap and water is most often recommended. If it is not seriously wounded, the skin usually heals more quickly through its own recuperative powers. A wrong guess will further injure the skin.

Next time you are shopping for cosmetics, pause and read the labels of the medicated products. Can you find the answers to these questions: Medicated with what? To cure what? And for whom?

HORMONES IN COSMETICS

Hormone creams have been introduced into the cosmetic market with great fanfare. Extravagant claims of skin rejuvenation have been made for the various creams and lotions containing hormones. They are usually inflated in price, also.

Scientific research has not discovered completely why the skin wrinkles as it ages. However, we do know that as the epidermis (outer layer of the skin) ages it usually becomes thinner and dryer. Locally applied creams containing hormones possibly counteract nature by thickening the skin somewhat and by holding water to the skin, but so will other simple emollient creams. The fatty layer below the dermis provides support for the skin. As a person ages, the fatty layer often diminishes, particularly in some areas of the face, with consequent wrinkling and changes in facial contour. No cream, hormone or not, will restore fat to the subcutaneous layer.

There has been some concern about the amount of concentration of hormones in various products. The Federal Drug Administration has established limits on the amounts regarded as safe. This limit applies to the individual product. It is within the realm of possibility that a consumer could use a variety of products all containing hormones, such as face creams, body oils, hand creams, and thus exceed the amount thought safe. This would produce systemic effects. This possibility must be kept in mind when such products are used.

In summary, cosmetics containing hormones should be carefully evaluated. They are generally expensive. They are directed toward the mature or "aging" consumer. They may cause side effects if a large amount of various products are consistently used. And they will not rejuvenate the skin.

NO MAKE-UP

There are many women who, for personal reasons, do not use cosmetics. These women must work a bit harder if they are to present themselves at their best. Their hair must always be shiny clean and attractively arranged, their skin must be immaculate, their teeth white and repaired, their eyebrows groomed. Their clothing should be carefully selected to enhance their delicate coloring yet not to overpower their personality. They must always wear a pleasant expression which reflects a zest for life and inner harmony.

sun and skin

Sunlight is a major cause of premature aging of the skin and skin cancer. Dermatologists continually warn people not to overexpose themselves to the sun. Most of the visible signs of aging, such as wrinkling, laxity, leathery texture, and pigmentary changes, are much more pronounced on the light-exposed areas of the body. To verify this statement, inspect the skin on your forearm with the skin on your upper underarm. It is the same skin! Weathering has made the difference in texture and appearance.

The natural color of the skin determines to some extent its sun tolerance. Black, yellow, and brown skins all seem to tolerate sun exposure better than fair skin. Unfortunately, it is the latter group that most often craves a suntan. The wavelengths of the solar spectrum that produce new pigment and suntan are the same ones that cause sunburn and the deleterious effects mentioned above. The two effects cannot be separated. Suntanning will damage the skin.

The commercial suntan lotions do not absorb all of the burn- and pigment-producing wavelengths; thus, they allow longer exposure to the sun and some tanning. Sun-screen preparations, which afford much more protection, are available for those who are especially sensitive to sunlight. Protection of the skin from sun is as important in cold weather as in warm. Skiers take warning! Sun reflecting from snow can cause terrific burns. This may happen even though you spent the entire day shivering on the "bunny slope."

Sun poisoning is another effect of overexposure. "Sun poisoning" is the lay term used to describe a variety of acute and chronic responses to the sun's rays. This problem arises when a sensitivity to the sun is developed. It is comparable to an allergy to the sun. Recovery from this sensitivity may take several years.

Artificial tanning preparations are available. These are chemical preparations that darken the skin without sun exposure. For some who wish to go bare legged in the summer, this may be a satisfactory solution. The products are continually improving and are medically safe. Some caution should be used in their application, however. A test patch for the reaction, both in color and sensitivity of your skin, is recommended. Some very jaundiced-appearing faces have resulted from careless application of these products, so take care. Remember, once on, it must wear off!

hair care

Hair care includes shampooing, brushing, combing, and styling. Individuals treat their hair with varying degrees of vigor. The average woman following fashion is often very rough on her hair. To style it, hair is often stretched around rollers, brushed vigorously to get out the setting marks, back-combed with vengeance, and sprayed until it crunches. Truly, a torturous regime.

Fortunately, hair can usually survive this treatment and keep growing. The damaged hair can be replaced slowly by the process of nature. The scalp, however, may rebel. The scalp is the skin that produces the hair which is so roughly treated. If the scalp is damaged, serious problems may occur. Scalp irritation may require the attention of a doctor and a very long healing process. If the irritation is deep enough, permanent hair loss may result.

How should the hair be cared for? Of primary importance is the shampoo. How often the hair is washed depends on the hair and the style worn. Healthy hair cannot be overwashed. Many girls wash their hair every two to five days because it gets oily. Frequent shampoos are even more important when scalp oiliness is accompanied by acne or dandruff, as it usually is.

What shampoos, conditioners, rinses, styling lotions, and hair sprays should you use? Any that you like if your hair and scalp are normal. There is a tremendous variety of products to select from, many designed for a specific purpose. Choose the ones that suit your needs best. Trying several brands often leads to an individual preference.

A word of caution: if your hair is oily, do not expect a shampoo labeled as oil-controlling to be 100 per cent effective. If it were, you might end up bald! The only effective way to keep oily scalp and hair under control is to wash it frequently with a drying shampoo.

DANDRUFF

This is a very common scalp condition. It is often a partner in the oily skin complex, along with acne. Interestingly, the tendency to have dandruff (*seborrheic dermatitis*) is hereditarily determined. Dandruff is usually worse in the winter; this is apparently related to the lack of sunlight and to artificial heat or dryness in the air.

Dandruff is not infectious or contagious—you cannot catch it or give it to anyone. It responds best to frequent shampooing with a product medicated for that purpose. Sulfur is the chemical most commonly used in such antidandruff preparations. Dandruff can be controlled, but it cannot be cured. If your problem is a serious one, it is best to seek medical advice.

nail care

Nails and their condition can say a great deal about you. Look at yours now. What is their message? Are they grubby, chewed to the quick, better sat on than seen? If so, change your ways. Nail care is a vital part of skin care and should be part of a weekly routine.

Caring for the nails consists of filing and shaping as needed and cleaning under the nails daily or whenever necessary. The cuticle should be gently pushed back from the nail after it has been softened by soaking (during the bath is a good time). Hangnails should be carefully trimmed away. All nail care should be done gently and carefully.

Buffing the nails brings a nice, natural shine to them and is preferred to polishing by many. If polish is desired, it should be a fashionable hue, color-keyed to the skin tones. Avoid polishes that claim to be permanent, as they are damaging to the nails. All polish should be kept in perfect condition on the nails, or it becomes detracting. Polish removal and exposure of the nails to air are important to the health of the nail. Wearing polish constantly is often damaging.

summary

Beautiful skin is directly related to diet, exercise, elimination, rest, and care. Cleansing the skin may be done effectively with either soap and water or cleansing potions. Soap, no matter what form, is always drying to the skin and therefore must be rinsed away completely. When selecting a cleansing lotion, the complete line of cleansing preparations should be used, so that the formulas will complement each other.

Cosmetics should be applied to enhance the natural beauty of the wearer. Skill should be acquired in using cosmetics, so that the best effects will be achieved. For the "natural look" currently popular, some sixteen products are needed. Application of cosmetics requires skill, patience, and time. Because of their nature and comparative low cost, certain cosmetics are subjected to rapid fashion change. Examples of these are lipstick, eye shadow, and nail polish colors, styles of false eyelashes, and eyeliner shapes and shades. Be sensitive to these changes and evolve with them—to avoid changing make-up styles is both dating and aging.

Medicated cosmetics are not necessarily good cosmetics. One must always question, medicated for what? Hormones added to cosmetics are very expensive and controversial. These preparations are the concern of the mature woman and should not be exploited as rejuvenators.

Medical studies have proven that excessive exposure to the sun is both aging and a primary factor in skin cancer. The "mahogany suntan" should be avoided by those who cherish their skin and its health; a light tan attained in easy stages is preferred. Always protect and moisturize your skin when it is being exposed to the sun.

Hair must be kept clean and groomed to be a complementary frame for the face. How often one's hair is shampooed depends on the kind of hair and the amount of grime it collects. Oily hair must be shampooed frequently. Dust and grime of certain environments will necessitate regular washings. Products to be used on the hair can be determined only by personal choice.

Hand and nail care is an important part of grooming. The condition of the nails is often used as an index in judging character and ability. The chewed and nibbled nails reflect a lack of self-confidence. The grubby and unmanicured hand reflects a lack of self-pride.

Skin care, grooming, and make-up are a vital part of your presentation of self. These are the elements that are often judged by those around you. How you care for yourself and how you present yourself may often be closely related to your "success" or lack of it in many situations. In the words of Helena Rubinstein, "There are no ugly women, only lazy ones."

suggested readings

American Medical Association. *The Look You Like.* Chicago: American Medical Association, 1967.

Cordwell, M., and M. Rudoy. *Hair Design and Fashion.* New York: Crown Publishers, Inc., 1967.

Editors of *Glamour* Magazine. *Glamour's Beauty Book.* New York: Simon & Schuster, Inc., 1966.

Editors of *Harper's Bazaar. Harper's Bazaar Beauty Book.* New York: Appleton-Century-Crofts, Inc., 1959.

Ford, Eileen. *Book of Model Beauty.* New York: Trident Press, 1968.

Hensley, M. B. *The Art of Make-up Skin and Hair Care.* New York: Hearthside Press, Inc., 1960.

Sauer, Gordon, M.D. *Teen Skin.* Springfield, Ill.: Charles C Thomas, Publisher, 1965.

Stabile, Toni. *Cosmetics: Trick or Treat.* New York: Hawthorn Books, Inc., 1966.

Uggams, Leslie. *The Leslie Uggams Beauty Book.* Englewood Cliffs, N.J.: Prentice-Hall, Inc., 1967.

8

emphasizing the personality area

each face is unique. No two faces are exactly alike, not even those of identical twins. The feature arrangement is more individualized by facial expressions. As one matures, the facial skin develops characteristics influenced by the total environment of the individual. Lines are etched on the face by both years and experiences. The faces of the very young are enjoyed for their unmarked beauty, while the faces of the mature are made interesting by the patterns achieved by years of living.

It is the face that identifies one. We recognize our friends and acquaintances not by hands or feet but by faces. The face is where the personality is expressed (Figure 8–1). The eyes have been romantically called the windows of the soul. The face is our most individual signature. Thus, the face is the area that should most often be emphasized in dress.

Bringing emphasis to the face or personality area is easily achieved in a number of ways. Items used to create this illusion may be grouped together and labeled the face-framing details. Face-framing details would include hair design, hats, jewelry, eyeglasses, necklines, scarves, and any other ornamentation used in the personality area.

159

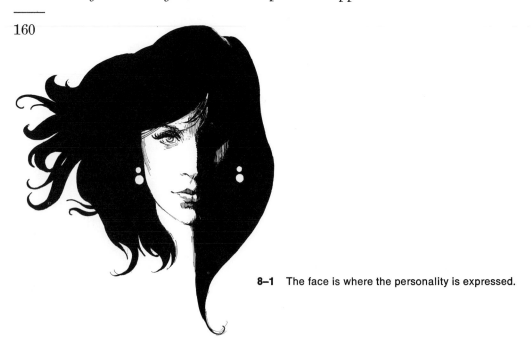

8–1 The face is where the personality is expressed.

The face-framing details are subject to the most rapid fashion change. This is probably because most of the details are comparatively inexpensive and thus faddish. Also, because the eyes are held by these details more than any other part of the ensemble, we may simply grow tired of seeing them. One must be sensitive to this fashion phenomenon and change with it. The woman who clings to the hair style, eyeglass style, or lipstick color of a decade ago is advertising both her age and her lack of awareness (Figure 8–2). Old college yearbooks vividly reveal this point. The Sweetheart of Alpha Xi Delta of twenty years ago looks rather strange by today's beauty standards. So does the middle-aged sweetheart if she is still wearing the hair style, make-up, and jewelry of her college days!

Because of the rapidity of change in the style and popularity of the various face-framing details, it is impossible to specify each in a text. It is much better for the student to understand the underlying principles for choosing each detail so that no matter what the mode of the day she may select that which will be the most becoming to her.

The fundamental art and design guidelines are continually incorporated into all adornment. Application of these to each fashion variation is the key to selection of the individual face-framing details. (See Chapter 11.) In selecting the items that bring emphasis to the personality area, one must constantly remember that these are only a part of the total look. These details must be evaluated with the entire ensemble so that the finished product presents a unified image. Thus, each of the face-framing details must be selected because its line, color, and texture harmonize with the total costume.

head, face, and neck conformation

The size and shape of the head, face, features, and neck should be analyzed in relationship to the conformation of the total figure. By studying pictures of oneself in many poses and by viewing oneself in a mirror from many angles, an understanding of the shapes and lines that compose this area of the body can be developed.

The head must appear to be in proper scale with the body if a pleasing relationship is to be achieved. Too small a head is not only out of balance but it contrasts with the rest of the figure to emphasize the size of the body. Too large a head distorts the relationship to the figure and makes one appear top heavy. The ideal length of the head is one eighth of the height of the body. The ideal width is two thirds of the head length measured at the eyebrow line. The ideal shape is oval. Very few heads are ideally proportioned. These dimensions are given for use as a standard of comparison. By understanding the deviation from the ideal, one may work to create the desired illusion.

Face shapes are difficult to determine. Reference books generally define

8–2 Continued use of make-up and hair styles of one's youth can be extremely dating in one's middle years.

8–3 Study your face shape from all angles.

faces by the geometric shapes of rectangular, square, oval, round, diamond, and triangular. Nature is never this exacting. Sometimes it's easier to describe a face than define it as a geometric shape. Tracing a face silhouette on a soapy mirror is helpful in defining its shape.

Features should be studied, both individually and in their relationship to the face and head. Pull the hair back into a pony tail and study both profile and full face (Figure 8–3). Start with the forehead profile; does it recede, stand straight, or bulge forward? Full face: Is the forehead wide or narrow? What is the hairline position on the forehead? How are the eyes set in the head? Are they deep set or do they bulge out? Are they wide set or close together? Ideally, the bottom of the eye should be about one half of the head length from the crown to the chin. Analyze the nose for length, shape, and size. Study the mouth; does it droop or pout? Are the upper and lower lips formed with the same amount of fullness? Is the mouth evenly centered in the bottom third of the face? Examine the chinline. Does the chin recede or jut forward? How many chins do you have? Facial portraits, both full face and profile, will help in this objective analysis.

After considering each feature individually, analyze them in relationship to each other and to the face. Try to determine the predominant lines in the shape of the features and face. Remember that any time these lines are repeated in the face-framing details, they will be emphasized. If the lines of the face-framing details are extreme opposites, facial lines will also be emphasized.

Study the neck in relationship to the total figure and the head. Does the neck appear to be long or short? Is it thick or thin? How is the head carried on the neck?

The classic face is said to have regular features. This is a very nebulous statement which can be refined to state that some arrangements of features are more pleasing than others. Often what pleases most depends on the fashion of the moment.

Individual beauty is created by the unique arrangement of features in each face. Feature variations should not be cause for despair unless they are seriously damaging to the personality (and then steps should be taken to correct the feature causing the problem). Individual feature arrangements are what make faces interesting. Consider some well-known women who have been called beautiful. Women such as Barbra Streisand, Diahann Carroll, Raquel Welch, and Jean Shrimpton fit this classification, and you can list others. What makes them beautiful? Each has a very different look, each has problem features, yet each is called a beauty.

Learning the techniques of dress and cosmetics helps to emphasize and express the beauty that each woman possesses. It should always be kept in mind that the face is a mirror of oneself. The expression of the face reflects how one feels about himself and the world around him. Happiness and peace are expressed in smiles, and any smiling face is a beautiful face. In the words of Chanel: "We are born with one face, but ... laughing or crying, wisely or otherwise ... eventually we form our own, along our own lines. A good face is composed of thoughtful laughter." [1]

hair styles

The hair style is one of the most important dress details, for it is truly face framing. The hair design is an integral part of the total silhouette. It should be selected to be in harmony with the age and activities of the wearer as well as with the conformation of the face and figure. Another important consideration in selecting a hair style is the amount of time a woman has to devote to hair care, plus her skill in handling the hair. For those with limited time, patience, or skill, a simple, easy-care hair style is a must. For those who have both time and talent, a more complicated hair style is possible. Every woman should learn to care for and comb her own hair, even if she does so only in emergencies, for such situations do arise.

The texture and condition of the hair will often limit the styles that can be achieved. This must always be an important consideration. Permanents add

[1] Gabrielle Chanel, "Collections by Chanel," *McCall's* (July, 1968), p. 43.

body to fine, limp hair and give it the illusion of increased volume. Straighteners soften and release or relax curl. Both permanents and straighteners change the texture of the hair, making it more manageable. A wide variety of conditioners are on the market. Their general purpose is to improve the health of the hair by reconstructing the hair shaft chemically. It should be understood that there is a direct relationship between diet and the health of the hair. A well-balanced diet is nature's best hair conditioner (see Chapter 6).

Hair coloring is closely keyed to skin coloring. Nature has a wide variety of skin and hair combinations, all of which are pleasing. Modern technology has made it both easy and tempting to alter nature's color scheme. Anyone considering changing her hair coloring should give the project careful study before beginning. Trying on wigs of various colors is a good, safe way to experiment. First of all, one needs to understand and analyze her own coloring in order to select a new hair color that will truly complement her beauty. Second, one needs to select the correct agents for both her hair and scalp. Third, and perhaps most important, directions must be carefully followed or disaster may result. While changing hair coloring is exciting and glamorous, many women have been bitterly disappointed and even disfigured because they did not understand the importance of the foregoing. Shocking, ludicrous hair colors or subtly mismatched hair and skin tones are both detractors of beauty. Damaged, weak, brittle hair with a "straw" or "cotton candy" appearance may result from wrong solutions. Painfully blistered scalp, even baldness, may be the product of incorrect technique.

Hair coloring changes naturally with the different stages of life. The vivid colors of youth generally begin to lighten or dull by the mid-twenties. Graying hair becomes a problem for many and often quite early in life. This natural lightening process should be remembered when one decides to assist nature with hair coloring. As one matures, the hair coloring should be lightened. Use of intense colors emphasizes the aging of the face and skin, while pastel colors have a softening effect. The color of the hair has a definite effect on the illusion created by the style. Masses of dark hair appear to have more volume than light hair and for this reason usually require more thinning and shaping. Light hair shows off the intricacy of the design of the coiffure, while dark hair conceals the design.

In selecting a hair design, the facial features and head conformation must be carefully considered. The hair should be styled to emphasize interesting features and minimize the less interesting (Figure 8–4). Thus, eyes may be emphasized by bangs, the mouth by guiches, and so on. A wide face may be narrowed by combing the hair forward, a narrow face widened by pulling the hair back. Generally, the hair should end above or below a feature that is to be minimized, such as a jawline or cheekbone.

A short neck is lengthened by a short haircut or upswept styling. A long neck appears shorter with a longer hair style that ends an inch or two below

No   Yes

No   Yes

No   Yes

8–4 Hair can be arranged to camouflage or emphasize face shapes.

the jawline. A small head appears larger when the hair is fluffed out. A large head may be made to appear smaller by the use of a controlled hair style.

Severe hair styles, those that are smoothly drawn back from the face, reveal each contour of the head. This type of styling requires the most perfect head shape and arrangement of features. Center parts also require even features, as they give the eye of the beholder a line with which to measure. Soft hair styles are much kinder to the wearer. Because of their free form, they may be

165

used to perfect the contour of the head. They have an irregular shape and therefore disguise the imperfections of the features.

The lines of the hair style should be analyzed carefully with consideration to head, feature, and figure conformation. Remember that repeating a line emphasizes that line; going to the extreme of the line also emphasizes it. Therefore, if you have a very round face, you should select a coiffure that is neither completely round nor straight. Long faces should avoid very straight lines and very round lines. Triangular faces should avoid fullness at the widest and narrowest points of the face.

The best friend your hair can have is a professional hair stylist. Styling, shaping, coloring, and pampering are best done by trained specialists. If you give the stylist a chance to understand both you and your hair by arranging several appointments before doing any drastic changing or the big date, you will probably be most satisfied. Shopping around for the stylist and salon that suits your needs is an excellent idea. Then let the professional take over. Relax and enjoy the appointment and don't make too many suggestions. Take advantage of the skill you are paying for, and you will most likely discover a variety of lovely hair styles.

WIGS AND HAIRPIECES

Wigs and hairpieces have found new popularity and acceptance. They are really fashionable, and many current hair styles could not be achieved without them. Modern technology has improved the quality and styling of both wigs and hairpieces, and public acceptance has made them fashionable.

Wigs and hairpieces may be styled in a tremendous variety of coiffures. They can be used to cover a wilted hairdo or to glamorize any kind of hair. They give a tremendous amount of freedom to their owners, who may engage in any vigorous sport or activity confidently, knowing there is a fresh hairdo sitting on the closet shelf.

A wardrobe of wigs can provide a variety of colors and length. Many celebrities depend on this instant glamour and change, and so may any woman.

Hairpieces, which have a variety of names (including wiglet, postiche, cascade, fall, switch), are designed to be added to one's own tresses. For this reason they must be carefully color matched.

Styling for both wigs and hairpieces should be developed by the same principles of selecting a natural coiffure. One may be more adventuresome with the false hair, but the end result should be becoming to the individual. Maintenance of hairpieces is important both to the length of service and to attractiveness. They should be cleaned and restyled regularly and stored on individual, styrofoam head forms.

necklines

Necklines, including collars and lapels, are also face-framing details of a costume. They must be selected with the same considerations as other parts of the ensemble. Since the neckline of a garment forms only part of the frame for the face, it must be selected with careful consideration for the other elements completing the frame, such as hair design or hat style.

The shape of the neckline is determined by the lines of the garment design. Again, the old rule holds true: do not repeat a face line in the neckline that you do not want to emphasize; do not emphasize face lines by using the extreme of their lines in a neckline (Figure 8–5). Square faces or jawlines are emphasized by square necklines or very round necklines. Round faces are emphasized by round necklines and also square necklines, and so on. The shape of the collar and lapels creates the same illusions.

The size of the neckline, collar, and lapels should be related to the size of the figure, head, and features. It is possible for a very small figure to have a large head and broad features or for a large figure to have a small head and tiny features. The scale of the face-framing details should be selected to complement both figure and face. Usually the best way to create unity between disproportionate areas is to select elements that will create a transition in size between the two. Thus, by selecting collars, lapels, or jewelry of a medium scale, the disproportionate face and figure are unified.

The neckline often is the most eye-arresting area of a garment. This effect is created either by color or décolletage. Bright or contrasting colors used at the neckline area attract attention. This is an excellent technique to use to create the illusion of a more slender figure, as the eye of the beholder is held by the neckline interest rather than by the figure silhouette. Thus, the size of the figure is camouflaged.

Décolletage, or low necklines, are always eye arresting, and, of course, the more daring the cleavage, the more emphasis placed there! Low-cut gowns should always be limited to casual, at-home, or evening wear. In selecting garments with an extreme neckline, the effects created by the movement of the body within the garment should be carefully studied. Such a line cut low in front, back, or underarm may be impossible for some figure types to wear without revealing much more than was intended. Study this in the dressing room before purchasing. A garment that inhibits movement for any reason becomes a straitjacket, which never has been or will be in vogue. Any gown that is to be worn dining should also be analyzed for its effect from the table up. The line of the table may cause some very unusual illusions.

8–5 Facial shapes can also be camouflaged or emphasized by necklines.

hat styles

Hats have several functions: they may be worn for warmth and protection; they may cover a wilted hairdo; they may be the finishing touch on an ensemble. Whatever the reason or occasion for wearing a hat, the hat should be flattering to the wearer.

When considering a hat, one should view it from all angles. All hat stores and departments have full-length mirrors. Use them! Study the hat in relationship to the total figure, the head, and the face. Choose only the hat that is becoming, no matter what its purpose—rain, sun, or church.

Hats go through fashion cycles just as do other accessories. The size, shape, and decoration of the hat are keyed to the trends in garments. The statement made by the hat must correspond to what is being said by all current fashion.

Hair styles are closely correlated to hats, both in popularity and styling. When elaborate or bouffant coiffures are fashionable, hats become less popular. A woman must decide between hat and hairdo. If the hair design was difficult to achieve, she is usually reluctant to crush it under a hat. The hair design must be appropriate for the hat. Casual hair styles do not complement sophisticated hats and vice versa. Usually the hair style must be subordinate to the hat.

The lines and the shape of the hat can create illusions about the height of the wearer. Any hat lines that lead the eye in an upward direction will give the illusion of height. Lines that lead the eye across terminate the height at that point, while lines that lead the eye in a downward direction give the illusion of shortening the figure.

A hat style that fits closely to the head and completely covers the hair is the most difficult to wear and requires the most perfect face. The asymmetric brim-line is the most flattering to all face shapes because of its irregularity. Hats that are worn on the back of the head allow the hair to soften facial features. As designs of hats are continually changing, it is best to keep these basic principles in mind rather than to discuss specific hat styles.

The color of the hat should be selected to add flair and interest to the ensemble. Avoid repeating the hat color again in the costume, as it loses its impact.

Texture is probably the most limiting element of a hat. Textures of the materials used in making the hat determine the season that it may be worn. Straws, veiling, and flowers are spring and summer textures. Velours, felts, and satins are fall and winter textures. Wearing a summer textured hat in the blustery weather of winter is indeed ridiculous. It would be more pleasing not to wear a hat than to wear one that is so inappropriate.

jewelry

Of all the articles of self adornment, man has always gained the most pleasure from jewelry. Possession of a "real" or precious jewel may give one a special thrill that is continually renewed with each wearing. The saying "Diamonds are a girl's best friend" is true, not only because of their monetary value but also because of the pride of ownership.

Jewelry has two broad classifications, referred to as "real" and "costume." Real jewelry is made from natural or genuine stones mounted in precious metals. Real stones are subclassified as precious and semiprecious. Among the precious gems are diamonds, pearls, sapphires, and rubies. These are very expensive because of their rarity and the skill required to cut them for maximum beauty. Semiprecious stones include amethysts, agates, opals, turquoises, and corals. Real stones are mounted in gold, silver, or platinum; these metals are referred to as fine, or precious. Scientists have developed manmade stones which closely resemble such natural stones as diamonds, rubies, and sapphires. Only close inspection by an expert can reveal the differences. Cultured pearls are not really manmade, as they result from the processing of natural pearls.

Costume jewelry was made popular by Coco Chanel in the 1920s. Chanel has continually used imitation jewelry in her collections, and the rest of the world has followed this lead. Costume jewelry may be wood, metal, paste, or glass. It has the single purpose of completing the costume; its monetary value is not important. Its color, shape, or design in relationship to the garment is the important factor. Some costume jewelry may rival "real" jewelry in price because of its design and beauty.

Whatever its value, the purpose of acquiring jewelry is the pleasure it gives. Each woman needs to develop her own philosophy toward jewelry. This is a very personal decision based on individual values. Jewelry should be pleasing to look at and add distinction to the costume it adorns. This is really the only criterion for choosing jewelry; if it pleases you, then it is right.

Fashion in jewelry changes. Some designs are ageless, while others are enhanced by updating. Often the settings of wedding and engagement rings signify the date of the ceremonies. The length of a necklace may date it. The design of a bracelet may be stylish only for a short period of time. Generally, the more valuable the jewelry, the more ageless it is. However, the quality of the original design is a more important factor than age. Resetting or restyling jewelry is an interesting experience and one that should be considered as part of wardrobe upkeep.

With collections of costume jewelry both the fashion of the moment and the age of the wearer should be considered. Costume jewelry is usually faddy. It is short lived because it appeals to a mass market and is usually inexpensive. It comes and goes in fashion, and when it is passé, it should disappear from your collection. Wearing out-of-date costume jewelry will not add flair to any ensemble. Some pieces of costume jewelry do not fit this category and can be favorites for years. A fashion-sensitive woman can easily make this judgment.

College women need to sort out their jewelry collections. Some jewelry may now be too infantile for you in either scale or design. Evaluate each piece. It is important to understand that jewelry designed for a child can never enhance a woman. Some of the collection may be plain junk; this is best discarded.

College women also need to put away high school rings and pins. These belong to a past life and have no part of your current life. If the pin or ring has sentimental importance, it is best worn on a ribbon around the neck and out of sight. Clinging to high school jewelry in college is considered immature by the majority of the student body.

Fraternity jewelry belongs to the college campus. Most fraternities and sororities have regulations for wearing their insignia, and, of course, these should be followed. When a girl accepts a pin, she should learn how she is supposed to wear it. Often the uninformed wear fraternity jewelry on jackets or coats, which is considered bad form by most national fraternities.

College jewelry, with the exception of recognition pins, should be put away at the end of college days and worn only for alumni gatherings. College jewelry, especially sorority and fraternity pins, have no place in the business world. Again, if the jewelry is of great sentimental value and must be worn, conceal it—it will be closer to your heart anyway.

glasses

Glasses are both eye arresting and face framing, and therefore they must be considered a fashion accessory. Face shape, coloring, personality, roles of the individual, and amount of wear are all important factors in selecting frames for eyeglasses.

The frames should be in scale with the face and should follow the principles of lines—they should not repeat the face shape or be the extreme of the face shape. Personal coloring will limit some choices of frames. The fair blonde usually is best in lighter hued frames, while the brunette looks best in darker frames. If you can afford it, a wardrobe of frames is desirable. However, this is usually too expensive for most. Therefore, those wearing glasses only part of the time are freer to select "kooky" or extreme frames; those wearing glasses constantly should choose the less extreme styles.

Frames of glasses are part of the total fashion picture and do change. Mature women should be careful not to be dated by their last visit to the ophthalmologist.

If you must wear glasses, learn not to hide behind them. Too many girls plop their glasses on their noses and think "Now no one can see me!" Actually, the eyes of these girls should be more accented so that their beauty is revealed. Their eyebrows should be carefully shaped in relation to the frames. Remember always that glasses bring attention to the personality area. Make them a fashion accessory and consider them in relationship to your total look.

summary

It is by our faces that we are known. By use of facial expressions and voice we communicate our personality from this area. It is the most individual part of us, and therefore the face or personality area should be most often emphasized by dress.

The face and head should be studied objectively with the rest of the figure conformation, so that an accurate understanding of their relationships may be observed. The face-framing details such as hair styles, necklines, hats, jewelry, and eyeglasses should be selected to enhance the personality area and draw attention to it. Selection of these details should be made with the total look of the ensemble in mind, so that continuity of costume is achieved. There should be one item that dominates the ensemble; the other items should be subordinated. Each detail of the costume should contribute toward the total image of the wearer.

suggested readings

Cordwell, M., and M. Rudoy. *Hair Design and Fashion.* New York: Crown Publishers, Inc., 1967.

Editors of *Glamour* Magazine. *Glamour's Beauty Book.* New York: Simon & Schuster, Inc., 1966.

Ford, Eileen. *Book of Model Beauty.* New York: Trident Press, 1968.

Hillhouse, Marion S. *Dress Selection and Design.* New York: The Macmillan Company, 1963.

Morton, Grace M. *The Arts of Costume and Personal Appearance.* New York: John Wiley & Sons, Inc., 1964.

Sassoon, Vidal. *Sorry I Kept You Waiting, Madam.* New York: G. P. Putnam's Sons, 1968.

Uggams, Leslie. *The Leslie Uggams Beauty Book.* Englewood Cliffs, N.J.: Prentice-Hall, Inc., 1967.

9

the ages of beauty

he beauty needs of women are closely related to the life cycle and must be revised as one passes through the different stages of development. Each reader of this text will find herself in one of the described stages. She may have experienced several of the cycles and be moving toward the next. Some of this material is a summary of what has been set down in previous chapters. It is suggested as a guide for a lifelong beauty program. Some of the recommendations will need modification for your particular situation. Fashions come and go, but beauty is a lifetime responsibility of each woman.

The life span of woman may be divided into different ages. Each age has its beauty problems and triumphs. Mothers should guide their children in the learning of the grooming routines required by each age. How well they learn and execute these routines will be reflected in their health and attractiveness as they mature. One must keep in mind that accepting one's age and stage in life gracefully is the cornerstone to true maturity. The "teeny-bopper" striving for sophistication looks as ridiculous as the grandmother dressed as a baby doll. Enjoy each age as you pass through it. Grow, mature, and develop so you will be ready to accept the challenges of the next age.

childhood years

Each child has a unique beauty which is the foundation for all attractiveness that is to follow. To nurture this beauty, a mother must provide love, good health habits, and a beautiful example. Love is a vital requirement for beauty at all ages. Love gives a sense of well-being, a feeling of importance, and builds self-respect and confidence. Love is a necessary element for the growth and development of all children; without it they wither and may even die.

The beginning years of every child are filled with phenomenal growth and maturation. Each child must be guided and protected through this period. They progress slowly from total dependency into individuals learning to choose their own way. In infancy the routine tasks of personal care must be carefully attended. As the child grows, many of its first learning experiences are related to personal hygiene. A wise mother will foster this interest and establish a foundation of good health habits which will last a lifetime.

The little girl is very interested in herself and in imitating those around her, especially her mother. This is an ideal time to instill simple beauty routines such as daily bathing, nail and hair care, and even clothing selection. In teaching personal routines to the very young, care should be taken to avoid overemphasizing physical beauty for its sake alone. No one advocates producing pretty faces with empty heads and hearts. Positive emphasis should be placed on good grooming as the foundation of personal care because it makes one feel better and healthier.

GROOMING

The daily bath is a fine place to start grooming tasks. This should be a pleasant time but not so filled with playthings that the task at hand is ignored. Personal bath things like bubble bath, soap, and brushes are nice for the child. The bubble bath should be a mild one designed for children so that it does not cause skin rashes. The technique of actually washing the body needs to be encouraged, as most children are by nature soakers. Nail care is easily done in the tub. Both finger and toe nails can be scrubbed with a nailbrush, cleaned gently with an orange stick or toothpick, and the cuticles pushed back. Brisk drying with her own fluffy towel followed by a dusting of baby powder brings out the *femme* in every little girl.

The proper sized toothbrush and a dentifrice that a child will use are important to dental hygiene. The child should be encouraged to brush after every meal. This usually takes a bit of adult supervision, as many children have an aversion to this and are indeed skillful at devising a number of techniques by which the teeth and brush never meet. A stern talk from the dentist may do much more than the same lecture from you. The child should start regular visits to the dentist shortly after the third birthday. Care of baby teeth is vital to the health and development of the permanent teeth.

Skin-care and cleanliness habits instilled in early childhood will have a great deal to do with the kind of complexion your daughter will have as an adolescent. Teach her now how to wash her face. Have her wet her face and gently massage with mild soap in upward and outward motions. Follow this with several rinses of warm, then cool water. Pat the face dry, do not scrub or rub. Follow with a mild lotion if desired. This type of care will encourage a beautiful baby-fine complexion for years to come.

HAIR CARE AND STYLING

Shampoo your child's hair as often as necessary. This will vary greatly with each child and her activities. Choose a mild shampoo that will not irritate the eyes. Rinse the hair well. A lemon or vinegar rinse will make the hair extra shiny; a creme rinse will eliminate tangles. Always wash the comb and brush along with the hair.

The hair style should be simple and easy to manage—it should also be becoming to the child. If you are not a genius with hair, have it cut and styled occasionally. Avoid hair designs for little girls that pull the hair tightly in rubber bands or clips, as this may cause loss of hair in the stretched area.

EXERCISE

Only a parent can know whether a small child really does get enough exercise. Your doctor can recommend, but only you can create the time, and playthings needed for the strenuous exercise of early childhood. Large muscle exercise is vital to the growth, development, and fitness of the child. The games of the young provide for this—running, jumping, climbing, hopping, skipping, sliding. Body control and coordination are dependent on such activities.

The early years are a fine time to begin formal lessons in swimming, skating, skiing, dancing, and other individual sports. The type of lessons would be dependent upon each family situation. Many kinds of lessons are available through community services at nominal costs. Such lessons have a twofold benefit: they provide exercise, and they also give the child the confidence that comes with doing something well. Children learn these things quickly and unself-consciously.

SLEEP AND REST

Proper sleep and rest are lifelong necessities, but even more important in childhood. Growing takes energy. The child in any phase of growth needs more rest and sleep. Children tend to vary greatly in sleep patterns. Understand your child and always provide ample rest and sleep periods. Learn the emotional symptoms that are created by fatigue and help your child avoid such difficult times. Fit your schedule around the child's rest times when necessary.

FOOD PATTERNS

The proper nutrition for your child will be recommended by your doctor, but as the child switches to table foods family food patterns take over. If you have never considered the subject of nutrition, this is the time to do some homework. You will not only benefit your child but yourself and other family members as well. Too many adults are completely ignorant of the basic nutrition needs of their own bodies. Eating patterns are learned in the family setting, so make certain you are helping your child to a healthy mind and body by serving the properly selected and prepared foods. (See Chapter 6.)

The Basic Four Meal Pattern is a wise guide to menu planning. Make a dedicated effort to serve plenty of the protein- and calcium-rich foods, such as meats and dairy products. Keep supplies of fruits and vegetables on hand for both mealtimes and in-between snacks. Introduce your child to the natural sweets like sun-dried fruits, honey, and all the fresh fruits. Avoid introduction of candies and soft drinks as long as possible and then help your child to understand that they should be eaten only occasionally and should never replace other foods in the diet.

Make mealtime a pleasant part of the day and avoid conflict or disciplining then. If your child is a finicky eater, learn to feed him when he is hungry and avoid appeasing him with a stick of gum until daddy gets home. The sweetness of the gum can completely satisfy him, and he really will not be hungry when dinner is served. If your child is pudgy and a lover of food, keep low-calorie foods for him and help him watch his weight by selecting body-building, low-calorie foods for his meals.

The important thing is to understand your child's food needs and cater to them. Encourage eating a wide variety of healthy foods just as you encourage good table manners. Help your child establish eating patterns that will be the foundation of a strong body, smooth skin, and pleasant disposition for an entire lifetime.

WARDROBE

The child's clothing needs are closely related to his stage of development and activities. The clothing should be comfortable and easily maintained. A versatile mix-and-match wardrobe is the most flexible and allows the child a great deal of freedom in selection. A coordinated color scheme will eliminate many adult "hang-ups" in the child's selection as well as reduce the need for a large quantity of clothing.

Children should be allowed some choice in selecting their clothes at the time of purchase. This does not mean they should have complete freedom of choice, for their inexperience would make this foolish. They should occasionally accompany you on buying trips and have the privilege of making a delimited choice. It is important to develop a taste in clothing in young children while they are still willing to listen to advice, as this may not be the case in a few years.

Most of all, help your little girl enjoy her womanly role. Certainly, there will be times when she will swing from a tree like a chimpanzee, roll in the mud with glee, and perhaps have the best batting average on the block. Great. This is a marvelous part of childhood which should be enjoyed to the fullest by both child and parent. But there will be other times when the feminine, girly side of her nature will emerge; nourish these. Her contentment with this role is the true foundation of beauty for the mature woman you desire her to be.

adolescent years

Adolescence is a very difficult period of transition from childhood to adulthood. It is a time of great growth and body changes as well as a time of extreme emotional stress. In the American culture it is a time of many decisions that will have a tremendous effect on the course of events during the rest of one's life.

The chronological age of the onset of adolescence varies with the individual. Recent studies show that the age of physical maturity is becoming lower, especially among girls. This is a time when many girls verbally reject all parental suggestions but emotionally wish very much for direction. The emerging young woman can be greatly helped through this very important time if she feels her beauty is shining through. To help the typical adolescent girl may try the patience of the most sainted, yet it is worth all the effort required. Guidance on the way from childhood to womanhood is the last major task of motherhood and demands all the skills and resources available.

GROOMING

As a girl enters adolescence, her grooming problems change, and she should be helped to develop good methods of dealing with them. It is important that parents realize that nature is taking its course, and, no matter how much they desire their little girl to remain a child, there is nothing that they can do to deter the process. Nothing, that is, without damaging the child's emotional development or destroying the family relationship. For these important reasons the adolescent girl must learn the importance of bodily cleanliness and begin the practice of using deodorants to cope with body odors.

Another must in our culture is the removal of superfluous hair on the legs and under the arms, and, in some cases, on the face. Someone once said that a young girl needs to start ridding her legs of hair just about the time her mother needs to start wearing glasses! Often the timing of the first hair removal is a family battleground. If it is regarded as a needed grooming practice, it may be easier for parents. The method selected for hair removal may vary from one area of the body to another. The legs may be shaved or chemically depilated. Excessive amounts of hair on the forearms may be bleached, singed, washed, or chemically removed. The underarms are shaved. The facial hair may be plucked, waxed, bleached, or removed permanently by electrolysis. Specific products are on the market for each process, and care in selection and use is mandatory. A small patch test is highly recommended.

Skin problems are equated with adolescence in the United States. Diet control and skin cleanliness are the best preventatives. If a problem does develop, prompt medical care may prevent many years of embarrassment, gallons of tears, and possibly permanent scars, both physical and emotional.

The teen years are not too soon to start using cleansing lotions and moisturizers. Night creams should really be a part of the daily grooming routine by sixteen or seventeen. These products often help combat oiliness. The girl with the oily skin will probably have some skin blemishes; the adolescent with dry skin may start to wrinkle before her twentieth birthday.

A weekly manicure becomes even more important at this time in life. Hands are judged by others as an index of what kind of person you are and what your habits may be. The grimy paw may have been charming in childhood, but it is unthinkable at this stage of development. Chewed and gnawed nails are not only unsightly but they tell the world how little self-confidence one has. Nicely shaped, manicured nails are within the reach of all. They take time, not money, and are well worth the effort.

The dental-care habits should be firmly established by now. After-meal brushing may require carrying a toothbrush with you, but why not? Regular dental checkups are important. Any straightening and orthodental work should be done in this period.

Most girls feel the need to do a great deal of experimentation with hair styles and make-up within this period. This is an important learning process, largely brought about by peer group pressures. One of the best ways to handle this stage is to encourage your daughter to learn proper make-up techniques and to set some limits on the things you will allow. A good lesson for any girl to learn is the importance of timing. The timing of extreme hair styles and make-up is much later in life, say about twenty!

EXERCISE

It seems unnecessary to mention exercise in adolescence, as adults often wonder if they are ever still. Yet, strenuous exercise is often neglected in this period of development, especially by fastidious girls who do not want to get "messed up." Participation in any kind of sport is important. Dancing is great exercise, particularly the way it is done now. Urge the adolescent to develop favorite individual sports that can be his for a lifetime. Exercise, whatever type preferred, will firm, trim, and tone the body. Teen-agers should learn to take exercise breaks while studying; it really revitalizes.

SLEEP AND REST

In this period of great growth, body changes, much social activity, and increased school loads, adequate rest is of vital importance. Insist on at least eight hours of sleep most nights. Encourage naps or a quiet time before big social events. When things pile up, such as parties during the holiday season or term papers, projects, and exams at the end of the term, help your teen-ager recuperate by tapering off activities for a few weeks following these times.

FOOD PATTERNS

The diet of the adolescent seems to change radically from the beginning to the end of this period. Many girls enter this period with ravenous appetites, eating constantly. As a result of this gorging, many gain a substantial amount of weight. Somewhere in the middle of the teens the crash or fad diet enters the scene, and by the late teens eating habits may be designed to maintain a fashionably skinny figure. The American teen-ager belongs to one of our most malnourished population segments—not because of deprivation, but because of choice of foods. Tragically, many of the teen-ager's skin, weight, and emotional problems can be closely related to faulty eating habits.

180

Again the Basic Four Meal Pattern is the best guide to food planning. Help your daughter understand the importance of eating habits to her health now and in the future. Find references for her to read on the relationship of food to skin, hair, nails, energy, and emotions. The public library has many of these books. Also help her understand that her nutritional status in adolescence has an important effect on the babies she may have. Hopefully, the good eating habits established in childhood will carry over into the teen years. But for too many high schoolers, candy, soft drinks, and French fries seem to be the most preferred bill of fare.

WARDROBE

This is the time in a girl's life when she acquires her largest wardrobe. Usually, little individuality is expressed in dress, peer group identification being more important. Clothing is very important to this stage of development. Quantity rather than quality is the general preference.

This is an excellent time to give a girl a clothing allowance and help her learn to manage it. Outfitting a teen-ager is a tremendous strain on many family budgets; often the clothing allowance will help a girl to understand this. In many cases a young girl should be encouraged to earn money to supplement that which the family can allow her. This is a great time for her to learn to sew. She should master this skill well enough to make some of her clothes and all of the alterations she requires. Sewing is an "in" hobby for millions of teen-agers and one of the best. It meets both aesthetic and economic needs. Once the fundamentals are learned, sewing is great creative fun, and the best route to a large wardrobe.

the college years

The late teens and early twenties are among the most challenging years of a lifetime. In our culture these are the years that set the patterns of the lifetime that is to follow. It is during this period that one emerges from the family setting to become an independent individual. As family ties are lessened, one begins the adventure of adulthood.

For many teen-agers, the first step away from home is to college. While the pattern of college life differs greatly with each campus, there is one vital characteristic necessary to all successful college students. This element is self-discipline—in managing time, energy, and money: the self-discipline to study what is required and fulfill course requirements; govern all interpersonal relationships; and to separate the mature from the immature.

Management is self-discipline in action. It involves setting up personal routines and practices, which will allow for the accomplishment of the tasks necessary to achieve certain goals. An essential part of the daily and weekly routines is to set aside times for personal care and beauty. These routines need to be a part of every college woman's schedule. Developing such routines into well-established habits will keep you at your most attractive and free your time and mind for intellectual or social pursuits.

The college years are the time when the "follow the herd" tendencies of earlier years depart and individuality is expressed more and more often. This expression of the unique self is found very often in dress and self-adornment. Certainly, college students follow fads, but more often because of the fun of it rather than for the necessity of peer group identification.

GROOMING

Personal grooming for the college woman is a continuation of the practices started earlier. Some more attention to moisturizing the skin may be necessary. Make-up techniques may be more sophisticated, as may hair styles. The important thing to remember in this age is to put away the high school look and develop the individuality of a mature college student. Hair styles should be simple and easily cared for during the school week. For special social situations, hair styles may be as extreme as your gown, if both fit the occasion and you. Some time before the end of college years, the girl who wears waist-length hair should get a good haircut and styling. Shunning this advice, the hair should be arranged in a disciplined way. Long, flowing locks are young and girlish; they are not appropriate for adult roles.

EXERCISE AND POSTURE

Finding sources of strenuous exercises after PE requirements have been met is very important. Find a sport you like to do and do it often. Walking or cycling around campus can fulfill this need, but you must do it with vigor and purpose. Carry yourself erect and shift the books so you do not develop a lopsided figure. Arrange your study desk and chair so that you may sit erect and thus become less fatigued. Take an exercise break during study sessions. If you are in your own room, do some strenuous calisthenics. If you are in the library, take a brisk walk around the building. You will feel better and be able to concentrate for extended periods of time if you incorporate this technique into your study methods.

SLEEP AND REST

One of the most difficult achievements of the college years is getting adequate sleep and rest. The demands of study, work, and social life push sleep hours to the bare minimum. This is something each person must understand about herself. Some can manage very nicely on very little sleep and rest, but others really need eight hours of uninterrupted rest each night. Learn to manage your sleep time as your body demands. Take care of this in a mature, responsible way. The rewards of proper rest are many, often including better grades.

FOOD PATTERNS

Many college women gain weight. This is usually due to irregular eating habits, dorm food, socializing, and nibbling while pursuing knowledge. This large intake of food and the reduced exercise pattern of many students lead to the addition of weight. Some college women completely reverse this pattern and exist on very little food, a great deal of nervous energy, cigarettes, and coffee. This latter pattern borders on starvation. If either problem is yours, you should reform.

As pointed out before, adequate nutrition is essential to healthy bodies, skin, hair, and teeth; it is also the foundation of emotional stability and has been related to scholarship. Following the food guide established by the Basic Four will contribute in a significant manner to college success.

WARDROBE

College wardrobes vary tremendously from one campus to another and also among the different groups found on each campus. In some areas the dress is very casual, while in others it is very fashionable. Some students employ the entire gamut of dress as suits their current purpose. Choice of clothing expresses the individuality of the wearer, but is also interpreted within the frame of reference of the observer (an important factor to remember when conferring with the instructor).

For those transferring from one campus to another, it is wise to wait until you are actually on the new campus before investing in a large wardrobe. Garments appropriate at the last school may not be acceptable at the new school. This is especially true for students transferring from one part of the country to another, or out of the country.

The college students nearing the end of their schooling should begin to give special consideration to the kind of clothing they will be wearing as they enter a career. A collegiate wardrobe may be woefully inadequate and inappropriate in the teacher's room, the business office, the laboratory, or the suburban setting. Do plan ahead and make the major expenditures of your last year with postgraduate days in mind.

marriage and motherhood years

Marriage is one of the most popular, demanding, and satisfying careers of all. Most young women aspire to marriage and motherhood, and the vast majority attain this goal. As our society changes, the roles of wife and mother are also changing. It is important that each woman decide for herself what kind of relationships she wishes to develop with her husband and children and then never settle for less. This takes a lifetime of effort and love and is extremely demanding. A woman must be prepared to give a great deal of herself to this relationship, but the wise woman saves a bit of herself for herself. She must retain an identity; she cannot live her life as Mrs. So-and-so or Johnny's mother; she must also be Mary So-and-so, who does something. The something in point can be anything, as long as it is satisfying to the woman. Some women find this something in the arts, some in volunteer work, some in creative projects; more and more are finding it in a paying job outside the household. It is the something that expresses your individuality and gives an identity to you.

This period of a woman's life is the most demanding. Whatever the status, the successful wife and mother must manage her time, energy, and resources. These roles are ones that usually evolve slowly. Each marriage is unique, and the interpersonal relationships involved pertain to that special family. This should always be kept firmly in mind when reading any advice. What is recommended must be tailored to your situation.

GROOMING

In the early years of marriage it is often easy to carry on with the routines established early in life. Special thought should be given to the consideration of your husband. It would be extremely vain and, in small, modern homes almost impossible, never to let your husband see you in varying stages of grooming. But this can be kept to the minimum. Some of the grooming practices such as facial packs, rollers, and reducing exercises might need a time change, say from Friday evening to Saturday afternoon when he is on the golf course. Most men

184 would rather believe you always look a certain way than become embroiled in the technicalities of how you arrive at it.

PREGNANCY

Pregnancy is a very special time in every woman's life. The physical and emotional changes require understanding on the part of both husband and wife. Being pregnant is a healthy condition, and, with morning sickness excluded, it should be regarded as such. All grooming practices should be carried on as always, but perhaps with a little more effort toward hair styling and make-up.

Each pregnancy should be carefully supervised by a physician who can advise and help you. One's habits of exercise and posture will be in evidence at this time. A body made strong by early health habits will function without difficulty during this period.

Your doctor will advise you as to diets, exercise, and rest. A woman would be foolish not to follow this advice most conscientiously. Your own health, and the health of your baby, for both the duration of the pregnancy and the years to follow, will depend a great deal on the regime you follow at this time.

Maternity wardrobes vary with fashion, although they may never appear too fashionable to you. They are usually limited in number of outfits, and so the clothing should be selected to fit the many roles of the expectant mother. They should be easily maintained and resist wrinkling. The colors should be the most complimentary hues. Grayed values and low-intensity colors will be more figure concealing. The design of the maternity clothing should place emphasis at the personality area. Eye-arresting details should be selected with care. Avoid such detailing as belts at the abdomen, buttons at bust points, and horizontal lines across the fuller parts of the figure. Long sleeves will detract from the size of the abdomen and give more width at the top of the figure, thus causing better balance. The skirt length should be fashionable, but in keeping with the mature role of motherhood. It should be kept in mind that numerous figure changes occur throughout the pregnancy. Clothing purchased at the onset will be expected to expand and change with the figure and therefore must be selected with this in mind.

Once the baby has arrived and been settled into the family routine, the new mother has a responsibiilty to the other family members that should be assumed. She should make every effort to regain the figure measurements she had before the baby arrived. The doctor can supply you with postnatal exercises and diets to help with this project. For too many years motherhood has been an excuse for lost waistlines; you can still mouth this, but no one will really believe you. The entertainment world is too full of excellent examples of svelte women who have had several children. If they can do it, you can too. All it takes is self-respect and self-control.

No matter how busy and fragmented your life becomes with the activities and responsibilities of homemaking and motherhood, you should always care about your personal appearance, for yourself and your family. Decide when you can do your grooming and do it. Many busy mothers may find that the only time the bathroom is free from interruptions is at 6 A.M.—so get up and use it in luxury! Greet your family in the morning with make-up on, hair combed, and fresh clothing. This sets an excellent example for them and has you ready to cope with any situation. Others find other times in the day for personal grooming better suited to their patterns of living. The excuse of being too busy to bother with personal appearance translates most simply as being lazy. We always have time to do the things we want to do.

MORALE BOOSTERS

Dedicated wives and mothers also owe it to their family to budget for their own beauty expenditures. This is not being selfish. A visit to the beauty parlor, a new bathrobe, luncheon in an elegant restaurant, or whatever, can be made to seem pure extravagance, but in reality this is a small price compared to the morale building it does. Your emotional health is important to your entire family; it is your duty to be as serene and contented a woman as you can be.

WARDROBE

Your wardrobe will depend on the kind of life you lead. Some women may be corporation wives with heavy social obligations; others may be suburban matrons for whom relaxed comfort is a way of life. Many will combine marriage and motherhood with a career. The list of possibilities is lengthy. Each must analyze the life she leads, the roles she plays, and the image she wishes to project, and dress accordingly. The most important factor to keep in mind is that fashions and styles change, and you must too. The clothing and hair styles of early matrimony need refurbishing as the years pass. Clinging to lipstick colors, hair styles, and fashions of high school and college are much more antiquating than calendar birthdays: This proclaims that you are not sensitive to the ongoing changes about you or receptive to new ideas. As Chanel advises,

Men count on maturity, women on youth. It is woman's misfortune. How long can youth last, how long can one remain sixteen? Certainly it is not the length of the skirt that will arrest time. Even sixteen year olds are not sixteeen for very long.[1]

[1] Gabrielle Chanel, "Collections by Chanel," *McCall's* (July 1968), p. 43.

the career years

It is estimated that the modern woman will work approximately twenty-five years of her life outside of her home. Today, there is such a variety of career opportunities available for women that it is impossible to guess the proper accouterments for each. Embarking on a new career, for the newly graduated college woman or the mature wife and mother returning after taking a "baby break," creates many problems. Each is being cast in an unfamiliar role. Each will be expected to look the part of the position she accepts. Each must analyze her personal appearance and decide what changes must be made to fit her for the new role. The old roles often continue, although some may need to be modified; and the new roles create special needs.

JOB INTERVIEWS

The most important step in starting a new career is the job interview. This is the time when first impressions must be the correct impressions for the job situation. As discussed in Chapter 1, dress plays a vital part in first impressions. The wise job applicant will make an effort to learn what kind of dress is appropriate or expected for each business establishment. In years past, interviewees were usually advised to appear in a conservative suit, hatted and gloved, with only the minuscule amount of make-up. This advice may still be good for many conservative businesses in some parts of the country. However, it may be very poor advice for a woman seeking a career in fashion, advertising, or other such businesses where flair, individuality, and progressiveness are vital. A bit of detective work on your part will help you know what type of dress will be best for your interview. It may also save you the effort of the interview; if you note that the women employees dress in a manner that you personally would resent or be uncomfortable in, it may not be the right place for you.

WORKING MANNERS

Once you have landed the job, it is important to remember that your dress and grooming must stay in keeping with the general policies of the company; you will often have a great deal of freedom, but this is something you should never take advantage of. Business dress is business dress. It looks as if the wearer is prepared to fulfill her obligations to her employer and not dressed for social activities. Personal and social life are very much apart from the business world, and the clothing appropriate for these kinds of occasions is too. Just as the cocktail dress is not worn to church, it is not worn to business. The obvious exception would be the woman who works in such a capacity that the after-five dress is her job uniform.

For social engagements after work, bring clothing to change into after the business day has ended. Clever use of accessories with basic clothing can often accomplish this. A totebag for carrying such things is preferable to an overnight bag. The totebag should be kept out of sight during the business day.

The executives in any business like their female employees to look feminine and decorative. It adds a pleasant atmosphere and also contributes in a positive way to the reputation of the establishment. These same bosses, however, do not like to know how their female employees maintain their beauty. So confine all combing, cosmetic applications, and manicuring to the lady's room. They are not paying you to do this, and you actually lessen your own attractiveness when you are continually seen repairing it.

EXERCISE AND POSTURE

The career woman usually needs to make a very special effort to get enough exercise. Most employed women do not exert themselves physically. You may be thinking, "When you come home as tired as I do, all I need is more exercise." Yes, you do! The fatigue you experience in most cases is mental fatigue, perhaps with a touch of boredom thrown in. Large muscle exercise continued over an extended period of time is important to your physical fitness now, just as much as it has been previously. Find the best form of exercise for you and do it. A jump rope could be a good solution, exercising with television instructors another.

If you have a position where you sit for long periods of time, your posture takes on even new importance. Sitting slows the circulation to the feet and legs. It spreads the hips. When the spine is not held erect, it can push the organs out of place. Adjust your chair to the proper height and sit tall. Change your position when you can. Get up and walk around. Perhaps instead of eating during your breaks a brisk walk would make you feel more alert and benefit your figure as well.

SLEEP AND REST

The patterns of sleep and rest should be well established for you by now. If your new career is a very demanding one, you may not be getting the rest you know you need. Nervous tension may be keeping you awake. You must

188 think through your own situation and make the necessary changes. Only you can make certain that you get enough rest, so do it. You will be a much better employee and a much happier person if you meet this basic need.

FOOD PATTERN

The Basic Four is still your guide. If you are eating a greater number of your meals out, make certain that you are getting a balanced diet. If you are beginning to add pounds, make some fast adjustments. The snacks at break time, the starchy lunch, and the cocktails after work can be awfully fattening. Review your calorie charts and begin playing the weight-watching game. Carrying your own snacks and lunches may not seem too sophisticated, but it has many advantages. You can eat less fattening foods, it costs less, and it can give you time to shop, walk, or relax. Perhaps you can lose that weight, save enough money to buy that new dress, and look smashing in it—all because you started "brown bagging" it.

WARDROBE

Your wardrobe needs will be directly related to your position. Some career women only need a couple of lab coats each year, others, special uniforms which are only worn on the job, and still others require a fantastic wardrobe. The best advice is to be sensitive to the attitudes of your employer and to the needs of your position. Clothing says a lot about you and can help you climb the ladder of success. It can make you look sharp as well as attractive. Clothing choices can also make you look like you do not belong to certain organizations. Think about it. What are your ambitions? What do you want your clothing to say about you? Could the way you dress help you get that promotion—or is that why you did not get it?

the middle years

The thirtieth birthday is a traumatic experience for most women. In our culture where the emphasis is on youth, it seems that to actually be thirty is to be over the hill. Yet, realistically, the achieving of thirty years is really a very insignificant milestone in the total life expectancy. A realization begins to develop soon after the birthday tears have dried. Being thirty is comfortable. Gone is the uncertainty of the teens and twenties. A new kind of self-confidence emerges, and one is able to accept herself as she is. Very few women who have achieved this stage would exchange it for younger years.

The middle years are the ones in which one should evaluate carefully all that one is and has achieved. It is during this time that the industry and struggles of past years begin to pay off. Careers of both men and women reach high levels of responsibility and reward, children become self-sufficient, interpersonal relationships mellow. It is a good time—the years of the command generation. This status and stature should be enjoyed to the fullest.

The middle years are also a time when one must learn to accept oneself, that is, the spiritual, emotional, and physical self. Once this has been accomplished, a delicious serenity can enter your life. The woman who fails this self-acceptance usually becomes a sad thing, pitied or ridiculed by those around her. A woman of forty trying to look and act twenty can never carry the act. She ends up looking and acting foolishly.

The aging process in many ways is a very kind thing. The harsh lines of youth are softened. The colors of the skin and hair begin to fade and soften. This should be considered when selecting cosmetics and hair coloring. The lines of the face take on character and individuality. The eyes reflect wisdom and experience. All the years of living are exhibited in bearing and actions. Acceptance of this new role and this physical self can lead to the most glamorous and exciting years of all.

The woman who is past her thirtieth birthday can be the most sophisticated, glamorous, and romantic creature alive. She has the self-confidence to be comfortable in clothing that is most becoming to her and usually the money to afford the kind of wardrobe that meets her needs. She can successfully wear extreme hair styles and make-up if she so chooses. The most beautiful dresses, the most beguiling hats, the most delicious lingerie are really designed for her, although they may be advertised on younger women. The brave new colors and color schemes again are hers to enjoy. Fashion, whatever the mode, is hers now. So, if you fit in this age, glory in this revelation while you have the appearance of youth and the convictions and poise of maturity.

EXERCISE AND POSTURE

The habits of exercise developed early in life should continue into the middle years. If exercise has been neglected in recent years, it is very important to begin a regular regime now. The body needs large muscle exercise to maintain its tone and flexibility. The heart, lungs, and circulatory system function better when large amounts of oxygen are brought into the system as the result of exercise. As a woman, you need exercise not only for good health, but for graceful body movements.

Exercising for five or ten minutes each morning upon arising is better than doing nothing. Choose the bending, stretching exercises that loosen the back, waist, and legs. It does add sparkle to the beginning of each day. Choose another form of exercise that you enjoy and do it. Find a friend that will golf, play tennis, swim, jog, or cycle with you and do it on a regular basis. A pleasant form of exercise and one that does much to refresh the spirit is walking. A wonderful companion for walking is the family dog.

REST AND SLEEP

Pamper yourself in this area—get enough rest and sleep. You should know by now exactly what it takes to keep you healthy, happy, and pleasant to be around. Rest before the big evenings. If things are becoming too pressured on the job, stay home and sleep one day; everyone around you will profit from a well rested you.

FOOD PATTERNS

Figure control with good eating habits should be your motto. Your body requires less food because your activities are less than they have been in the past. The female body chemistry is geared to storing food excesses as fat tissue. So beware. Each year of your life you should evaluate your eating habits, maintain the Basic Four Meal Pattern, but modify the amounts consumed. Be a weight watcher. Get to your best weight, then take the vow: three pounds on, three pounds off.

WARDROBE

The variety of roles your life demands will dictate the kind of wardrobe you must have. Quality of clothing, rather than quantity, may become more important to you. You may establish trademarks of dress that become you, by selecting certain designs or accessories and always wearing them. Consider the elegance of the understated look. Follow fashion only to appear contemporary, using your clothing as a showcase for you. Always select what is best for you, what makes you comfortable, what pleases you. Chanel gives sage advice to this age: "Originality is personal. A dress adds taste and measure. Elegance is not the prerogative of those who have just escaped adolescence, but of those who have already taken possession of their future." [2]

[2] *Ibid.*, p. 43.

the senior years

The greatest gift of the twentieth century to all womankind has been the gift of life. A life span that has been doubled by modern science and technology is a magnificent present, and it should be treated as such. The added years of life are to be treasured, enjoyed, and lived.

As a woman progresses through the cycles of life, she should give some thought to the kind of "old lady" she wishes to be. Retirement years, if they are to be enjoyed, must be planned and anticipated. Often this time in one's life requires tremendous changes in one's routines and habits. It usually means a move from the large family home into smaller quarters; this may be in the area one is familiar with or perhaps in a brand new area. Sadly, one often loses the mate of a lifetime. Children usually have neither the time, energy, or resources to be of much assistance during this time. If a woman is to enjoy her gift of added years, she must be independent and self-reliant.

This is the time in one's life to do all the things one never had time to do before. To be busy and creative should be the goal of all during this time. Explore the community around you. Find the things you like to do and do as much as you can. Fit the new things to you; do not expect to become a social butterfly if you have never been one; rather, expand the talents you have long enjoyed.

Accept the limitations that age has placed on you gracefully. But keep in mind that an active and alert mind is the best company anyone can offer oneself or others. Keep informed of the events around you. Listen to others and contribute your wisdom. Enjoy your reveries into the past, but do not bore others with them. Try to seek out young people and establish a rapport with them.

Enjoy the benefits of time. Nature has mellowed your face, your hair, your body. Accept this. Soften your make-up, hair coloring, and clothing. You will find you have a beauty that only years of living can achieve. The lady of seventy with the face lift, bright hair, and too fashionable clothes fools no one but herself. Accept your maturity; it really is a precious gift. Consider this advice of Chanel: "A face of 50 should show something. If it looks like 20, empty, without a line of experience ... it looks moronic. Should Lincoln have had his wrinkles removed?" [3]

GROOMING

Your personal care should be immaculate. Laziness in this area has never been acceptable and is even less so now. If it takes a little longer, who cares—

---

[3] *Ibid.,* p. 43.

you have the time. Make yourself as pleasant to be near as you can. Have your hair styled in a soft, becoming, easy-care style. Use the amounts of make-up that you are accustomed to using, only try a little softer effect. If your eyesight has dimmed, make a special effort to check the art work with your glasses on to make certain you see what everyone else is seeing. Avoid any downward lines in the face make-up or hair style; these can drag your features into a gloomy expression.

EXERCISE AND POSTURE

Do some exercise. What you have been doing for the past twenty years will probably be fine. Do not get carried away with a strenuous new routine. Walking may be the most enjoyable form of exercise. It can be delightful and keep you informed of the lovely things that happen as the seasons go by.

Make an effort to keep your head held high, your body erect. Sit, stand, and walk as straight as you can.

SLEEP AND REST

You may need more sleep and rest than ever before in your adult lifetime. If you do, take advantage of the extra time you now have and sleep and rest as you need to. Adequate rest will make you a much more pleasant person to be around. Little things will be less irritating and other people less crotchety. This is important to your physical and mental health, so indulge yourself.

FOOD PATTERNS

The amount of food you require has been diminished by fewer body demands, but the variety of foods you need has not changed. Consult your doctor on the kind of diet you need and follow it. Many problems of the elderly are related to malnutrition. Special conditions do require special diets, and these should be carefully observed. Lifelong patterns of eating are very hard to modify, but if this is your challenge, accept it as such.

WARDROBE

This is the time in your life you really can wear whatever you wish and still be quite lovely. Your individualism carries you beautifully. Softer fabrics and pastels or muted colors will be the most becoming; body-concealing clothing more flattering than body-revealing clothes. As Chanel more bluntly put it: "Don't expose a lot of flesh unless it is young and firm. It is barbaric to see old women wearing dresses showing a great deal of bosom." [4]

A secret of remaining forever youthful, regardless of the years on the calendar, is flexibility. Open your mind to the world around you, be informed, read, think, and, above all, listen. Evaluate what you learn in your own frame of reference. Most important, be receptive to new ideas. These new ideas will come from all around, especially from your children. Think about them and form an opinion based on new thinking, not on what you decided twenty years ago. Put new ideas into action. When plans have to be changed, be graceful about it. Be willing to give and bend with the situations. Such flexibility of thought and action is the key to youthfulness and the key to being a desired companion.

summary

All the world's a stage,
And all the men and women merely players.
They have their exits and their entrances;
And one man in his time plays many parts.
His Acts Being seven ages.

> *Shakespeare*
> As You Like It
> *II, vii*

Enjoy each act and savor each age to the fullest. Grow, change, expand, and evolve as you gain in years and stature, always remembering that a truly successful person lives life in his own way.

suggested readings

Editors of *Glamour* Magazine. *Glamour's Beauty Book.* New York: Simon & Schuster, Inc., 1966.

Editors of *Harper's Bazaar. Harper's Bazaar Beauty Book.* New York: Appleton-Century-Crofts, Inc., 1959.

Ford, Eileen. *Book of Model Beauty.* New York: Trident Press, 1968.

[4] *Ibid.,* p. 43.

194

Gam, Rita, and Walter Goodwin. *The Beautiful Woman.* Englewood Cliffs, N.J.: Prentice-Hall, Inc., 1967.

Morton, Grace M. *The Arts of Costume and Personal Appearance.* New York: John Wiley & Sons, Inc., 1964.

Powers, John Robert. *How to Have Model Beauty, Poise, and Personality.* Englewood Cliffs, N.J.: Prentice-Hall, Inc., 1964.

Waterson, Barbara Johns. *Pull Yourself Together.* New York: Simon & Schuster, Inc., 1967.

Wilkens, Emily. "The Seven Ages of Beauty," *Family Circle* (August 1968), p. 54.

10

---

social graces

the social graces of each person are an expression of individuality. The way one moves and speaks, his manners in relationship to all others are trademarks or identifying characteristics. These are segments of personality which are used as tools to describe and catalog one. How are you labeled by those around you? How would your friends, teachers, family, employers, and other associates describe you? Would they say you are friendly, charming, gracious, confident, warm, thoughtful, and polite? Or would you be described in other terms? Do you always treat your family members in the same way as you do your friends, or do you have a double standard—one for home and one for public? Social graces are the qualities that express refinement. They are an expression of thoughtfulness and consideration for others and are much to be desired by one who wishes to fulfill his social role in our society. Social graces can be acquired by everyone who sincerely wishes to possess them. They cost only time and effort. Their rewards are without number.

Gracious body movement and a pleasant voice are important in presenting a pleasing image. No matter how lovely the ensemble, coiffure, and make-up, the illusion of beauty strived for by a woman can be completely shattered by awkward movements and postures. A dissonant voice, poor speaking habits, and incorrect grammar can be equally as devastating. Actions and voice use are social expressions that are regulated by a society.

Manners may be defined as ways of behaving with polite standards. Etiquette is the conventional requirement of social behavior or the proprieties of conduct established by any class or community. Manners and etiquette are never old-fashioned or stuffy. They are the elements of socialization that make the human existence pleasant. The most beautiful women in the world can be made ugly by gross or uncouth actions. The most plain man can become charming through pleasing manners and etiquette.

Age has absolutely nothing to do with social grace. Babies must be trained to become socially acceptable. They must learn manners and etiquette along with everything else. The mature of each age cycle always incorporate social graces into their lives and relationships.

To be well presented, each one must practice the social graces continually. Personal conduct and interpersonal relationships should reflect this considerate behavior. Social graces are the unpurchasable accessory that completes each man and woman whatever the accouterments.

vocal and facial expressions

The most gracious characteristic one can have is a genuine interest in others. This interest is of utmost importance in establishing rapport with anyone. Genuine interest is the basis of friendship. It is also an essential element in the art of conversation. If one is interested in what the other is saying, the conversation flows. Most people like to talk about themselves and the things they know and do. Questions that bring out this information are fundamental to small talk. The give and take of ideas and concepts are the roots of lively conversation. The ability to talk to people is an essential social grace.

When conversing with anyone, it is vital to look at him. This does not mean a constant eye contact which may be uncomfortable over a long period of time, but an interested and alert reaction, which is natural. Many people do not realize the importance of eye contact. Eyes that are wandering around the room or are glued to the floor cannot express interest or reaction. If you want people to really register what you are saying, you must direct it to them. Eye contact supplies this direction.

Development of the voice and diction is important. If the voice has unpleasant qualities, such as high pitch or raspiness, it is irritating. Clear pro-

nunciation and correct word usage are as important as an adequate vocabulary.
Verbal communication is one of our most precious talents—learn to use your
voice so that it is truly representative of the person you are. College students
have a wonderful opportunity to take classes in speech which can be highly
beneficial to every facet of their lives.

Develop the practice of smiling. It is hard to understand why so few people
show their pleasure with a smile. A happy or pleasant expression on the face
makes one much more approachable. All people of all ages respond to a smile;
it makes them feel good. Smiling comes from within, but it must be done with the
entire face to look genuine. The eyes must register happiness as well as the
mouth. The lines of the individual face form the smile. The expression formed
is special and enhancing to each face.

One should be certain that the teeth are clean and in good repair, or the
smile can be distracting. Exposure of the gums is to be avoided when smiling.
For certain mouth shapes it may take some practice in front of the mirror to
avoid the gums. Practicing saying the vowel sounds in an exaggerated manner
can also improve a smile. The individual sounds create a variety of expressions
which can be incorporated into a smile.

Think of the people you know of various ages and analyze their smiles.
How do you feel about the ones that do not smile? Do they appear sad, sullen,
woebegone, or miserable? Think about the people you know that do smile, and
contrast their image with the nonsmilers. To which category do you belong?

MAGIC WORDS

Some of you will remember watching the television show *Captain Kangaroo,*
a delightful show for children. One of the lessons that the good Captain con-
tinuously taught was the use of the "magic words"—please, thank you, excuse
me. This lesson of childhood should always be remembered. When used often
and sincerely, these words truly are magic. They are kind words that evoke
courteous responses.

Whenever someone does something for you, say "thank you." This someone
may be a stranger opening a door for you, your mother who has done something
for you, a friend who has promptly returned something he borrowed from you.
Who it is is not important; your extension of this courtesy is.

"Please" should be used whenever you are making a request of someone.
This someone could be your little brother, whom you are requesting to remove
his filthy tennis shoes from your clean rug, or your fiancé, whom you are asking
to pass the salt. The word "please" changes a command, which may be very
brusque, to a request.

"Excuse me" or "pardon me" should be used when you must impose a discourtesy on someone. This act may be walking in front of them, interrupting them, or leaving them. By saying "excuse me," you are requesting their permission to do whatever you need to do.

These "magic words" are verbal manners which should be deeply ingrained in your speech patterns. Use them easily, often, and sincerely. They are the terms that help you express your consideration of others and label you a kind and gracious person.

LITTLE THINGS THAT COUNT

Learn to give and receive compliments. If you honestly admire something, say so. Do it in a manner that best suits how you feel and how you express yourself. Do not try to be anything you are not when giving a compliment. A direct and simple expression of admiration is the best kind.

For many, receiving a compliment is more difficult than giving one. Never argue with the one offering the compliment. For example, can you think of a time when someone said he really liked your outfit and you responded by pointing out how old it was, the ill fit, and how shabby it had become? What you are doing, in essence, is attacking the taste of the person complimenting you. It would be much more appropriate for you to smile and say "thank you," thereby expressing pleasure for your admirer's thoughtfulness. Since you selected this outfit to wear, why argue?

It seems the more personal the compliment, the harder it is to accept it gracefully. It is very difficult for many to have attention directed toward their person. A comment about their attractiveness, clothing, or skills embarrasses them because of a certain lack of confidence. This really is an enigma, since the shy person has probably worked very hard developing what is being admired. Always remember: a sincere smile and a simple "thank you" are the best responses to any compliment. Such a reply is easy to offer, and it shows you as a sensitive and gracious person.

WRITTEN EXPRESSION

A written note of thanks is a most thoughtful gesture. It represents an extra measure of effort on your part to express appreciation. The occasions evoking a thank-you note are limitless. Any time someone does a nice thing for you, it may be acknowledged with a note. A dinner or party, a gift or flowers, a wonderful date, even a particularly nice birthday card—all of these are appropriate reasons for a thank-you note. This is a very friendly gesture that is sometimes forgotten in the rush of modern life, but it is one that is always appreciated.

There are certain times when a thank-you note is mandatory. When you have been a house guest, the thank-you note becomes a "bread-and-butter" letter. It should be sent promptly and directed to the persons responsible for making your visit possible. In the case of a family, all members should be included. This sometimes may require more than one note—one for the parents and one for your friend.

Wedding and shower gifts must always be acknowledged by a handwritten thank-you note. Printed ones are not proper. You must express your own thanks in your own manner. This is necessary even though you have verbally thanked the giver. These notes must also be sent promptly. This is one of the ways a new bride is judged as she assumes her new role. It really is important. One frustrated mother of the bride once placed a thank-you note in the newspaper because of the delinquency of her daughter in this matter. This is not recommended form, but it does reveal how important this note is.

Guides for selecting stationery and certain forms of notes for various occasions are outlined in all of the etiquette books. Reference to these can help assure that your thank-you notes will be correct and representative of good manners.

The basis of social graces is really common sense—taking the time and effort to treat all those around you exactly as you would like to be treated. We each appreciate the thoughtfulness and kindness of others. When someone does something nice for us, we are pleased; returning the favor pleases them in return. These gestures should be spontaneous and done only because we want to. Kindness becomes something else when it is done out of duty or for personal gain.

When you last gave a party, what happened? Did all the guests acknowledge your invitation so you knew exactly how many to plan for? Did they enter into the planned activities with enthusiasm? Did they seem to enjoy the refreshments? Did they offer you their assistance? Were they considerate of the other guests? Did they thank you and your family when they departed? Did they phone or write a thank-you note to express appreciation? When you were last a guest at a party, could you honestly answer yes to all of the above? If you expect such behavior in others, shouldn't you require it of yourself? This is really what social grace is all about—the golden rule applied to social situations.

protocol with escorts

There are certain courtesies that should be extended by men to women, such as opening doors, offering assistance, walking on the street side of the sidewalk. Sadly, many men offer these gestures only to be rebuffed by a boorish woman. Always be aware that an escort should do certain things for you and be ready to graciously accept these courtesies.

A gentleman opens a door for a lady. This may be a complete stranger or her escort. If the door opener is unknown to her, a smile and a "thank you" are in order to acknowledge his thoughtfulness. If the gentleman is her escort, the smile is always in order; the "thank you" will depend on just how many doors he has opened during the evening. Sometimes the smile alone implies the "thank you."

A lady waits for her escort to open the car door for her. Too many women leap out of passenger cars even before they have been properly stopped. These same women are so anxious to get where they are going, they often leave their escorts far behind as they race along. This makes them appear very aggressive and unmannered. A lady will exit from a car on the driver's side only for two reasons: she is driving, or it is impossible to get out the passenger side. Sliding under the steering wheel of the car is both awkward and unrefined.

If an escort is not in the habit of opening car doors or extending other courtesies, a lady will need to use her feminine charms to encourage him. If she really cares about the man, a talk about manners and courtesies is in order. Girls may discover that men have a few gripes about some of their actions, too.

AUTOMOBILE MANEUVERS

Graceful body movements should be incorporated into all activities. Today's cars combined with today's fashions often present a real challenge to a lady. When getting in or out of a car, you must use your leg muscle strength if you are to be graceful. If a gentleman is assisting you, fine, but it is your strength that gets you in and out. His hand should be used only as a balance. Otherwise, he might pop you out of the car like a cork out of a bottle!

To get into a car gracefully, plan your movements and practice them until you can achieve a flowing motion. To enter the front seat, stand first facing the front of the car so that you enter the car sideways. It is perfectly permissible to balance yourself by grasping the car roof, the steering wheel, or perhaps the door. The next phase of entering a car may be done in one of two ways— both are graceful when done correctly. The first method works well for sports cars and long legs. Place the foot nearest the car on the car floor, slide hips onto seat, pull in head and shoulders, and then bring the other foot into the car with you. The second maneuver to accomplish the same thing is to sit on the edge of the seat and swivel the legs, shoulders, and head into the car in one easy movement.

Getting into the back seat of a car should always be done sideways. This prevents exposure of the broad backside. Face the front of the car. Step backward into the car with the near leg. This leg acts as a fulcrum as the body slides back into the seat and the other leg follows into the car. Getting out of the back seat is just the reverse of this movement.

The exit from the front seat is most graceful when you have moved close to the edge of the seat. Swing the door open and pivot the body until it faces the open door and the feet are on the curb. Execute a modified deep knee bend, and you are out. It is possible to get out by placing the outer foot on the curb, sliding out the head and shoulder, and, as you are straightening to standing position, bringing out the lower torso and the other foot and leg. This last technique can be very exposing, so care should be made to cover the space between the knees with a purse or hand.

SIDEWALK MANNERS

When walking along the sidewalk, the woman should always walk farthest from the street. This custom arose in the Middle Ages when housewives were in the practice of tossing their household garbage into the street. The man walked close to the street to protect his lady from the cascading debris. In these days of garbage disposals, the custom still holds and shows respect for the female. When walking with a lady, it is often necessary to change positions as you turn corners. The man should cross behind the woman and resume the outside position. When he does this, the lady should move over so that he is not forced to walk in the gutter.

When walking with a man, the lady should take the man's elbow or arm if she needs support or just feels friendly. A man should never propel a woman down the street by her arm. For many strollers, holding hands is fun, romantic, and probably the most graceful way to walk with a man. Holding hands is fine and very acceptable; any more entwining is not.

DINING

When dining in public with a male escort, a lady should become her most feminine and dependent self. As a man opens the restaurant door, the woman enters and hesitates. The escort should take over and make the request for the table. A lady follows the maitre d' to the table. Either the maitre d' or the escort helps her with the chair or indicates where she is to sit. A lady sits gracefully and does not argue with the seating arrangement. Follow the lead of the host when ordering. If there are some doubts about price range, ask him to order for you. A lady makes all requests to her escort, who relays them to the waiter. One should concentrate on one's date and direct most of one's attention toward him. Of course, if you are in a group, you will participate in con-

202 versation with all. The conversations a lady has with the service people should be held to an absolute minimum. A "please" or a "thank you" is most acceptable, but a long, flirtatious discourse is very rude. Your part as a dinner guest is to be interesting and interested in your date. When the check comes, a lady should be rather oblivious to the money exchange; this is the man's responsibility.

If you must leave the table for any reason, excuse yourself discreetly. If you are in a group, it is not necessary to take a friend or two with you. Make-up repair beyond a quick lipstick addition should not be done in public, ever, and this includes restaurants.

Leaving the restaurant should be done quickly, without table hopping. If you see friends, a smile of acknowledgment and a few words of greeting are all that are correct in this situation. If the lady has a coat, it is best carried to the foyer of the restaurant before putting it on, with the assistance of her date.

any social situation

In any social situation you should always understand the rules of etiquette and try to apply them. However, your own sensitivity should be more of a guide than any written rules. If someone is doing something you know to be incorrect, never call attention to this and embarrass him. At certain times you will be forced to follow along and do things that are not quite in keeping with the technicalities of etiquette. Do this graciously and gracefully. It is much more important that you do not hurt anyone's feelings, or make them feel awkward and uncertain, than it is for you to be absolutely correct. In fact, for you to call attention to this would be a greater discourtesy than the original one. Again, use common sense when applying rules of etiquette to each individual situation. Do what will show you to be a kind, thoughtful, and gracious person, and you will always be correct.

personal decisions

Social life in the United States demands that each individual make certain decisions about personal behavior. The values instilled by early training are tested at this time, as the final decision rests with the individual. Drinking of alcoholic beverages and smoking are the kind of decisions referred to. Each person has to make this choice. For many the social pressures are very great, and a number of adults smoke and drink, not because they really want to, but because the crowd does. Analyze your position and then do what you really want to do. Every grade school child has been exposed to the pros and cons of drinking and smoking, so there is no need for discussion here. However, if you do elect to either drink or smoke, learn the social graces of both. These are described in all etiquette books. Drink and smoke in as gracious a manner as you can, and always be sensitive to those around you who most whole-heartedly disapprove of both.

Another adult choice that must be made by young people is what may be nicely labeled public demonstrations of affection. Most college campuses have students who are complete extroverts when it comes to affection. A kiss good-bye for a fifty-minute class sometimes looks long enough to suffice for a whole war. Young people in public places such as parks, beaches, and movie houses carry on private little orgies in full view. What do you do? If two people are truly in love, their shared affection is a private matter. It does not need to be exhibited. Each should have enough respect for their relationship not to be put on public display. How do you react when you observe such behavior? What is your impression of the participants? Could this be you?

In this chapter the authors have discussed the social graces important to them and ones they have observed being neglected by college students. There are many others that could be included and many directions given. However, each library and bookstore has a variety of etiquette books which delve into these subjects. They make excellent reading and references. Try them.

With friends, family, and classmates start a discussion about social behavior of others that is a source of irritation to each of you. It may be things like gum chewing, picking the face, sprawling instead of sitting, grooming in public, eating techniques, and so on. Make mental notes of the conversations, and then be especially sensitive to your own actions for a while to see if you are guilty of these things. Do not let it be said of you: "Pat would be a great person if only . . . ."

suggested readings

Barry, James. *A Man's Guide to Business and Social Success.* New York: Milady Publishing Corporation, 1966.

Gam, Rita, and Walter Goodwin. *The Beautiful Woman.* Englewood Cliffs, N.J.: Prentice-Hall, Inc., 1967.

Munson, Mary Lou. *Practical Etiquette for the Modern Man.* New York: The Taplinger Publishing Company, Inc., 1964.

Post, Emily. *Etiquette: The Blue Book of Social Usage.* New York: Funk & Wagnalls Company, Inc., 1965.

204   Powers, John Robert. *How to Have Model Beauty, Poise, and Personality.* Englewood Cliffs, N.J.: Prentice-Hall, Inc., 1964.

Tolman, Ruth. *Charm and Poise for Getting Ahead.* New York: Milady Publishing Corporation, 1967.

Vanderbilt, Amy. *Amy Vanderbilt's Complete Book of Etiquette.* Garden City, N.Y.: Doubleday & Company, Inc., 1967.

Vogue's Book of Etiquette and Good Manners. New York: Condé Nast Publications, Inc., 1969.

Whitcomb, Helen, and Rosalind Lang. *Charm.* New York: McGraw-Hill Book Company, Inc., 1964.

11

---

design in dress— elements and guidelines

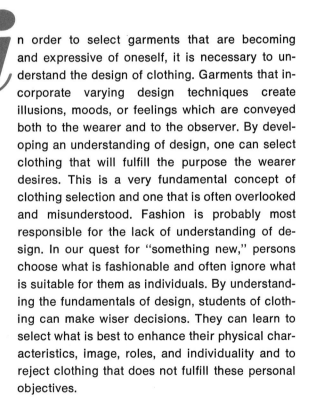

n order to select garments that are becoming and expressive of oneself, it is necessary to understand the design of clothing. Garments that incorporate varying design techniques create illusions, moods, or feelings which are conveyed both to the wearer and to the observer. By developing an understanding of design, one can select clothing that will fulfill the purpose the wearer desires. This is a very fundamental concept of clothing selection and one that is often overlooked and misunderstood. Fashion is probably most responsible for the lack of understanding of design. In our quest for "something new," persons choose what is fashionable and often ignore what is suitable for them as individuals. By understanding the fundamentals of design, students of clothing can make wiser decisions. They can learn to select what is best to enhance their physical characteristics, image, roles, and individuality and to reject clothing that does not fulfill these personal objectives.

understanding design

Design is defined as any arrangement of lines, shapes, textures, and colors. These are often referred to as the fundamental and plastic elements. They are fundamental because they are the basics with which the designer must work and plastic because they can be manipulated with infinite variety. The problem of creating design is in choosing and organizing the fundamental or plastic elements. Good design shows thoughtful arrangement of materials used to produce desired effects.

The design guidelines, discussed later in this chapter, can be applied to the organization of the elements to achieve the effects preferred. Because these guidelines represent personal value judgments, they should be evaluated and used as such. Those that are of value to the individual can be used as guides in appraising the design of clothing.

STRUCTURAL AND APPLIED DESIGN

There are two kinds of design—structural and applied. All garments have structural design because they are created by construction details when put together, including seams, collars, pockets, and the color and texture of the fabric (Figure 11–1). Any detail that is an integral part of the garment is structural design. This structural detail may be either very elaborate or very plain. In clothing, structural design is most important because it is the fundamental component of the garment. Garments that rely on good structural design for their interest and appeal are the most pleasing, and they are often the most expensive.

Some garments may have applied design (sometimes called decorative design), which is surface enrichment added to the garment. It consists of trims such as sequins, beading, embroidery, applique, rickrack, and piping. It often includes buttons without buttonholes and flaps without pockets. Applied design is often used as a less expensive method to achieve design interest. In mass production applied design is sometimes used to cover shoddy workmanship. Ready-made garments which do not have appropriate or effective decorative designs in buttons, bows, scarves, and trims can often be enhanced by eliminating these details entirely or by replacing them with more suitable trims. Existing garments in the wardrobe can be radically transformed by the use of decorative design.

Applied design can be evaluated by use of the following criteria.

11–1 All garments have structural design. This gown is void of any applied design; it relies upon cut, construction details, and fabric for interest. (Courtesy Du Pont Company)

11–3 The applied design shown here is related in texture to the fabric, and in scale and shape to the area in which it is used. The Ceil Chapman design is fashioned in twilled satin Qiana nylon. (Courtesy Du Pont Company)

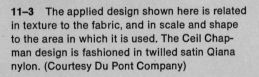

11–2 The applied design is related to the structural lines of this garment. It appears to grow out of and reinforce the basic construction lines. (Courtesy Eastman Chemical Products)

1. The decoration or trim should reinforce the basic design concept created in the construction of the garment. This is achieved when the placement of the trim is related to the structural lines of the garment (Figure 11–2). Decoration placed without consideration of the basic garment lines often produces a disorganized impression.

2. Applied design is most attractive when it is related in scale and texture to the textile of the garment (Figure 11–3). Compatible combinations of textures include
fine embroidery—finely woven fabrics
sequins—shiny, fine textures
rickrack—medium-weight cottons
embroidered tapes—medium-weight cottons and wool
raffia—homespun cottons and linens
crewel embroidery—heavy woven and knitted fabrics.

3. Applied design, when used in limited areas, will produce an organized impression (Figure 11–4). Overuse of decoration usually detracts from the total effect of the garment. When trims are very eye arresting, they are most effective concentrated in one or two areas. Applying bands of peasant embroidery at the neck, wrists of long sleeves, and yoke is overdoing it and obvious; a disunified impression may result.

4. Trims should create an interesting color harmony with the garment fabric. Colors can be selected to match, blend, or contrast. When the garment

11–4 The use of applied design in limited areas is eye appealing without being confusing. (Courtesy Eastman Chemical Products)

fabric is a print, repetition of a predominant color used in the print will unify the applied design.

5. The applied design is expected to be related in the size of the area that it occupies. Small areas such as cuffs and collars can accommodate trims of limited size; large areas such as yokes, the skirt, and bodice can adequately utilize large-scale trims.

THE DESIGN ELEMENTS—LINE AND SHAPE

The design elements significant to dress design are line, shape, color, and texture. The latter two mentioned are discussed in following chapters. Line and shape are treated together because line divides the areas, thus creating shapes both within the garment and in the outline of the garment on the body.

Lines create impressions, and skillful use of line can create visual illusions. Line can be used in a garment to make you look taller, shorter, heavier, or thinner. Line and the shapes and spaces that line creates can make hips look small or large, shoulders broad or narrow, and waists thick or thin. The effects that line produces will be related to other factors, such as fabric color and texture, the shape of the body wearing the garment, and the degree of contrast that enables a line to be noticeable or not. The effect that line produces is also affected by what we have been preconditioned to expect.

The design lines of a garment may follow the contours of the body or be in opposition to it. The lines of a garment define its outline; they also divide the space within the silhouette to create shapes. Lines connect one part of the garment with another and provide a pathway for the eye to follow. Lines can create moods or feelings.

There are two kinds of lines—straight and curved. Straight lines can take three directions—vertical, horizontal, or diagonal. A curved line may be extreme or subtle.

Straight lines are in opposition to the body. The use of straight line in clothing design is very often softened by the texture of the fabric selected; when a soft fabric such as jersey is incorporated into the design, straight lines take on body curves. Stiff fabrics maintain the straight line. Straight lines in clothing are achieved from fabric design—stripes and plaids; structural lines of cut and seaming pleats and tucks; and trims, such as buttons, braids, laces, and embroidery.

A straight line may be vertical, horizontal, or diagonal. Each direction of line creates illusions and must be judged on the individual to learn exactly the effect in a particular garment design. Interestingly, visual illusions are not experienced by all people to the same degree, and some people may not perceive them at all. Perception of illusion varies among individuals because of experience, association, imagination, attitude, and cultural differences. What we have been conditioned to expect plays an important part in how we perceive. Illusions are errors of the visual sense, the intellect, or judgment. Lines, shapes, colors, and textures may form illusions that will distract the eye or make accurate judgments impossible. We can use illusions to produce certain effects, but we cannot be sure that the effect will be recognized in the same manner by everyone.

Vertical lines *generally* add height or length. This is the favorite line of those who wish to appear more slender. Vertical lines in clothing are found in fabric design, construction line, sleeve line, trim, and fasteners. Noticeable vertical lines which divide skirt or pants and bodice or shirt areas can reduce the apparent visual width of these spaces. For example, a plain skirt, undivided by vertical seams, usually appears wider than a skirt having one or two vertical seams in the front and back sections. The angle and spacing of the two vertical seams vary in their effect of slimness. (See Figures 11–5 and 11–6.)

A most important fact to remember about vertical lines is that when they are repeated in quantity they can add width. What effect the vertical line has depends on the spacing and the background contrast of the verticals (Figure

11–5 The amount of vertical spacing and the angles produced by the lines have varying effects on the figure when these spaces are made noticeable by contrast. What makes the visual effects vary in the identical figures?

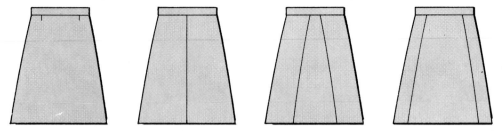

11–6 The same skirt silhouettes with different space divisions create varying visual effects on the figure.

11–7). Closely spaced parallel lines may lead the eye in an upward direction, but as the space between the lines is increased and if there is a variation in spacing the eye begins to measure width. To judge the effect of vertical lines, it is best to study the garment on the figure. Double-breasted garments almost always add width because of the distance between the vertical lines (in addition to the bulk of the double layer of fabric).

Horizontal lines *generally* add width or breadth. Just as repeated verticals may sometimes add width, some horizontal spacing can produce illusions of height. (See Figure 11–8.) Horizontal lines in clothing are found in fabric design, waistlines, yokes, belts, hems of skirts, sleeves, and trims. (See Figure 11–9.) The horizontal lines usually carry the eye across the body. This means that when a horizontal line is emphasized in a garment design, the eye of the beholder measures the width of the area. Widths of waists are measured by

11–7 The direction the eye moves when observing vertical lines will depend in part on the spacing and the background contrast between the verticals. What impression do these lines give? (Courtesy Celanese Corporation)

belts; widths of hips are measured by hemlines of jackets, sweaters, or over-blouses; apparent widths of bosoms are increased if the hemline of the sleeve ends at the fullest part of the bust; widths of legs are measured at the level of the skirt hem. Widths are also measured by comparison to other widths of the body (Figure 11–10). For example, a wide shoulder line will make a wide hip line less noticeable than a narrow shoulder line (Figure 11–11). A waist cinched in tightly will make a hip and shoulder line appear wider by contrast. Hip width is also measured by hem width. A skirt that flares gently and becomes wider at the hem than at the hip gives an illusion of a smaller hipline than a straight skirt. Greatest width is achieved when the horizontal line is emphasized by a contrast in color, as found in blouses and skirts of different colors.

Diagonal lines assume the characteristics of the vertical or horizontal line as the degree of slant approaches each extreme. The degree of the slant of the diagonal line determines the illusion created (Figure 11–12). The extreme diagonal as found in the bouffant skirt adds width; the very subtle slant of the diagonal as found in the A-line skirt adds length. The use of diagonal line in clothing design is often very pleasing. It is one of the best lines to incorporate when trying to camouflage poorly proportioned parts of the figure. Diagonal lines give a feeling of movement or action.

213

11–9 Horizontal and vertical movement is often created by placement of contrasting trim. (Courtesy Celanese Fibers Marketing Company)

11–10 The width of the arm or leg is measured by comparison to the width of the sleeve, pant, or skirt. Compare the effect created by sleeve and pant styles in these three figures. In *A* the arm and leg appear slimmer than in *B* and *C*. *B* seems fuller than the other two.

214

A　　　*B*　　　*C*

11–13 A dot pattern arranged in a zigzag fashion produces erratic movement of the eye across the fabric. This increases the illusion of body size. (Courtesy National Cotton Council)

A zigzag line is a series of diagonal lines connected. It forces the eye to shift its direction abruptly and repeatedly in an erratic and jerky movement. This type of line is found most often in fabric design. Because of the eye activity, zigzag lines tend to increase the mass or size of the area covered (Figure 11–13).

Curved lines generally follow the contour of the body and are becoming. However, when the curve becomes exaggerated toward a full circle, it becomes very active and may easily be overdone in a costume. A restrained curve is graceful, flowing, and gentle. A gradual transition in the change of direction of a curved line adds pleasing quality to the design. Just as straight lines can conform to the body contour through fabric textures, so do curved lines. The effect is emphasized if the body is extremely curvy. (See Figure 11–14.)

216

The Silhouette

Lines of a garment create an overall outline of shape, which forms the silhouette of the garment. Often the silhouette gives the first impression because it is usually seen by its contrast to a background, and it is readily seen from a distance. The silhouetted form of the clothed body reveals the shapes of various parts of the figure and garment, such as the sleeve, the skirt, and the bodice.

Designers throughout history have developed only three basic types of silhouettes, and they have used them repeatedly with variations. These are the straight or tubular, the bell or bouffant, and the back fullness or bustle. High fashion uses exaggerated shapes of the silhouette, while mass fashion uses more modified shapes. The silhouette changes slowly with fashion. At the present time more than one silhouette is concurrently fashionable. Although one silhouette may dominate fashion, it is possible for the individual to use the shape that is most flattering to her and still be in vogue.

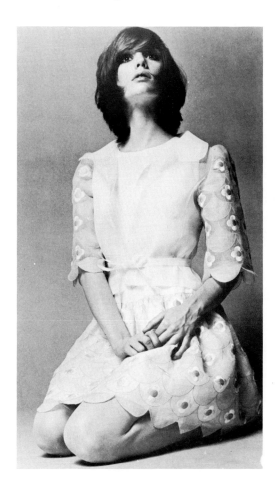

11–14 Predominately curved lines produce the effect of width. Curves are often used to express femininity and youthfulness. (Courtesy National Cotton Council)

Clarity of Line Definitions

The outline or silhouette of a garment and the body within it is evident when there is contrast with the background. But often not all internal structural lines are noticeable due to a lack of contrast to emphasize them. Some garment designs do not show a definite line direction, even though the design is composed of many straight lines or curved lines. The internal lines may not be noticeable in garments made of printed fabrics, especially dark prints or those having a great deal of color contrast within them. (See Figure 11–15.) With some fabrics in solid dark values in which the seams are pressed very flat or the nap covers the seam, the line becomes negligible. Internal lines become less distinct as the distance from which they are viewed increases.

Lines are made noticeable by panels of contrast (Figure 11–16), welt seams, lapped seams, and trimming or piping (more so when the piping is in a contrasting fabric) (Figure 11–17). Line direction is then emphasized.

11–15 The impact of the line design is related to the degree of contrast to the background. The structural lines of this garment are obscured by the fabric design. (Courtesy Cotton Producers Institute)

11–16 The structural lines of the garment are reinforced by the contrast of colors used. (Courtesy Simplicity Pattern Company)

11–17 White piping defines the indistinct line of the collar, lapel, and front closure. (Courtesy National Cotton Council)

219

Application of Line

In applying lines in clothing designs, there are two guides that are important to understand and apply: (1) repetition of line emphases and (2) contrast to line emphases. For example, if you are very tall and slender and you repeat this vertical line in your clothing, you will emphasize your height and slimness. If you go to the extreme and select very round lines or horizontal lines, you will emphasize your height and slimness by contrast. In the selection of necklines, a square jawline will be emphasized by repeating the square or contrasting it with a circle. A pointed chin will be emphasized by repeating it with a V-line or contrasting it with a half-circle. Bell-bottom trousers are impossible on the full hip-thigh figure because the width of the hemline repeats the width of the hip-thigh and emphasizes it; in this figure type the small waist often emphasizes the size of the hips by contrast.

If you have a problem area you wish to minimize, simply remember not to repeat this line and not to contrast this line. Use the lines that are less extreme. They will be kinder to your figure and create a desired illusion.

guidelines for the selection of design in dress

The design principles are rules or laws that are used in art forms to judge good design. These principles are used at times to guide the painter, the sculptor, and the designer when they compose or evaluate their work. There is some disagreement among artists as to what these principles are, but the principles used most often in textbooks of clothing selection are balance, proportion, scale, rhythm, emphasis, harmony, and unity.

The authors of this text have taken a different view regarding the use of each of these principles and their application to dress design. It is our opinion that all of these principles do not meet today's requirements for good design. Standards which were established in the past need rethinking in terms of present-day apparel. A person needs only to look through the work of designers who have gained fame in the past fifty years to find that the traditional principles were often not only disregarded but the opposite of what the principles stood for was frequently used.

Innovations of style would be extremely limited if designers adhered strictly to the art principles. The artists during the last half of the nineteenth century, known as the Impressionists, met critical response and rejection because their new use of paint application and color were not consistent with practices then in vogue. Today, the works of the Impressionists are considered very valuable and are held in high esteem.

Fashion currently worn has, perhaps by habituation, become acceptable, whether art principles were followed or not. In the 1950s the large, full extended shoulder line, worn with pencil slim skirts, defied the principle of good proportion. People became used to this line, accepted it, wore it, and enjoyed wearing it. The misuse of proportion in this example is the distinguishing factor that made this style different from styles previously worn. (See figures from the Tournament of Roses in Chapter 3.)

Another example can be found in the misuse of the principle of balance. Balance is the grouping of objects, shapes, and colors around a center in such a way that there is equal attraction on either side of the center. If a person wears a scarf tied at the side of the neckline permitting both ends to lay over to one side of the center, she is in effect breaking the law of balance, but few would argue that the effect is displeasing. Pepper said, "There is an allure in a certain degree of unbalance in dress quite distinct from the demureness and propriety of symmetry and balance." [1]

The possibilities of not having good balance in clothing are not especially great because clothing covers a relatively small area and the body is often in motion rather than being static and stationary. On the other hand, poor balance may apply to the decoration of a room because it is a large, stationary space and the eye can perceive the weight of the objects and the color arrangement more easily.

As mentioned previously, there is much disagreement among artists as to exactly what the basic art principles are. Criteria of excellence vary historically, and these standards reflect the period and the person making them.[2] A survey of books on art criticism will lead to many different sets of principles, each set depending on the judgment of the writer. Pepper reported

The hypothesis of the existence of certain perfect aesthetic relations among aesthetic materials is becoming psychologically less and less tenable. Whatever the law of habituation signified in detail, it offers a wide range of evidence for an extensive spread and growth of appreciation for aesthetic materials rather than a fixed selection of certain elements to the exclusion of others. That is, psychologically it is improbable that certain proportions are aesthetically better than any others in any absolute sense....[3]

Principles are no more than judgments of individuals based on their personal values and tastes, which are not universal but very individual. One value level is not necessarily superior to another, as witnessed by the changing values of man through the ages.

Knobler, in *The Visual Dialogue,* observed judgments made of art in this manner.

[1] Stephen Pepper, *Principles of Art Appreciation* (New York: Harcourt, 1949), p. 83.
[2] Frank Seiberling, *Looking into Art* (New York: Holt, 1959), p. 274.
[3] Pepper, *op. cit.,* p. 195.

The question of absolute values in the area of aesthetics has concerned philosophers for centuries. Many aestheticians have attempted to construct value systems for the arts. None of them have proved adequate. Inevitably, the judges are confronted with the application of the rules they have constructed, and it is at this point that major problems arise, for it is impossible to eliminate the personal responses of the viewer from his function as a judge.[4]

What it comes down to is the fact that the individual needs to form his own personal requirements for good design. These will be based on his environment and will be an expression of his own personal tastes and values. The criteria accepted should be a projection of oneself and thus should have more meaning and application for one's personal needs.

In clothing selection there is a need to combine the *aesthetic* qualities that we desire—the *functional* and *practical* components of design—in order to judge whether an article of apparel is satisfying to us. A design must be aesthetically pleasing to most of us, but it must be more than that: it must be functional and practical to meet our value standards and expectations. We want many qualities from a garment—fit, comfort, easy care, a reflection of the current fashion, and enhancement of both physical and nonphysical qualities.

Both aesthetic characteristics and functional properties are interwoven in such a complex manner that it is difficult to separate them. For example, a garment selected for aesthetic reasons must maintain its shape as it is worn to be truly beautiful. If clothing wrinkles, strains, frays, wilts, or pulls apart, it will no longer be considered attractive. A dress on a hanger may be appealing, but on a body in motion it must fit, provide comfort, hold up, and enhance the wearer to be considered truly pleasing.

In establishing some workable guidelines for the selection of apparel, the term *principle* will not be used, because it implies rules and rigidity. Instead, we will use the term *guidelines*. As stated previously, it is necessary for each person to form personal guidelines which will apply to his unique needs. The authors have developed some ideas which may provide a starting point for your thinking. These guidelines may not include all of the possible requirements you individually desire, or they may include ideas you do not consider important. Like principles, values, and tastes, these guidelines are arbitrary rather than universal.

In the process of setting up these guidelines, we have to combine

Body shape	Roles
Personal coloring	Values
Personality	Goals

[4] Nathan Knobler, *The Visual Dialogue* (New York: Holt, 1966), p. 18.

with

Fabric (color, texture, and design)   Cut (lines, shapes, and styles)

which results in

Image (appropriateness, mood, expression)

The many ways in which fabric, cut, and theme are combined create an endless variety of garments. Consumers are equally as varied. The object of these guidelines is to combine all of the elements required in a satisfactory garment and relate them to the needs of the individual. In other words, the authors have endeavored to develop guidelines that will become the criteria for individual selection of all clothing.

guidelines for apparel selection

1. Performance
2. Image
3. Emphasis
4. Scale
5. Theme

PERFORMANCE

A knowledge of fiber quality, garment construction, and adequate garment labeling is important in evaluating performance. (See Figure 11–18.) A garment performs because it

Functions for intended use	Maintains its shape
Fits properly	Requires minimum maintenance
Provides comfort	Is constructed adequately for intended use

A garment performs because it functions for the activities for which it should be used. All apparel must provide sufficient ease to enable us to accomplish daily routines such as getting on and off buses, in and out of automobiles, walking, and standing. Some garments will require additional room for movement when their use is intended for active sports, house cleaning, or gardening.

11–18 Performance of clothing is related to design, materials, and construction. Fit, comfort, durability, and easy maintenance are requirements for children's clothing. (Courtesy National Recreation and Park Association)

A garment performs because it fits properly. Styles with normal waistlines remain in place; cutaway necklines fit snugly enough to conceal shoulder straps and undergarments. Correct fit means that bust darts point to the center of the area of greatest fullness, not above or below. Sleeveless garments are cut high enough under the arm to conceal the bra or slip. Fit is adequate so that it does not reveal rolls of flesh held in by tight foundation garments. Seams do not pop because of strain, and straight skirts do not stretch in the seat and lose their shape.

A garment performs because it is comfortable to wear. Cut and fabric are designed to suit seasonal temperatures. Requirements provide for warmth, coolness, and protection from rain, snow, and sun (Figures 11–19 and 11–20). The garment is comfortable to wear because it feels good on the body—it does not bind, pull, irritate the skin, or feel constricting.

11–19 Garment performance for some apparel includes meeting the need for protection from the weather. (Courtesy Men's Fashion Association of America, Inc.)

11–20 Garment performance needs are related to the conditions under which they are to be used. This Eskimo is primarily interested in warmth and protection from severe weather. (Courtesy Pan American World Airways)

The garment performs because it keeps its shape through wearings and cleanings. It maintains its original freshness for an adequate period; it does not muss, wrinkle, or look bedraggled during wear. Bias-cut skirts hang perpendicular to the floor.

The garment performs because it meets individual demands for easy care and maintenance. Time and money required for cleaning and upkeep should be considered at the time of purchase.

The garment performs because it is constructed adequately for its intended use (Figure 11–21). Seams do not give; zippers remain closed; and hems, hooks, snaps, and buttonholes function. Facings, seams, hems, and the network of lingerie straps do not shadow through to the outside. Garments intended to be worn on a short-time basis, such as bridal attire and fad clothes, need only function for a limited time, so the lasting quality of the construction of these garments is not vital.

IMAGE

The image expressed by the garment is ideally consistent with

The self-concept of the individual

The body structure

Current fashion adapted to individual requirements

Group and community clothing practices

Roles and activities of the wearer

Age of the wearer

Personal requirements such as originality, distinctiveness

The clothing we select reflects our characteristic traits, values, attitudes, interests, and tastes—it is an extension of the image we have of ourselves. The garment is a symbol of how we want others to react to us (Figure 11–22).

The image expressed by the garment is consistent with our body structure and our own concept of a physical ideal. Our ideal does not have to be that of Miss America. A tall, angular girl may not want to appear shorter or fuller; a short person may not want to appear tall. Twiggy made a fortune with her less than ideal figure. We select styles that we believe will accentuate physical assets and divert attention from areas we want to camouflage. We should accept and work within the bounds of our physical structure rather than try to gain an unreachable ideal. The application of color, texture, and line can be used to produce illusions of the way we wish to look within moderate and reasonable limitations.

11-21 Functional for the intended use, this garment performs in many ways. It is made of a soft absorbent fabric to provide comfort. Elastic-backed pants encourage independence. Cotton seersucker makes it easy to maintain. (Courtesy National Cotton Council)

11-22 The image that a garment expresses is ideally consistent with the self-concept of the individual. Our clothing choices are a symbol of how we want others to react to us. (Courtesy Men's Fashion Association of America, Inc.)

The image expressed by our clothing reflects current fashion trends, but current fashion is adapted to our physical and nonphysical characteristics. If fuchsia is the color of the season but fuchsia makes you look ghastly, avoid it. Current fashion features a choice of styles at the same time, and we should select only those that are appropriate for us. People who cling to styles long after the period when they were considered fashionable have a "dated" look. Hair styles, make-up, fads in colors and styles, shoe shapes, shoulder widths, and skirt lengths are features that become dated fairly rapidly. People who must wear their clothes for a long period due to economic or personal reasons can select styles that are classic and dateless.

The image expressed by the garment is consistent with and acceptable to local group and community clothing practices. It is often necessary in certain situations to respect existing clothing customs. This is of special importance to newcomers in a community and to business people. Acceptance or rejection may depend upon how you fit into the group and whether you meet the standards the group expects in clothing as well as in personal characteristics and behavior.

11–23 These youthful styles express the ages of the girls wearing them. A sophisticated style on a young girl is inconsistent with the image of her age. (Courtesy Simplicity Pattern Company)

Acceptance or rejection may be based upon clothing, as this is the first obvious symbol of the wearer; behavior may be assumed by others by this symbol.

The image that the garment expresses is a reflection of the roles of the wearer and the activities for which it will be used. The various roles in which we are engaged have clothing requirements which must be considered when we select clothing. Role is identified by dress. The places we go and the things that we do require clothing appropriate for the activity.

The garment expresses the image of the age of the wearer. A sophisticated style on a young girl is as inconsistent as a baby-doll look on a mature woman (Figure 11–23). The impression contrasts with the age of the wearer and therefore accentuates the years, or lack of them.

The image of the garment will meet individual personal requirements. Some people want their image to suggest originality and distinctiveness, while others do not want to be noticed but want to blend in with the crowd.

EMPHASIS

Emphasis is dominance or a concentration of interest in one area of a costume which prevails as the center of attention and is more eye arresting than any other part. All areas may be interesting, but not all areas should have equal strength of interest. This implies the use of subordination in other parts so that one area may be emphasized. (See Figure 11–24.)

Placement of emphasis should not be at any area the individual wishes to minimize. The face or personality area should most often be emphasized. This is the part of the person that is most unique and individualistic—the real you. Emphasis at the personality area may be achieved by color and texture contrasts, necklines, jewelry, scarves, ties, hair styles, and make-up. Only one item must be the most important or dominant, and all other ornamentation is subordinate to it.

Sometimes interest may be concentrated at the waistline, bust, hip area, hands, legs, or feet. Hands are emphasized by long sleeves, especially when cuffed; bracelets; and rings and bright or unusual nail polish. Poor grooming of the hands, lack of manicure, or chewed nails can bring negative emphasis to this area.

Legs and feet are made dominant by unusual hem lengths, design detail at the hem, textured or colored hosiery, and elaborate footwear. Color contrasts, texture, or cutwork in shoes is eye arresting and should be evaluated carefully.

Parts of the torso, bust, waist, and hips become areas of interest when garment lines or ornamentation fall at these areas. Emphasis is achieved by the use of color, line, texture decoration or trim, or by the absence of fabric which reveals the skin. The methods used to obtain emphasis are

11–24 The placement of interest at the personality area is achieved by a large, contrasting, and unusually shaped collar. (Courtesy Celanese Corporation)

Repetition or concentration

Unusual lines or shapes, textures

Decoration on a contrasting background

Contrast or opposition

Progression

Repetition or concentration may be achieved by rows of tucks, gathers, ruffles, buttons, or trim in one area, or by concentration of jewelry, such as rows of beads, chains, or pins. (See Figure 11–25.) Repeated cut-out areas of fabric and concentrated areas of bareness such as the midriff, décolleté front, or low back necklines produce areas of concentrated interest. Emphasis gained by repetition or concentration as well as the other four methods implies that these

11–25 Emphasis is achieved by decoration on a plain background and concentration of embroidery. The dress on the right utilizes unusual sleeve shape as a means of interest. Designer Jeanne Lanvin has used large subordinate areas of undecorated fabric in order to permit dominance of the design. (Courtesy National Cotton Council)

devices are used in one area and that other areas are subordinated to this. Repeating rows of trim in many different areas will not accentuate any area, thereby producing confusion.

Unusual lines and shapes by virtue of their uniqueness are eye arresting. Unusual shapes of collars (Figure 11–25), sleeves, pockets, jewelry, outsized buttons, belts, and trims can be used to localize interest. Textures and fabric designs that depart from the ordinary may be the focus of attention. Elaborate, complex, or eye-arresting fabric design is best displayed by simple garment design, so that the fabric and garment design do not compete with each other for attention (Figure 11–26). Because of high labor costs the majority of ready-to-wear garments feature simply cut and uncomplicated lines in combination with unusual textures and prints, which emphasizes the fabric.

The placement of decoration on a plain, contrasting background permits

231

11–26 Unusual fabric design is allowed to dominate when simple styling is used in the structural design. (Courtesy National Cotton Council)

the decoration to be dominant. The use of a figured pin such as a cameo on a print dress does not allow the jewelry to dominate. Trims, embroidery, appliqué, jewelry, buttons, and belt buckles, when used on a contrasting background, are emphasized and become areas of interest.

Contrasts of color, line, shape, and texture will create emphasis. Some unifying factor must be used to connect these contrasts, or the result may be confusing.

When contrasts are kept close together in placement, the continuity of the idea comes into better focus. An example is the use of color contrast in hat and scarf rather than in scarf and shoes. The scarf and shoes are relatively far apart, which weakens, or destroys, the effect of the color contrast. Contrasts that are used many times lose their impact.

Shape contrasts in designs are more strongly emphasized when their value or color differs from the background. Yokes, collars, cuffs, and panel shapes will be more effective when their edges are outlined in a contrasting trim or when these sections are of themselves a value or color contrast.

Texture contrasts provide a means of emphasis. The combination of textures creates excitement for a costume. The use of all shiny, all dull, or all heavy textures in the same costume produces monotony; variations are more interesting.

Progression means a change in size. Emphasis can be achieved by progression in ruffles, contrasting bands, buttons, and other trims. Progression may be achieved by value change from light to dark or by the use of related color harmonies.

SCALE

Scale in clothing design is the comparison of the size of any of the parts of the garment with each other and with the body. (See Figure 11–27.) This includes the size of the collar, lapels, buttons, belts, trims, handbag, jewelry, and the texture and design of the fabric. Size relationship is of special concern to the very petite or the very large person.

A large collar worn by a person with a tiny neck and face may provide too much contrast in size and make the neck and face seem smaller than they actually are. A huge handbag carried by a tiny person has much the same effect. A tiny handbag carried by a large person, by contrast, will emphasize her size. Contrast of size is a means of obtaining emphasis, but if scale is too extreme for the wearer the use of this type of interest may not be desirable.

11–27 Compare the effects of the size and shape of these white bib designs upon body length and width. (Courtesy National Cotton Council)

11–28 The scale of the applied design must be related to the size of the area the design occupies and to the size of the person wearing the garments. (Courtesy National Cotton Council)

Scale is of concern to the person who makes her own clothing with regard to the selection of details of pattern, fabric, and trim. These should be related to the stature of the wearer as well as to each other (Figure 11–28). For example, some garments are styled with a narrow flap which provides a background for buttons. The selection of the button size must relate to the size of that area. Trims used on cuffs, collars, and pockets must be related in width to the areas they occupy. Scale in prints and texture is discussed in Chapter 12.

THEME

Theme is a single idea or motif expressed by all parts of a garment or a costume and it results in a total look. In planning a costume, consideration must be given to each area; line, color, texture, and the feeling of the design should be consistent and reinforce each other. This means that the elements of design have a sort of family resemblance. All parts and details of the garment and accessories express a theme, and this motif is consistent with the role and

11–29 The theme of the entire outfit is effectively expressed by all of the parts. The fabric texture is related to the structural design, the shoes and "knee highs" reinforce the theme. The garment was designed for school wear and is appropriate for that function. (Courtesy National Cotton Council)

personality of the wearer. (See Figure 11–29.) Hair style and make-up are of equal importance in the expression of an uninterrupted idea.

Theme is not achieved when the original purpose of the garment or accessories is ignored. This error is often made when women carry a street purse with after-five apparel or when tennis shoes are worn with tailored suits. Sporty type of sweaters and wraps are often worn over dresses that do not express this casual theme.

The purpose for which the garment is designed, such as sportswear, at-home attire, beach apparel, and the place where it is worn are part of the theme. Beach wear used at school or after-five garments worn on the job are not related to the intended use of the garment. Too casual or too formal attire for the occasion is always inappropriate.

The theme of the garment is expressed in the structural design and the fabric (Figure 11–30). Supple fabric must be used for soft lines when the style requires concentrated fullness or drape; stiff fabrics with body must be selected for styles needing shape and support. Incompatibility of fabric and design is a common error of the amateur dressmaker.

11–30 The structural lines utilize the geometric shapes of the fabric design and result in the continuation of a single idea. The fabric texture has adequate firmness to support the design. (Courtesy Cotton Producers Institute)

Textures must have some relationship to each other if they are to strengthen the impression of the theme. For example, wooden beads with homespun dresses, straw baskets with sportswear, and glitter jewelry with evening wear show a theme relationship of textures.

The concept of theme does not mean that there can be no variety or contrast. Some artists call this unity with variety. Without variety the costume would be monotonous indeed. Line, color, and texture provide three different elements by which variation of theme may be achieved. Variety, because it is an expression of a different idea, must have a valid connecting form or transition to the contrasting area. Overuse of variety with any one of the elements will result in instability of the total look—the continuity of the theme will be lost.

Each detail of the costume, including the garment, accessories, make-up, and hair style, must be coordinated for an effective expression of a theme. This theme must be consistent with the roles and personality of the wearer to result in the achievement of a total look.

summary

The design elements of line and the shapes and spaces that line creates, texture, and color, when arranged by the application of organizing guidelines, can produce desired effects in dress design. Line, an important design element, can be straight or curved, and it can take a vertical, horizontal, or diagonal direction. Each line contributes to the total impression of a garment. In selecting clothing, the lines of each garment must be studied on the figure to understand the illusion created in a particular design. Clever use of lines can camouflage figure faults and lead the eye of the beholder to the area of desired emphasis.

Judgments of garment designs should be made in terms of both aesthetic qualities and functional components to result in a wardrobe that will meet personal needs and expectations. How well a garment performs and the image the garment expresses are related aesthetically and functionally. Emphasis is used to focus attention on areas preferred by the individual by means of repetition; by unusual lines, shapes, and textures; and by decoration, contrast, and progression. Scale is of special importance to the very tiny or the very large person. The theme or motif expressed by the garment results in a total look when all components of a costume and the individual reinforce each other.

The woman who truly comprehends the importance of good design in clothing and its application to her figure also understands the man who observed: "A dress on a woman should be like an address on an envelope—something to direct the message to where she wants it to go." [5]

[5] Hugh Allen, in the Knoxville *News Sentinel,* as quoted in "Quotable Quotes," *Readers Digest,* **92**:145 (May 1968).

suggested readings

Brockman, Helen L. *The Theory of Fashion Design.* New York: John Wiley & Sons, Inc., 1965.

Chambers, Bernice. *Color and Design.* Englewood Cliffs, N.J.: Prentice-Hall, Inc., 1951.

Hillhouse, Marion S. *Dress Selection and Design.* New York: The Macmillan Company, 1963.

Horn, Marilyn J. *The Second Skin.* Boston: Houghton Mifflin Company, 1968.

Morton, Grace M. *The Arts of Costume and Personal Appearance.* New York: John Wiley & Sons, Inc., 1964.

12

fabric designs and textures

*f*abric design and texture are both very important considerations in clothing selection. The visual effects created by these two elements can greatly influence the appearance of a garment on the figure. Fabric design and texture are interrelated and yet separate. The fabric design includes all elements of the design that make a visual impression—the construction method, the color, and the pattern. Texture is the surface interest of the fabric. It is a part of the fabric design but important enough to be considered separately. Texture is created by the construction techniques used in making the fabric.

fabric design

Design in fabric is achieved by a great variety of techniques. It may be created as the fabric is made, or it may be applied to the finished goods. The selection of fabric with any kind of design requires careful appraisal of all the elements that combine to form the finished product. These elements include the pattern or allover design, the

239

shape and arrangement of individual motifs and background areas, and the treatment of color and the visual aspects of texture. When the fabric is fashioned into a garment, the style of the garment must also be considered.

When selecting fabrics, the light source is of great importance to the appearance of color. Daylight and phosphorescent and incandescent light all produce different effects. When possible, the fabric should be studied in both natural and artificial light. Many stores have a variety of light sources for checking this effect. Always consider the light source that will be used when the garment is worn.

Distance also influences the appearance of a pattern. Certain combinations of colors may take on a different hue from various distances. Oftentimes tiny patterns seem to blend into the background. Examples of this are fine checks, stripes, and dainty floral patterns. Large motifs can appear spotty or blotchy when viewed from a distance.

MOTIF

A motif is an individual unit of a pattern. The pattern is the overall design created by the compilation of the individual motifs. Motifs are classified according to style as geometric, realistic, stylized, or abstract.

Geometric Motifs

Geometric motifs include plaids, checks, stripes, and circles. Some geometric motifs are formed with yarns dyed before weaving and some are printed. Patterned fabrics made from yarns dyed prior to weaving insure that the pattern will be "on grain." This means that the design formed by the colored yarns is in a horizontal (filling) and vertical (warp) pattern, as these yarns form the grain of the fabric. When such fabrics are fashioned into garments, the pattern should be placed on the body so that the design looks straight and hangs correctly (Figure 12–1).

Plaids, checks, and stripes printed on a fabric after it is woven are often crooked; that is, the pattern is not straight with the grain formed by the vertical and horizontal threads. These fabrics create problems in construction because the finished product will either appear to be crooked on the body or hang improperly. When purchasing fabric or garments of printed, geometric designs, check to see if the pattern runs true with the grain and if the motifs are aligned. If they are not, the fabric should be rejected because it will always result in an unsatisfactory garment.

Realistic Motifs

Realistic motifs duplicate nature or some manmade object. They include florals that look as if they belong in a garden, lemons that hang on a tree, toys that belong in the nursery, and animals that abound in the forest.

12–1 Geometric motifs of plaid, stripe, and check must be cut "on grain" so that the design looks straight and hangs correctly on the body. (Courtesy Men's Fashion Association of America, Inc.)

Motifs such as these do not show imagination or creativity on the part of the fabric designer and are therefore less exciting than motifs that result from an artist's interpretation. The realistic treatment of subjects is obvious, and frequently the obvious becomes very monotonous.

Realistic designs attempt a three-dimensional form in order to copy reality. Because of the perspective achieved, they do not respect the flatness of the fabric. Devices used to make a two-dimensional design appear as three dimensional are shading, overlapping of objects, diminishing sizes, and texture. The use of these techniques makes the motif and pattern appear to advance and not remain flat.

Imitation of reality is not generally the effect one wishes to achieve in dress. Because these motifs are obviously reproductions of nature or manmade objects, they are not particularly suitable for apparel.

Stylized Motifs

Stylized motifs are variations of natural forms. For example, when floral or leaf motifs are used, they show imagination—not imitation—on the part of

12–2 Stylized motifs are variations of natural forms that reveal the imagination of the textile designer. They remain two dimensional and relate to the flatness of the fabric. Helga's bolero dress utilizes the stylized design effectively. (Courtesy California Fashion Creators)

242   **12–3** Abstract motifs predominate in combination with stylized mushrooms in a dramatic black and white shirtdress of jersey. (Courtesy Celanese Corporation)

the artist. This group of motifs is successful on textiles, because it remains two dimensional and therefore relates to the flatness of the fabric. (See Figure 12–2.)

Abstract Motifs

Abstract motifs include splashes of color and shape; they have no counterpart in nature or manmade objects. The effect produced by them is much like that found in paintings by Mondrian and Pollack. These motifs are very pleasing when used in fabric design. (See Figures 12–3 and 12–4.)

12–4 Plaid becomes abstract in a gown designed by Mr. Blackwell. (Courtesy California Fashion Creators)

244   Warp prints belong in the classification of abstract motifs. These fabrics use groups of multicolored warp yarns woven with solid filling yarns. The effect produced is a blur of soft, hazy colors, often in random groupings.

Combinations of Different Motifs in a Pattern

When different motifs are combined in a fabric, they should be related to each other in shape and size if unity is to be achieved (Figure 12–5). This does not imply that they should be alike, for this would produce monotony. Some variation and some similarity produce interest. Unrelated shapes and sizes

12–5 When two or more motifs are combined in a fabric, they should be related to each other. The shape of the motif used here is related, producing similarity. Variation can be achieved with a change in motif size. The grouping and concentration of the motifs effect unity in Helga's shirtdress. (Courtesy California Fashion Creators)

12–6 Motif shape is emphasized by value contrast from the background areas in Alex Colman's flower print. (Courtesy Cotton Producers Institute)

destroy harmony. When many different motifs are combined, there will be greater coherence to the total effect of the design if one shape or size dominates and the others are subordinated.

Motif shape is emphasized by value contrast from the background areas (Figure 12–6). If there is little value difference, the motif is not easily discernible. To illustrate, pink polka dots on a pale yellow background will not appear as bold as black polka dots on a white background.

Pattern and Pattern Arrangement. Pattern is made up of the arrangement of motifs. These may be considered formal—showing a regular methodical repetition of the motif or informal—having irregular placement of motifs.

When motifs are placed, the background areas, called negative spaces, become as important a consideration as the motif itself. The negative areas should show thoughtful spacing of the motifs, whether the arrangement is formal or informal (Figure 12–7). If the negative space is greater or smaller than the area occupied by the motif, the spacing will be more interesting than if it is equal to the motif. When the negative area is greater than the motif, it helps to give it strength. Too much negative area generally makes the motif lose its importance. Not enough negative space makes the motif appear crowded and prevents the single motif from dominating in the design. Equal divisions of motif and negative areas are often displeasing to look at, particularly when strong contrasts are used.

12–7 Negative areas should show thoughtful spacing of the motif. When the negative area is greater than the motif, it gives the motif strength. (Courtesy Catalina)

12–8 In order to avoid spottiness, the arrangement of the pattern should show movement from one motif to another. (Courtesy Catalina)

12–9 Fabric designs with a great deal of movement can be tranquilized by the use of solid color. (Courtesy Cotton Producers Institute)

In order to avoid spottiness, the arrangement of the pattern should show some movement from one motif to another (Figure 12–8). This should not be overdone so that the pattern fatigues the eye. For example, repeating checks or stripes of great value contrast are difficult to sew on because of the great amount of movement. Fabrics that have a great amount of movement can be tranquilized by combining them with a solid-color fabric (Figure 12–9).

TEXTURE AND PATTERN

If the pattern is to dominate, the texture of the fabric must be subordinated. Complicated weaves compete with patterns, allowing neither to dominate. The concept of emphasis must be observed in the selection of fabrics.

Fine-textured weaves are enhanced when the pattern has the effect of delicateness; textured fabrics may use heavier and less refined patterns. A theme is developed when pattern and texture appear to belong together.

FABRIC DESIGN RELATED TO GARMENT CONSTRUCTION

Apparel constructed of a distinctly patterned fabric should show coordination of the fabric to garment cut and design. Gross distortions often result when little consideration is given to the fabric pattern. Some of the most displeasing effects, perhaps because they are so obvious, occur in garments made from plaid fabrics (Figure 12–10). Unmatched seams and too many seams break the continuity of the plaid units. Darting, particularly in the bodice, is often done at an unbecoming angle. Curved seams which do not repeat the angularness of the fabric make matching of seams virtually impossible. These all result in distortions to the design.

Motifs whose shape, size, and spacing demand continuity by matching are often broken by too many seams and unmatched units. The placement of motifs on the body should not appear in unbecoming places. When widely spaced, realistic motifs are arranged informally, it is of particular importance that their placement on the body be considered. Such motifs as roses with realistic thorns rising from the seat of the skirt are painful to see. Flowers blooming at the bust line or a large cabbage rose isolated over the abdomen all call unnecessary attention to those areas of the body.

Geometric fabric patterns with angular lines such as plaids, checks, and stripes suggest dress designs with straight lines that are tailored and sophisticated. Dots and curvilinear patterns imply curved or transitional lines that are feminine in feeling.

Either the pattern of the fabric or the structural lines of the garment should be allowed to dominate. If the garment lines are most important, they are best combined with a plain fabric (Figure 12–11). If the fabric is most important, the design lines of the garment should remain simple (Figure 12–12). If both have equal appeal, a lack of emphasis will be effected and the total impression will lose impact.

12–10. Garments made of plaid look best when the continuity of the plaid unit is not broken by seams. Patterns match vertically (side seams chevron and shoulder seams match) and horizontally. Notice that the openings overlap to complete the plaid unit vertically at the lower button. (Courtesy Men's Fashion Association of America, Inc.)

12–11 When the structural lines of the garment are dominant because of their special interest, the fabric must be plain. Georgette Trilere uses silk for an elegant sculptured dress. (Courtesy California Fashion Creators)

12–12 When fabric design is intended to dominate, the design lines of the garment must remain simple in order to achieve emphasis for the fabric design. (Courtesy Celanese Corporation)

EFFECT OF FABRIC DESIGN UPON THE FIGURE

Research regarding preferences of fabric design and color-related physical characteristics was conducted by Compton with college students.[1] The findings revealed that personal physical factors such as eye color, hair color, and weight did not influence the selection preferences of clothing fabrics. Significantly, this research showed that the groups tested did not consider the importance of physical characteristics in their preferences of patterned fabrics. Is it possible that people do not wish to admit their physical shortcomings, or do they fail to realize that fabric patterns have a visual effect upon the figure? It is obvious to the observer that physical characteristics can be enhanced or camouflaged by the selection of certain fabrics. Fabric designs that make an already full figure larger will not produce a flattering effect. Patterned fabrics that result in concealing irregular body contours can be used to advantage.

scale, arrangement, and color

The scale or size of the motif, its arrangement, and the colors used are three factors that strongly influence the effect the fabric has upon the figure. Ready-to-wear garments are best judged on the body, and yard goods can be draped over the figure to suggest the effects. Factors such as light source and viewing distance should be considered if intelligent decisions are to be made.

When the scale of the pattern is related to the size of the wearer, attention will not be called to deviations from the average figure. Very small overall patterns can be worn by almost all women without producing unfavorable effects. These patterns blend into a nondistinct design and do not increase or decrease apparent figure size, provided the properties of color are kept in mind. These patterns are especially effective on the large figure because of the variations of color and textures. A plain, undecorated fabric is figure revealing; a small overall pattern is figure concealing.

Small, distinct motifs, spaced so that the motif dominates the design, look well on the petite or average figure (Figure 12–13). Women who do not wish to call attention to a figure that is tall and large or short and full will avoid this group because the extreme contrast of the body to the scale of the pattern will emphasize their figure size.

Fabrics that call attention to body proportion are bold designs of large-scale plaid or large motifs that do not form an allover pattern because of great amounts

[1] Norma H. Compton, "Personal Attributes of Color and Design Preferences in Clothing Fabrics," *Journal of Psychology,* **54:**191–95 (1962).

12–13 Small, distinct motifs which are spaced so that the motif dominates the design look well on the petite and average figure. (Courtesy National Cotton Council)

12–14 Motifs showing strong horizontal movement may add width to the figure. The border design, sleeve fullness, skirt fullness, and contrasting belt add width to the figure. (Courtesy Simplicity Pattern Company)

of negative areas. Women having good proportions and who are medium to tall in height are enhanced by these designs. A petite figure will appear small because of the contrast in scale. A large, heavy person will seem larger because of the emphasis by repetition of size.

Plaids come in small-, medium-, and large-scale units. The larger the scale of the unit, the greater the apparent width to the figure. Small plaid units do not adversely affect the apparent size of the small or average figure. Medium-scale plaids can be worn by all women, and very large-scale plaids are suitable for the average or tall. Large, full figures and petite figures can utilize medium-scale plaids with close value contrasts. The greater the contrasts of colors or values, the greater the apparent width.

Circular motifs add width and fullness to the figure. Border designs at the hemline, waistline, or hipline also increase figure width.

Motifs showing a strong vertical movement usually add height to a figure, and those showing horizontal movement may add width. (See Figure 12–14.) This is particularly true when there is great contrast in values and colors and when motifs are arranged somewhat isolated from each other.

251

12–15 Patterned fabrics convey feeling as the result of motif, arrangement, and color. This geometric fabric design is forceful and sophisticated. (Courtesy Penny Baker, Inc., Dow Badische)

Sharp color contrasts used in prints will enlarge the visual appearance. The use of light values and bright intensities adds weight, whereas dark values or dull intensities will not call so much attention to body size.

selection of patterned fabrics related to individuality

Patterned fabric conveys various feelings as the result of the motif, arrangement, and colors used (Figure 12–15). Some adjectives for patterns are forceful, exotic, demure, conservative, nondescript, sophisticated, quiet, loud, gay, somber, refined, and feminine.

Attention should be given in fabric selection to one's individual characteristics. Do people actually make selections of fabric design according to its relationship to their personalities? Results of Compton's research [2] on color

252

[2] *Ibid.*, pp. 191–95.

12–16 Two different yet related plaids are used by Helga. The unifying factor is the color repetition in the two plaids. A more simplified plaid is used in the dress. (Courtesy California Fashion Creators)

and design with college students showed a definite relationship between design and color preferences and personality and interests. Students who preferred small designs scored higher on the good-impression personality measure than students who preferred large designs. The good-impression personality test measures characteristics that present persons in the best light possible—that is as being unaffected and modest. Those characteristics reveal themselves through preferences for smaller, less bold designs by students desiring to make a good impression.

Students preferring small designs also scored higher in interest in merchandising than students who preferred large designs. Students with high-femininity scores preferred small designs more than those with low-femininity scores.

The research indicates experimental evidence that people do select clothing fabrics to express themselves and that clothing is used in helping an individual to conform to an ideal self-image.

Are the adjectives you use to describe yourself related to the words that describe the patterned fabrics in your present wardrobe? Do the adjectives that describe your fabrics also describe the image you wish others to have of

253

12–17 When two prints are combined in a costume, one unifying factor is used to unite the designs. The Helga fashion uses one fabric motif with different background contrasts. (Courtesy California Fashion Creators)

254

you? Relate the patterned fabrics illustrated in this chapter to the personal characteristics of the students in your class and explain how each selection expresses a student's individuality.

USE OF DIFFERENT PRINTS IN ONE COSTUME

To successfully combine two prints in one costume requires analysis of the fabric designs. Some ready-to-wear garments are designed by the use of coordinated fabrics. These are intended to go together because some factor unifies the theme for a total effect. Techniques used to successfully combine two different patterned fabrics include

1. One color that predominates between two different prints (Figure 12–16)
2. One fabric motif that may be repeated with different background designs in two pieces of fabric (Figure 12–17)
3. One patterned fabric, greatly subordinated in attention-getting power, that combines with a patterned fabric having a more pronounced design

12–18 The fabric of this Ernst Strauss pants suit is combined with a repeating large-scale motif in the head scarf. (Courtesy California Fashion Creators)

The latter is seen in suits using a subtle tweed for the jacket and a plaid for the skirt that uses the same background colors as the jacket. Whichever technique is used in combining two different fabric patterns, one should be dominant in design, and a unifying theme such as color or motif should unite the two fabrics. (See Figure 12–18.) Accessories such as fabric-patterned shoes, handbags, scarves, and gloves have limited use with more than one item in the wardrobe. They are shown to best advantage when worn with apparel of solid colors.

SUMMARY

The inclusion of patterned fabrics in the wardrobe provides it with variety and interest. Thoughtful selections include consideration of the design as related to the physical characteristics and to the expression of personality traits one wishes to convey.

The cut and construction of the garment should reinforce the essence of the pattern of the fabric. This is done by repetition of straight or curved lines and by limited use of seams, which should not break up the continuity of distinct and large-scale designs.

Coordination of different fabric designs in the same costume requires skillful selection if a coordinated effect is to be achieved. A unifying factor such as color or motif repetition and use of one dominant pattern will help to successfully combine the two fabric designs.

texture

PERCEPTION OF TEXTURE

Texture is an element of design that describes the surface appearance and feel. Fabric, metal, leather, and straw—each has a distinctive texture. The descriptive words used to characterize textures are comparative: both burlap and sailcloth are coarse textures, but their degree of coarseness differs. Textures are also comparative to other textures with which they are combined and to the person wearing them. Some adjectives used to describe textures are smooth, heavy, fine, crisp, and glossy.

Texture is a sensory impression understood by sight as well as touch. The visual aspect of texture is perceived by the eye because of the degree of light absorption and reflection on the surface of the material. Lustrous textures are seen in satins and dull textures in fuzzy wools. Texture has the definite physical dimensions of weight, size, bulk, and shape. These are also visually perceived. The opaqueness of dress linen and the transparency of handkerchief linen are recognized by sight.

The tactile aspects relate to the hand of the fabric. The coarseness, softness, rigidity, or clingyness are recognized by feel. Hand determines how some fabrics will respond to a given style. Some textures literally speak to the designer as to how they should be used. Firm twills, linen, and worsteds call for crisp tailorings; silk jerseys and chiffon are effective in draped designs. Softly tailored garments need pliable fabrics of crepe, shantung, and dress weight wool flannel. Texture is only fully comprehended by touch, but it is not necessary to feel an object to understand its tactile qualities as sight can recall the memory of touch. Thus, we can feel with our eyes and pass this on to our sense of touch.[3]

Each fabric has many textural characteristics which describe

Feel	Soft-crisp
Feel	Smooth-rough
See and feel	Thick-thin
See and feel	Clingy-rigid
See	Shiny-dull
See	Opaque-transparent

These characteristics will determine how the fabric may be used.

COMPONENTS THAT DETERMINE TEXTURE

Texture is determined by the arrangement of the component parts in fabric. These are the fiber, the yarn construction, the weave, or other methods of making fabric and the finish given to the fabric.

Fibers are hairlike strands of raw materials which are spun into yarns and woven into cloth. Fibers of wool can produce soft textures; fibers of linen can produce crisp textures. Both of these textures are the result of the inherent characteristics of the raw materials used. The short, fuzzy fibers of cotton will produce fabrics that will absorb light and be dull; the long, smooth filaments of reeled silk will make fabrics that reflect light, giving a shiny appearance.

Yarns are composed of fibers that are short lengths twisted together or long filaments laid or twisted together. The manner of joining fibers and filaments into yarns can result in the formation of distinctive textures. A yarn given a low twist will produce a shiny texture, as found in satin; a highly twisted yarn will form a rough texture, such as crepe. Yarns organized by thick slubs give

[3] Lorenz Eitner, *Introduction to Art; An Illustrated Topical Manual* (Minneapolis: Burgess, 1961), p. 41.

shantung; those that are looped or coiled produce stretch fabrics. Yarns having a little twist can be brushed after weaving to produce a nap or fuzzy texture.

Fabric is formed by putting yarns together by some method such as weaving, knitting, crocheting, felting, and braiding. Some fabrics, called film fabrics, which are often used for rainwear or which simulate leather, are formed by chemicals that are extruded in sheets instead of filaments.[4] The way yarns are put together to form fabric determines the texture. A satin weave of loosely twisted yarns, woven so that the yarns float across many threads, produces visual effects which will reflect light and give a shiny texture. The diagonal design formed in gabardine, denim, covert, and drill is the result of a twill weave. The pattern of knits is formed by the way the loops of yarn are formed. Knits absorb light and are dull textured unless a plastic yarn is used.

The finish given to cloth after it is constructed can impart or change texture as well as other qualities. The durable press finish which makes a fabric smooth and wrinkle-free usually stiffens the texture and makes it less pliable than fabrics not given this finish. Organdy is produced by the addition of a sizing mixture which gives stiffness to the fabric. Embossed fabrics, which are characterized by their three-dimensional designs, are formed by passing the fabric through rollers having embossed designs. Flocked fabrics have short fibers attached to the surface by means of adhesives.

The texture of fabrics is affected by the characteristics of the raw material used and the production processes involved from the fiber stage to the finish applied in the making of cloth. The textures determine how the cloth will be used. Garment design that does not consider the texture characteristics is not satisfactory.

FASHIONS IN TEXTURES

Textures as well as silhouettes and colors have periods of popularity. The design of garments determines which textures will be required; therefore, changes in fashion bring changes in texture. Many designs are inspired by the textural characteristics of the fabric.

Because texture and pattern styling must be compatible, the reappearance of textures as well as lines occurs periodically. Tailored styling trends require crisp, firmly woven fabrics to enhance the precise line. A fashion for femininity and ruffles demands textures that express this quality in soft and drapable fabrics or crisp and sheer ones. Gabardine was in fashion during the early 1950s; then it reappeared in the mid-1960s. Sheer chiffon, voiles, and crepes, worn in the flapper era, returned to fashion in 1967. Some years in fashions call for bulky, fuzzy textures and others for smooth, soft, or firm.

[4] Marjorie L. Joseph, *Introductory Textile Science* (New York: Holt, 1966), p. 289.

12–19 The fabric texture determines how the garment should be designed. The multicolor knit of metallic yarn suggests a simple A-line silhouette for the most effective use of this texture. (Courtesy Penny Baker, Inc., Dow Badische)

Some designers determine their line by what the fabric textures suggest. They manipulate the material to determine the hand and how it will react to draping, pleats, folds, or tucks. This helps them to decide how the garment should be designed (Figure 12–19). Many designers drape the final fabric to be used on the model rather than using muslin, which has different characteristics. Women who make their own clothing often find that they become more inspired by selecting the fabric first and then finding a compatible pattern.

Some textures are classics; they remain in popularity year after year. These are usually textures that are neither very rough nor very smooth, very thick or very thin. They belong in the middle and are not extreme. Print cloth, percale, dress-weight flannel, and dress-weight linen have all been fashionable for a very long period. These textures are not particularly exciting, but their appeal is lasting because people do not tire of them as quickly as of the extreme textures.

SELECTION OF TEXTURES

In selecting textures, one should consider what will enhance physical proportions, skin, hair textures, and personality. This includes selecting combinations that will provide contrast and at the same time carry out a predominant textural theme or idea. The result will be unity of the total look and of the purpose for which it is to be used.

EFFECT OF TEXTURE ON PHYSICAL PROPORTION

Because textures have the physical properties of weight, size, bulk, shape, light absorption, and reflection, some fabrics produce illusions that dwarf or enlarge the figure, whereas some textures add neither weight nor bulk to apparent body size. When considering which textures to select, lay them across the shoulders if they are to be worn near the face and stand away from a mirror to see the effect they produce.

The fabrics that are grouped together in the following discussion are related by one common characteristic such as softness, large scale, or stiffness. Each fabric possesses a combination of characteristics which must be considered in regard to the effect they produce. A fabric may be soft, bulky, and shiny. A person may want the softness but not the shine or bulk, as these two characteristics may not be advantageous to a particular figure. It will then be necessary to find another soft fabric that does not include these two characteristics. Depending upon the effect a person wishes to achieve, careful selection of textures can function to produce a desired impression.

SCALE OF TEXTURES

All fabrics have scale. The size relationship of the pattern formed by the texture determines the scale.

Obvious scale differences are seen by comparing the wale of corduroy in fine, or baby wale, medium, and wide varieties. Some tweed fabrics which have a small-scale pattern are not so easily discernible as those having coarser yarns and large-scale patterns. Rep fabrics which have a thick filling yarn vary from a fine scale of broadcloth to heavy, as in bengaline. Nap length of wools relates to their scale. The size of the yarn and the needles used in knitting produces the differences in the scale of their textures. When the scale formed by the pattern of texture is tiny, the pattern is reduced when seen from a distance, and it is perceived as an overall effect. The textural effect of very large-scaled patterns as wide-wale corduroy, Erin Isle knits, and wool fleece remains identifiable when viewed from a distance.

The selection of scale of textures should be considered in relationship to the size of the person. A contrast in texture will emphasize form.[5] Petite figures using large-scale textures get lost in the texture because of the extreme contrast of the fabric to the figure. Their petiteness is emphasized. Very heavy people wearing large-scale textures will, because of the repetition, appear heavier.

Large-scale fabrics include

Monk's cloth	Mohair
Hopsacking	Some quilted fabrics
Bulky knits	Wide-wale corduroy
Fleece	Some tweeds
Chinchilla wool	Bedford cord
Some homespun	

SOFT AND CLINGY FABRICS

Fabrics that are soft and drapable cling to the body and reveal every contour. Unless additional treatment is given in the construction of garments made from these fabrics, their use should be limited to those people having ideal figures of any height.

Soft, clingy fabrics include

Satin	Silk, rayon, and acetate jersey
China silk	Velvet
Thin, supple silks	Batiste
Chiffon	Organza
Handkerchief linen	Challis
Soft silk and rayon crepes	Voile
Georgette	Lawn
Bemberg sheer	

[5] June King McFee, *Preparation for Art* (Belmont, Calif.: Wadsworth, 1961), p. 263.

12–20. Silk chiffon, a soft, clingy fabric, has been made firm by underlining and quilting. The scale of the texture has increased with this treatment; shadows are produced, which give a new dimension to the fabric in this suit designed by Irene. (Courtesy California Fashion Creators)

The quality of softness and adherence to the body can be changed by the addition of underlining or bonding to the outer fabric (Figure 12–20). The degree of firmness of the underlining will determine how stiff the outer fabric will be. It is possible for the less-than-perfect figure to use these textures if they are properly handled in this manner to provide the firmness needed to change the clingy quality of the outer fabric.

STIFF FABRICS

Textures that are stiff stand away from the body and hide figure irregularities. Excessively stiff fabrics appear to add bulk and weight to the body. Extremely stiff fabrics can be worn to advantage by persons who are average-to-tall in height, having either ideal or thin figures. These textures should be avoided by those having very petite figures because they make them appear dwarfed by the contrast. Overweight people will look heavier in these fabrics because of the bulk of the excessive thickness. A moderate amount of stiffness in fabrics is desirable for the overweight figure because the cloth does not cling to the body revealing its contours.

Excessively stiff fabrics are

Burlap	Plastics that simulate leather
Bengaline	Leather
Brocade	Organdy
Tapestry	Organza
Some bonded fabrics	Taffeta
Laminated fabrics	Tulle
Stiff hopsacking	

Moderately stiff fabrics include

Some bonded fabrics	Bonded jersey
Dress- and suit-weight linens	Double knit
Silk linen	Tropical worsted
Durable press	Worsted
Medium-wale corduroy	Gabardine
Indian head	Twill

BULKY FABRICS

Some textures add volume to the figure by virtue of their weight and bulky nature. These fabrics, like those in the stiff group, may by contrast be overpowering on the very slight, very thin, or petite figure. The slender person can effectively use these textures.

Bulky knits	Angora
Fuzzy wools	Heavy bonded and laminated fabrics
Bengaline	Hopsacking
Wide-wale corduroy	Homespun
Bouclé	Mohair
Terrycloth	Felt
Tapestry	Quilted cottons
Whipcord	

SHINY TEXTURES

Textures that are shiny reflect light and make the person wearing them appear larger. The color is also intensified by shine. Pile fabrics of velvet, plush, velour, corduroy, velveteen both reflect and absorb light. Shadows occur due to multiple reflections of light on the pile. The average figure and the girl who wishes to appear larger can wear these textures effectively. The softness and clingingness of satin reveal any figure irregularities, and the stiffness of some shiny fabrics limits their use on tiny persons.

Shiny fabrics include

Plastics	Polished cotton
Velvet	Metallic
Velveteen	Glossy silk
Satin	Patent leather
Sateen	Sequins

DULL TEXTURES

Fabrics that absorb light and are dull do not enlarge the figure. These textures are suitable for all figure types, provided they do not possess other qualities such as bulk, softness, and crispness, which would contribute undesirable characteristics.

Among the dull fabrics are

Crepes	Felt
Gingham	Challis
Percale	Hopsacking
Raw silk	Sailcloth
Flannel	Dress-weight wool
Silk linen	Madras
Jersey of rayon and wool	Cotton suiting
Linen	Tweed
Piqué	

TEXTURES THAT ARE NOT EXTREME

Figures that are not ideal will find that the selection of textures that are not very thin or thick, very soft or stiff, or very shiny will not call attention to figure irregularities. Textures found in this middle group rather than at the extremes are not as interesting, so that other features such as color and line, must be used to add interest to the ensemble.

Fabrics found in the middle group are

Serge	Chambray
Gabardine	Gingham
Wool jersey	Silk broadcloth
Flannel	Seersucker
Velveteen	Percale
Crepe	Dress-weight wool
Linen	Nonbulky medium-scale tweed
Shantung	Bonded fabrics that are not bulky or shiny
Broadcloth	Underlined fabrics that are not stiff

TEXTURE RELATED TO SKIN AND HAIR

Skin and hair have texture just as every other material object. There are degrees of fineness and coarseness which must be kept in mind when selecting fabric and jewelry textures to be worn next to the face.

The extreme contrasts of coarse skin and hair textures with fine fabrics can produce disastrous effects to skin appearance. People having coarse or aging skin which is less fine should select the middle range of textures which are neither very fine nor very coarse. Such fabrics as piqué, crepe, jersey, medium knits, dull silk, linen, and dress-weight wool are medium textures.

Women blessed with fine-grained skin can use such fabrics as voile, sateen, satin, organdy, polished cotton, batiste, dimity, China silk, finely woven silk, and plastics. They can also wear the middle and rough textures most effectively.

Glasses frames and jewelry worn next to the skin such as necklaces and earrings should be considered for textural qualities if the skin is very coarse grained. Shiny metals and large pearls are best used by individuals who have smooth and fine-to-medium-fine skin. In the medium range of textures in jewelry are baroque pearls, satin-finish metals, tortoiseshell, and seed beads.

Hair textures are not as important a consideration as skin textures. Materials used for hats should be complementary to hair textures. Shiny felt, shiny leather, satin, and finely woven straw will emphasize coarseness of hair texture. Most furs, velour felt, coarse leather, felt, and medium-textured straws all fall into a medium-textured category, which can be worn by all.

EXPRESSING PERSONALITY THROUGH TEXTURE SELECTION

The ability to select textures that reflect the self-concept of an individual is achieved when there is an understanding of the character or idea projected by the textures. The distinctive individual qualities of some textures typify particular moods and feelings. A variety of fabrics must be examined carefully in order to be able to identify the character they project. The response felt by handling and feeling burlap differs from that to velvet.

Personal preferences based upon past experience will undoubtedly play a large part in the selection of textures that a person feels comfortable wearing. One should not overlook the possibility of using some different and exciting textures which mirror personal qualities, enhance appearance, and give personal satisfaction. Some people feel more confident in the medium textures of percales, more exotic and sophisticated in the coarse textures of rough tweeds, more feminine in satin and chiffon.

Fabrics that some consider to project the image of sophistication, boldness, and self-confidence are

Burlap	Solid-colored plastics
Heavy homespun	Wide-wale corduroy
Velour	Thickly slubbed raw silk
Plush	Thick, spongy knits
Upholstery or tapestry	Crocheted fabrics
Satin	Felts
Tweedy tweeds	Quilted fabrics
Bengaline	Heavy lace
Ottoman	Transparent fabrics
Moiré	Lamé
Leathers	Metallic fabrics
Heavy fleece	

Fabrics that may express femininity are

Tulle	Velvet
Fine lace	Flat crepe
Dimity	Chiffon
Dotted Swiss	Organza
Organdy	Silk, rayon, and acetate jersey
Soft silk	Gingham
Angora	Voile
Wool challis	Fine-wale corduroy
Soft-wool suiting	

Textures that often provide a sporty, informal, and casual feeling are the rough, coarse fabrics, such as

Tweeds	Plastic
Pigskin	Ostrich
Cowhide	Ticking
Brushed cowhide	Seersucker
Reptiles	Bulky knit
Simulated leather	Denim
Wide-wale corduroy	Sailcloth
Homespun	

Fabrics known for their formal and dressy character are often smooth, soft, velvety, lacy, and transparent textures, as found in

Textured cottons	Sequins
Sateen	Glittery fabrics
Organdy	Eyelash
Voile	Taffeta
Satin	Velvet
Lamé	Brocade

HARMONY IN TEXTURE COMBINATION

In the years past textbooks of clothing selection considered suitable combinations of textures to be used together. Today we are in a period that defies tradition—an age of strong contrasts where boldness and bravery and adventure are in fashion in dress as well as in behavior. We find contrasts of textures used that would not have been considered in "good taste" years ago. Glitter jewelry is worn with street clothes, heavy leather boots are not confined to wools but used with lightweight cottons as well, sheer blouses are matched up with leather skirts. In spite of a trend for bold contrasts, some combinations appear to be more compatible than others. Contrast is necessary in order to avoid sameness and monotony; however, a predominant texture idea should be evident so that a theme is achieved.

Combinations related to weight (the thickness and thinness) and those related to firmness (crisp and soft) do not present particular problems, but combinations related to the image, feeling, or personality of textures should be carefully considered. Refer to previous lists for the groupings that carry out a predominant idea. Delicate lace and fine embroidery harmonize with fine, sheer fabrics which are listed under fabrics expressing femininity. Coarse cotton lace and heavy crewel embroidery would be too great a contrast with many of the fab-

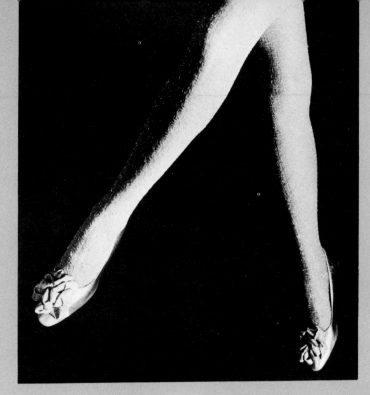

12–21 Textures appear in fashion hosiery. Gold and silver metallic yarns are used to produce this unusual texture for evening wear. (Courtesy Penny Baker, Inc., Dow Badische)

12–22 The "crocheted" look of metallic yarn produces an unusual hosiery fashion with an abundance of textural interest. (Courtesy Penny Baker, Inc., Dow Badische)

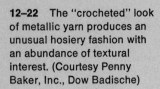

12–23 Textures predominate in these eye-arresting "knee highs" and shiny shoes. (Courtesy Penny Baker, Inc., Dow Badische)

rics on that list. Cotton lace combines well with percale, velveteen, and piqué; crewel embroidery has qualities in common with homespun, heavy knits, and monk's cloth. Sequins convey formality for evening wear and are better applied to silks, satins, taffeta, and laces rather than to straw purses, heavy knits, and medium-weight cottons. Tweed skirts and jersey blouses have a similar character, whereas tweed skirts and satin blouses do not.

When making decisions regarding textural combinations, stand away from them. Distance will diminish the effect the combinations present up close. They may blend together and appear too similar in texture to provide needed contrast.

Contrast of Textures with Accessories

The selection of accessories for a costume provides an excellent way to use contrast of textures. An all-smooth or all-coarse, all-dull or all-shiny, textured ensemble would be unified, but it would be terribly dull and unrelieved.

The combination of a hopsacking dress, straw basket, rafia shoes carries out a textural theme but lacks contrast and is uninteresting. Variety in texture combination adds excitement, but a thoughtful selection is required. A soft wool dress accessorized with reptile shoes, fur felt hat, and silk scarf brings into the costume a variety of compatible textures.

Small, delicate evening and late-day purses of fine fabric or fine leather do not go with casual campus clothes, nor do large saddle leather or rough straw suggest wear with elaborate or dressy apparel.

Purses and shoes do not have to be of identical texture to be used together. It is more important that they express the same feeling. Gloves provide a variety of textures in knits, crochet, fabric, and many types of leather.

Hosiery is available in a wide assortment of textures from the traditional fine knit and mesh to coarse ribbed, net, and crocheted. Coordination of these textures with the garment is essential. The heavily textured hosiery is best worn with medium-to-coarse dress fabrics. They convey the image of these materials, and they usually clash with fine textures because of the extreme contrast. It must be remembered that heavily textured hosiery will enlarge the appearance of the legs and call attention to them, more so when the color contrasts with the skirt. (See Figures 12–21, 12–22, and 12–23.)

summary

The selection of textures for garments and accessories must be related to skin and hair texture, personality, physical proportions, and the occasion for which they are to be used. All of the components should have a predominant textural idea in order to achieve the impression of belonging together. Enough contrast should be used in order to make the ensemble interesting.

suggested readings

Compton, Norma H. "Personal Attributes of Color and Design Preferences in Clothing Fabrics," *Journal of Psychology,* **54** (1962), 191–95.

Eitner, Lorenz. *Introduction to Art: An Illustrated Topical Manual.* Minneapolis: Burgess Publishing Company, 1961.

Hillhouse, Marion S. *Dress Selection and Design.* New York: The Macmillan Company, 1963.

Hollen, M., and J. Saddler. *Modern Textiles.* New York: The Macmillan Company, 1964.

Horn, Marilyn J. *The Second Skin.* Boston: Houghton Mifflin Company, 1968.

Joseph, Marjorie L. *Introductory Textile Science.* New York: Holt, Rinehart & Winston, Inc., 1966.

Labarthe, Jules. *Textiles: Origins to Usage.* New York: The Macmillan Company, 1964.

13

color

think about color. Have you ever really considered how important it is to you? Look around you right now and see how much color there is. Are the colors that surround you bright, interesting, pleasant; are they dull and faded; or are they garish and inharmonious? How are you reacting emotionally to this color atmosphere? If there are others with you, look at their coloring. Is their personal coloring complemented by the colors they are wearing and their background? How do you use color? Are you always confident that your color choices are correct, pleasing both to you and others? Or do you make expensive color mistakes? What do you really need to know about color to present yourself at your best?

Color is an integral part of our daily living; its use is as old as man. Early men used color to decorate their bodies. (Modern cosmetics fill a similar role.) Color was once a status symbol, and rigidly enforced sumptuary laws regulated its use. The ancient clan plaids of Scotland used color in intricate combinations to identify family groups.

In the United States since World War II the range of color has exploded to a dramatic rainbow. Prior to this time, because of prevailing custom and the lack of technology, color use was

271

severely limited: kitchen appliances were white, cars were black, and most other utilitarian objects were nondescript colors. In recent times color has been used to perform a great variety of functions, many of which are so much a part of our lives that we assume it has always been so.

In the merchandising of almost every product and service color plays an important role. Advertising displays utilize its ability to sell. Product packaging employs color to both promote and identify items. Business machines are color keyed to facilitate their use. Complicated wiring systems use color identification to simplify installation and maintenance. Various vocations and professions use uniforms of color to identify their members. Nurses, policemen, clergymen, servicemen, and many others are readily identified because of the color of their apparel. Navy blue, green beret, and red cap have become part of our vocabulary because of this identification of occupation by color of uniforms. Fire engines, police cars, school buses, traffic signals, and information signs are all identified by color. Emotions may be expressed with color. "In the pink," "feeling blue," "black with rage" are examples of color describing feelings. Many members of racial groups prefer to be identified by their color: black, brown, yellow.

Popularity of colors for interior decoration has passed through the entire palette. A person following this field can make educated guesses as to the exact year or period in which the colors used were in vogue.

Wearing apparel for men, women, and children has also joined the color parade. This is most recently apparent in the men's clothing, especially sportswear. Today many of the most conservative men have pastel shirts, multihued business suits, bright ties, and even brilliantly patterned underwear. Women's garments have an endless variety of fashionable color combinations. Once the consumer learned that material of bright color was durable, children's clothing became a part of this rainbow.

As our population has become more accustomed to seeing and using color, they have become more and more sophisticated about its use. Not everyone has become a color expert, but people are enjoying and using color more than ever before. Today, the Joneses ride in a bright orange car, the Millers have avocado green appliances, and the Smiths live in a muted violet house. When one family has all the colored items just mentioned, the effect seems quite garish; however, by the phenomenon of habituation, we often learn to enjoy such bizarre effects. The modern student of color must acknowledge that the traditionally rigid rules of color combination have been made obsolete by an acceptance of individual color preferences.

color systems

Many different systems are used to organize color. These systems are based on the effects of color or the materials used to make it. The painter and the dyer combine pigments. The physicist mixes light. The physiologist studies the eye-brain color effects. The psychologist evaluates emotional responses to color. Each color system uses different primary or principal hues, and each has its own terminology. Primary colors are combined to produce other colors. Each primary color has its complement or opposite. The systems vary in their color notations; however, exact duplication of a color is possible because of the precise notation given to each color in some of the systems. The color systems currently most popular and studied most frequently are the Prang, the Munsell, and the Ostwald.

THE FIRST SYSTEM

In 1660, Sir Isaac Newton conducted experiments to illustrate that all color is contained in light and that color does not exist in the absence of light by passing a light through a prism which refracts or bends the light rays into a spectrum of colors. Newton counted seven colors in this spectrum—red, orange, yellow, green, blue, indigo, and violet.

Physiologists later studied the process by which color is seen by the human eye and translated by the human brain. This is extremely complicated. The color reflected from an object is determined by the composition of the object. Light striking an object may be reflected, absorbed, or pass through it. Surface transparency or opacity will determine the pattern of the light. Colors not reflected are absorbed by the object and are not visible. For example, a green fabric is green because its chemical colorant absorbs all colored rays of light except green which it reflects. In this manner all other colors are reflected. Black is the absence of all color or light. White is a combination of all colors in light. Gray is a mixture of black and white.

THE PRANG SYSTEM

The Prang system of color is based on the mixing of pigments. It is the oldest and simplest theory and is most often used by the artist or painter. It is based upon the three primary colors—red, blue, and yellow—which are placed equidistant on a color wheel. These primaries are combined to produce the secondary colors. Thus equal amounts of the same intensity of the two primaries red and blue produce violet; blue and yellow produce green; red and yellow produce orange. The intermediate colors are formed by mixing neighboring colors.

Primary colors: red, yellow, blue

Secondary colors: purple, green, orange

Intermediate colors: yellow-green, blue-green, blue-violet, red-violet, red-orange, yellow-orange

274   The color wheel can be expanded by continuing the process of mixing equal amounts of the same intensity of neighboring colors.

THE MUNSELL SYSTEM

The Munsell system uses the spectrum of the physicist. It is based upon five principal colors, called hues in this system, which are placed equidistant around the color wheel. These are red, yellow, green, blue, and purple. The intermediate hues are yellow-red, green-yellow, blue-green, blue-purple, and red-purple.

The Munsell color system uses a three-dimensional sphere having as its vertical axis the scale of values. The value scale is in seven steps from white at the north pole to black at the south pole. The horizontal axis carries the chroma or saturation. The saturation is greatest at the outer end and decreases to neutral at the center. In the Munsell system each value and chroma change has a numerical notation, thus making it valuable in exact duplication of color.

THE OSTWALD SYSTEM

The Ostwald system is based on hue black and white rather than hue value and chroma as in the Munsell system. The Ostwald color solid is made up of two cones placed together, with their points opposite each other in a north-south relationship. This is called the double cone.

Eight value steps from white at the top to black at the bottom are located on the center axis of the double cones. The complementary hues are placed horizontally in an east-west relationship. Colors between the center axis and the hue to the far east or west are formed by mixing the pure hue with black or white. The solid represents 24 hues. The four basic hues are yellow, red, ultramarine blue, and sea green. The intermediate colors are orange, purple, turquoise, and leaf green.

The commonly used systems discussed above can be further studied in numerous texts, including those listed in the references at the end of this chapter. The system used in this text and presented later in this chapter is the Color Key System. It is easily understood and particularly suitable for the selection of colors for the individual.

dimensions of color

In order to discuss color, a knowledge of color terminology is necessary. Describing color is difficult because each color has so many variations, and each individual sees color in a highly personalized manner. The terms "hue," "value," and "intensity" or "chroma" are used to describe color. By developing a good comprehension of these dimensions of color one can better understand the application of color.

HUE

Hue is the family name of a color such as red, blue, or green and distinguishes one color from another. There is a name for any hue regardless of its value or intensity. Hue is often used interchangeably with the word "color."

Hue is further described as being warm or cool which depends on the hue's position in the spectrum of colors. When light is refracted by a prism, wavelengths of color result. The long wavelengths of red, orange, and yellow are warm, whereas the short wavelengths of blue and violet are cool. Green is between warm and cool, becoming warm when combined with yellow, as in yellow-green, and becoming cool when combined with blue, as in blue-green.

Further, the warmth or coolness of a color carries with it an apparent psychological association which can produce certain sensations and reactions. The yellow, orange, and red hues visible in the sun or fire are often associated with the sensation of heat and warmth. The blue hues of the sky reflected in the water and the purple shadows of twilight convey the idea of coolness.

The properties of warmth and coolness are important in the selection of hues in clothing. They can produce the illusion of relative importance and size. Warm colors—red, yellow, orange—are said to be advancing. That means they appear to move toward the observer; they appear closer, larger, and more important than other colors. Cool colors—blue, blue-green, or violet—are receding. They create the illusion of being farther away, smaller, and less important. Warm hues emphasize the body size and contours; cool hues minimize these proportions. This color information should be considered when selecting clothing for various figure types.

VALUE

Value describes the lightness or darkness of a color. The hue remains the same, but the addition of white or black changes the value of the color. As an example, when white is added to the hue red, a white-red or pink results. This new color is described as having a high value, that is, it is lighter than the original hue. When white is added to a hue, the result is called a tint of that color. When black is added to red a black-red results. This new color is described as having a low value, that is, it is darker than the original hue. Black added to a hue creates a shade of the original color. A good place to observe value orientation of hues is on black and white television.

The application of value in clothing selection is most important. Exciting, dramatic, and clever figure camouflage can be achieved by the use of color values in an ensemble.

Light or high values reflect light and make an object seem to stand out. Thus the light or high values make a figure appear larger than when it is attired in dark or low-value colors. The strength of this effect depends on the amount of contrast with the background. Most of the environment in which we live consists of middle values. White, being the lightest value, and black, being the darkest value, generally are in the greatest contrast to the background. Therefore, white or very light, black or very dark clothes should not be worn by those who do not wish to call attention to their figures.

The value of hues in clothing has an effect on skin coloring. Dark values drain color from the skin. Pale or very fair-complexioned people will find that wearing dark values will make them appear more colorless. Those with a great deal of color in their skin will find that dark values help to tone down their complexions. Light values reflect color onto the skin and are a good choice for those who wish to enhance pale personal coloring, but not for those who desire to tone down their coloring.

When considering the value of a color in relation to clothing, remember what nature does with flowers. The lovely blossoms are light and bright so that they will be contrasted against the foliage which is generally dark and dull. When you wish to emphasize, use the light and bright; when you wish to minimize, use dark and dull.

The placement of value contrast on the figure is important because the eye focuses on the area of sharp contrast. If the value contrast is placed at an area of a figure problem, this will be emphasized. As an example, consider dark slacks with a light cardigan sweater. The line of value contrast will fall on the hipline, and say "Here world, look at this!" If hips are a problem area it would be wiser to wear dark-value slacks and a dark-value sweater. The lower the value contrast, the less the emphasis.

White or very light pastel shoes are in direct contrast to dark, suntanned legs or dark hosiery, thus the feet stand out because of value contrast. This also happens when the light shoe is contrasted against dark floor coverings. Because of the advancing quality of light values, white or light shoes also seem to increase the size of the foot.

Closely blended values have very little contrast and therefore do not outline contours. Middle values are the least attention-demanding because they contrast least with the background and thus are the most camouflaging. Nature follows this guideline of values with the protective covering of many animals. Their coloring blends with their natural habitat.

When all colors are the same in value, the lack of contrast is uninteresting and monotonous. Personal coloring should be analyzed for its value. Wardrobes should be planned to present a variety of color values based upon personal coloring, while the effects of high and low values on the figure are kept in mind.

INTENSITY OR CHROMA

Intensity is the term used to describe the purity of a color. It is also defined as the amount a hue departs from neutral gray. Intensity is expressed as the strength or weakness, the brightness or dullness, or the degree of saturation of a color. High-intensity colors are pure, strong, brilliant saturated colors. Low-intensity colors are weak, grayed, and dull.

In clothing selection intensity is important because of the illusions it can produce. When it is understood, color intensity can be an effective tool for creating both camouflage and flair in the wardrobe.

Bright, high-intensity colors are advancing; they make the figure appear larger. Weak or low-intensity colors are receding; they are less conspicuous and make the figure appear smaller.

When the use of colors of high intensity is considered, the relation to personal coloring must be carefully analyzed. Hues that have an intensity greater than that of the hair color will rob the hair of some of its color. Most eye coloring, except brown and hazel, is intensified by a hue that matches it in intensity. Brown eyes benefit most from contrasting shades of high intensity. Hazel eyes are like chameleons and reflect the color of their environment in direct relation to its brilliance.

High-intensity colors bring out or force their complement. This means that a high-intensity green will force the red complement in any area of color close to it. This happens very often with skin coloring. A brilliant green dress can make a blushing or ruddy complexion look crimson. The complements of violet and yellow have the same effect. A violet garment may bring out the yellow in sallow complexion almost to the point of making it look jaundiced. This effect does not always have to be negative; a bright orange pin can intensify lovely blue eyes, or a green gown can brighten rosy cheeks. Sometimes the intensity of a color is increased by combining it with a staple color such as black or white. A very intense color may have a more subtle effect if it is placed next to an analogous color. Bright orange appears less firey when placed next to yellow than it does next to its complement blue. These tricks of intensity of color should be evaluated whenever color and designs are selected.

A classic color rule, the law of color areas, defines the ratio of high-intensity color to duller colors in a costume. It states that bright, saturated colors should be used in small areas, and less intense colors should be used in large areas. Fashion sometimes ignores this dictum and features entire garments of very high intensity, yet the rule is still a very good one that the wise woman will use in selecting her clothing for several reasons. Figure size can be minimized by following this rule. By using high-intensity colors as accents in the personality area, the eye of the observer is attracted and held there, thus the figure silhouette is ignored. This small amount of high-intensity color, when selected to accent eyes, hair, and skin, has more impact and drama than a larger area would.

influences on color

Color cannot be considered alone because of the wide number of factors that affect its appearance. A single color takes on many different properties as it is manipulated for various purposes or observed in changing environments.

RELATION TO OTHER COLORS

As colors are organized into different patterns, designs, or garments, the appearance of one hue may be altered by the proximity of one or a group of other colors. A color may be intensified or dulled simply by its relationship with surrounding colors. This effect is often created because of a contrast in intensities of the involved colors or may result because of the composition of the colors used. Color harmonies are used to achieve pleasing combinations of hues. Preference for a particular color harmony depends on social and cultural factors which are learned. Personal likes and dislikes cause a variety of responses to different color harmonies. No hard and fast rules should govern the use of color harmonies, but traditionally organized patterns of color merit study if only as a point of departure for personal improvisation. It must be kept in mind, however, that successful harmony depends on many factors, including the color pattern of the individual, the size of the area in which the color is used, its location, and the selection and combination of the value and intensity of the hue.

The traditional color harmonies are divided into related and contrasting groups. Related colors and related color harmonies are composed of at least one color in common. Yellow is related to orange and to green because it is common to the composition of these colors. Contrasting colors or color harmonies have no colors in common. Thus red, blue, and yellow are contrasting colors.

RELATED COLOR HARMONIES

Monochromatic Harmony. One color is used with value and intensity differences for monochromatic harmony, for instance, light pink, dark maroon, and watermelon. If value and intensity gradations are too close together, the effect may appear to be a mismatch. These schemes require noticeable differences to achieve the variation of value and intensity necessary to avoid a fatiguing and monotonous effect.

Analogous Harmony. Colors appearing next to each other on the color wheel such as yellow-orange, yellow, and yellow-green make up an analogous harmony. When one of the hues is allowed to predominate and when values and intensities are varied, striking effects can be achieved. This harmony creates movement and excitement because of the vibrating effect of adjacent hues. A variation of this harmony which produces a dramatic effect combines three analogous hues with an accent of the complement of one of the hues. Thus, yellow-orange, yellow, and yellow-green would be used with violet to produce an analogous scheme with a complement.

CONTRASTING COLOR HARMONIES

Complementary Harmony. Complementary colors such as yellow-orange and blue-violet are opposites on the color wheel. Simple complementary schemes of two colors can be extended by using several different values and intensities. When complementary hues are used in their pure strength, they intensify each other and produce sharp contrasts. Lowering the value tends to reduce the contrast and lessen their power to intensify each other.

Double Complement Harmony. Two hues adjacent on the color wheel are used with their complements, such as yellow and violet with yellow-orange and blue-violet.

Split Complement Harmony. The hue is used with the colors on each side of its complement. Thus, yellow would be joined with red-violet and blue-violet.

Triad Harmony. Three hues placed equidistant on the color wheel are used as yellow, red, and blue.

Tetrad Harmony. Four hues equidistant on the color wheel are joined, for example, red, blue-violet, green, and yellow-orange.

LIGHT SOURCE

A factor affecting color is the light source under which it is viewed. The type of light will affect the depth of the color. Incandescent light, fluorescent light, sunlight, candlelight—all have different effects on color. Sometimes this effect can be predicted and sometimes it cannot. The best way to test color is to view it under the light source with which it will be used most often. Generally, bright sunlight changes the intensity of a color. As the intensity of daylight changes from morning to night, the degree of the color alteration also changes. Artificial lights come in different color tones such as yellow, white, rose, and so on. Each of these lights has a different effect on color. Generally, a warm-hued light source intensifies red, yellow, and orange, whereas it neutralizes blue and violet. A cool-hued light source usually intensifies blue and violet and neutralizes red, yellow, and orange.

DISTANCE

The distance from which a color is viewed can change its effect. Because of the amount of color used and the hue combination, proximity to the colors influences their appearance. In some allover designs of tweeds, tiny stripes, or checks the mixture of colors blends together to form new combinations when viewed from a distance; the individual colors making up the design lose their original color identity. When this blending occurs, more accurate color matching of fabrics and accessories can be achieved by observing them from a distance rather than at close range.

TEXTURE

Texture changes color. The same dyes used on different textures will produce a range of colors. Shiny fabrics such as satin reflect the light, thus the colors become brighter or more intense. Dull textures such as flannel absorb the light and cause colors to become less intense. Shoes, stockings, garments, hats, and scarves are all made of materials of different textures; for this reason they can seldom be perfectly color matched. The textures involved reflect or absorb light differently, thus changing the value or intensity of the color.

PERSONAL COLOR PATTERN

When colors are selected for personal adornment, individual coloring should be a main consideration. Skin, hair, and eye coloring (in order of importance) should be evaluated carefully. Colors worn should complement personal coloring. All colors worn should have the same undertones as are found in the individual coloring. Undesirable tones in the skin can be subdued by using analogous colors in the personality area. Desirable skin coloring can be enhanced by using complementary colors. The value and intensities of the colors worn should vary and be in pleasing harmony with the personal coloring.

BODY AREA AND SHAPE

The size and shape of the individual should influence color choice. Warm hues, light values, and bright intensities create the illusion of increased body size. Cool colors, medium values, and low intensities help decrease the apparent body size. Low-value and less intense colors in major areas of clothing with high-intensity colors as the accents in the personality area will focus the eye of the observer away from the figure and thus create a camouflage.

AGE

Age also should be considered when making color choices. As one ages, the skin and hair coloring becomes less intense. Harsh, bright colors are generally less attractive on the older person. Just as nature softens personal coloring by the aging process, so the mature individual should soften color choices. Vivid colors contrast with fading skin and hair coloring and thus emphasize age.

PERSONAL REACTIONS

Recent research has delved into psychological reactions to color. Although there are still many questions to be answered in this area, it has been established that response to color is very individual. One reacts to color in a certain manner because of the experiences and associations he has had with that color. Each man, woman, and child has a high degree of color sensitivity. Some are more aware of this sensitivity than others and react more violently to it. People may actually become physically ill, excited, soothed, or depressed by exposure to certain colors. It is not exactly understood why these intense emotional responses to color are evoked or why they vary so much with the individual. Attitudes toward color may be the result of some childhood experience (either pleasant or unpleasant), lack of experience or association with color, or a psychological phenomenon. Each individual has certain colors and combinations of colors that are more pleasing to him than others. For this reason any dogmatic approach to color for the individual is misleading. The individual needs to experiment with color in relation to both his physical and psychological self and discover color and color harmonies most pleasing to him.

color key [1]

As was discussed earlier, a number of technical color systems such as the Ostwald, Prang, and Munsell theories are widely used to explain the physical properties of color. However, the authors of this text feel that confusion arises when the individual attempts to apply these systems to selecting the most desirable colors for himself. What is needed is a simple device that will personalize all colors so that one may know immediately what to select or reject.

A recently developed system is Color Key, a working tool for both the professional and lay person which individualizes the choice of color. By understand-

[1] The Color Key System used by permission of Robert C. Dorr and Ameritone Color Key Corporation.

ing and using the Color Key System, the individual quickly becomes a color expert adept at always choosing and combining the best colors for himself and those around him.

The Color Key System was developed by Robert Dorr. Drawing on a rich experience of working with color in the hotel, department store, fashion, home furnishing, textile, and education fields, he was able to develop a practical approach to color selection. This theory is supported by all existing color systems and by testing and research with hundreds of thousands of persons of all races ranging in age from eight to eighty. Research which supports Color Key was conducted by Dr. Robert Beardmore at California State Polytechnic College.

The Color Key System is based on three facts. Understanding these facts can eliminate guesswork from the selection of color for any purpose.

First, Color Key is based on a scientific way of relating basic pigments of one color with those of another. In this manner all the colors of the spectrum have been separated into only two palettes. These two palettes are labeled Color Key 1 and Color Key 2. All the colors in Key 1 are technically and visually perfect for use in multiples with each other. The same holds true for the colors in Key 2. The reason for this is that the colors that harmonize with one another are scientifically related by the basic pigments in their composition. The Color Key System is based on this relationship.

Second, it has been established that each person during his early teens forms a pattern of color choice that remains constant throughout his entire lifetime. Not only do we show a definite preference for certain colors, we are physically more attractive and comfortable with these choices.

Finally, the color of anything we see is composed of the primary colors red, blue, and yellow, plus black and white. Each individual's natural coloring is made from these same colors. It has been proven that when an individual, male or female, selects the key he prefers, the colors in that key are his most becoming and comfortable. The preferred Color Key represents color proportions that are related to the individual's own natural coloring.

HOW DO YOU DISCOVER YOUR COLOR KEY?

Study carefully the illustrations showing the two Color Keys (Figures 13–1 through 13–4). Notice that there are reds, purples, blues, greens, and yellows represented in each key. Notice also that there are no unkeyed or what is commonly known as neutral colors. See the pink-beige in Key 1, the yellow-beige in Key 2; the snow-white in Key 1, the cream white in Key 2; the jet black in Key 1, the off-black in Key 2. Can you see how the keys differ? Study the model's natural coloring. Consider how the personal coloring of the model relates to the background of color surrounding her in the picture.

1 Light Skin. The blue undertone of the skin gives people with this coloring a rose-pink ~~complexion~~. The natural eye and hair colors always blend with the flesh tones. These ~~people~~ may successfully wear all colors represented in Color Key 1.

2 Light Skin. The yellow undertone of the skin gives people with this type of coloring ~~a~~ peach-pink cast. The natural eye and hair colors repeat this yellow tone. People with this ~~c~~oloring may successfully wear all colors represented in Color Key 2.

~~In~~ the various races there are many different skin shades. Each coloring may be color ~~keyed~~ by studying the undertones of the skin. Each skin has an undertone of blue or yellow, ~~and~~ this undertone is the key to Color Key. Once the undertone has been established, ~~the~~ Color Key is identified. (Photos courtesy Tommy Mitchell and George Szanik)

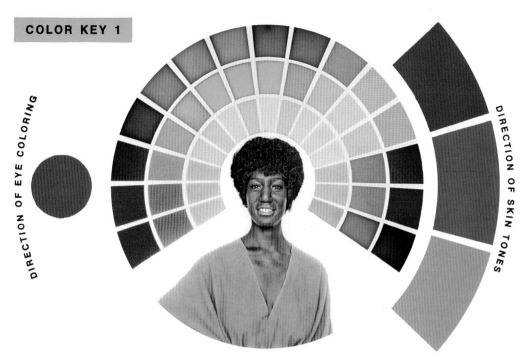

13–3 Dark Skin. The blue undertone of some dark skins gives a beautiful umber cast and classes it as a Color Key 1. The natural eye and hair colors repeat the blue undertone. Persons with this kind of coloring may successfully wear all colors represented in Color Key 1.

13–4 Dark Skin. The yellow undertone of some dark skins gives a lovely golden glow and classes it Color Key 2. The natural eye and hair colors repeat the yellow undertone. People with this coloring may successfully wear all colors represented in Color Key 2.

color key

13–5 and 13–6 These settings illustrate how the same room can be pleasing in either Color Key. The secret to successful application of color is to use colors of the same Key for each project. (Interiors by Ester Laartz; courtesy Ameritone Paint Company)

13–7 and 13–8 Robert Dorr's Bel Air cottage landscaping illustrates the subtle difference of Color Key. The house exterior is Color Key 2. When Color Key 1 flowers are changed to Color Key 2, the difference becomes quite noticeable. As an extra bonus, the Color Key 2 flowers may be used as successful accents in the Color Key 2 interior of the home. (Courtesy Ameritone Paint Company)

Now choose for yourself the group of colors you prefer. Do not be influenced by any single color, but choose the entire group of colors. Do not be swayed by the dress you have on or the color scheme of your present home. Decide for yourself by answering this question: *If I had to live with one key the rest of my life, with which one would I be happiest?* You have now discovered your Color Key. The only color selection mistake you can make in the future is by combining colors from one key with those of the other.

Choice of one key does not mean that you dislike the other; it simply means that you prefer one group of colors to the other. Even in your chosen key there may be some colors you do not wish to wear. No one says you must. Do not let a color prejudice confuse your selection. Choose your key from the entire range of colors. Understand, however, any color in your key will look well associated with you, should you choose to wear it. All the colors in the key you have chosen are flattering to you. They are your "best colors." They will enhance your appearance and present you at your best.

Study the illustrations again. Note that each key has both warm and cool colors, clear as well as grayed tones. In each key all colors are represented except one. The colors missing are orange in Key 1 and magenta in Key 2. These colors are the indicant of the Color Key System.

HOW DOES THE COLOR KEY SYSTEM RELATE TO YOUR PERSONAL COLORING?

The Color Key System works for men and women of all races—yellow, red, black, or white. In selecting color, the skin, hair, and eye pigmentation should be considered. The theory scientifically relates all colors with those found in the individual's skin, hair, and eyes. Using this method to select color automatically insures that the choice will be complementary to each individual's skin, hair, and eye coloring.

The skin pigmentation of all peoples is composed of red, blue, yellow, black, and white. These are the same colors that compose Color Key. In the white race Key 1 people, because of the prominence of blue in their skin tone, have a rose-pink complexion. They prefer, look better, and are happier when associated with colors from Key 1. Key 2 people, because of the prominence of yellow in their coloring, have a peach-pink skin tone. They like the colors found in Key 2 best and are most attractive and happiest surrounded by them. Skin tones are consistent even as the skin weathers, tans, and ages. After the initial sun or windburn, the skin darkens in its own key. As the skin ages, the undertones become darker, lighter, or remain consistent as the body chemistry adjusts. Aging will never cause a change in Color Key of the skin.

Color Key in the yellow, red, or black races is distinguishable not by the darkness of the skin but by the undertones. A Key 1 skin has a predominant blue undertone which gives the skin a beautiful umber cast. A Key 2 skin has a yellow undertone which gives it a golden cast.

Eyes are a fascinating index to true coloring and one that is most consistent. Eye color does not fade or change with age. Unless eye color is altered by disease or the use of contact lenses, it remains the same from infancy on. The skin and hair color change with age; eye coloring does not. Blue and brown eyes are found in either key. Bright blue eyes are Key 1; gray-blue eyes are Key 2. Red-brown eyes are Key 1; and yellow-brown eyes are Key 2. The colors comprising the hazel eye and unusual eye colors such as green and violet must be observed carefully in order to define their composition which will then determine the key to which they belong.

Hair colors are Color Keyed also. All colors are represented in both keys. It is the undertone of the hair color that establishes in which key it belongs. The blue or smokey undertone of Key 1 claims the platinum blondes, auburn reds, jet blacks, snow whites, and the smokey blue or purple tints. The golden undertones of the honey blondes, rust reds, chestnut, off-blacks, and cream whites belong to Key 2. Remember this especially when you help nature with the color of your hair. Always choose an artificial tint in your Color Key. When you gray, you will do so in your own key, snow white in Key 1 and cream white in Key 2.

Always keep in mind that the colors from your own key are your most flattering because they are related to your natural coloring. Never be influenced by fashion to change your Color Key, as you will not look or feel your best in the other key. Colors not of your key will tend to make you look older by emphasizing facial wrinkles, shadows, and blemishes. For visual proof of this statement, drape a length of fabric or toweling around your shoulders covering your clothing. Select a bright orange from Key 2 and a bright magenta from Key 1 for this purpose. The difference will be vivid. If the drape is in the wrong key, your skin will be shown at its worst. Wrinkles, shadows, blemishes, freckles and pigmentation are all intensified by the incorrect Color Key. By switching from one drape to another quickly, the "magic" of Color Key is dramatically illustrated. For this test to be most effective, the face should be devoid of make-up.

COLOR KEY COMBINATIONS

Use your knowledge of Color Key for every purchase where color must be considered. All cosmetics should be selected in your Color Key. Accessories such as shoes, handbags, hosiery, and jewelry should be Color Keyed along with the entire wardrobe. All items of exterior and interior design and decoration should be Color Keyed.

All the colors found in one key may be successfully combined with all the other colors of that key. Applying this knowledge, you can develop endless varieties of chic color harmonies individualized by you. Each combination selected from your key will flatter your personal coloring and present you at your best.

The one thing you may never do is to cross Color Keys. That is, you may never combine the colors in one key with those of the other key. Yes, you do find these combinations of crossed keys in the marketplace, but they are harsh, jarring, and offensive. Remember a great number of articles for every purpose are available commercially that are not tasteful, pleasing, or even desirable. These items should be avoided by the discriminating person. You will find that any item that violates the Color Key rule by crossing the two keys is always inharmonious. The combination of the two keys will be short lived, whether it be in a dress fabric or a wallpaper pattern. These combinations do not wear well visually and therefore are soon discarded.

APPLICATION OF COLOR KEY

For your beauty and use of color, understanding of the application of Color Key is essential. The Color Key Coordinator has been developed to assist in every facet of color selection. The Color Key Coordinator is a holder that contains a number of color chips representing each Color Key. If you develop the habit of always comparing the color of an item you are considering with the keyed color chip related to it, you will always be able to select the "right" color. The Color Key Coordinator is purse size and may be conveniently carried with you whenever you are choosing color. (For information on acquiring your own Color Key Coordinator, see the end of the chapter.)

If you apply your knowledge of Color Key to your wardrobe, you will find that it seems to increase in size. This is because everything you buy will be perfectly Color Keyed to go with everything else. Sweaters, coats, and jackets will blend with dresses, blouses, skirts, and pants. Shoes and handbags will mix with gloves, hats, and scarves. In clothing selection texture and design may limit some combinations of apparel, but a Color Key–selected wardrobe will be in color harmony.

Textures such as leather, velvet, satin, and paint have an effect on color. Textures such as patent leather or satin that reflect the light make the color appear lighter. Textures such as velvet or corduroy that absorb the light make the color appear darker. Artificial light will also affect the color. This effect of light on color varies with the kind of light, the colored surface, and other surroundings. By referring directly to the colors in your Coordinator, you can be certain of exact color. Even the professional person, who deals constantly with color, cannot make decisions about color without testing. Regardless of the textures and the lighting, if you have selected the items in your Color Key, they will remain flattering to you.

Be aware that there are no unkeyed colors in this system. The beiges of Key 1 are different from those in Key 2, as are the blacks, browns, navies, and whites. For example, snow white of any fabric has a blue undertone which makes it Key 1. Cream white has a yellow undertone, which makes it Key 2. The white of 100 per cent wool always belongs to Key 2. This is because as white wool is worn and ages, it becomes more yellowed and thus very flattering to a Key 2, but not a Key 1 person. Robert Dorr, the creator of the Color Key System, stated: "There are no neutral colors, therefore, never use a color that goes fairly well with everything and very well with nothing."

On occasion colors you are trying to match may be somewhat grayer in tone than the chip in the Color Key Coordinator. Bear in mind that all colors in both keys can be grayed a fraction without throwing them into the opposite key.

When choosing hosiery, check to see if it is in your Color Key. Textured or opaque stocking colors will be found on the Color Key Coordinator. Beige or natural-colored hosiety should be Color Keyed by matching skin tones or the colors recommended for foundations on the Coordinator. Often very inexpensive hosiery has a red tone to it that becomes redder as the stockings are laundered. This red-blue undertone is Key 1 and should be avoided by Key 2 people. If your natural-colored stockings are always carefully Color Keyed, you will never find yourself with the "wrong stockings."

All cosmetics should be in your Color Key. Foundation colors should match the skin or be slightly darker. Eye liner, mascara, brow pencil, and shadows are Color Keyed in the same tones as hair coloring. These eye make-ups may vary in value and intensity, but their undertones must be Color Keyed. Rouge, blusher, lipstick, and nail enamel also should be Color Keyed. Cross keying the reds used in these cosmetics creates unflattering effects which make the facial wrinkles and blemishes more pronounced, or emphasizes the pigmentation of the face making it appear more florid or sallow. Careful selection of nail enamel will enhance the beauty of the hand by complementing the skin tones. A Key 1 nail polish is a rosy pink with a bluish undertone. A Key 2 nail enamel is a peach-pink with a golden cast. Properly keyed nail polish always blends with all your Color Keyed wardrobe and therefore eliminates forever the frustration of a speedy polish change.

Each of us desires to have bright, healthy white teeth. But snow-white teeth belong only in Key 1 faces. Tooth enamel of Key 2 people is cream white, as is the rest of their coloring. This is a very important point to remember when having any type of corrective dentistry done. Key 1 tooth enamel set into a Key 2 set of teeth will always look false and therefore unattractive.

Jewelry can also be Color Keyed. Rose, white gold, silver, and platinum are considered Key 1. Yellow gold is Key 2. Each of the precious stones such as the diamond, emerald, ruby, and pearl can belong to either key. A person truly sensitive to color will carefully consider this aspect before selecting jewelry.

As stated previously, Color Key is applicable to all men, women, and children. The very young may vacillate somewhat in their choices, but the pattern of color preference is firmly established by the teen years. When selecting gifts for others, it is most thoughtful to consider their Color Key. The gift in your key will not be nearly as pleasing as one in their own key. Wives very often select their husband's apparel; if the spouse happens to be a different key and she ignores this—poor man!

The entire home environment should be Color Keyed. (See Figures 13–5 through 13–8.) The landscaping that surrounds the home and provides its public setting should be selected in the Color Key of the exterior. Dramatic effects on a very small budget can be accomplished simply by selecting all flowering plants and bushes in the Color Key of the house. Cut flowers can be used in the house in perfect harmony with room settings.

Color Key should be used in selecting all home furnishings and interior design. A family will look and feel better surrounded by the colors that are best for them. All building materials are Color Keyed. You will discover that some bricks are Key 1 with a bluish cast, while others are Key 2 with a yellow tone. All stones, woods, metals, glasses, paints, and other such material belong to one key or the other. If you are building a home or business, careful attention to the Color Key of each detail can create a beautifully harmonious product. If you are refurbishing a building, you must work with what has already been installed. Study fixtures such as built-ins in the kitchen and bath to determine their Color Key. Even if this is not your personal key, carry out the new color scheme in the key presented by the old, irreplaceable items. This may seem somewhat of a contradiction to what has been said before, but crossing keys is more offensive than working in the opposite key. When decorating a home where the other Color Key must be used because of the building materials that cannot be changed, it is best to use less dramatic color combinations and seek those that approach the desired key.

Ideally, a woman's home should flatter her. Interior designers state, in theory, that the personal rooms of the home should be in the key of the lady using them. When possible, the living area, kitchen, and master bedroom should follow this rule. When there are differences in keys among family members, it is wisest to create the color schemes in the key of the one using them the most. Never attempt to compromise within a single room by crossing Color Keys. The result of this attempt to compensate will please no one.

SUMMARY OF COLOR KEY

Color Key is a key to individualized color selection. If you always stay within your Color Key, you will be making wise color choices. Do not let a personal color prejudice inhibit your use of the valuable tool. All colors are represented in each key with the exception of orange in Key 1 and magenta in

Key 2, so that you have complete freedom to pick and choose what pleases you most. You can combine any color of one key with any other colors in that key. Thus, you may have complete confidence to build your own personal color harmonies. The only rule to remember is never cross keys in your color choices.

A survey revealed that 60 per cent of the people in the United States preferred the colors in Key 1, while the remaining 40 per cent liked the colors of Key 2. This figure varies, however, with geographical areas. In certain southwestern and southern areas 40 per cent preferred Key 1 and 60 per cent Key 2.

Professionals dealing with color in any form, but especially those in fashion industries and interior design, must learn to work in both keys. They should help their clients establish their own Color Key and then carry through in this key for their mutual satisfaction with the project.

Color Key can open doors to a new dimension of life through exciting use of color. You can surround yourself with the colors that are right for you, the ones that enhance your physical and emotional self and thus present you at your most beautiful. Further information regarding teaching aids and the purse-size Color Key Coordinator may be obtained from Color Key Coordinator, 23975 Crosson Drive, Woodland Hills, California 91364.

suggested readings

Birren, Faber. *Principles of Color.* New York: Van Nostrand Reinhold Company, 1969.

Burnham, R. W., R. M. Hanes, C. James Bartleson. *Color, A Guide to Basic Facts and Concepts.* New York: John Wiley & Sons, Inc., 1963.

Fabri, Ralph. *Color, A Complete Guide for Artists.* New York: Watson-Guptill Publications, 1967.

Horn, Marilyn J. *The Second Skin.* Boston: Houghton-Mifflin Company, 1968.

Sargent, Walter. *The Enjoyment of Color.* New York: Dover Publications Inc., 1964.

14

personalizing dress with color

Personalizing dress individualizes the costume. In a country where most of the clothing is mass produced, personalizing dress is vital to avoiding a carbon copy image. A variety of accessories such as jewelry, scarves, hats, handbags, shoes, and gloves combine with the elements of color, texture, and fabric design to achieve a personalized ensemble. Most women intuitively select their items of adornment; unfortunately, this method sometimes leads to chaos rather than to a total look. The art of accessorizing is an important part of clothing selection and personal appearance is therefore worthy of consideration.

Color, texture, and fabric design are combined to create the total look of a costume. Careful study of the chapters dealing with each of these subjects is important to the understanding of relating each element to a specific costume. This chapter presents guidelines for using color in accessorizing apparel. The selection of garments, fabric designs, textures, and exact colors must remain with the individual and her personal wardrobe. The student is urged to experiment with the guides set forth here, but in no way to be inhibited by them. Personalizing dress obviously can only be done by the individual.

color coordination

No other element of fashion varies quite so much as color. This is due to a number of reasons, including the reaction of dyes with fibers and the low cost of changing colors in manufacturing. As a result of this manipulation, a color may be high fashion one season and no fashion the next. As both a consumer and a woman who wants to remain fashionable, it is necessary to understand the fundamental principles of combining color for flair and economy. In the discussion of the Color Key theory it was learned that any color could be successfully combined with any other color in the same key. Exactly how these combinations can be made most exciting and effective needs to be considered carefully. For the following discussion of color application, it is necessary to define the terms that will be used to describe both color and accessories.

color and accessory terms

Fashion Color. The basic colors—red, yellow, blue, green, orange, and violet—are the basic colors from which all others are derived. Each fashion season presents a variety of colors which differ subtly from the year before. Fashion colors are rarely the pure primary colors but rather are variations of them.

Staple Color. These are basic colors that may be combined successfully with all other colors. Staple colors for cold weather are black, black-brown, and navy. Staple colors for warm weather are beige and white. The cold weather staple colors may be worn in warm weather if desired; however, the reverse is not true. Beige and white accessories are not appropriate in cold weather.

Flair Color. This may be any color other than the staple colors. Flair color is used for contrast and accent. Flair accessories are selected in flair colors.

Flair Accessories. These include such items as scarves, dickeys, collars and cuffs, belts, jewelry, and hats. These items are selected in the flair colors and used in the costume to achieve flair and accent.

Standard Accessories. These include shoes, handbags, and gloves. If the handbag and gloves are of the same material as the shoe, they are considered as a unit. It is not necessary to match these three items; it is wise, however, to have at least one set in a staple color that will go with most wardrobe items.

Personality Area. This is the face and head area. The true uniqueness of each individual is expressed by the face. For this reason the personality area should be emphasized most often in dress.

Related Colors. These are colors that have a common color in their composition. Orange and purple have red in common; green and orange have yellow in common; purple and green have blue in common.

Unrelated Colors. These are colors having no common colors, also defined as complements. Examples are yellow and purple, red and green, blue and orange.

Value. Value is the lightness or darkness of a color. Value changes are achieved by adding black or white to a color. When white is added, a tint of the color is made in fashion; this is called a pastel. When black is added, a shade is created. Low-value or grayed colors tend to be more body concealing than high-value colors. Varying the values of colors used in a composition can make a more interesting harmony.

Intensity. This is the brightness or dullness of a color. Strong, brilliant, saturated colors are called high-intensity colors. Weak, grayed colors are called low-intensity colors. High-intensity colors are more figure revealing. Varying the intensity of colors used in combination makes a more interesting composition. The higher the intensity of a color, the smaller the area it should be used in. High-intensity colors are best used for accent.

number of colors worn at one time

A limited number of colors must be worn at one time, or the effect created becomes garish, spotty, and cluttered. The eye of the beholder notices color and color contrasts. If too many colors are worn, the eye busily travels from one area to another over and over again, giving the beholder the impression of a large mass. If the colors worn are not placed in the costume with some relationship to each other, the total image created is spotty and disorganized. This misuse of color detracts from the attractiveness of the wearer. Indeed, it often makes it impossible to find the wearer in the rainbow being worn.

A good rule to employ when combining color is never to wear more than three distinct colors at one time and preferably only two. This includes the fashion and staple colors. When colors are repeated, they should be located in the same area of the body; that is, all above the waist, at the waist, or all below the waist. It should always be kept in mind that the most important area to emphasize is the personality area. Of course, for variety it is fun sometimes to call attention to a good feature such as a small waist or pretty legs, but these areas should usually be subordinate to the personality area.

Shades of the same color may be used and counted as one color. Gradation from one color to another color may be used and counted as two colors. When selecting prints or plaids, count the colors represented. Most good design does not include more than three distinct colors; it may have several shades of each color, however.

how to use flair colors and accessories

Adding interest and individuality by the use of varied accessories in flair colors is one of the most exciting ways of personalizing dress. A collection of flair accessories should be developed and added to each season. It is a good idea to plan the purchase of a few flair accessories each time a garment is added to the wardrobe. In this manner the accessory collection will continue to grow, and the items will be fresh and current. It should be remembered that many accessories are classic in design and may be worn for years, but that some are true fads and should be discarded when they are no longer appropriate.

Presented here are some guidelines for using flair colors and accessories in personalizing dress. Remember that the examples are illustrating only one costume. The student should use her own creativity when dressing and employ the following as guides only. All colors represented are selected from the same Color Key.

1. When the main costume color is a staple, the flair color should be a bright, clear color for definite contrast. Avoid dark, grayed colors for flair color, as the ensemble will have a dull, funereal appearance.

Example:
  Dress: Black wool
  Standard accessories: Black kid
  Flair color: Lime green in silk scarf

Example:
  Suit: Navy wool
  Standard accessories: Black kid
  Flair color: Blouse in pastel pink, lapel pin in emerald green

2. If the main item of the costume is a fashion color, the staple colors may be used as flair colors. This accessorizing is pleasing but not too creative.

Example:
  Dress: Cherry red wool
  Standard accessories: Black kid
  Flair color: White pearls

3. When the main costume is a fashion color, a monochromatic color harmony may be used. This is achieved by using variations of the fashion color for flair.

Example:

>Dress: Royal blue silk
>Standard accessories: Navy blue kid
>Flair color: Light blue hat and scarf

4. When the main costume is a fashion color, a related color may be used for flair.

Example:

>Dress: Soft orange crepe
>Standard accessories: Beige kid
>Flair color: Bright pink scarf

5. When the main costume is a fashion color, an unrelated color may be used for flair.

Example:

>Coat: Dark purple wool
>Standard accessories: Black kid
>Flair color: Yellow scarf and pin

6. When the main costume is a print or plaid, select one of the design colors for use as flair.

Example:

>Dress print: Red, white, and blue cotton
>Standard accessories: Navy blue kid
>Flair color: Red bracelet and earrings

Some garments present special problems which make it impossible to follow the three-color rule; for example, a garment that contains three distinct colors such as a bright green dress banded at the neckline in yellow and orange. To pick up the yellow or orange of the trim would be to use too bright a color for accessories and would place the areas of color too far apart (at the neck, hip, and feet). To have standard accessories dyed to match the bright green of the dress would be expensive and perhaps too much of one color. In a case such as this it would be best to add a fourth color. Choose standard accessories in the staple color that pleases you the most.

Another problem example where a fourth color could be added would be the suit in a brilliant color such as yellow with a coordinated blouse that adds two or three more colors. Again, the most interesting total look would be achieved by understating the standard accessories and selecting them in a staple color which would not call attention to them.

WHERE TO USE FLAIR COLORS

The flair colors should be used most often in the personality area. When communicating with another, it is desired that the eyes of the beholder be attracted and held at the personality area. If accessorizing of dress emphasizes other parts of the body, the impact of the individual personality is greatly lessened.

Belts in flair colors should be limited to slender figures over 5'5" in height. This is because the horizontal line of the belt measures the figure for width and also cuts the apparent length of the figure. A thick body build will appear heavier with a contrasting belt. A short figure will appear shorter with a color contrast at the waistline.

Blouses, sweaters, jackets, and vests may be in a flair color only if they divide the body in a becoming area, that is, the horizontal line created by the contrasting color of the garment should not divide the body at a wide point such as the hip line. The short-and-thick figure type should avoid this type of contrast, as it will cut height and emphasize thickness. For this figure type, blouses, sweaters, jackets, and vest are best selected in the same fashion color as the garments worn with them.

Shoes, handbags, and gloves are most attractive in staple or a dulled fashion color. Eye arresting as these items are because of their movement, they detract too much from the personality area if they are in bright flair colors. These standard accessories are best selected in a color that does not emphasize their size or detract from the total ensemble. As a general rule, shoes should be as dark as or darker than the hemline. Handbag and gloves are considered as a unit if they match in color and texture. Thus, matching shoes, handbag, and gloves are considered a unit. Remember, however, it is not necessary to match exactly the standard accessories. In fact, a more interesting appearance is created when these items do not appear to be made of the exact same materials. When handbag and gloves differ from shoes, they should be selected to match some other item in the costume. It is preferable that the handbag or gloves are not the flair accessory. This is because of the area where they are generally carried. Too much emphasis would be placed in the middle of the torso, an area that is generally not the most attractive on any figure.

Jewelry is an excellent choice for flair color, and placement of the jewelry can be most imaginative. Do not be afraid of wearing a favorite piece of jewelry over and over. It can become your individual trademark. Do be careful not to wear too many articles of jewelry at one time unless a special eclectic look is desired. Styles of jewelry as well as the way of wearing them are tied closely to fashion, so be alert to changes.

Hats come and go in fashion popularity, but they can always be worn, and in some social situations they are still considered mandatory. The flair color can be used most effectively here; a hat frames the personality area and puts the flair color in excellent relationship to the face. When choosing a hat for the flair accessory, it is most effective to understate the other parts of the ensemble.

Scarves are also closely tuned to fashion. When they are in, they are wonderful for adding flair color. An endless variety of ways of wearing scarves can be created with a little imagination. Scarves, while never cheap, are an inexpensive way of giving a slightly out-of-fashion garment a new lease on life.

Hair ornaments come and go in popularity also. When they are fashionable, they can add a great deal of fashion for a very small investment. Be cautious not to affect a too "little girl look" with these ornaments. And do be certain to consider them in relation to the other parts of the total look.

Fresh flowers are sometimes used for flair color—this is a custom that can be charming. A bunch of violets pinned to a lapel can seem like a breath of spring. The size and placement of the flowers should be carefully considered, however. Generally speaking, the more unusual the blossom, the fewer flowers should be worn. A perfect rose is more effective than a rose corsage. Local custom will also determine how flowers are worn. In Hawaii blossoms in the hair are lovely, but not so in the downtown area of a busy metropolitan city. The gift corsage sometimes presents special problems to the girl who has carefully accessorized her gown. Corsages are properly worn with the stems pointed toward the ground from whence they came. If the gift corsage does not complement the costume you have selected, pin it to your handbag and carry it.

Repeating the eye and hair color in the costume intensifies their color. This is emphasis through repetition. Selecting an unrelated color of the eye or hair will also emphasize them. This is emphasis by contrast. Be careful not to wear colors of higher intensity than the hair, as it will make the hair color seem dull.

Avoid using flair colors for hosiery or shoes. This attracts too much attention to the foot area and detracts from the personality area. If shoes and hosiery are the same color as the skirt, a long, unbroken line is created that adds to the apparent length of the leg. Contrasting colors of hosiery break this line and appear to shorten the figure. Colored hosiery should be worn only by those who wish to draw attention to the shape of the leg and ankle.

illusions created by color

Interesting effects can be created in dress by incorporating the illusions made by some kinds of colors. Experiments can be devised to test these illusions and their effect on your figure. Working with large fabric drapes or clothing of different colors and textures can illustrate exactly the image projected by wearing these colors and textures.

The figure size is increased by light colors; all pastels and white or light colors will make the figure look larger. Bright or high-intensity colors have the same effect. For the slender woman who wishes to make her figure appear fuller, these colors are an excellent choice.

Dark, grayed, or medium-value colors decrease the size of the figure. Note that black is not one of the colors that decreases size. Black outlines the figure in strong contrast to most backgrounds and thus reveals it completely. Students with any figure irregularities should avoid black clothing, particularly when it is form fitting. The same concept is true of black hosiery. It outlines each contour of the leg and makes it appear heavier.

Warm colors—reds, oranges, yellows, or those colors found in firelight—generally make the figure appear larger. Cool colors—blues, purples, or those colors found in twilight—generally decrease the size of the figure. The value and intensity of each color must be considered for this effect to hold true. An electric blue of high intensity would appear to increase the size of the figure, while a grayed, muddy red would seem to decrease the size of the figure.

Colors have a definite effect on body temperature. Light colors reflect heat, thus they are more comfortable in warm weather. Dark colors absorb heat and therefore are warmest to wear in cold weather. A black coat will continue to feel warm for a long time after it has been removed from the body. This is because of the stored or absorbed heat. Interesting cultural use of this color phenomenon is found in the light dress of the people of the tropics and the dark dress of those living in cold regions.

Texture of fabrics affects the color. This is why it is so very difficult to color match various articles in an ensemble. Fuzzy, nap, and pile fabrics absorb color and decrease its intensity: woolens, velvets, corduroys, and terry-cloth fabrics will never have the highest intensity of color. Smooth, shiny fabrics reflect light and increase the intensity of the color: chintzes, satins, and *peau de soie* fabrics can have colors of very high intensity.

Colors can also have a definite effect on the appearance of the skin. Dark colors absorb color from the skin and pale it. Black, being the darkest color, does this the most dramatically. Light colors, in turn, reflect color into the skin. The amount of these effects varies with the individual coloring. It should be noted that bright, high-intensity colors are the most aging. So, as the years add up and the skin begins to show the birthdays, harsh colors should be avoided. Proper use of your Color Key will help you make color choices that are kindest to your complexion.

summary

Color is a vital element in any ensemble. Accessorizing with flair color when done properly creates exciting, personalized costumes. Understanding the various illusions produced by color combined with texture and fabric design can give each person a powerful tool to employ in the art of dress camouflage. Colors in fashion are subject to rapid change, yet carefully selected flair accessories are a real bargain. The Color Key System presents many colors that can be worn by each individual. The authors have suggested many guidelines to assist the student in personalizing dress by use of color knowledge.

To put this new color knowledge to work, create the following individual color index.

1. Use strips of cardboard approximately 1½ × 6 inches to build the base for your color index. Fasten these strips together so that they can be fanned out or folded closed. See Figure 14–1.

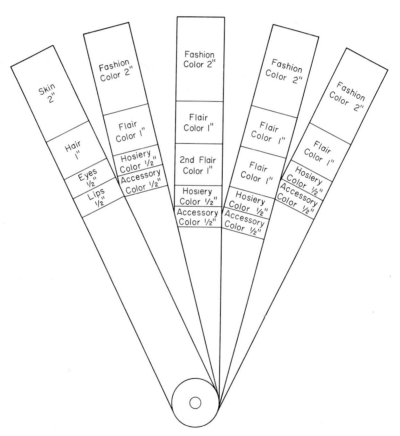

14–1 The personal coloring index. Directions for creating this visual of your individual coloring are given in the text.

2. From magazine illustrations, find colors that exactly match your skin, hair, eye, and lip coloring. Mount these on one cardboard strip in the following proportions and locations.

Skin color, 2 inches   at top of strip
Hair color, 1 inch   second from top of strip
Eye color, ½ inch   third from top of strip
Lip color, ½ inch   fourth from top of strip

3. For the next four or five strips, select fashion colors in various fabrics and textures. Mount these on the top 2 inches of the individual strips.

4. Select flair colors to coordinate with the selected fashion colors. Mount these fabrics in a 1 inch section under each fashion color.

5. Select fabrics to represent hosiery and accessories (staple/flair). Mount these in a ½ inch section under the flair colors.

6. Check each color selected in the problem for its Color Key. Remember that only the undertones in one's personal coloring should occur in the colors selected for adornment.

suggested readings

Bopst, Harland. *Color and Personality.* New York: Vantage Press, Inc., 1962.

Burnham, R. W., R. M. Hanes, and James C. Bartleson. *Color: A Guide to Basic Facts and Concepts.* New York: John Wiley & Sons, Inc., 1963.

Horn, Marilyn J. *The Second Skin.* Boston: Houghton Mifflin Company, 1968.

Smith, Charles N. *Student Handbook of Color.* New York: Reinhold Publishing Corporation, 1965.

Spears, Charleszine W. *How to Wear Colors.* Minneapolis: Burgess Publishing Company, 1965.

Wolf, Thomas H. *The Magic of Color.* New York: The Odyssey Press, Inc., 1964.

15

wardrobe planning

the only good wardrobe plan is the one that suits your individual needs. You are the only person who can devise this plan. Of course, you can gather suggestions for your wardrobe planning from many sources—such as this text, popular magazines, and clothing classes. But the ideas garnered from each reference must be put into action by you before they have any merit.

Your existing clothes collection, your style of life, and the dollars available for clothing expenditures all affect the initiating of a wardrobe plan. Anticipation of new and changing roles and activities are also an important consideration in planning. The test of your planning lies in how well your wardrobe fits the clothing needs in your life. Only you can do the planning; only you can know how successful your plan is. The person who never states "I haven't a thing to wear" has planned his wardrobe well. He has appropriate clothing for all the occasions in his life, a wardrobe tailored to fit his individual needs.

wardrobe planning begins in your closet

No one develops an ideal wardrobe without really working at it. Most people have an accumulation of garments which have been acquired over a period of time for various reasons. Of this accumulation some have given much satisfaction and have been worn with pleasure, whereas others have been unsatisfactory, for a wide variety of reasons. These are the clothes that are seldom worn and usually pushed to the back of the closet and ignored.

The first step in wardrobe planning is closet cleaning. Go through all the clothing you own. Try each item on and analyze it. Decide what you like or dislike about each item. Separate the articles into groups: the clothes you like, the clothes that need repair or alteration, and the clothes that have not been worn for at least a year. Put the first group back in the closet, get busy with the second group, and give the last group to your favorite charity. (This makes you feel noble and helps them.)

Carefully consider the clothing from your collection that you like. Analyze these garments for fit, comfort, color, and design. These favorite garments are the basis of your wardrobe planning. Future clothing investments should follow the guidelines established by these favored articles of clothing.

YOUR ROLES AND ACTIVITIES

Where you go, what you do, and the style of life you lead have a great deal to do with the kinds of clothing you need. A student attending a commuter college will have clothing requirements that vary from the student enrolled in a resident college. The career woman has clothing needs that differ from those of the homemaker. The working mother has apparel requirements that the socialite does not.

Consider your various roles and the kinds of clothing that each requires. The activities you participate in will also help you know your clothing needs. List all the kinds of things that you do for play, for pleasure. How many different kinds of clothing do your activities require? Can some of the clothing meet the needs of other roles and activities? (See Figures 15–1, 15–2, and 15–3.)

What is your style of life? Is it a very casual or informal style in which clothing is selected for comfort and durability? Or is it a formal type of life in which clothing needs are specific? Does your life have a great deal of variety which demands many different kinds of clothing?

15-1 Texture and design permit this ensemble to serve many activities and to meet unexpected weather changes. (Courtesy Cotton Producers Institute)

What are your clothing values? Do you enjoy clothing and fashion? Are you happiest with lots of beautiful, fashionable clothes? Are clothes of less importance to you than other factors in your life? Is a small, functional wardrobe the best for you?

These are the kinds of things that will give you clues to your wardrobe planning. Carefully consider all the factors influencing your life and activities. Develop a plan for apparel selection that is tailored to fit your individual needs.

15–2 Go-anywhere fashions by Michel Gama for Patou can be worn around the clock. The black cassock dress on the left is especially versatile for late-evening activities. (Courtesy Celanese Corporation)

Resources Available

After you have decided what you like and what you need, the next stop is to purchase the articles of clothing you desire. The amount of money available to you for this project will determine how rapidly your wardrobe plan will go into effect. The financially independent person, of course, has a great deal more money available for clothing than a family member. Studies reveal that about 9 per cent of the total family income is generally allotted for clothing expenditures. Women in their late teens and early twenties generally spend the largest percentage of their income on apparel. Actual dollar expenditures for clothing vary from as little as less than $100 a year to over $35,000 per annum, spent by those on the current Best Dressed List.

Those desiring to build a wardrobe must develop a priority list of their needs—that is, they must decide what items they need most and purchase these first. It is usually wisest to mix large and small expenditures and to purchase some things each season. A written plan is very essential to organized wardrobe development. How detailed your written plan is, of course, is up to you. Whatever works best for you is the right written plan. Consider the total needs of your wardrobe when developing your list. You will get a great deal of satisfaction from marking off your purchases.

15–3 Designer Stanley Nelson's fashion of giant houndstooth check in a classic daytime suit will meet fashion requirements for the most diverse schedule. (Courtesy National Cotton Council)

Building a wardrobe is a continuing process. Once the basic needs are met, the less essential items can be purchased. As the fashion scene changes, items of apparel should be reevaluated. As items are discarded because of wear or obsolescence, they should be replaced. Plan to make these expenditures over a period of time.

individuality in dress

THE SECRET OF THE WELL-DRESSED WOMAN [1]

The art of dressing is an art as complex and elusive as all the others. It, too, has its principles and traditions, known only to persons of taste because they harmonize with their inmost feelings. This art has little in common with money.

303

[1] Paul Poiret lived from 1880 to 1944. This article appeared in *Harper's Bazaar* when he was at the height of his influence just prior to World War I. His advice is as timely today as it was then. It is reprinted by courtesy of *Harper's Bazaar* from *Harper's Bazaar: One Hundred Years of the American Female* (New York: Random House, 1967).

304   *The woman whose resources are limited has no more cause for being dowdily dressed than the woman who is rich has reason to believe she is beautifully gowned. Except insofar as money can procure the services of a good dressmaker, of an artist who can judge his customer's style and garb her accordingly, the wealthy woman stands no better chances of being correctly dressed than the woman who must turn every penny before spending it.*

The contrary is very often true. Whereas the rich woman can satisfy her least caprice in a most haphazard fashion, the woman of average means, simply because she is actually forced to think about her wardrobe, is more apt to realize what is suitable to her and what is not. She learns how to choose and what to select. She acquires the art of dressing well.

And it is not an easy art to acquire. It demands a certain amount of intelligence, certain gifts, some of them among the rarest, perhaps—it requires a real appreciation of harmony of lines, of colors—ingenious ideas, absolute tact, and above all, a love of the beautiful and clear perception of values. It may be résuméd in two words—good taste

Taste is by no means developed by riches; on the contrary, the increasing demands of luxury are killing the art of dressing. Luxury and good taste are in inverse proportion to one another. The one will kill the other as machinery is crowding out handwork. In fact, it has come so far that many persons confuse the two terms. Because a material is expensive they find it beautiful; because it is cheap they think it must be ugly.

To give you an example. All women whose wealth may be measured beyond a certain figure invariably appear with a string of pearls around their necks. Pearls are essentially becoming to certain types only, and cannot possibly be suitable to all women, but they seem to have become a visible sign of social caste. To how many women does a pearl necklace add any beauty? How many women choose their pearl necklaces for reasons of good taste and style, that is to say, in order to set off the beauty of their coloring?

At the theater, in restaurants, you see hundreds of women more adorned than Indian idols. The most sparkling with jewels, the most expensively garbed, are never the most beautiful. Quite the contrary. Those who are most loaded down with precious stones, necklaces, bracelets, and rings rarely attract my attention. Sometimes I try to force myself to admire them. But it is impossible for me to feel anything more for them than for the dazzling setting of a jeweler's window, and the women who appear thus dressed in their fortune only would not appear one whit less attractive to me if they wore it in their hair as curling papers made out of banknotes!

Unfashionable to Follow Fashions

The well-dressed woman is the one who picks out her gown, her adornments, simply because they make her appear more pleasing, not because other people are wearing that style or because it will be a palpable proof of her husband's bank account. Because one woman chooses to emphasize the purity of her Grecian profile by winding a band of gold around her hair, why should twenty the next day and five hundred the day after that do their hair in the same style? But that is the way fashion sways women today. The only well-dressed women are those who dare and create original ideas, not those who servilely follow fashion.

In order not to appear entirely out of harmony with her surroundings and the place where she lives, a woman is obliged to follow fashions to a certain extent. But let that be within certain bounds! What does it matter if tight skirts be the fashion if your figure demands a wide one? Is it not more important to dress so as to bring out your good points rather than to reveal the bad? Can any idea of being fashionable make up for the fact of being ridiculous?

I dined the other day in a fashionable restaurant. At the tables around me I noticed at least half-a-dozen women whose hair was dressed in exactly the same way, with the same number of puffs and switches. All were dressed in equally expensive goods, although I was not able to judge of the colors because they were all equally overloaded with beading, embroideries, gold, silver, or steel ornaments, with laces and fringes.

These women, who, I imagine, were neither sisters nor friends, were all shaped in the same mold, that is to say, in the same kind of corsets, and they all wore jewels, pendants, and necklaces that, if not exactly alike, were at least of the same type. Every woman had adapted her body, her movements, and her taste to the commonplace desire of being fashionably dressed. And in looking at them I could not help thinking that in case of a panic their husbands or brothers or friends would be perfectly justified in mistaking one for the other.

Instead of hiding their individuality, why did not each woman try to bring out her personal type of beauty? One woman would have been more attractive without the puffs and switches; another would have been more beautiful in black; jewels were out of place on the third.

A Definition of the Well-Dressed Woman

But, curiously enough, women fear being called original or individual, but never hesitate to make fools of themselves in following the latest fashion. A woman will submit to any torture, any ridicule, if she believes she is worshipping the absurd goddess Fashion. Every year a certain very limited number of types of styles are seen, and almost all women may be classified under one of them. Only those who do not fit in under any particular heading are worthy of being called well dressed.

I cannot help feeling a vague contempt for those who ask at the beginning of the season, "What is to be the favorite color?" Choose the color that suits you, madame, and if someone tells you that red is to be worn, dare to wear violet and consider only what is suitable to you, *because there is only one single rule for the well-dressed woman, and the old Romans expressed it in one word—*decorum—*which means "that which is suitable."* That which is suitable!

Choose whatever is suitable to the time, the place, the circumstance, the landscape, the place you are staying, whether it be a large city, a village, or a watering-place!

15–4 This projection of glamour is fashioned in drapable and clingy crepe. Billowing sleeves are finished with crystal-beaded cuffs. The cinched waist is emphasized by the full bodice folds. The unusual treatment of the hat provides mysterious allure to complete an image of romance. (Courtesy Celanese Corporation)

Choose whatever is most in harmony with your character, for a dress can be the expression of a state of mind if you but try to make it. There are dresses that sing of joy of life, dresses that weep, dresses that threaten. There are gay dresses, mysterious dresses, pleasing dresses, and tearful dresses.

dressing for the occasion

306   Clothes are a form of artistic expression. They create definite moods and feelings through the personality of the garment. Clothes can project such images as glamour, romance, casualness, sportiness, severity, femininity, and masculinity.

(See Figures 15–4 through 15–8.) Clothes, being an art form, use the elements of design, texture, and color to express mood and feeling. These same elements delimit the garments by determining where they will go and for what occasions they are appropriate. Some clothing styles are very limited and indicate explicitly when and where they are appropriate. Other styles, because they are more subtle, are appropriate for a variety of activities, times, places, and individuals.

Apparel that strongly expresses where and when it can be worn is called "personality clothing." These articles have strong identifying characteristics which restrict them to a specific use, such as for sports or for formal attire. This type of clothing is expensive not only because of the initial outlay but because of the limited number of wearings it generally gets. Garments that have no strong identifying characteristics are labeled "nonpersonality clothes" (also known as basic clothes). "Nonpersonality" clothing is not easily remembered and therefore may be worn often with assurance. It has few, if any, design

15–5 Sporty casualness is the message of this outfit. Tailored lines combine with fabric textures to emphasize the mood. (Courtesy Eastman Chemical Products)

15–6 Ultrafeminine describes the image projected by this soft ruffled design for evening wear fashioned in metallic yarn. (Courtesy Penny Baker, Inc., Dow Badische)

15–7 At-home attire is characterized by sophistication of both fabric design and line. The bold, stylized, Persian design makes an unusual and striking impression. (Courtesy National Cotton Council)

15–8 Simplicity of dress typifies the youthful look of these ensembles.
Fabric textures support the mood of the clothes. (Courtesy Catalina)

details to distinguish it and therefore it may be accessorized in many ways
(Figure 15–9). Nonpersonality clothes are appropriate for many activities, times,
and places. Because of their versatility, they are basic to any wardrobe. Nonpersonality clothes are used a great deal; therefore, the money expended upon
them is well utilized.

Three elements determine to which category a garment will belong: texture,
cut, and trim. Each piece of clothing must be individually analyzed to determine
if it is a personality or nonpersonality garment. Certain fabrics such as satins,
laces, and velvet are always "personality." The more unique the cut of a
garment, the more "personality." Eye-arresting trims are "personality." These
details tell you where and when the garment is appropriate.

Nonpersonality clothes are made of smooth and flat textures. The cut of
these garments is never extreme or body revealing, and they usually are devoid
of trim. However, if there is trim, it is understated and inconspicuous, such as

15–9A A "personality" coat dress communicates when and where it can be worn. The shiny textured fabric rather than the cut and styling place it in this classification. (Courtesy Du Pont Company)

B "Nonpersonality dress." Basic lines and untextured fabrics do not limit the use of a dress to a particular time of day or occasion. This type of dress can be the most versatile in the wardrobe. It can be given personality by use of accessories.

hand picking. Because of their "nonpersonality," these garments are appropriate for many times, places, and occasions. When in doubt about what to wear, it is best to select the understated look of a nonpersonality garment.

Appropriate clothing for all occasions may be either personality or nonpersonality. The type of garments you prefer will depend on your personal preferences and on the amount of money you have available for clothing purchases. Listed below are the general classifications of clothing for special occasions. You may wish to select all personality or all nonpersonality clothes for these occasions. Remember the personality clothes are the most limited and therefore the most expensive. Nonpersonality clothes are more versatile, being appropriate for many occasions. Most wardrobes contain both types of clothing; the choice belongs to the individual.

STREET AND BUSINESS WEAR

Clothing considered appropriate for street and business wear has a covered or protective look (Figure 15–10). It is a utilitarian type of clothing which requires little care or concern while being worn. It should create a feeling of efficiency. This does not mean that it cannot be attractive; it simply means that while you are engaged in these activities, the garments you are wearing should be a background for you.

The color choices for street and business wear vary with the occupation, the geographic location, the local customs, and the fashion. Generally, darker hues are a more chic choice than lighter colors. Stark white is very often considered inappropriate; this is because it is too eye arresting on the street and too institutionalized for business.

With the wide variety of occupations available and the numerous clothing philosophies of employers, it is impossible to set down rigid clothing rules for the working person. The best guide is what is worn by the other staff members.

15–10 Business and street-wear clothes are subdued in color and design but they need not lack dash and excitement, as shown by this tailored skirt and weskit combined with a soft surah blouse. (Courtesy Celanese Corporation)

Some firms are extremely conservative in attitudes toward dress, while others are extremely avant-garde. The best-dressed employee is the one that can express his individuality within the limits defined by the employer.

Both personality and nonpersonality clothing have a place in this area of dress if they harmonize with the surroundings. The worst mistake any employee can make is to report for work dressed as if ready for a party. If you must leave from work for an evening engagement, bring the date clothes in a totebag ready for a quick switch. This is the time when an accessory change for a non-personality outfit can be the most effective. A flexible and versatile wardrobe is best for both street and business dress.

CASUAL OR SPORTSWEAR

American women, particularly those living in suburban areas, have truly embraced casual or sportswear. Into this classification fall sweaters, blouses, skirts, pants, and understated dresses. They usually are durable, easy care, comfortable, and suitable for a wide variety of times and activities, going from early morning until late evening, from PTA breakfasts to the local cinema. The non-personality type of dress adds even more flexibility to casual clothing. This type of clothing may be suitable for street and business depending on the locale; it is generally too informal for big city life.

CAMPUS WEAR

The local campus decrees what is suitable classroom attire. Fashion magazines are full of school fashions that would be out of place on many campuses. The best guide is an on-the-spot check of what is being worn. With this fashion knowledge you can then choose the attire you wish to wear.

Clothes selected from street and business attire or casual wear are all appropriate for the campus. The coed should adapt a type of dress that is most becoming to her. With the lessening of dress codes on most campuses, many girls have fallen into the trap of always wearing clothing selected for comfort rather than for appearance. If you do not look your best in pants, why wear them? If everyone else on campus seems to be affecting the sloppy look, must you? (See Figure 15–12.) College is a time to become an individual, not only in your thinking but in your dress also.

ACTIVE SPORTS

Each sport has a proper costume (Figure 15–13). These uniforms are truly classic in style. You should adopt an outfit that is appropriate for both the

15–11 This contemporary female adaptation of the "Civil War Look" by Teal Traina is classified as casual sportswear. This type of fashion has been popularized by suburban women because of its versatility. (Courtesy Celanese Corporation)

15–12 A ladylike cousin to the denim jeans family is this knit shirtdress, perfect for campus wear. (Courtesy California Fashion Creators)

15–13 Each sport has a proper costume. This tennis dress of traditional white is designed with both glamour and freedom of movement in mind. (Courtesy Eastman Chemical Products)

314 sport and you. Remember that the novice is conspicuous enough, so do not attract any unnecessary attention to yourself by the manner in which you dress. The extreme styles of clothing for any sport belong to the expert. Until you have mastered the skills required of any sport, choose more conservative attire.

AFTER-FIVE

This is the category of party clothes, which may be either personality or nonpersonality, as you prefer (Figure 15–14). Generally, these clothes are the most flamboyant in your wardrobe. They may be as extreme as your own personality will allow. You should be sensitive to those around you, however; some people are made uncomfortable by too much high fashion. If you are a single girl, you have much more freedom in selecting after-five wear. If you are a married woman, you really should consider your husband's attitude toward this

15–14 This after-five dress belongs to the "personality" category because of the unusual texture. The fabric is hand-crocheted, metallic yarn made in Lisbon by Castillo. (Courtesy Penny Baker, Inc., Dow Badische)

attire, especially in social situations where his business acquaintances are present. (See Figure 15–15.)

FORMAL WEAR—WOMEN

Formals differ from after-five wear in that they generally are more décolleté. They may be short or long. The only occasions that require a long gown are opening nights at the theater, diplomatic dinners, a Queen's reception, and an inaugural ball of a President! If you do not have occasion to wear a formal too often, it is best to select a classic design. This type can be worn over many, many years and remain lovely. A matching or blending jacket is also a good idea, as it eliminates the added expense of an appropriate wrap. To be most versatile, a formal should not be strapless, as this type of gown is not suitable for dining. It also should not be too bouffant, as you must be able to enter and

15–15 Anthony Muto's after-five gown of Qiana nylon expresses sophistication and femininity. Design details such as a plunging neckline and a waist-cinching sash support the image. (Courtesy Du Pont Company)

316 exit gracefully from vehicles and not take up more than one seat in the theater. Formals can be any color you choose, but you are wisest to select a color that will stay in fashion.

FORMAL WEAR—MEN

The traditional and most conventional evening clothes for men have basically been the same for years and will probably remain so. Fashion and fads come and go, such as peaked lapels for a dinner jacket being popular at one time and shawl collars at another, and they are not necessarily inappropriate (Figure 15–16). But when in doubt a man can always wear classic evening dress with confidence, knowing he will be correct and never criticized. Traditional evening dress, including accessories, is limited to black and white, with midnight blue being the only acceptable departure from this rule. Of course, the community custom, the occasion, and the man's age may make further departures possible. A dress suit—white tie and tails—permits no variations at all. Semiformal evening dress—black tie and dinner jacket—often does. The trousers worn with any dinner jacket should be black or midnight blue. Evening dress should never be worn before 6 P.M.

AT-HOME CLOTHES

At-home clothes can be anything you want. These are the clothes that express the real you (Figure 15–17). You may wish to wear the kooky and wild

15–16 Formal wear for men with a new approach to the traditional tuxedo. (Courtesy Men's Fashion Association of America, Inc.)

15–17 At-home attire can express the real you. This Leo Narducci hostess pajama features a giant mushroom print. (Courtesy Celanese Corporation)

15–18 A dramatic, poncho pants set for "at home," where you can wear exactly what you please. (Courtesy Cotton Producers Institute)

garb that makes high fashion so wonderful or choose these clothes for their simplicity and comfort. At home is the place to wear exactly what you please (Figure 15–18), and this is what this type of clothing should always be.

The only caution in this area of dress pertains to entertaining. As a host or hostess in your own home, you may not only wear what you wish but you must also inform your guests of what they should wear. Guests should know from the type of invitation issued what kind of garb they are expected to wear. If they are in doubt, generally they will ask. In your role as host or hostess, it is most unkind to tell your guests to wear one type of clothing while appearing in another type.

wardrobe essentials for women

Every wardrobe contains articles of clothing that are essential. Included in this grouping are coats, some dresses and suits, shoes, handbags, gloves, hats, and lingerie. Some of these items may not be essential to your particular wardrobe, but they are all considered vital to a complete wardrobe. These articles are more flexible and adaptable if they are nonpersonality items. If possible, it would be ideal to have each item suitable for wear in both cold and warm seasons.

Remember the reason that some women do not have anything to wear, although they have a closet full of clothes, is that clothes tell us where they will go. Developing a wardrobe of nonpersonality clothes will correct this situation, as these clothes can go most places and with most other things in the wardrobe. In planning a wardrobe, start to build with the nonpersonality items and add the personality items later.

Listed here are some things to look for when purchasing various apparel items. These articles of clothing would all fall into the nonpersonality category, but this does not mean that they need be drab or uninteresting. The color, fit, and accessories will give them flair and individuality. The purpose of these items is to build a nucleus of clothing that will complement and blend with everything else in the wardrobe. These items should be budgeted as large expenditures. You should buy the best quality you can afford. Many of these items should be in your wardrobe from seven to ten years.

NONPERSONALITY COAT

This is the coat that goes with everything. It is the backbone of the wardrobe. The coat collar will influence the whole wardrobe, so it should be selected wisely (see Chapters 13 and 14 on color). This coat will be a major expenditure and should last from seven to ten years in the wardrobe.

Style: Tuxedo, mandarin, or shawl. These three styles are always fashionable.

Fabric: Flat nap, firmly woven wool. Very little, if any, surface interest.

Coat length: One inch longer than the dress length. It should have some fullness so that it can be worn over full-skirted dresses.

Sleeve length: Long, straight sleeves with no cuff. The sleeves should have some fullness so they will be comfortable when worn over other long sleeves.

Buttons: The fewer the buttons, the better. The buttons should be inconspicuous; self-covered are the best. Buttons limit how much the coat can be worn. For example, bone or rhinestone buttons tell you where the coat can go.

Pockets: Slit pockets in the side seam are best.

Trim: It is best if there is none; however, some detailing in the same fabric is permissible. Any fur trim must be completely and easily removable.

Color: Staple color, of your choice.

Lining: Same color as the coat. Patterned linings clash with some garments.

NONPERSONALITY SUIT

Style: Classic or dressmaker.

Fabric: Firmly woven, lightweight wool, wool double knit, flannel, or worsted. For warm weather, lightweight, nonwrinkle fabrics.

Jacket length: Three to four inches below waist. Avoid extreme lengths, as they become dated.

Skirt width: Easy fit for comfortable movement.

Sleeve length: Full length, no cuff.

Buttons: Three-button closing with buttons ending just above the bustline. The jacket should look good both buttoned and unbuttoned. Inconspicuous or self-covered buttons are best.

Pockets: Slit in the side seam or none.

Trim: None unless in self-fabric.

Color: Any solid color; avoid white and pastels. Grayed or medium colors have the longest wearing qualities.

Lining: Same color as the suit.

The suit can be worn with many varied types of accessories, so that it may be dressed up or down.

NONPERSONALITY DRESS

Style: Should not point toward any time of day. Moderate neckline, some sleeve, skirt not too tight or too full. Choose the style that is best for you.

Detail: Very little if any; this dress is to be accessorized in many ways, so should have no pattern.

Fabric: Very little surface texture, firmly woven, nonwrinkle, soil resistant.

Color: Any color suitable for you. Solid colors are more versatile than patterned fabrics.

SHOES, HANDBAG, GLOVES

These three items should be coordinated but not necessarily matched. They may be of the same fabric or leather and be of the same color. Each wardrobe should have these items in the staple color selected for the basic coat. These should be of the best quality you can afford, for with care they will last for many years. Each of these items should be selected for simplicity of design. They should have no extra ornamentation which will limit their use or date them.

HATS

Whether or not you wear a hat depends very much on the kind of life you lead and local fashion. A hat may be worn to certain social affairs and usually to church.

If a hat is worn, it should be a "hatty" hat. Avoid the wisps of veil, ribbon, and flowers that look as if you could not make up your mind. A hat is selected to complement your entire person, so check it from all angles before deciding (including from the full-length rear view). The hat should complement the costume and the occasion. The texture of the hat is its most limiting feature. Do not wear pastel straw hats in cold weather or fur hats in hot weather.

LINGERIE

With the technological explosion in this area of apparel, it is impossible to set down firm and fast rules. This apparel should be carefully selected for fit and comfort. Bras and girdles should always be fitted by a trained expert. Periodic refitting is a wise idea, as the body changes shape as one matures. These garments must fit the figure in many different ways; incorrect fitting can cause permanent damage to delicate muscle tissue.

The market in this field is continually changing, and wonderful new ideas are constantly becoming available. Individual preference decrees exactly which garments are worn and in what combination. Comfort and the appearance of outside apparel over the undergarments should be the guide in selection of these garments.

Lingerie must never be visible through fashion clothes unless this is part of the garment design. Dark lingerie with light outer clothing is not sexy, just poor taste. Little rosebuds and bowknots showing through bodices are just as bad as polka dots or tiger stripes discernible under light-colored slacks. Bumps and bulges showing the outlines of undergarments distort even the most expensive outer fashions.

Properly fitted undergarments selected in solid black and white are the best ways to avoid the *faux pas* mentioned above. Remember that dark clothes require dark underpinnings, light clothes need light undergarments, and the two colors of lingerie should never be integrated!

predicting fashion trends

Learning to study the current fashion scene for clues to future trends is an important part of wardrobe planning. Of course, no one can state exactly what will become fashion. Fashion is dependent on the buying public, which is made up of the people who choose the styles that become fashion. But skills can be developed to discern the advances made by certain styles on their way to becoming fashion.

Generally speaking, a fashion has a seven-year life span. It takes two years for it to come in, three years to enjoy popularity, and two years to fade away. Buying on the incoming trend assures much longer wear and use than buying when the fashion is on the wane.

Texts for the study of new fashion are magazines such as *Harper's Bazaar, Vogue, Mademoiselle, Glamour,* and *Seventeen.* The European fashion magazines such as *Linea Italiana* and *L'Officiel* are excellent references also. The trade newspaper, *Women's Wear Daily,* contains technical and merchandising information along with fashion reports from many metropolitan areas in the world. Some fashion publications for men include *Gentlemen's Quarterly, Esquire, California Men's Stylist,* and *The Daily News Record.* Scrutinize these publications carefully. Look at the colors and combinations of colors featured. Notice the textures used. Study the silhouettes and design lines. Note the garment lengths, sleeve cut, shoulder lines, neck treatments, and waist placements. How is the look put together? What are the shoe styles, and how are they combined with hosiery? What other accessories seem to be featured? How many times do certain styles appear? Do the styles vary greatly from what has been fashionable? What are the models featured in the advertisements wearing? How do these looks compare with the ones featured in the magazine?

What you see in the high-fashion magazines is adapted and modified before it is accepted as fashion. Much of high fashion never becomes fashion. Yet high fashion is one important source of all fashion. It is the one kind of fashion influence that may be studied and analyzed in detail.

Fashion evolves very gradually, and the student must be very observant to discern the subtle clues of change. Picking fashion trends in advance is fun and profitable. By spending clothing dollars on incoming fashion trends, the longevity of the investment is assured. New styles are also featured in clothing stores, in both displays and fashion shows. For some, studying actual garments is better than looking at them in high-fashion magazines; it is often easier to see the subtle nuances of fashion change.

clothing customs

While the total fashion picture is a continually changing one, some areas of the United States cling to clothing customs that are part of their tradition. Subtle local conventions of dress prevail in many areas, as do food patterns, types of architecture, and speech patterns. When traveling or relocating to a new area, one should be sensitive to the new environment and respect its customs of dress.

In many suburban and rural areas, casual cothing is worn for all but very formal occasions; in many metropolitan areas clothing of a more dressy nature is preferred. Dress customs on the East and West Coasts and in some parts of the South are more high fashion than those of other parts of the country. Mass media and modern transportation have, of course, penetrated and informed the isolated areas by providing visual images of what people are wearing around the world and also the means to get to where fashions are sold. But the fact remains that local customs of dress are still prevalent. Some areas are extremely conservative and slow to adopt a new look. Other areas are less conventional and welcome a strong, individualized appearance. Within all communities are subgroups, both social and business, which have their own clothing traditions. Clothing differences in each geographic area reflect the modes of living, tastes, economic and social status, values, attitudes, interests, and activities of the inhabitants.

In the past clothing customs were more sharply defined than they are today. A New Yorker or San Franciscan was able to identify the tourist by his dress. Some visitors were marked by their pastel suits, white shoes, and absence of hats and gloves. Male tourists were conspicuous because of their bright sport shirts, summer suits, and light-colored shoes. Today there is a national trend toward the wearing of more casual dress of the entire color spectrum.

Many subtle differences remain to identify the clothing habits of various geographic areas. A covered-up look for women for street wear continues to be the custom in northern metropolises. In many southern cities an informal and less covered appearance is acceptable. Pants and shorts are seen on many women in suburban shopping centers; this attire would be considered inappropriate in some metropolitan areas. In many small towns the dress is far more conservative than in the large city. The wearing of furs, jewels, and ostentatious clothing is often contrary to what many small-town people consider good taste. Big-city citizens often wear clothing at night that reveals what they felt necessary to cover by day.

It is impossible to pinpoint geographical areas and their clothing customs with complete accuracy. These customs do evolve with the times, but it is well established that differences do occur. The student of clothing can discern upon close observation what is accepted and not accepted in each area.

When making a change to a new geographical location, it is wisest to wear rather conservative clothing until the local customs can be investigated. Remember that acceptance of a newcomer may be largely based upon the first impression and that clothing is an important part of that impression. The manner of dress will be interpreted in the frame of reference of the observer. By wearing classical clothing in subdued colors and a minimum of jewelry, with an understated hair style and make-up, a woman will be properly attired. Once you understand the clothing customs that exist, you can express your individuality with more assurance. By following this conservative approach, you may appear slightly dull to some, but you will avoid a *faux pas* that might take years to live down.

If your clothing philosophy will not allow you to adapt to the local customs of a new environment, the consequences of not being accepted must be faced. The importance of social acceptance or rejection is a highly personalized matter. In an employment situation (yours or your spouse's) gaining the approval and respect of the townsfolk may be essential. Acceptable dress, by their standards, may be a key to this acceptance.

the travel wardrobe

In this wonderful age everyone can expect to travel. Planning a travel wardrobe is an essential part of the preparation and contributes greatly to the success of the trip. Every travel wardrobe has certain criteria to be considered: it must meet climate changes, be wearable for many types of occasions, be attractive

15–19 A travel wardrobe should include basic items that can be accessorized in many ways. These knits would make ideal travel clothes, as each piece can serve several uses. (Courtesy Catalina)

and comfortable, wrinkle free, and easily maintained. It must provide adequate clothing changes without being a burden to carry. If the wardrobe is selected to fulfill these basic needs, it can travel all over the world for months at a time and be most appropriate. (See Figure 15–19.)

Clothes in the existing wardrobe should be the basis for planning what needs to be added for travel. Apart from the money-saving factor, clothing that has been worn has already been tested for personal satisfaction and maintenance. Shoes that are known to be comfortable are a much wiser choice than brand new ones. A purse that has withstood the rigors of daily use has already proven its durability. When purchasing the needed new items for your trip, allow some time for wear before you depart. These newer items can then be checked out for service and comfort.

A good travel wardrobe is one you can carry yourself—baggage handlers are often the scarcest when you need them the most. And public transportation seldom waits for anyone; it may be necessary for you to carry your bags and run for a plane, train, or bus. Each time your bags are handled, money for tips is required. The more experienced the traveler, the more condensed his belongings. One suitcase and one handbag are the recommended amount of baggage. This allows you to be more mobile and independent because you are not weighted down by extras.

The clothing selected for a travel wardrobe should be nonpersonality essentials which do not know time or place. Select clothing can be accessorized with weightless items. Work out color harmonies, so that each item is coordinated with the others. Coat and sweaters should be selected to go with all other items.

Each item of apparel should have many uses. A coat of opaque, easy-care fabric can double as a robe. This coat should be an all-weather coat, good looking enough to go from train and rain to dining and dancing. Skirts and blouses and pants and shirts can be mixed and matched for variety. When planning clothes for a long trip, keep in mind that you will be making grand entrances in many places where no one has seen any of your wardrobe. The clothes will become monotonous to you, but not to anyone else.

Study the customs of the places you plan to visit. Do not take clothing that will be inappropriate. In some areas sleeveless dresses are just as offensive as pants on women. Learn these things in advance, so you will not take useless items and risk being a rude tourist.

Fabrics that travel especially well are knits. They do not wrinkle, and they can be packed into the suitcase by rolling rather than by folding. Good travel fibers are wool, polyester, acrylics, nylon, and permanent-press blends. By selecting clothes made of these fibers, you can eliminate the necessity of carrying a heavy travel iron. Any packing wrinkles which do develop can be "hung out."

You must be able to maintain a travel wardrobe yourself. It is both very time consuming and expensive to depend on others to do it for you. Washable clothing should dry wrinkle-free when hung on a hanger over the bathtub. Other clothes must resist wrinkling and spots. Providing your own clothesline and detergent in plastic bags makes your laundry chores much easier.

Shoes are vitally important to travel. A wise selection can reduce shoe needs to two or three pairs for a trip lasting several months. One pair should be suitable for dress as well as touring. One pair should be selected for solid comfort and be sturdy enough to endure miles of walking and sightseeing. The third pair might be sandals if warm weather is anticipated. Women's sandals should be selected so that they may be considered somewhat dressy and appropriate for evening wear.

The handbag featured for travel is usually an oversized one which can become extremely heavy and tiring to carry. A smaller leather purse with several zippered compartments to accommodate billfold, traveler's checks, passport, keys, pad, pen, and a few personal items is all that is really necessary. A type of handbag that has an adjustable shoulder strap is a good idea, for it frees both hands for carrying luggage or taking pictures.

PACKING

The lightest weight suitcases are made of canvas and have zippered openings. Those with firm sides and soft top and bottom give the greatest packing space. The zipper must be well inserted, for if this fails the bag is useless.

Pack in layers. Place the heaviest items on the bottom first. This will include shoes wrapped in plastic bags, drugs, cosmetics, which should be transferred to small, nonbreakable bottles, and film. Underwear can go on top of this.

To pack suits and dresses, make a separate compartment for them. Cut out a layer of heavy cardboard about one inch smaller than the area of the suitcase. Fix two long grosgrain ribbons to each end of the cardboard by cutting slashes about one inch in from the edge of the cardboard. Thread the ribbon through the slashes. When these garments are stacked on the cardboard and the ribbons tied, they all remain in place. It is easy to get to items on the bottom by lifting the entire bundle.

When folding dresses and suits, button them and fold accordion-style from the skirt up, with the sleeves folded over last. Keep the surface the size of the cardboard insert. If a garment tends to wrinkle, lay one atop the other and fold the two together as one.

Plastic food bags are helpful for keeping underwear separate. They take less room than the type you buy at the notions counter, they are much less expensive, and the items packed can be seen readily. Carry detergent flakes in several layers of plastic bags, closed by a rubber band. Carry extra bags for wet bathing suits and laundry which did not dry. A shower cap can double as a carrier for your face cloth. An evening bag can be used to carry jewelry.

If luggage is not packed tightly or is not full, there is a greater chance of wrinkles forming. Stuffing hosiery, underwear, and toilet-seat covers in the cracks will help eliminate this problem.

In your small handbag put all the items it takes to make you comfortable. This would be a change of clothing or night wear, cosmetics or razor, hair-care equipment, medicines, and other personal items vital to your existence. When you travel from one place to another, keep this bag with you. Often luggage that is checked through on public transportation vehicles is delayed or lost. By carrying these items, you can avoid some of the inconveniences which will befall your fellow tourists.

conclusion

Wardrobe planning takes some time and some effort, but its rewards are great. The properly planned wardrobe is customized to your individual needs and therefore can be done only by you. The life you lead and plan to lead, your values, attitudes, and interest toward clothing—all influence your clothing choices. What you have in your wardrobe at present, your anticipated needs, and the monies available for clothing influence your planning.

suggested readings

Chambers, Helen, and Verna Moulton. *Clothing Selection.* Philadelphia: J. B. Lippincott Company, 1969.

Erwin, Mabel, D. and Lila A. Kinchen. *Clothing for Moderns,* 4th ed. London: The Macmillan Company, 1969.

Horn, Marilyn J. *The Second Skin.* Boston: Houghton Mifflin Company, 1968.

Juster, Harry. *Clothes Make the Man.* New York: Bartell Macfadden, 1965.

Tate, Mildred T. and Oris Glisson. *Family Clothing.* New York: John Wiley & Sons, Inc., 1961.

Trahey, Jane (ed.). *Harper's Bazaar: 100 Years of the American Female.* New York: Random House, Inc., 1967.

Vogue's Book of Etiquette and Good Manners. New York: Condé Nast Publications, Inc., 1969.

16

fit in clothing

t he manner in which clothing fits your body is an important factor in clothing selection. It determines whether an appearance of quality and beauty is achieved by the apparel. Even the most carefully constructed garment made of the finest fabric cannot give the appearance of quality if it fits poorly.

On the stage both comic and pathetic roles are often characterized by dressing the actors in ill-fitting clothing. In the role of the comic, the clown wears oversized pants and shirts that can be counted on to draw laughs. The role of the pathetic character, dressed in clothing that is too tight or too loose, evokes pity. Although these are examples of the extremes in the fitting of clothing, they illustrate a point. Improper fit can never make us appear attractive or give our clothing a look of quality. Proper fit can give one a feeling of physical comfort and great self-confidence.

Apparel presented in fashion showings is fitted to the model who will wear the garment to insure that it will be presented in the best manner possible. If our personal standards of fit meet those used by professional models, our clothes will make us achieve a more attractive appearance.

fit in motion

To determine whether a garment fits, it must be observed from all angles in front of a triple, full-length mirror. Underclothing and height of shoe heel should be the same as that which will be worn with the garment. This is very important because underclothing can change the fit and hang considerably. French couture houses make underclothing for each gown to insure correct fit of the outer garment.

Remember that a garment is both worn and seen in motion as well as standing still. Check to determine if it looks attractive and feels comfortable while you are sitting, standing, walking, and bending. If it is an active sports garment, such as a bathing suit, tennis outfit, or ski pants, bend, twist, and reach to decide whether it is comfortable and does not strain when these movements are made. Women's wraparound skirts and coat-dresses should be carefully observed while walking and sitting in order to judge whether the overlap and underlap are of sufficient width and do not reveal underclothing.

fit determined by style, use, and preference

The design of a garment, its use, and your personal requirements will determine its fit. The amount of ease, drape, length, shoulder placement, and closeness to the body which the garment has should be considered. Some garments are designed to be somewhat loose on the body; others are intended to fit more snugly. The amount of ease allowed is always a matter of personal preference. Some people prefer ample ease, while others feel more comfortable in closely fitted garments. It must be remembered, however, that a very tight- or a very loose-fitting garment will affect the appearance of the figure contours. Often a very thin person who wears a very loose-fitting garment will, because of extreme contrast, look thinner. A moderately close-fitting garment, when worn by a thin person, generally does not effect a thin look because there is no extreme contrast. A heavy person in a somewhat loose fit looks less heavy because of the lack of contrast between the silhouette created by the garment as compared with that of the body. You can experiment with this principle by comparing sleeve widths and lengths on the arm and pant styles on the legs. Legs and arms look larger in close-fitting styles than in loose-fitting lines. Tight-fitting garments will also reveal body defects by emphasizing their contours. Defects can be concealed by the use of adequate ease and of textures that do not cling to the body.

sizing of clothing for women

Shops and stores have clothing grouped together by categories known as Misses, Junior, and Women's, or half-sizes. In some lines there are groupings of Teen, Petite, and other subdivisions as well. These are figure divisions rather than age groupings. However, the larger sizes grouped as Women's feature styles intended for the mature woman and are not often youthful in design. They are cut for the figure with larger bust, waist, and hips. The Junior group is designed for a height of 5 ft, 2 inches, and under. These are sized in odd numbers such as 9 and 11 and are youthful in style. Half-sizes are cut for the short figure but for one that is fuller in the bust, waist, and hip. Misses are intended for the woman of average height and proportions and are numbered evenly as 10, 12, and so on.

Size numbers do not represent the same sizes with every manufacturer. As the price goes up, the size sometimes gets smaller in number. This usually is because of the quality of construction in the more expensive garment. A woman may wear a size 14 in an inexpensive dress and a size 10 in an expensive costume. For this reason, you may have a range of sizes in your closet. (Sizing and fit for men are found in Chapter 17.)

JUDGING FIT ON THE INDIVIDUAL WOMAN

Many women are not aware of what constitutes a properly fitting garment. Make a general observation of the grain direction of the fabric. If grain is not correct, further consideration should not be given to the dress. The cloth must be cut on true grain; that is, the lengthwise grain is intended to be exactly perpendicular to the floor at the center front and center back, and the cross grain is parallel to the floor across the chest, upper back, and hip area. There are exceptions to this, such as bias cut, which may appear in the entire dress or parts of the dress. Bias-cut skirts provide flare at the bias area. If a dress is intended to be cut on strength of grain and it is off just a little, the garment will not hang properly, and alterations become either impossible to make or inadvisable. The dress should not be purchased.

Examine each area of the body for diagonal wrinkles. These indicate a problem. Follow the diagonal wrinkles to their source, and you will usually find the cause. Sometimes horizontal wrinkles appear. This usually means the garment is too long for that section of the body.

Check the neck, shoulder, and upper sleeve area. It is important that these areas fit properly because they are the most difficult and costly to alter. Notice where the armhole-seam and shoulder-seam length coincide with the body. Some garments are designed with extended shoulder length so that the set-in sleeve begins at the edge of the shoulder. This is found in most tailored shirts and shirtdresses. The sleeve does not have extra fullness in the sleeve cap because it is not needed with the extended shoulder. Sleeves that are set in at the ball-and-socket joint have extra fullness eased into the sleeve cap to accommodate the upper arm muscle.

In the same area notice if the lower armhole is cut deeply enough to be comfortable but not so long that the hemline is raised when the arms are raised. The shoulders must fit comfortably. The length and slant of the shoulder seam coincide with the body underneath. The area across the upper back section must have enough width so that a person can move the arms forward sufficiently to drive a car, or to place arms forward on a table or desk without undue strain at the back armhole seam.

The collar at the neckline should fit the back and sides of the neck snugly unless this section is designed to definitely stand away from the body. A scoop-neck dress must fit snugly around the chest area so that it does not gap when bending forward or moving the arms.

Sleeve width should be adequate to cover the heavy upper arm muscle and not silhouette the bulge. When arms are at the sides, no diagonal wrinkles should appear in the sleeve area. Sleeve lengths vary. Wrist-length sleeves reach or cover the prominent wrist bone unless the garment is designed to accommodate a cuff that is intended to show below this area. Elbow darts or fullness should be located at the elbow. If a long sleeve is designed with one dart, this is directed to the elbow joint; if it has two darts, the space in the middle of the two darts should meet the elbow. A three-darted sleeve has the middle dart pointed to the elbow. The arm is slightly bent when checking this area.

The fullness in the bust area is provided for by the use of darts, gathers, or curved seams. Full-body curves require darts that are deep at the base; small-body curves need darts that are proportionately smaller at the base. Therefore, a person with a large bust will need deeper darts than the smaller busted person. The reason for this is that deep darts create more fullness than shallow darts. This dart principle will apply to any area of the body, such as the hip and shoulder. Darts must *point* to the area of greatest fullness. They do not extend beyond the area of greatest curve. Bust darts are directed to the point of bust. If they come above or below this area, they do not release the fullness where it is needed. The underarm bust dart comes within 1½ to 2 inches of the bust point. Waistline darts directed to the bust end ½ inch below the bust point, and long diagonal French darts which start at the hip side seam end at, or just short of, the bust point.

When princess styling is used in garments, the fullness required at the bust area is provided by means of curved seams. The fullest part of the curve must coincide with the fullest part of the bust. This would be an impossible alteration because the fabric is cut into the curve, and it is not possible to change this.

If bust fullness does not meet the fullness provided in the garment, all that may be needed is to adjust the brassiere straps. If this does not help, the darts must be altered (this cannot be done if dart has been slashed or fabric distorted). One of the most common fitting problems is incorrect placement of bust darts.

Vertical ease across the bust and waist must be adequate so that the dress does not draw across this fleshy area. Some dresses are worn so tightly that the dress acts as a foundation garment and reveals folds of flesh. This is never very fashionable.

The waistline of a fitted garment or of one that has a seam at the natural waistline meets the waist at the smallest area. If the waistline of the dress hits above or below this area, the garment will never be comfortable.

Gathers are also used to give fullness. Gathers below the bust or above the hip area should be placed to allow fullness where it is needed. Gathers over the abdomen will add visual fullness to an area where it may not be flattering.

Vertical fullness at the hip and thigh area is adequate if it allows room for movement and provides space so that the skirt does not ride up toward the waist. If a skirt is tight, it will move up and cup in the seat area. A straight skirt should have at least 2 inches of ease in the hip area; you should be able to pinch ½ inch out of each side seam. Another method of testing is to lift the skirt upward above the hip line; it should slide down into place easily. Front and back hip darts are directed to but do not extend beyond the full part of the body curve.

Side seams should fall straight down toward the ankle from the hip. The center front and center back are also perpendicular to the floor. This can be checked by using a plumb line much like masons use when building. Place a weight at the end of a string. Hold the string at hip level at the sides, center front, and back. Because of gravitational pull, the weight will fall, making the string perpendicular to the floor. The seams should follow the string. If the side seam pulls forward, the thigh may need more room than the skirt front allows or the back may be flat below the waist, not filling in the room allowed at the skirt back. A dress with a waistline seam or a skirt can be raised at the waist back to bring this seam in a line perpendicular to the floor. A dress without a waistline seam could only be altered from the side seams. The front seam would need to be let out or the back seam made deeper, or both. Inadequate seam allowance usually makes this impossible. If side seams are directed toward the back of the string, there is probably not enough skirt back fullness to accommodate the derriere.

Skirts with pleats should not spread at the pleat when a person is standing. If this occurs, the skirt is too tight. The same applies to slash and set-in pockets.

Skirt length is determined by fashion, a woman's legs, and her age. A skirt is equidistant from the floor on all sides unless the style dictates otherwise.

Coats fit with sufficient ease so that they may be worn over a suit or a dress with sleeves. Armholes must be deep enough to accommodate the garments worn underneath. Suit jackets must allow for a sweater or blouse to be worn under them. Full-length coats should be about 1 inch longer than the dress length, so that the dress is not visible as the body moves.

When checking the fit of slacks, sit down to see if the crotch is long enough. If it is too long, it will be baggy in the seat. If it is too short, the back waistline will drop down. If slacks are too tight in the thigh, wrinkles appear in the front crotch area. If the slacks have a crease down the front as design detail, this must hang in a straight line. No diagonal wrinkles should appear in the pants in a standing position.

TO ALTER OR NOT TO ALTER

Some alterations are possible, others are not. Alteration costs are always high, and this may boost the price of the garment considerably. If major changes need to be made in the areas of the shoulder sleeve and neckline and in lined garments, it may be wisest not to buy the garment. It may not be possible to alter certain garments for several reasons. Some alterations interfere with design lines that cannot be changed. Some alterations may change the general proportions and the scale of the individual sections so that they do not look aesthetically right for the body. Some manufacturers may not have allowed the necessary seam allowance needed for letting out seams. Many garments have slashes in darts and seam allowances which were used for matching seams. Lack of fabric use would make it impossible to let out these areas. Fabric construction and finishes may not permit alterations. Some fabrics leave holes when former stitching lines are removed. Removing a press mark in hems and seams is a major problem with some fabrics such as durable press, crease-resistant finishes, taffeta, and some synthetics and blends.

If you understand how to make alterations, it is possible to have the needed changes pinned at the store and do them yourself. Changing hem lengths and taking in seams are minor alterations and usually can be done without difficulty by a person who has some knowledge of sewing.

Personal weight change is often noticed first by a difference in the way clothing fits. It is difficult to keep up with the necessary clothing adjustments when great weight changes occur, but it is especially important that this be done. Both comfort and appearance will be enhanced if alterations are made. Remember that clothing that fits too tightly or too loosely will exaggerate body defects and call attention to them.

summary

The correct placement of fabric grain should be first checked when deciding whether to buy a new garment. Fabric cut off grain will never be satisfactory, and these garments should not be considered. The placement of garment fullness must coincide with body curves. Darts are directed to the full curves of the body and do not extend beyond them. Appearance of wrinkles indicates the garment is too tight, too loose, or too long for the area in which they appear.

It is not advisable to have some garments altered because of design, expense, and fabric construction. Durable press and some synthetics and blends leave impressions of removed stitching lines which are not possible to remove.

Proper fit will make a garment look as though it were created just for you. An attractive appearance can never be achieved unless the garment fits correctly. Without proper fitting, a look of quality cannot be attained.

suggested readings

Bishop, Edna B., and Marjorie S. Arch. *Fashion Sewing by the Bishop Method.* New York: J. B. Lippincott Company, 1966.

Brockman, Helen L. *Theory of Fashion Design.* New York: John Wiley & Sons, Inc., 1965.

Erwin, Mabel D., and Lila A. Kinchen. *Clothing for Moderns.* London: The Macmillan Company, 1969.

Siemen, Esther. "Principles of Fittings." Springfield, Ill.: University of Illinois, College of Agriculture Extension Service in Agriculture and Home Economics, Springfield, Ill.: 1962.

Sommerfield, Edna. *Fitting Dresses.* Washington, D.C.: U.S. Department of Agriculture, Farmers' Bulletin No. 1964.

17

family clothing needs and buying guides

ach one of us is aware of specific requirements that we expect our clothing to satisfy. The amounts and kinds of garments we buy hopefully will serve our individual social, emotional, physical, and aesthetic needs. The types of clothing we purchase depend on such factors as age, geographic location, local customs, sex, occupation, roles, activities, and income. Within the family the problem of meeting the clothing needs of each individual is compounded because of the requirements of each of the several family members. An understanding of these individual requirements is essential if satisfactory clothing purchases are to be made.

Further, it is important to have reliable information regarding the workmanship and fiber quality of specific items which are to be purchased in order to obtain maximum value for the money spent. Increasing apparel prices make it necessary for the average consumer to be knowledgeable about both clothing needs and practical guides for buying.

The clothing needs and buying guides included in this chapter are intended to help the consumer obtain maximum value for money spent on clothing for the individual family members. The articles of clothing described are selected to encompass only the major and most often purchased garments rather than the entire family wardrobe. Listed within this chapter in the suggested readings are books and pamphlets which can be referred to for more exhaustive and comprehensive buying guides for all articles of clothing.

infant wear

Clothing requirements from birth to six months are few. The principal clothing needs of the newborn infant are for warmth, comfort, and cleanliness. (Figure 17–1.) Clothing should be easy to maintain, light in weight, soft, simple to put on and take off. The type of clothing needed will depend on geographic location and heating conditions of the home.

The baby's principal activity for the first few months is sleeping. This gradually tapers off, so that by one year sleeping will occupy only half the time.[1] Babies sleep in diapers, shirts, and a short jacket called a sacque. The use of these garments eliminates the need for a complete change when diapering. Some babies sleep in gowns or sleepers. A sleeper is a garment that has accommodation for the feet. (See Figure 17–2.) Sleepers styled with space for each leg can be purchased with two pairs of pants. Those which hold both legs in the same space are shaped somewhat like a bag and are available in styles with a hem which can be let down for growth. Sleepers ensure that the baby will keep warm after the covers have been kicked off. A garment called a "sleep-and-play set" can be used for all baby activities; this is made of two-way stretch terrycloth or cotton knit (Figure 17–3).

Shirts and diapers form the basic wardrobe for the baby. Cotton shirts can be found in styles with or without sleeves, slip-on, or double-breasted front openings (easier to put on and take off) with snap enclosures. Some shirts have waterproof tabs for pinning the diaper to the shirt.

Diapers are available in a wide variety of fabrics, shapes, and sizes. It is more economical to purchase the largest size diaper that can be used throughout the entire period of diapering. Gauze diapers are not bulky, they dry quickly, and they are soft and absorbent. They are available in prefolded styles, which save time and storage space. Regulation-style gauze measures 27 × 27 inches. Birdseye is absorbent, but it is bulky and does not dry as fast as gauze. Flannelette diapers are soft and warm, but they are bulky and do not dry quickly. Cotton knit diapers are tubelike in shape and fit more like panties. Diaper liners can be used with any style diaper; they reinforce the diaper, giving greater protection.

[1] Mildred T. Tate and Oris Glisson, *Family Clothing* (New York: Wiley, 1961), p. 172.

17–1 A baby's clothing needs encompass warmth, comfort, and cleanliness. A soft velour, terry sleeper zips down the leg for easy diaper changing. (Courtesy Kiddie Kover, Jayvee Brands)

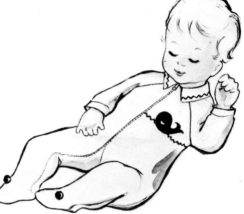

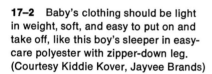

17–2 Baby's clothing should be light in weight, soft, and easy to put on and take off, like this boy's sleeper in easy-care polyester with zipper-down leg. (Courtesy Kiddie Kover, Jayvee Brands)

17–3 Matched five-piece layette set includes two-piece sleeper, blanket, bib, and hat made of cotton-textured terry-cloth. (Courtesy Kiddie Kover, Jayvee Brands)

Disposable diapers which were formerly used only for travel have become regular diaper wear for many babies. These are made of several layers of cellulose material. Some brands feature a hydrophobic liner (which remains dry) that draws moisture away from the baby's skin to the adjacent layers, thus keeping the baby dry. Diapers with an outer plastic covering eliminate the need for waterproof pants. The plastic layer must be removed before disposing the diaper into the toilet.

Diaper costs vary. Buying your own supply and laundering them at home is the least costly. The use of diaper liners, diaper service, or disposable diapers may increase costs considerably. These conveniences must be evaluated in terms of the time and money available.

The stretch "sleep-and-play sets" previously mentioned are but one type of the many garments made of stretch fabrics now available for babies and young children. These garments, of nylon, cotton, and rayon, have replaced many of the traditional clothes. They reduce the need for concern with the baby's exact size—stretch clothing is only available in two sizes: 0–12 months and 12–24 months. They eliminate binding, because they stretch gently with the baby's growth. Most garments are one piece and have front openings. It is easy to care for stretch apparel, and no ironing is required. They are available in shirts, pajamas, play sets, and stockings.

The suggested needs for the first six months are

3 dozen diapers	*For the crib*
3–4 long or short sleeve shirts	1–2 blankets
3–4 cotton-receiving blankets	5–6 sheets
6 sacques or kimonos	2 mattress pads
1 wrapping blanket	*For the bath*
1 sweater and cap	3 towels
1 dress-up outfit	3 face cloths
2 waterproof pants	
2 stretch coveralls	

creeper age

The creeping baby needs clothes for protection (Figure 17–4). Dresses, while pretty and feminine, are an impediment to creeping because they get in the way and do not offer adequate protection. (Figure 17–5.) Overalls shield tender knees from floor and carpet burns. Reinforcements in the knees of pant legs will

17–4 For the creeper set, a two-piece no-iron knit, knee saving for the child and labor saving for the mother. (Courtesy Kiddie Kover, Jayvee Brands)

17–5 Girl's "diaper set" of no-iron batiste with matching pants in a most feminine style. (Courtesy Kiddie Kover, Jayvee Brands)

17–6 "All-boy" styling of no-iron batiste polyester and cotton. (Courtesy Kiddie Kover, Jayvee Brands)

17–7 A sleep-and-play set of wash-and-wear fabric—features plastic-covered soles and zippered front for easy dressing. (Courtesy Kiddie Kover, Jayvee Brands)

17–8 When temperatures drop, a snowsuit is a must. Attached hood cannot stray and get lost. (Courtesy National Recreation and Park Association)

provide for greater durability. Snappers or grippers on the crotch of overalls save time when diaper changes are necessary (Figure 17–6). Garments of firmly woven or knitted fabrics with appropriate seam finishes will give good service for rough wear and many launderings. (See Figure 17–7.)

In cold weather zones a snowsuit, mittens, and hood will be necessary (Figure 17–8). Snowsuits having a closely woven outer fabric will provide good protection against the cold and wind. Linings should be durable in both fabric and construction. Twill, poplin, and taffeta fabrics are made of cotton, nylon, or polyester; these fabrics are light in weight and have little bulk. Look for labels that indicate water repellency and care required. Washable snowsuits should be labeled. This will mean that both linings and outer fabric can be laundered.

During the creeping ages soft-soled shoes may be worn if protection from the cold is needed. Shoes should be about ½ inch longer than the toe, and stockings should be ½ inch longer than the foot.

Training pants are often worn when toilet training begins. This is at about eighteen months, but the time will depend upon the child. Training pants will continue to be worn until toilet training is accomplished. These pants are made of two-way stretch fabrics which fit snugly at the hip. Center panels of two, three, and four layers provide for absorption and protection.

toddler age

The principal clothing concern in the toddler age is the selection of shoes. When walking begins, flexible-soled shoes having rough soles of ⅛ inch thickness are worn. They may have either a slight heel or no heel, and they will be full and puffy in the toe area. Shoes should be ¼ inch wider than the foot and ½ inch longer than the big toe. Greater length and width than this will not be comfortable. The toe should be wide enough to permit the toes to spread when the body weight rests upon them. The toe area should be deep enough to avoid flattening and pinching. The instep is ample to allow the blood to circulate. If the instep is too tight, the developing foot presses the bones of the arch out of shape and cramps the foot. The shoes should fit snugly at the heel in order to grip the foot firmly and prevent heel rotation when walking. The heel is the part that balances and controls the foot.

As the child grows and begins to run about, the soles of the shoes will be about ¼ inch thick and the heel ¼ to ⅜ inch high. The inside line should be straight, and the length is about ¾ inch longer than the foot.[2] Some parents

[2] Household Finance Corporation, "Better Buymanship—Use and Care of Shoes," Chicago, 4th rev. ed., Bulletin No. 5, pp. 12–13.

17–9 Toddler's jumpsuit of machine-washable corduroy features feminine trim. (Courtesy Kiddie Kover, Jayvee Brands)

17–10 Two-piece toddler garment of machine-washable cotton jersey features plastic-covered toe and sole covers. (Courtesy Kiddie Kover, Jayvee Brands)

dress their children in tennis shoes or sneakers exclusively. These shoes do not have support and should not be worn all of the time. However, some tennis shoes and sneakers have supports built into them, making them similar to a regular shoe.

Children do not often complain when their feet hurt, as they cannot localize pain. Ill-fitting shoes may not be detected unless parents are alert to behavior that might indicate a shoe-fitting problem. These symptoms include less general activity and less activity in games. A child who walks carefully by putting his feet down flat rather than taking a normal, springy step or a child who removes his shoes often has a shoe-fitting problem.[3]

Shoes that fit well help to build good body skills in balance, climbing, and running.[4] Shoes need replacing as they are outgrown, and, in a rapidly growing child, this may be as often as every two months.

[3] U.S. Department of Health, Education, and Welfare, "Your Children's Feet and Footwear," Children's Bureau Folder No. 41, rev. (Washington, D.C.: Government Printing Office, 1957).
[4] James L. Hymes, Jr., "Enjoy Your Child, Ages 1, 2, 3," New York Public Affairs Pamphlet No. 141 (1962), p. 11.

from three to six

Clothing requirements for children from three to six years of age must provide for the activities of sleep, rough play, school, and occasional dress-up. Due to growth and increased activity, these ages bring an increase in clothing expenditure to almost double that of children under two years. For these reasons it is wise to purchase quality rather than quantity. Features to look for when shopping include self-help, growth, safety, and comfort for the child.

SELF-HELP FEATURES

Control of the large and small muscles takes place between the ages of two and six years. A child can partially dress himself by the third year if the clothing selected will help him with this task. By the fourth year he needs little assistance. The selection of clothing that features self-help is a means by which we can teach children independence. Children can be encouraged to dress themselves by use of the following self-help features.

1. Place hooks and rods for hangers at a level easily reached by children
2. Lay clothing out in the order in which it is to be put on
3. Mark shoes for the right and left foot
4. Mark the front or back of the garments
5. Select garments having
   Front openings
   Large armholes
   Large necks on slipovers
   Zippers rather than buttons
   Large buttons and snaps rather than small ones
   Stretch fabrics with no closures
   Panties that slip down easily

GROWTH FEATURES

During the ages from three to six years the pace of physical growth is reduced somewhat from the previous period. Buying clothing with growth features will enable a garment to be worn over a longer period of time. Some growth features include

1. Long straps on overalls
2. Tucks near the hemlines of dresses and slips
3. Stretch fabrics
4. Deep hems on skirts and pants
5. Two-piece garments
6. Indefinite waists

SAFETY FEATURES

Between 1,500 and 3,000 deaths occur each year as a result of burning clothing. Approximately 150,000 injuries occur yearly, to children and older people mainly, because of this fire hazard.[5] Some clothing is more fire prone than others. The rate of burning is affected by the type of fiber, the fabric construction, and the design of the garment. Fibers of cotton, rayon, and silk catch fire easily and burn rapidly. Most synthetic fibers such as acetate, nylon, acrylic, and polyester do not burn easily, but they melt, causing the sticky substance to adhere and burn deeply into the flesh. Blends of natural and synthetic fibers can both burn readily and melt. Wool is both difficult to ignite and slow to burn. The construction of a fabric also affects the way it burns. Open and loose weaves are more flammable than tightly woven fabrics. Sheer and lightweight fabrics ignite more rapidly and burn faster than heavy, durable weaves. Fuzzy-surfaced fabrics with a brushed nap catch fire easily and burn at a fast rate. Design of clothing affects burning: loose-fitting garments which permit air to reach both outer and under surfaces of the garments permit fire to spread rapidly. These include loose-fitting sleeves, ruffles, and flaring skirts.

Costumes used for Halloween and other activities which may bring them near flame sources should be labeled flame-proof. Costumes that are made at home can be treated with a borax–boric acid solution.[6] These finishes are not permanent—garments must be retreated after either dry cleaning or wet cleaning.

Parents often buy larger sizes of clothing with an eye to growth or have a child wear "hand-me-downs" that are too large. This is a dangerous practice, because loose-fitting garments catch on things such as branches of trees and parts of bicycles, causing serious accidents.

Other safety features include

1. Reinforcement at the knees to prevent skin burns
2. No drawstrings at the neck

[5] *Los Angeles Times,* October 6, 1968, p. 22.
[6] U.S. Department of Agriculture, "Making Household Fabrics Flame Resistant," Leaflet No. 454 (Washington, D.C.: Government Printing Office, 1967).

17–11 Clothing for play must be durable and offer protection in long sleeves and pant legs. (Courtesy National Recreation and Park Association)

3. No unnecessary ribbons or bows that can get caught

4. No cuffs on pant legs that may cause children to trip

5. Bright colors that permit motorists to see children

COMFORT FEATURES

Children, as well as adults, feel more comfortable in certain types of garments. Fabrics that are soft and absorbent contribute to comfort. Other comfort features in children's garments include

1. Garments that are sized correctly and fit the body and limbs

2. Straps that stay up on the shoulder

3. Pants and panties that do not restrict the waist or leg—red marks on the body mean that the garments are too tight

4. Bows that do not come untied

5. Lightweight garments

6. Textures that are not scratchy or itchy

347

7. Seasonally appropriate clothing

8. Clothing that offers protection from bruising, such as long sleeves and long pants (Figure 17–11)

9. Garments that hang from the shoulder

10. Shoes and stockings that are the correct size

CLOTHING LIKES AND DISLIKES

Children, as well as adults, have their favorites in clothing. They may also have definite dislikes for certain garments. Their tastes tend toward primary, saturated colors. Boys and girls from the ages three to ten prefer red to any other color.[7] Decorative features such as ornaments and appliquéd designs in the form of flowers and animals appeal to children. Velvety and furry textures such as fleece, terrycloth, and fur are often stroked and patted. A definite dislike is shown to harsh and scratchy textures; these should be avoided as they can irritate a child's delicate skin.

Children like garments that are familiar to them. Often it is difficult for them to give up a garment which is no longer wearable because of a strong attachment.

Qualities of becomingness, appropriateness, durability, conformity, size of wardrobe, cleanliness, and neatness are important to mothers but not to their offspring.[8] The fact that a garment may be unattractive on, or that a party dress is inappropriate for rough play, is of no concern to youngsters. They do not recognize having a large or a limited wardrobe if their clothing consists of "hand-me downs." What is important to them is a liking for the garment itself, regardless of the source.

Very young boys and girls are not aware that their clothing conforms to that of their playmates. It is not known at what exact age the desire to conform in dressing occurs. The need to dress as others becomes evident when the child refuses to wear something that differs from what the other children are wearing.

Preschoolers who are interested in mud puddles and dirt care nothing about getting it on their clothing. It is not normal for a child to be overly concerned about keeping clean. This type of child often has difficulty in group adjustment.[9] Mothers who are anxious about their children getting dirty restrict a child's attitude concerning play. Part of being a child is experimenting in mud puddles, clay, paints, and other messy media (Figure 17–12). These are learning experiences for children, and they should not be hampered by soil-conscious adults.

Does clothing have an effect upon the mood and behavior of a child? Ryan

[7] Mary Shaw Ryan, *Clothing: A Study in Human Behavior* (New York: Holt, 1966), p. 213.
[8] *Ibid.,* p. 216.
[9] *Ibid.,* p. 16.

17–12 Part of being a child is experimenting in mud puddles, clay, paints, and other messy media. This Australian child takes great delight in finger painting. (Courtesy Australian Consulate)

feels that statements regarding the effect of dress on behavior are the result of casual observation and that there is no evidence that these observations are valid for children in general. There is no experimental evidence at this time to indicate these statements about behavior are generally true; therefore, they should be considered as hypotheses.[10]

ages six to eleven

Clothing needs for elementary school children vary in some respects from those of the preschoolers, although many requirements remain the same. This period is a very active one physically; sports rate high in interest for both boys and

---

[10] *Ibid.,* p. 217.

17–13 Elementary school children are very active physically; sports and games rate high for boys and girls. Note the clothing conformity of this group. (Courtesy National Recreation and Park Association)

girls (Figure 17–13). Clothing plays an important role in social development, as definite ideas about clothing likes and dislikes are developing. This is an age of belonging to a group, and what the group wears is very important.

Sports are the chief pastime of elementary-age boys and girls. Leadership and popularity are frequently found among those children who have developed skills in games and sports.[11] Durable clothing must be provided which will withstand the strains of vigorous exercise. Garments should be cut so that they are comfortable and do not restrain activity. Dresses and shirts should have adequate fullness across the back; pleats at the center back or yokes with fullness will provide for strenuous arm movement without tearing the garment. Dresses that hang from the shoulders provide more freedom than fitted dresses (Figure 17–14). The armscye of dresses should be at least 1 inch below the armpit.

350

[11] *Ibid.*, p. 222.

Clothing is important for the social and emotional development of the child 351
(Figure 17–15). Pronounced ideas about what will be worn appear sometime
during this period. These ideas will be related to what their playmates and
schoolmates wear. There is a strong need for children to dress like their group.
The "gang" is a significant part of their lives, and the feeling of group belonging is strong. One of a child's greatest fears is that of being ridiculed by the
peer group. Clothing may be an object of ridicule when it differs from what
friends are wearing. Dressing differently may give rise to feelings of inferiority
and insecurity. For many children the dislike of wearing "hand-me-downs" may
be that it does not conform with what the group wears more than the fact that it
has been used by others.

Because of the need for conformity in dressing as their friends do and the

17–14 Garments should be
cut so that they do not
restrain activity. Dresses
that hang from the shoulders
provide more freedom and
growing room than fitted
styles. (Courtesy Celanese
Corporation)

17–15 Clothing is important to the social and emotional development of the child. This boy, dressed in an Indian costume, enacts a role, much to the delight of his fans. (Courtesy National Recreation and Park Association)

fact that children now have some definite ideas about how they want to dress, it may be helpful to them and to you to take them shopping when buying their clothing. A sense of importance and freedom is given them if they are allowed to help select their clothing.[12] For younger children, a preselected sample could be presented from which they can make their selection. This age group is not so concerned as to whether the garment looks attractive on them as much as to "Are the other kids wearing it?"

Activities such as baseball leagues and scout troops give children the opportunity to belong to organized groups. The wearing of uniforms, pins, and badges visually identifies them with a group. They enjoy wearing these uniforms and look forward to the days on which they can be worn. (For some children, this is every day.)

Unfortunately, interest in what is worn does not extend to appearing neat and well groomed. Some girls, at seven years of age, like to look neat, but this

[12] Walter Neisser, "Your Child's Sense of Responsibility," New York Public Affairs Pamphlet No. 254 (1957), p. 14.

may not appear until later. During the eighth year girls usually take more responsibility in clothing care, such as hanging up garments and reporting needed repairs. For boys this takes a little longer.

Skills in dressing are not fully developed in the early elementary age period, and some clothing is not designed with independence in dressing in mind. Dresses that close down the back are hard to manage. Until a child is eight years old or thereabouts, assistance in dressing may be needed and should be offered. Feelings of self-consciousness may develop if children need to ask for help. Shoes may be difficult to tie, and some hair styles such as braids need assistance. At about ten years both boys and girls like to manage their own hair, but they still need reminding about taking a bath.

By the eleventh year most children begin to take some interest in the opposite sex. Their bodies are developing toward maturity, and they may be very self-conscious. There may be a strong desire for privacy. At about twelve years girls begin to wear brassieres. Most garment manufacturers produce a training bra, a specially designed garment for the youthful and developing figure. There is no specific cup size; the entire cup section is made of stretch fabric which gives as the figure develops.

Children are not interested in whether a garment is becoming to them—they need help in the selection of designs. Opinions and attitudes that are formed early in childhood are often lasting; therefore, it is important to teach children the value of looking their best in clothing that enhances them. Developing good taste in clothing can begin by dressing them attractively and appropriately for their activities; exposure and good example are ways of learning which can be understood by the child. Growth in body width may not catch up with growth in length for a while. The selection of lines that will minimize the problems of skinniness or chubbiness may help to reduce feelings of self-consciousness which might arise from these problems of growth. Shy children should not be overdressed or dressed in loud colors which might add to their embarrassment. Drawing attention to their clothing may cause shy children to withdraw even more.

the teen years

Role participation increases in the teen years; therefore, clothing continues to be a significant factor in the satisfaction of emotional and social needs. Vitally aware of how they look, teen-agers are often critical about their clothing and personal appearance; they worry about their figure or physique, facial features, skin, hair and the wearing of glasses. The clothes they wear affect how they feel and how they act, as clothing satisfaction has a significant effect upon their moods and actions. Their self-confidence is increased when they know that they are well dressed (Figure 17–16). Some boys and girls will change clothing several times before they depart for school in the morning until they arrive at a look which satisfies them.

Social approval is of great concern to the teen-ager; this is commonly equated in obvious terms with how they appear to others physically rather than with the more hidden qualities of their personalities. One of the most important factors in the selection of teen-age clothing is that it conform with what is worn by the peer group (Figure 17–17). Often this does not meet the same standards that have been established in the family. One study on clothing disagreements has shown that conflicts between girls and their parents are often due to differences in opinion regarding their ideas about personal appearance, habits, and manners more than any other matter.[13] The areas of clothing disagreement in the upper-status families concerned selection of formals, shoes, coats, suits, jeans, shorts, and accessories. In the middle status disagreements were over formals, shoes, and grooming, and in the lower status, undergarments. A teen-ager feels the strong need to conform rather than be the object of teasing and possibly ostracism from the group.

In families where dress behavior is completely unacceptable, parents must try to help the teen-agers understand the underlying reasons of why they wish to dress in a defiant manner. They must be made aware of the possible negative reaction and the consequences to this reaction from others. Sharp criticism or ridicule will produce more antagonism than a quiet suggestion and a gentle approach to the problem.

Dress in the school situation has been the subject of concern in the junior and senior high school. School officials believe that students feel and act better when they are neatly dressed. School dress codes have been established in many schools to set standards in dress in the hope that improved behavior will result. Some schools bar wearing cowboy boots, motorcycle jackets, and T-shirts and prescribe hair lengths and cuts for boys. For girls there are regulations for length and tightness of skirts, arm covering, and make-up. Sheer blouses, exposed toes, and hair curlers are abolished. Although these codes do not solve the problem of helping students understand why they dress the way they do, they are enforced because better behavior is expected by school administrators when students are properly dressed.

Recently many schools have dropped dress codes as a result of the revolution in dress. Most schools are happy to be out of the "fashion business" and accept the tastes of the students. For many West Coast schools the only dress rule is that shoes must be worn to class. Interestingly, in schools where there has been a relaxation in dress regulations, after a few weeks of bizarre or extremely informal dress most students return to a more appropriate school attire.

[13] H. Angelino, L. Barnes, and C. Shedd, "Attitudes of Mothers and Adolescent Daughters Concerning Clothing and Grooming," *Journal of Home Economics* (Dec. 1956), p. 799.

17–16 The clothes that teen-agers wear affect how they feel and how they act. Self-confidence is increased when they know they are well dressed. (Courtesy Simplicity Pattern Company)

17–17 One of the most important factors in the selection of teen clothing is that it conform with what is being worn by the peer group; often this means pants for social functions. (Courtesy Simplicity Pattern Company)

Some high schools have "dress-up days" when students deviate from the normal school dress. In a study done by Wass and Eicher, the girls questioned felt that clothing affected their behavior. They acted more grown-up and better behaved; they felt more feminine and confident in dressy clothing. The girls also expressed feeling more comfortable when they wore slacks and bermudas.[14] The effect of dress on behavior is often noticeable at high school dances. When the dance is to be a dress-up affair rather than very informal, the students are observed to be better behaved and more courteous.

The relationship between personal appearance and popularity was the subject of an interesting study.[15] The results revealed that popularity was influenced by a girl's dress. Students who listed the names of the best-dressed girls also listed the same names as being the most popular. The same study also showed that appraisal of a new student was first derived from dress; after they got to know the individual, personality, general attitudes, and beliefs were considered.

SPENDING AND SHOPPING BEHAVIOR

A large proportion of teen-agers are wage earners. In one midwestern school 65 per cent of the high school students earned money in addition to receiving an allowance.[16] Whether teen-agers get their money from allowances or jobs, the buying potential of this group is sizable. There are twenty-five million teen-agers between the ages of thirteen and nineteen in the United States. Eleven billion dollars is spent on goods and services in the teen market every year, mostly for clothing and cosmetics.[17]

National and local advertising is geared to the youth market. Department stores feature teen-age boutiques and devote a large share of space to clothing and accessories for this group. Many stores have fashion boards of young people for the purpose of promoting sales. Magazines such as *Glamour, Mademoiselle,* and *Seventeen* are directed at the teen market and do much to promote fashion among the older girls of this group. They provide hints on beauty and grooming together with advertising products.

Teen-agers usually select their own clothing. They shop with either their mothers or friends. About one half or one third of the time they are accompanied by their mothers or other family members. Help is usually needed when buying expensive items such as suits and coats.[18] Not much planning is involved

[14] B. Wass and Joanne B. Eicher, "Clothing Related to Role Behavior," *Michigan Quarterly Bulletin,* **47:**206–13 (1964).

[15] Suzanne H. Hendricks, Eleanor A. Kelley, and Joanne B. Eicher, "Senior Girls' Appearance and Social Acceptance," *Journal of Home Economics,* **60:**167–71 (March 1968).

[16] M. Zunich and A. Fults, "Teenage Economic Behavior: Earning and Saving," *Journal of Home Economics,* **59:**739 (Nov. 1967).

[17] *Ibid.,* p. 732.

[18] Tate and Glisson, *op. cit.,* p. 283.

before buying. They either buy something when there is a special occasion or when they see something they like. Shopping is usually done in department stores, and garments are purchased on the first trip.[19] There is not much evidence that teen-agers shop around for the best buy before making a purchase.

The qualities that are most important to teen-agers are fit for girls and style for boys.[20] Construction is not often considered. The reason for not showing consideration for construction may be that teen-agers are not aware of what qualities to look for. Many people do not realize the importance of fabric, cut, and construction upon the total appearance or the expected wear.

Because growth during the early adolescent period is so rapid, a minimal wardrobe is advisable at any one time. Two-piece outfits such as sweaters and blouses and skirts may extend the wardrobe over a longer period of time because of uneven growth of different parts of the body. If shoulders and bust grow faster than the hips, a skirt may be worn longer by adding a new top. The use of one-piece dresses may mean discarding them because of growth in one section of the body.

INNOVATORS OF STYLES

Creation of styles is found among teen-agers. This group has introduced and popularized many styles such as Nehru jackets, leotards, bulky knit sweaters, leather jackets, pierced ears, and certain types of jewelry. Many designers get their ideas by observing youth. Designer Bill Blass says, "All fashion stems from kids." [21]

Teen-agers are great followers of fashion and fads. The popularity of certain faddish styles is usually concentrated in small groups. Fads are usually demonstrated in the use of accessories. The cost of following fads can sometimes be rather high when taken over a period of time.

special clothing needs—maternity

The psychological benefit of maintaining an attractive appearance during pregnancy is of great importance to the feeling of well being of the mother-to-be (Figure 17–18). Fortunately, today's fashions in maternity clothing provide a wide choice of well-designed and expandable apparel.

Following the guidelines of good design, maternity clothing is selected to

[19] Ryan, *op. cit.,* p. 279.
[20] Tate and Glisson, *op. cit.,* p. 284.
[21] Bill Blass, *U.S. News and World Report,* **64**:74 (May 20, 1968).

17–18 The psychological benefits of maintaining an attractive appearance during pregnancy are of great importance to the feeling of well being of the expectant mother. (Courtesy Toni Lynn)

17–19 One-piece maternity dresses that hang from the shoulders are often more comfortable than a skirt, which relies upon the waist to hold it up. (Courtesy Toni Lynn)

include colors and lines that will minimize width. This means using vertical lines that are spaced so that they do not accentuate width and colors that blend rather than contrast with the background. Separates that do not provide too great a contrast between the two sections of the top and skirt can provide more variety than dresses. On the other hand, one-piece dresses in a solid color or print may be more slimming than two-piece separates. One-piece garments which hang from the shoulders are often more comfortable than a skirt, which relies upon the waist to hold it up (Figure 17–19). The jumper is well suited to both comfort and slimness, and blouses from the existing wardrobe can be worn. Slacks and skirts can be purchased with expandable waistlines (Figure 17–20).

Interest can be focused on the face by using interesting collars, scarves, and jewelry. A contrast in color for these accessories will bring additional attention to them. (See Figure 17–21.)

A criterion more important than appearance is comfort. Pregnancy may be

17–20 Maternity slacks can be purchased with expandable waistlines. The long overblouse can be used with skirts as well as slacks. (Courtesy Toni Lynn)

17–21 Emphasis in maternity clothes is best focused at the personality area and away from the expanding body. (Courtesy Toni Lynn)

accompanied by excessive perspiration. Absorbent fabrics, such as cotton and wool, are more healthful than closely woven, nonabsorbent synthetics, which leave a layer of perspiration between the garment and the skin. This could result in chilling. Both under and outer clothing should be selected with absorption in mind. High-quality fabric used in durably constructed garments is of great importance during this time. Minimum-care fabrics not only save the mother's strength but give a better appearance by not showing muss and wrinkles. Seams constructed so that they will withstand the strain are essential.

Garments that restrict circulation should be avoided. This includes garters and panties with tight elastic bands at the leg and waist area. Maternity corsets which support the uterus can be adjusted to figure changes. Broad-strapped brassieres will provide support and comfort. Adequate cup size should be considered.

Shoes that support the arches are important as increased weight may cause flattening of an unsupported arch. High heels tend to throw the pelvis out of alignment, which may cause backache. Heels having a broad base will support the body, and there is less danger of turning the ankle and falling.[22]

Girls often begin wearing maternity clothing before it is necessary. This is regretted by the time the period of pregnancy is over, because they tire of wearing such a limited wardrobe. During the first three months of pregnancy, any change in the body proportions remains almost unnoticeable. The time to begin wearing maternity clothing varies in individuals, but expandable outer clothing is usually not needed until the fourth or fifth month.[23] If three quarters of the entire wardrobe is purchased during the fourth month, strength will be saved, as shopping becomes more fatiguing further along in the pregnancy.[24]

Maternity clothing is designed to provide for six or seven added pounds at the time a woman begins wearing them to ten to fifteen more before pregnancy is over.[25] Rapid expansion and body changes occur after the twenty-sixth week. During the last two weeks of pregnancy the baby drops lower, and the waistline is lowered.

Clothing for maternity wear should be attractive, comfortable, and easy care. Designs should be selected with lines that will minimize the added weight and change in physical proportions. Clothing that is comfortable and made with proper support contributes healthful benefits. Durably constructed garments are necessary as added strain is put on them. They should be constructed so that they will provide good service throughout the entire pregnancy period.

recognizing quality in women's wearing apparel

The quality of a garment is determined by the characteristics of each of its components. Every element from the fiber used to construct the fabric to the last finishing detail will influence the final appearance of the garment. To the discerning eye, quality is evident in the external appearance of a garment. The details that are not seen from the outside, such as interfacings, linings, and construction techniques, are all clues to quality. These elements affect not only how the garment looks but how it will retain its shape and wear.

FASHION FABRIC

Fashion fabric is the exterior layer of a garment. It must have eye appeal to attract the attention of the buyer and also to be attractive on the figure. The

---

[22] M. E. Breckenridge *et al., Growth and Development of the Young Child* (Philadelphia: Saunders, 1969), p. 118.

[23] Tate and Glisson, *op. cit.,* p. 47.

[24] Doris Ruslink, *Family Health and Home Nursing* (New York: Macmillan, 1963), p. 128.

[25] *Ibid.,* p. 129.

construction of the fashion fabric will determine its wearing qualities. A variety of natural and synthetic fibers are currently used in producing fashion fabrics. The type of material, its qualities, and the properties selected for the construction of the textile will do much to determine its wearing qualities. If the fiber is made into a yarn and then woven, the construction of the yarn will be another factor in determining the characteristics of the textile produced.

A woven cloth may have a firm or loose weave. Generally speaking, firmly woven fabrics give better wear. Loosely woven cloth often gives more interesting textural effects, particularly when constructed from novelty or complex yarns.

The quality of the fashion fabric is also dependent on the dyes or methods used to add color to it. Some color techniques fade when exposed to sun, atmosphere, cleaning, or wear. The labels on the garment should give information regarding colorfastness. The consumer also may build up a knowledge of color performance from past experience.

Finishes are added to the fabric in the final steps of production. There are a variety of finishes developed for specific purposes; they often affect the performance of the fabric. For example, a finish to prevent wrinkling may make ironing difficult if wrinkles are set by the heat in the dryer; soil-resistant finishes sometimes stiffen the fabric so that a familiar textile takes on new characteristics; durable-press finishes create some abrasion and spot-removal problems. These fabrics are easy care but do not wear as long as they would without this finish.

Bonding of fabrics has become very important in the garment business; it allows for greater freedom of design, particularly with hard-to-handle fabrics. Bonding is a process by which a backing is attached to the fashion fabric, thus providing stability and durability for the fashion fabric. Some bonded fabrics come unbonded after several cleanings. The number of cleanings anticipated in the lifetime of the garment should be considered when buying a bonded fabric. Some fabric manufacturers will guarantee their bonding process against this separation. This information is available on the "hangtag."

Some fashion fabrics have design or texture direction. These must be taken into consideration in the construction of a garment or the beauty of both fabric and design will be distorted. Fabric designs such as plaids, large checks, stripes, or distinctive motifs must be cut and sewn together so that the design is not distorted (Figure 17–22). The fabric design must be matched in the construction of the garment (Figure 17–23). If the design is in the texture, such as a twill weave, the garment must be constructed so that the diagonal line flows in one direction. In some fabrics—velvet, velveteen, corduroy, some satins—a change in color depth will be obvious unless the nap of the fabric is placed in the same direction.

Particular care should be taken to observe how certain fabric motifs are placed on the figure. Daisies that outline the bosom, bull's-eyes located in the seat, or arrows pointed to the pelvic area are examples of poor design placement. These are not only silly and vulgar but they usually generate ridicule.

17–22 Plaids must be cut and sewn with precision to avoid distortion of the design. (Courtesy National Cotton Council)

17–23 For the desired effect, fabric design should be matched in the construction of the garment. (Courtesy Penny Baker, Inc., Dow Badische)

Fabrics used on the inside of a garment fulfill one of several purposes. If they are supportive and build shape and design into small areas of the garment, they are called interfacings. If they are supportive and add stability and durability to the fashion fabric, they are called underlinings. If they are decorative and enclose construction details, they are called linings. The fabrics used for interfacings, underlinings, and linings are a significant factor in the quality of the garment.

Construction fabrics should be fastened securely and finished appropriately for the design of the garment. They should not wrinkle or distort the fashion fabric in any manner. These construction fibers determine how long a garment will maintain its shape and fit and how long it will wear.

CONSTRUCTION DETAILS

Stitch length should be appropriate to the fabric used. Generally, small stitches indicate quality, but some fabrics such as synthetics, blends, or permanent-press require larger stitches in order to avoid seam puckering. Thread color should match the fashion fabric; thread endings should be secure so that they will not pull out.

A good seam width is about ⅝ inch wide so that it can stand the stress of wear without pulling or fraying out. The seam should be pressed open smoothly unless design detail indicates otherwise. Seams should not show signs of pucker or pulling. Fabrics that tend to ravel should have an appropriate seam finish to prevent this.

Hems should be invisible from the right side of the garment. A hem of 1½-to-2 inches is appropriate for most garments. Too deep a hem looks "home-sewn" and distracts from the design of the garment. An exception would be a deep hem on a sheer fabric. A narrower hem is required for shaped skirts and some fragile fabrics. The hem finish should be appropriate for the fashion fabric and not overstitched so that it shows on the right side of the garment.

Check to see if sleeves are set in smoothly without signs of puckering. There should be comfortable ease in the fit of a sleeve so that it does not draw or pull when on the figure. The grain line for a set-in sleeve should be parallel and perpendicular across the center upper arm. (See Chapter 16 on fit.)

The collar must be placed on the garment so that both sides are symmetrical, unless indicated otherwise by the design. The undercollar should not be visible from the right side. The collar should have well-defined edges and a good shape.

Ease or fullness allowed in a garment indicates quality. The overall fit of the garment should have adequate and comfortable room for movement. A garment should never bind or constrict the figure. Adequate ease should also be found in the fullness of gathers, pleats, and tucks. (See Figure 17–24.)

Sleeve set in smoothly, no pucker

Edges well defined

Flat seams pressed open, no pucker caused by stitching

Seam width not skimpy

Seams finished if fabric requires

Undercollar seam hidden

Good quality interfacing

Buttonholes:
Machine type—close even stitches, no loose threads
Bound buttonholes in high-cost garment

Fabric design matched at seam

Hem ridge and stitches do not show from right side of garment

Hem depth allows for alteration. Hems of A-line or circular skirts eased in

17–24 Signs of quality are important clues for the consumer to check before buying.

FINISHING DETAILS

All fasteners should be properly placed and securely attached. Quality in a garment is indicated by the choice of fasteners, such as buttons. Buttons should be in harmony with the texture and color of the fashion fabric as well as with the design of the garment.

Buttonholes must be properly placed and of the correct size to accommodate the buttons. Bound buttonholes are a sign of quality, but not all fabrics are suitable for them. Machine buttonholes should have close stitches, and the threads should be secured to prevent raveling.

Zippers should zip. Unless otherwise indicated by design, the zipper should be well covered by the fashion fabric. It should be installed in such a manner as to stay closed; often a small hook and eye are placed at the top of the placket to insure this. In quality garments the zipper is "hand picked" (installed with small hand stitches to make it more invisible).

Decoration and trim should be in keeping with the quality of the garment. The placement and quantity of the applied design should add to the beauty of the garment. Check all applied design to see that it is appropriately placed and securely attached.

Pressing is extremely important to the appearance of the garment. The presser in a garment industry is one of the highest paid workers because a garment can be ruined by improper pressing. Each detail of the garment should be pressed into position. There should be no overpressing effects on the right side of the garment, such as dart impressions or pocket imprints. The garment should be smooth, well shaped, and ready to wear.

relationship of price to quality

The price paid for a garment is often equated with the quality one expects to receive from it. High-priced garments are expected to be high-quality garments, but this is not always true. You have heard the statement, "You get what you pay for." Although the price tag may be an indication of quality, several factors influence the price of a garment.

A garment may be expensive because the fabric is costly. High-quality virgin wool, finely woven silk, and linen are more expensive than most cottons, synthetics, and blends. Garments made from these fibers will cost more at the onset. In order to be sold in a particular price range, the manufacturer may use high-quality fabric or high-fashion fabrics and cut corners on the amount of fabric used, the construction, or the finishing details.

The exclusiveness of the design will influence the price. If few garments are cut, this will be reflected in a higher price. Price is affected by the garment design. The number and shape of the pattern pieces boost the price. Odd shapes and many pieces which involve more seaming will cost more than simple patterns of few pieces.

The amount of handwork also affects the price. Linings applied by hand, covered snaps, handstitched zippers, and hand hemming involve high labor costs.

The price of the trims used such as fur, lace, and ribbon contributes to the final cost of the garment. High-quality buttons are expensive; for example, use of four buttons priced at three dollars each will add twelve dollars alone to the total cost of a garment.

The mark-up is the difference between the wholesale price and the selling price. The amount of mark-up will depend on the store that sells the garment. The mark-up on high- and low-priced garments and the percentage this represents of the market is shown below.[26]

Wholesale Price		Retail Price	Per cent of Market
High price	$95.75	$200.00	2
Low price	3.75	5.69	65

[26] Helen L. Brockman, *The Theory of Fashion Design* (New York: Wiley, 1965), pp. 14–15.

men's wear

A greater amount of available money, increased leisure time, and the influence of youth are three factors that have made men fashion conscious in recent years. Increasing numbers of men are now doing their own shopping rather than sending their wives to the store. They want to coordinate their suits, shirts, ties, socks, and shoes. The president of Macy's, David L. Yunich, said that for a long time 80 to 90 per cent of men's clothing was purchased by women, but this practice is rapidly changing.[27]

This trend is bringing about changes in merchandising emphasis. Designer's names (formerly confined to sales appeal for women's wear) are being stressed by the big houses of men's apparel. Greater style choices are available (Figure 17–25). Rapidly changing tastes mean that stock cannot be ordered six months ahead as was the previous practice. Boutiques for men's fashions have sprung up in both department stores and small independent shops. Fashion shows of male apparel are regular features in some department store grill rooms, and both men's and women's apparel are modeled together in tearooms. Many members of the couture who designed exclusively for women are now concentrating on men's fashion—Yves St. Laurent, Hardie Aimes, and Pierre Cardin, to name a few. Two thirds of Cardin's 1967 gross sales of $22 million came from his male line.[28] Between 1955 and 1965 the number of newspapers covering men's wear jumped from 100 to 800.[29]

SHOPPING FOR MEN'S WEAR

Many general criteria for the purchase of women's wear can be applied to the purchase of clothing for men. Fabric quality, general construction, and style influence the price. Inner construction details, the quality of interfacings used, linings, and the amount of handwork influence the cost as well as the quality.

MEN'S DRESS SHIRTS

Styles include many variations of collar shapes, neckband widths, cuff designs, sleeve lengths, body shapes, colors, and fabrics (Figure 17–26).

[27] David Yunich, *Daily News Record* (May 27), 1969, p. 1.
[28] Male Plumage '68, *Newsweek* (Nov. 25, 1968), p. 75.
[29] *Ibid.*, p. 70.

17–25 Greater style choices are available for men today than in recent times. Men are stressing individuality in dress for various roles. (Courtesy Men's Fashion Association of America, Inc.)

17–26 Men's dress shirts include many variations in collar shapes, fabric textures, and colors. (Courtesy Men's Fashion Association of America, Inc.)

Collars: Collars may be rounded or pointed in varying degrees of length of tips and of spread between the tips (Figure 17–27). Longer collar tips with a close spread are flattering to round-shaped faces; short spread collars that are round are becoming to long, thin-shaped faces. Collars are fused so that they remain permanently stiff, or they may have stays to keep the collars flat. Some shirts have removable stays. Others may have soft collars that button down. Neckbands are narrow, medium, or deep to conform to neck lengths and widths.

Cuffs: Cuffs may be barrel, convertible (single), or French (double) (Figure 17–28).

Body shape: Shirts that are tapered reduce bulk at the waist and hip area and are preferred by slim men. Portly physiques prefer the untapered cut for comfort.

Construction features to check when buying (Figure 17–29):

1. Even collar points
2. Uniform stitching on collar

17–27 The amount of spread between collars is a styling detail that influences the appearance of face shape. (Courtesy Men's Fashion Association of America, Inc.)

A. Barrel

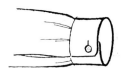

B. Convertible

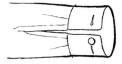

C. French

17–28 Three cuff styles found on men's dress shirts. *A.* The barrel cuff is single; it laps and buttons. *B.* The convertible cuff is single; it may use either buttons or cuff links. *C.* The French cuff is double; it requires cuff links.

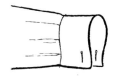

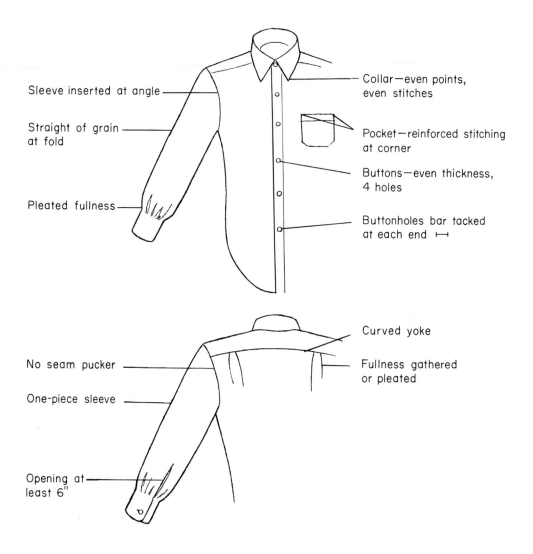

Sleeve inserted at angle

Straight of grain at fold

Pleated fullness

Collar—even points, even stitches

Pocket—reinforced stitching at corner

Buttons—even thickness, 4 holes

Buttonholes bar tacked at each end ⊢⊣

No seam pucker

One-piece sleeve

Opening at least 6″

Curved yoke

Fullness gathered or pleated

17–29 Points to check when buying shirts.

3. Cut on grain—the fold at the top of the sleeve should be on grain

4. Sleeves cut in one piece rather than two

5. Sleeve inserted at an angle for greater room for movement and comfort

6. Fullness at the cuff pleated rather than gathered

7. Cuff placket on grain and at least 6 inches in length for ease in ironing

8. On higher priced shirts, a row of stitching in the inside center of cuff holds interlining in place

9. Seams free from pucker

10. Matching of patterns, plaids at center front, pockets, and collar points

11. Pockets evenly stitched and reinforced at corners

370

12. Four-holed buttons of uniform thickness

13. Buttonholes with close stitching, backstitching at each end

14. Deep yoke, curved at back fullness at back, pleated into yoke in more expensive shirts, and gathered into yoke in less costly shirts

Fit

Shirt size represents the neck and sleeve length. Measure the circumference of the neck around the middle and the sleeve length from the center of the back neck, across the shoulder, and over a slightly bent elbow to the wrist.

A shirt that fits correctly shows ½ inch of the collar above the jacket. The shirt sleeve extends ½ inch below the jacket edge. The armholes are wide enough for freedom; the collar fits the neck comfortably, and tabs lay flat. Check shoulder, back, and chest for ample fullness.

Fabrics

One hundred per cent cotton will be the most absorbent and comfortable, particularly in warm weather. Unless labeled wash-and-wear, cotton will require ironing.

One hundred per cent synthetic, such as polyester, dries quickly, does not require ironing, but is not absorbent and will be uncomfortable in warm weather. This may be compensated for by a more open weave or knit.

Blends of synthetic and natural fibers, 65 per cent polyester and 35 per cent cotton, or blends of 50 per cent polyester and 50 per cent cotton, provide the advantages of both fibers. They require little or no ironing and provide more absorbency.

The chief advantage of durable press is the elimination of ironing, provided the fabric is laundered correctly. The disadvantages are a firmer, harsher hand than untreated fabrics and less durability. Inspect the seams of durable-press garments for puckering due to improper stitching techniques. These fabrics require fewer stitches per inch and less stitching overall. Sleeve openings will have a continuous facing rather than a flat placket.

Check labels and hangtags for fiber content, finishes, and care instructions. Note the amount of residual shrinkage. Labels that say preshrunk without giving the percentage of residual shrinkage are of no value.

MEN'S SUITS, SPORT COATS, TROUSERS

Style choices in suits include straight, boxy, fitted, or flared silhouettes. They may be double or single breasted, regular, high waisted, or have vents at side or back. The various pocket styles are bound, welt, patch, or flap. Lapels are notched, peaked, or shawl, either narrow or wide. Jackets may be unlined, partially lined, or fully lined. Trousers come with or without cuffs, beltless or with belt loops. (See Figures 17–30 and 17–31.)

Fabric choices are as varied: cottons, silks, synthetics, and blends. Finishes can be wash-and-wear or durable-press. Durable-press garments must fit without any letting-out alterations, because the seams, when let out, will not press flat.

The quality and price of a suit will depend on the outer fashion fabric, the materials used for interfacings and linings, and the amount of handwork involved in making the suit (Figure 17–32). Unfortunately, much of the quality is hidden by facings and linings and cannot be seen. Quality may not become evident until the garment is worn and cleaned. Check the following construction features for quality when buying.

Suit and Sport Jackets
1. Plaids and patterned fabrics match at center back, side seams, across the front, at pockets, welt, and flaps
2. When lapel is creased, it pops back into place when hair canvas has been used for interfacing
3. Buttonholes with even, close stitching, reinforced at the ends
4. Buttons firmly attached with adequate shanks to prevent buckling when buttoned
5. Pockets lined in a durable fabric and reinforced openings
6. Exposed seams turned and stitched or bound
7. Lining not seen below the coat hem
8. Armholes taped to prevent stretching. Shields in armholes

Trousers, Slacks
1. Belt loops firmly stitched
2. Interfacing at waist of noncrushable fabric to prevent wrinkling
3. Pockets of generous size, reinforced at ends. Linings of closely woven, durable fabric; pocket facing deep enough to keep lining from showing
4. No piecing in crotch in high-quality garments. Facings extended to reinforce crotch line
5. Inseam with adequate allowance for letting out

These points should be checked for fit (Figure 17–33).

Suit and Sport Jackets
1. Collar hugs neck, shows ½ inch shirt collar at back
2. No wrinkles across shoulder back or bubbles under collar area

17–30 Suit style choices are varied in silhouette. This wide-lapel, double-breasted jacket with semifitted waist styling gives emphasis to a broad shoulder area. (Courtesy Men's Fashion Association of America, Inc.)

17–31 The gray flannel suit takes on a new look with a suppressed waist and square shoulders. (Courtesy Men's Fashion Association of America, Inc.)

17–32 The quality and price of a man's suit are related to the fashion fabric, interfacings, linings, and the amount of handwork in the tailoring. Most suits are given a final fit on the customer, and alterations are made at the time of purchase. (Courtesy Men's Fashion Association of America, Inc.)

3. Full-cut armholes for movement

4. No wrinkles across chest area

5. Lapels lay flat to chest, do not gap

6. Front hangs straight when buttoned

17–33   Areas to check for fit in a man's suit are illustrated here.

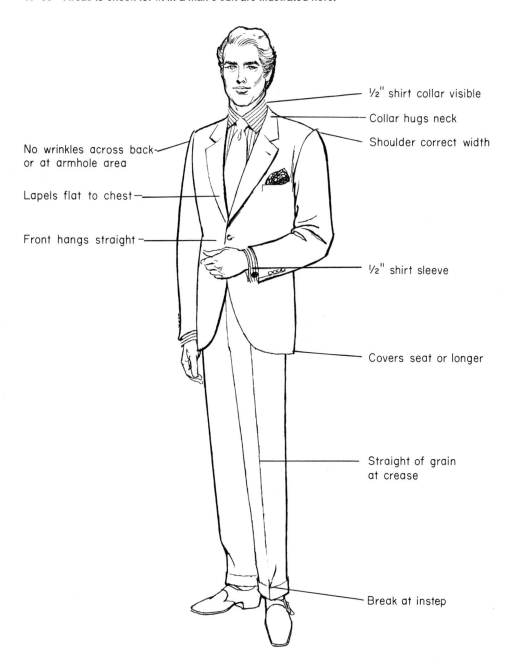

½" shirt collar visible

Collar hugs neck

Shoulder correct width

No wrinkles across back or at armhole area

Lapels flat to chest

Front hangs straight

½" shirt sleeve

Covers seat or longer

Straight of grain at crease

Break at instep

7. Sleeve shows ½ inch shirt cuff

8. Vent hangs straight

9. Jacket covers seat or is longer in some styles

Trousers, Slacks

1. Waist fits comfortably

2. Pleats, if any, lay flat

3. No wrinkles when standing

4. Crease straight with grain at front

5. Adequate seat fullness

6. Length breaks at instep

labeling

Information is attached to apparel by means of a cardboard tag or a cloth label stitched into the garment, which designates the name of the manufacturer and the generic name of the fiber content of the garment. This information is required by law under the Textile Fiber Products Identification Act of 1960. In blends, the percentages of the fibers used must also be indicated. If the consumer is knowledgeable about the characteristics of fibers, the information will indicate to some degree the performance which can be expected of the fabric and the cleaning care required. (See table on pages 410–12.) However, the fiber content is by no means the only factor that indicates performance of a fabric. The yarn structure, cloth construction, dyes, finishes, and construction of the garment—each contributes to the quality of the garment and the care required. Unfortunately, no labeling is required to help the consumer make decisions regarding these aspects.

Some manufacturers provide additional information which is of value to the consumer, including cleaning and pressing instructions, shrinkage control, colorfastness, special finishes applied, and guarantees or seals of approval. Labels should be read and kept on file for future reference, so that correct cleaning procedures can be used. Notation must be made on these labels to identify the garment to which it corresponds, or they will be of no value.

Guarantees are only as good as the reliabilty of the person making the guarantee. The guarantee may be between the consumer and the manufacturer or between the consumer and the retail store which sold the product. The guarantor can contest the claim, which would involve legal action. Guarantees should be read carefully to determine exactly what is guaranteed.

legislation of textiles

Protection is provided to the consumer through various legislative acts pertaining to textiles and fur products. These provisions require accurate labeling in regard to fiber content and to protection from the use of dangerously inflammable fabrics.

The Textile Fiber Products Identification Act of 1960
This requires labeling that encompasses the following.

The percentage of each fiber present designated by generic name

The listing in order of predominant weight

The manufacturer of the product

If imported, the textile fibers used and the name of the country where the product was processed or manufactured.

Wool Products Labeling Act of 1939
This act requires that all fiber content must be given by percentage of new, reprocessed, or reused wool. Formerly a product of reprocessed or reused wool could be sold under the impression that it was new wool. The terms wool, new wool, or virgin wool designate that the fibers are being manufactured for the first time.

Reprocessed wool has been through the manufacturing process previously and has been reclaimed and returned to the fiber stage for processing a second time. It has never been used by a consumer. Reused wool has been reclaimed from products that were used by consumers.

Fur Products Labeling Law, 1951
Giving misleading names to furs is prohibited by this law. The label must indicate the animal the fur was taken from, the country of origin, and whether the pelt has been used, damaged, or is scrap fur. If the fur has been dyed or bleached, this must also be indicated.

Flammable Fabrics Act of 1953
This legislation prohibits sale of highly inflammable fabrics or wearing apparel. Standards which have been set up regarding flammability must be met. This legislation has kept highly dangerous fabrics from reaching the consumer.

consumer aids

An abundance of information is available to the consumer that gives factual data regarding specific clothing purchases. When the shopper knows what features to look for, better judgments of value and quality can be made. Listed below are some books and pamphlets which can be obtained by writing to the addresses given.

Consumer Information (Price List 86, 2nd ed., 1965) is a booklet of publications, including those pertaining to clothing and fabric. It may be obtained free by writing to the Superintendent of Documents, Washington, D.C. 20402. There is a nominal charge for the pamphlets listed in the booklet.

Consumers' Research publishes the *Consumers Bulletin,* in which branded and trademarked items are tested and evaluated. It also publishes the *Consumer Bulletin Annual.* These may be obtained through Consumers' Research, Inc., Washington, N.J. 07882.

Consumers Union publishes *Consumer Reports,* which also tests and evaluates branded and trademarked items. An annual buying guide is also published. The address is Consumer Union of the United States, Inc., 256 Washington St., Mount Vernon, N.Y. 11055.

Consumers All: The Official Consumer's Guide, originally published by the U.S. Department of Agriculture, 1965, is a paperback book now published by Pocket Books, Inc., N.Y. It consists of articles by people known well in their field and covers many aspects of clothing and care of clothing, in addition to housing, furnishing, equipment, food, and gardening.

The Household Finance Corporation (Prudential Plaza, Chicago, Ill. 60601) publishes "Your Clothing Dollar" and "Your Shopping Dollar," among ten money management booklets.

The Celanese Fibers Marketing Company publishes *Textile Topics,* available to home economists. Address the Consumer Editor Department, Celanese Fibers Marketing Company, 522 Fifth Ave., New York, N.Y. 10036.

PROFESSIONAL ORGANIZATIONS CONCERNED WITH CONSUMER PROBLEMS

The National Institute of Drycleaning, Inc. (309 Burlington Ave., Silver Spring, Md. 20901), provides services to their industries through their test laboratories, courses, and publications. A bulletin, *Fabric Facts,* is available to home economists.

The American Institute of Laundering (Certified Seal Laboratories, Drawer 940, Joliet, Ill. 60434) publishes material on fabric care.

The American Home Economics Association is a professional organization for home economists devoted primarily to the support of programs for protection of the consumer and to the direction of programs in consumer education. The association promotes informative and descriptive labeling and advertising of consumer goods and services; their interest in developing quality and safety standards is of benefit to the consumer.

TESTING LABORATORIES

Some companies maintain testing laboratories for the purpose of preserving quality in the products they sell. Some of these include J. C. Penney, Montgomery Ward, Sears Roebuck, Macy's, Gimbel's, and Marshall Field and Company.

suggested readings

Chambers, Helen, and Verna Moulton. *Clothing Selection.* Philadelphia: J. B. Lippincott Company, 1969.

Consumers All: The Official Consumer's Guide. New York: Pocket Books, Inc., 1965.

Wingate, Isabel, Karen Gillespie, and Betty Addison. *Know Your Merchandise.* New York: McGraw-Hill Book Company, Inc., 1964.

18

---

shopping

In an urban society such as ours, selection of consumer goods is an important task. Very few households produce the major share of items required by the family or its individual members. Since a substantial portion of the income is spent on goods purchased in some manner, examination of shopping practices merits study. Most of us have developed shopping patterns that lack skill. While the primary concern of this text is clothing selection, much of the information given in this chapter can be applied to any item found in the marketplace.

To assist and influence the customer, merchants employ a variety of selling techniques. The packaging of products, the display of merchandise, the pricing of items, the store image, the advertising methods, even the floor plan are all thoughtfully designed to attract customers and sell goods. The merchant must constantly employ a variety of merchandising methods to attract, hold, and increase his volume of customers.

The individual, in turn, has the privilege of selecting from a vast array of stores and merchandise. The customer is always in the lead position in a relationship with a businessman, but too often individuals fail to press this advantage to the fullest. No matter what the circumstance, the customer is the buyer, the merchant the seller. The customer has the opportunity to select or reject what the merchant is selling. This is what we commonly call shopping. The shopper should understand merchandising and selling so that he may always receive full value for the monies spent.

promotion and advertising

Advertising means different things to different people. To a housewife it may mean the weekly specials at the supermarket. To a teen-ager it may mean peer identification with products promoted by a favorite disk jockey. To a businessman it may mean selling campaigns. To a child it may mean singing commercials on his favorite TV program. These concepts all represent different forms of advertising.

The true purpose of advertising is to move goods and services. It does this not only by making people aware of products and services but by creating in the consumer a desire to have them. Advertising also attempts to convince the consumer that one product is the most desirable of all those available.

Advertising sometimes attempts to put pressure on the individual to make purchases irrationally or emotionally rather than intelligently. A wise shopper must develop the skill to distinguish advertising that is informational and factual from that which appeals only to the emotions.

The consumer is exposed to an average of 1,600 advertisements each day through television, radio, newspapers, brochures, magazines, outdoor signs, cards, personal letters, and product packaging. Of this exposure, it is estimated that only seventy-five are noticed, and of this number only five can be considered informational advertising. The vast majority of advertisements are designed to sell a product by emotional persuasion.[1]

Motivational research is the technique used by advertising agencies to discover the human factors that convince customers to buy. These studies, developed by psychologists, are utilized to learn the anxieties and desires of the consumer. With this information more effective appeals can be used in advertising. Very often, instead of selling a product directly, an idea which fulfills a need is sold. This type of emotional advertising often is directed to hidden fears or promises to satisfy the concealed hopes of the consumer. For example, products for personal hygiene generally advertise "social security" rather than the qualities of the soap, deodorant, or toothpaste.

[1] Leland J. Gordon and Stewart M. Lee, *Economics for Consumers,* 5th ed. (New York: American, 1967), p. 162.

Most advertisements use a variety of techniques of emotional persuasion designed to appeal to our basic needs and values. These may be social, psychological, physical, or economic in nature. Numerous advertisements are directed toward the human desires for

1. Emotional security—youthfulness, glamour, belonging, sex appeal, prestige, or status
2. Convenience and comfort—ease of care, upkeep, or use
3. Safety and health—best for yourself and those you love
4. Financial gain—wise buy, bargain, economical, shrewd investment, snob appeal [2]

While the main purposes of advertising are to sell a product or gain acceptance of an idea, scores of different approaches have been developed. For the consumer, recognition of the underlying purpose of an advertising campaign can assist in establishing the credibility of the information distributed. Specific purposes of advertising are

1. To increase the use of a product (frequency of use, frequency of replacement, variety of uses, units of purchase, extended length of buying season)
2. To attract a new generation
3. To present a special merchandise offer
4. To coordinate a family of products
5. To become familiar with the organization behind the product
6. To render a public service
7. To dispel wrong impressions
8. To meet substitution
9. To reach the person who influences the purchaser

The vehicle that carries the advertising is spoken of as the medium. Chief advertising media may be classified as

Newspapers	Outdoor advertising
Magazines	Transportation advertising
Radio, television	Point-of-sale displays, motion pictures
Direct-mail advertising	Premiums and special offers

[2] *Ibid.,* pp. 179, 385.

advantages and disadvantages of advertising

It is said that advertising is a reflection of the standards and values of society. The pros and cons directed at advertising are numerous.

ADVANTAGES

Advertising makes people aware of new products and services. It also informs them where they may be purchased. These may be time- and labor-saving products such as durable-press garments or laundry equipment, which can ease the burden of wardrobe maintenance.

Informative and descriptive advertisements enable people to make some comparison between products without leaving their homes. Newspaper ads are an important source of shopping information. A study made in two cities showed that 67–70 per cent of the respondents looked at ads regularly and that 41–48 per cent found them "very helpful." [3]

Advertising is necessary to the economy because it moves goods and services which in turn provides employment in all phases of manufacturing, distribution, promotion, and selling. Advertising creates a high living standard by virtue of the mass production of goods which can be sold at prices people can pay. Advertising pays for a large part of the expenses involved in the publication of newspapers and magazines. It also pays for radio and TV programs which provide entertainment.

DISADVANTAGES

Advertising influences people to overextend their budgets and misuse credit. The appeals and temptations to have products people cannot afford put a serious financial burden on their income.

Advertisers control the media that they use. A survey conducted by the Society of Business Magazine Editors revealed that 50 per cent of the respondents were influenced in their editorial policy by their advertisers, to some degree.[4]

---

[3] Stuart Rich, *Shopping Behavior of Department Store Customers* (Boston: Harvard University—Graduate School of Business Administration, 1963), p. 69.
[4] Gordon and Lee, *op. cit.*, p. 165.

Advertising encourages obsolescence by making consumers dissatisfied. It is obvious in the area of fashion apparel that promotion of the frequent changes of styles creates wardrobe obsolescence long before signs of wear appear.

False claims, exaggerated claims, misrepresentations, and promotion of dangerous products by some advertisements is detrimental to the consumer and can result in serious injury when harmful products are promoted.

EVALUATION OF ADVERTISING

A revealing evaluation can be made by clipping several advertisements from magazines and newspapers of clothing and cosmetic items. Underline in red all copy based on emotional appeals. Underline in black copy that is informative. One can readily see whether the advertising is of real help to the consumer. Further analysis can be made by jotting down to what needs and values the appeals are directed, such as emotional security, health, convenience, comfort, status, power, prestige, or financial gain.

Consumers are in a better position to make intelligent decisions regarding the purchase of goods and services when they understand the motivational appeals made by advertising. They must be able to distinguish factual and informative copy from that which appeals to the emotions and that which makes ambiguous claims.

types of stores

The type of store in which people prefer to do business is based upon personal attitudes and values. Some shoppers consider this activity as recreational; others regard it as an undesirable chore; and many view it as a bargain hunt. There are shoppers who are willing to pay higher prices to be in pleasant surroundings with soft carpets, subtle lighting, and the advantages of service and convenience. These services include sales help, credit, delivery, dining facilities, and pleasant restrooms. Others shoppers consider these as frills and of little importance, and they prefer to look for values at shops with lower overheads and few services. Most shoppers will select stores that carry the quality of merchandise they wish to have at the price they can afford to pay. Many shoppers shop for specific items in a special type of store. This is due both to the habits of the consumer and also to the image of the store. Stores that are accessible and those with adequate parking facilities are important considerations for most everyone. (See Figures 18–1 and 18–2.)

18–1 A modern street scene of shops in the African city of Zanzibar.
(Courtesy Pan American World Airways)

18–2   A typical scene of Tokyo shoppers. Note westernization of dress. (Courtesy Qantas)

18-3 Japanese department store. Tokyo has twenty large department stores offering practically everything for daily use. Note dress of two cultures. (Courtesy Consulate General of Japan)

DEPARTMENT STORES

Many different items are carried under one roof; hence the name, department store. A department store may be part of a large chain with volume buying power, or it may be a one-family operation. Department stores cater to a wide variety of clients from the most wealthy to the poverty-stricken. Each store creates an image and develops a reputation for quality of goods and services and for price range. Department stores provide many types of services, from dress alteration to wedding planning and from interior design to drapery making. Sales personnel are usually well trained and knowledgeable about their department. Telephone orders, credit, charge accounts, and delivery service are extended to the customer. It is often advantageous to the department store customer to use them, as the costs of these services are included in the cost of the merchandise rather than as a separate charge. The department stores have gained public confidence. Their reputation for accepting returned merchandise and standing behind the products they sell has created customer loyalty. (See Figure 18-3.)

DISCOUNT STORES

Discount stores operate on a high-volume, rapid-turnover principle. They offer fewer services to the customer than the department store. Most discount stores are self-service, although there are sales personnel available for assistance. Low prices are the chief feature of a discount house. However, the customer must know quality and prices to ensure a good buy. Discount stores charge for all services, including delivery. Sometimes it is difficult to return unsatisfactory merchandise, and some houses have a posted policy against returns of any kind. A wide variety of merchandise is available from the discount store, and there are many excellent buys. Parking space is usually most generous.

MEMBERSHIP STORES

A membership store is pretty much a combination of a department and discount store. The memberships are sold to a particular group of people who then have the privilege of shopping in the store. Membership stores work on the large-volume, rapid-turnover, reduced-prices policy. These stores generally offer fewer services than department stores but stand behind their merchandise better than discount stores.

SPECIALTY SHOPS

A specialty shop carries a limited amount of exclusive merchandise and caters to a small clientele. This kind of shop builds a reputation on goods and personal services. Very often they specialize in only one item such as dresses within certain size and price ranges, lingerie, handbags, hosiery, and men's haberdashery.

There is an evident trend by shoppers toward a preference for the small specialty shops. The popularity of the smaller units in the department stores supports this trend. Each of these small specialty shops caters to limited tastes and creates a special image.

THE BOUTIQUE

The boutique is a small shop that features a strong fashion image. The success of this type of retailing is due to the trend for individuality in dress. These shops feature a few carefully selected fashions in each style, priced from a few dollars to $1,000 or more. Boutiques may have their own designer or use a free-lance designer. They also use ready-to-wear manufacturers, but they do not depend upon mass-produced ready-to-wear. Custom clothes can be purchased in some boutiques.

The boutique especially appeals to the young and young in spirit. Background music, fashion-conscious young salespeople, the invitation to browse, and the whimsical interiors all contribute to make shopping an exciting adventure. The display equipment is movable and can easily be arranged to accommodate new ideas and groupings.

Many department stores have boutique departments. These are small areas of floor space with all the features and attractions of an independent boutique. The atmosphere is one of a small shop that caters to individual tastes. Carefully selected items are displayed together, and the shopper can purchase an entire coordinated outfit in one area.

techniques for intelligent shopping

Intelligent shopping should result in receiving value and satisfaction for the money spent. The following techniques are recommended.

1. Plan purchases rather than buy on impulse
2. Know value and quality
3. Shop comparatively for major purchases
4. Know your requirements and do not be influenced by others
5. Be cautious of sale items
6. Understand the uses and costs of credit
7. Return unwanted merchandise immediately
8. Demand satisfaction for defective merchandise

PLAN PURCHASES RATHER THAN BUY ON IMPULSE

Planned purchases enable the consumer to bring unity into the wardrobe by having outfits that carry out a theme. They also enable the consumer to budget buying expenses over a longer period. This in turn can cut down on the use of overextended credit and costly carrying charges.

Impulse buying means making purchases of items we did not intend to buy. The odd item purchased on impulse which does not go with anything else in the wardrobe represents an unnecessary expense. Although impulse buying should be discouraged, there are times when buying unplanned merchandise results in an asset to the wardrobe and gives the shopper a lift. A shopper who does not often find apparel that pleases her may find an ideal item that was not on the shopping list. This item may not be available later on. The shopper should take time to evaluate quickly an impulse buy to discover whether the item will

Fit into the existing wardrobe?

Necessitate buying additional items for it to be used?

Represent the image of the user?

Have a place to be worn?

Be suitable in color, line, and price?

Stores take advantage of impulse buyers by placing eye-catching displays in prominent areas such as at the store entrance, near elevators and escalators, and at cash registers. Surveys show that 70 per cent of purchases in self-service stores are made on impulse and 35 per cent in service stores.[5]

KNOW VALUE AND QUALITY

The consumer is informed by use of buying guides, articles, newspapers, and government bulletins as to how to evaluate fabric and workmanship in garment construction. Merchandise should be carefully inspected before making a purchase. By knowing what to look for, the buyer can compare values on the basis of quality, style, and price and arrive at better decisions for the best buy for the money. An informed shopper reads labels and guarantees.

SHOP COMPARATIVELY

Compare major and expensive items. Price differentials on the same quality merchandise are found in various shops in the same locality. Mark-up on merchandise varies because of overhead expenses, volume of sales, and turnover of merchandise. Studies reveal that women shop around more for better dresses and children's clothing than for large appliances.[6] It is a questionable use of time, energy, and transportation to shop comparatively for minor items.

Know Your Requirements

Unnecessary purchasing can be avoided if the shopper knows her needs and is not persuaded by either salespeople or friends to buy something about

---

[5] *Ibid.,* p. 385.
[6] Rich, *op. cit.,* p. 100.

which she is uncertain. Many people are unable to make up their own minds and so succumb to the urges of others. When a person asks a salesclerk if a garment looks good, the answer is going to be an obvious one, yet this is a common practice. If in doubt, it is best to put off the purchase, think it over, and then decide.

The consumer who is aware of clever selling techniques will be less inclined to make unnecessary purchases. Perhaps the highest pressure selling occurs at the cosmetic counter. When a woman goes in to buy a lipstick and leaves with several other items, a clever salesperson has been influential. Flattery is a means often used to make sales. Showing a customer a garment that is not on display makes him believe that he is the first person to see it. Another technique called a multiple-sale occurs after a customer has purchased a dress and an additional sale is often made by the suggestion of a related item such as a purse, hosiery, jewelry, or perhaps even another dress. Trading-up takes place when you have purchased an item of higher cost than the one you originally intended to buy.

BE CAUTIOUS OF ITEMS ON SALE

Because an item is on sale, many people think they are getting a bargain. The fact that an item is on sale may mean that it is not wanted, either by the store or by the manufacturer. Some merchandise may be a bargain, but it may also be a "white elephant." Decide whether the item is a style that is going out of fashion or whether the garment will become obsolete in a short time. For items such as undergarments and sleepwear sales can benefit the budget.

Some sales are not legitimate. This occurs when merchants make fictitious mark-ups to make the sale price look good. "End of the Season Clearance Sales" on clothing items occur after Christmas in January for inventory; the end of April for the arrival of summer stock; after July 1 for the arrival of winter stock; and late in November for the arrival of Christmas merchandise. Some stores feature sales of "special purchase" merchandise which is not the regular store stock. It may be of a lower quality than usually carried and should be carefully inspected.

UNDERSTAND THE USES AND COSTS OF CREDIT

The costs of credit are high. Stores accepting credit run the risk of loss on bad debts, and this loss is often met by higher priced merchandise. Additional charges on accounts extending over thirty days should be clearly understood by the buyer. Revolving or budget accounts quote 1 to 1½ per cent per month on the unpaid balance. This amounts to from 12–18 per cent per twelve-month period.[7] If you bought a $240 coat and made twelve payments of $20 per month, the interest charge on the $240 coat is $53.20 at 1 per cent and $59.30 at 1½ per cent. As of September 1, 1969, the federal government has required that all stores inform their customers in writing exactly what the credit charges are.

RETURN UNWANTED MERCHANDISE IMMEDIATELY

It is the consumer's responsibility to return unsatisfactory merchandise promptly. This merchandise should be in the best possible condition. Returned goods involve an expense for the store, as they must be either reticketed and returned to the stock or sent back to the manufacturer. When returning unwanted merchandise, be friendly, courteous, and firm. Ask to see the store or department manager or buyer rather than complaining to a clerk without authority to make the exchange. A smile and consideration for the store employee usually get far more satisfaction than a rude or hostile approach.

DEMAND SATISFACTION FOR DEFECTIVE MERCHANDISE

Satisfactory adjustments for defective merchandise should be demanded. Reputable stores will accept these goods without question, while other stores may be less responsible. Some stores advertise an "all sales final" policy, which should warn the shopper to inspect all goods carefully before purchase. If the store does not give you proper satisfaction and you honestly feel they are being evasive or cheating you, your best recourse is to discuss the matter at your local Better Business Bureau.

shopping for clothing

How do you shop for clothing? Have you ever really considered this? Clothing expenditures represent a very large part of most budgets, so that careful examination of the practices of spending these monies should be of interest to all. Think about how you usually shop for apparel items. Do you shop in a variety of stores, comparing price and quality before buying? Or do you always buy at the same stores? Do you have a wardrobe plan, or do you just buy what pleases you on impulse? Do you wait for sales and then buy only the marked-down items? Or do you use clothing shopping for a psychological lift or reward? Do you make all the decisions about your purchases, or do you let salespeople or friends talk

[7] *Consumers All: The Official Consumer's Guide* (New York: Pocket Books, 1965), p. 159.

you into purchases? If you are like most, you use a combination of the above methods with perhaps a few personalized twists.

How successful are your shopping methods? Clothing purchases reflect personal values. The clothing philosophy we develop must meet our individual requirements to be satisfactory. Clothing is used to satisfy psychological, aesthetic, economic, physical, and social needs. The emphasis placed on both needs and values varies with the individual. The answer to how successful your shopping techniques are lies in how satisfactory your wardrobe is to you. Does your clothing fit your personal needs and style of life? When you analyze your wardrobe, do the "successes" outnumber the "failure" purchases? Are you satisfied with your shopping methods? Do you feel that you get the full value for your money, or do you have some doubts?

As a guide for making clothing decisions at the time of purchase, the following questions have been developed. This list is not intended to be comprehensive. It is meant to serve as a guide for on-the-spot decision. Add to the list any considerations that are important to you. For added meaning, the relationship of the question to the fulfillment of the value or need is included.

Need or Value	*Question at Point of Purchase*
Economic	Is this what I started out to buy?
	Does it fit my price range?
	Is it well constructed and styled for the price?
	Will it be easy to care for?
	Will it give long service?
	Does it fit into my wardrobe?
Physical	Is it comfortable?
	Does the movement room fit the activities it will be used for?
	Does it suit the climate in which it will be worn?
Psychological	Am I deciding for myself or being pressured into buying?
	Do I feel right in it?
	Does it represent my self-image?
Social	Does it suit my roles?
	Where can I wear it?
Aesthetic	Does it enhance my appearance?
	Is it fashionable?

summary

The true evaluation of shopping skills is the degree of satisfaction derived by the consumer. If you are pleased with your purchases and feel you are getting full value for the money spent, then you are a good shopper. However, if your

18–4 The shop comes to the door in some areas of the world. A pine-
apple vendor paddles up to the customer in Bangkok, Thailand. (Courtesy
Pan American World Airways)

purchases do not fulfill your expectations or fit into your style of life, then there
is room for improvement of shopping skills.

The consumer should become familiar with the variety of products on the
market and the differences between them. Advertising plays a large part in ac-
quainting the consumer with the product. Advertising has the specific purpose
of moving goods from manufacturer to consumer. A wide variety of advertising
and selling techniques are employed to accomplish this purpose, and the wise
shopper will be acquainted with them. The shopper should also understand the
various purposes and policies of the numerous stores selling goods. Each store
has a specific image and caters to a certain clientele. Understanding the purpose
of the store enables the consumer to select the specific goods that the store
handles best. (See Figure 18–4.)

Each shopper should develop a personal list of shopping techniques which
are suitable to his needs, values, and style of life. Critical to the success of any
shopper is the ability to make the right decisions at the time of purchase.

suggested readings

Aspley, J. C. *Aspley on Sales*. Chicago: Dartnell Corporation, 1967.

Blum, M., and J. McLean. *Shopper's Handbook.* Ithaca, N.Y.: Cornell University, New York State College of Home Economics, 1961.

Canfield, B. *Salesmanship Practices and Problems,* New York: McGraw-Hill, 1959.

Consumers All; The Official Consumer's Guide. New York: Pocket Books, Inc., 1965.

Gold, Annalee. *How to Sell Fashion.* New York: Fairchild Publications, Inc., 1968.

Kleppnes, Otto. *Advertising Procedure.* Englewood Cliffs, N.J.: Prentice-Hall, Inc., 1950.

Schoenfeld, D., and A. A. Natella. *The Consumer and His Dollars*. Dobbs Ferry, N.Y.: Oceana Publications, Inc., 1966.

Swinney, John Bayly. *Merchandising of Fashions.* New York: The Ronald Press Company, 1942.

U.S. Department of Agriculture. *Family Economics Review.* Washington, D.C.: Government Printing Office, 1968.

19

care and maintenance of the wardrobe

are and maintenance of the wardrobe are probably the most neglected aspects of the study of clothing. However, this is an area that must be considered for several reasons. The length of "life" of the items in the wardrobe can be greatly extended by proper care and maintenance. This extension of wearability helps to stretch the budget allotted to clothing. Also, management of the wardrobe through care and repair keeps all clothing fresh and ready to wear, thus allowing you to always be immaculately dressed.

label file

Garment hangtags describing fiber content and care found on purchased garments should be kept for future reference. These labels can be fastened to an index card along with notations that will identify the garments to which they belong. Information such as the price of the garment and the date and place of purchase can help in appraising the garment long after it has been purchased. A file box containing the labels should be placed

395

near the laundry area, where it will be available when you need to refer to it for cleaning instructions. This file should be kept current by periodically removing cards of discarded clothing. It should be a working file and referred to often.

daily and periodic care

Daily and periodic care of clothing helps to extend wearing time and ensures that clothing is always ready to be worn when needed. After wearing, inspect garments for rips, loose snaps and hooks, and other breakdowns. Either make the necessary repairs right then or put the garments aside for a more convenient time for mending and pressing.

Spots given attention when they are fresh are far more easily removed than those that have aged and set into the fabric. Commercial spot- and stain-remover preparations give excellent results, but reading and following the directions for use are a must. Be sure that the fiber content of the garment and the cleaning agent are compatible.

Daily care may involve brushing, airing, and pressing before storage. This is of particular importance for the care of wools. Garments made of wool also need a rest between wearings in order to maintain their shape, so give them at least a day off after wearing them.

Good hangers are important for the support of garments. Wire hangers which are returned with clothes from the dry cleaners do not provide adequate support for garments. They often cause distortion of the fabric in the shoulder and sleeve cap area. Padded hangers can be purchased, or wire hangers can be padded at home by covering them with tissue paper and fabric scraps or crocheting. Skirts and pants can be clamped to wire hangers with snap-type clothespins.

One way to avoid wrinkles forming while garments are stored in the closet is to allow sufficient room so that clothes are not crowded or packed in tightly. They should be permitted to hang straight. Some garments crush less if stuffed with tissue paper. This may entail some reorganization, such as finding another place to store garments not worn often. A double row of rods which runs halfway through the closet can double the space for short lengths such as shirts, skirts, and jackets, thus leaving the remainder of the rod space for full-length garments.

Check shoes for scuffs in need of touching up. Shoe trees help to preserve the shape of shoes that are fully enclosed. Open or sandal-back styles can be stuffed with paper. Metal shoe racks are available, and these can help in holding the toe shapes. Run-down heels need prompt attention to prevent the entire shoe from becoming permanently distorted. Heels in need of repair present an unsightly appearance which detracts from the total image.

Periodic care involves brushing out pockets, repairing clothing in need of mending, and cleaning soiled clothing. Garments in need of dry cleaning can be put aside until a number of clothes need the same treatment rather than making frequent trips to the cleaners. If you use the services of a dry cleaner that delivers, this is no problem. Reliable cleaners are a rarity in some locations. The symbol of The National Institute of Drycleaning displayed in a cleaning establishment is one of the best guides to quality work. Word of mouth recommendations of satisfied customers are also excellent references.

DRY CLEANING

Whether a garment is washable or dry-cleanable depends upon several factors—the fiber content, fabric construction, type of dye, finish, garment construction, and trim or decoration. A fabric with the fiber of cotton may be washable, but the trims applied might not withstand washing, thus making the garment dry-cleanable only. This is a factor to consider at time of purchase.

The consumer has the choice of using either the coin-operated, self-service cleaner or the professional dry cleaner. Your choice will probably depend on your budget, the value and conditon of the garments, and the past performance you have experienced with either one.

The chief advantage of using the self-service establishments is the low cost per cleaning load. The disadvantage is the lack of professional help in removing spots and stains and knowing whether the garments are dry-cleanable. Pressing or touch-up must be done by the individual after cleaning. Many garments which are still serviceable may not be worth paying the price asked by the professional dry cleaner. This might include children's outer wear of wool, sweaters, and simply designed garments.

When self-service cleaning is used, separate the light- and dark-colored garments and the fragile and heavy clothing, and do these in separate loads. Check pockets and brush lint from cuffs and pockets; remove buttons, belts, and trims unsuited to cleaning. After drying is completed, remove the clothing immediately and hang them on hangers.

A professional dry cleaner will detach noncleanable accessories, remove spots and stains (he can do this even better if you tell him what caused it), clean, dry, and finish clothing under conditions best suited for the garments. Commercial pressing equipment and a skilled presser will restore garments to the best possible condition.

WET CLEANING

Home Laundry Equipment

Modern laundry equipment represents sophisticated engineering and technology. The drudgery and most of the guesswork are eliminated. (See Figure

19–1 For some people, doing the family laundry means washing the clothing in a nearby stream, as this Indian family at Tavuni must do. The drudgery of the task is reduced by the camaraderie of the group. (Courtesy Qantas)

19–1.) For washing machines, various price ranges and models are available. Some equipment has cycles for prewash and soak and special cycles for delicates and wool; automatic dispensers for detergent, bleach, and softeners will discharge the proper amount at the proper time. You can select the amount of water for the size of the load, control water temperature for wash and rinses, and choose the speed for agitation and spin dry for the kind of load, depending on the amount of soil and type of fabric.

Dryers can be regulated by selecting the temperature best suited for the various fabrics and finishes. Some drying equipment has electronic controls which stop the dryer automatically when clothes reach the right amount of dryness. Automatic dampening devices are found on some models, as well as signals that warn you to remove the clothes from the dryer before they wrinkle.

Coin-Operated Equipment

398

People who do not own laundry equipment may use coin-operated machines, either in apartment houses or in commercial establishments. Most commercial equipment has fixed cycles, and the selection for agitation and water temperature is limited.

Commercial multiload dryers utilize one temperature, and it is not recommended that synthetics and knits be used in these dryers. Durable-press garments dried in these dryers should be removed as soon as they are dry to prevent wrinkling. Persons that use coin-operated equipment should always use a disinfectant in their wash to prevent the spread of bacteria.

DISINFECTANTS

Bacteria can survive on garments whether they are washed in hot water or cold, although more so in cold water. People who use coin-operated laundry equipment can pick up bacteria on their laundry from the machine. Illness of one family member can be transferred to others by bacteria on clothing whether the laundry is done at home or elsewhere. The addition of a disinfectant can reduce bacteria to a safe level. Many women use cold water for their entire family wash. Because more bacteria survive in cold water, the addition of a disinfectant is advisable.

The Agriculture Research Service of the U.S. Department of Agriculture gives four types of disinfectants that will reduce the bacteria to a safe level in home laundering.[1]

For Use in Hot, Warm, or Cold Water
1. Liquid chlorine bleach (containing 5.25 per cent sodium hypochlorite) added to wash cycle, 4 oz (½ cup) for front-loading machines and 8 oz (1 cup) for top-loading machines. Chlorine bleaches cannot be used on spandex, silk, wool, colors not fast to bleach, and some wash-and-wear finishes.

2. Quaternary disinfectants added to rinse cycle, 3 oz (6 tablespoons) for front-loading machines and 4 oz for top-loading machines.

For Use in Hot or Warm Water
3. Pine oil disinfectants (70 per cent pine oil) added to wash cycle, 4 oz for front-loading machines and 6 oz for top-loading machines.

4. Phenolic disinfectants (3 per cent of active ingredients) added to wash or rinse cycle, 5 oz for front-loading machines and 8 oz for top-loading machines.

Trade names for these products are available in *Consumers All: The Official Consumer's Guide.*[2]

[1] U.S. Department of Agriculture, "Sanitation in Home Laundering," Home and Garden Bulletin No. 97 (Washington, D.C.: Government Printing Office, 1967), p. 5.
[2] (New York: Pocket Books, 1965), p. 372.

laundry products

Supermarket shelves are bulging with varieties of laundry products which give excellent performance in cleaning clothes. Being faced with the many choices available can be a confusing experience. Some products such as soap or detergent are essential; other aids including bleaches, fabric softeners, enzyme products, and fabric finishers aid in getting better results and may be considered as necessary for certain laundry problems. Regardless of which product is chosen to be used, it is important to read and follow all the label instructions carefully. Use a standard measuring cup to get the exact amount; guesswork may result in serious, irreparable damage to fabrics. Some products cannot be used in combination with other products because of chemical reactions resulting in the formation of new compounds, which may damage the fabrics or give off harmful fumes.

SOAPS AND DETERGENTS

Soaps are natural cleaning agents composed of fats, oils, and alkali along with compounds used to increase sudsing, soften hard water, and generally improve cleaning. Soaps are rarely used in home laundry today. The chief reason for the decline in popularity of soap as a cleansing agent is its reaction in hard water. When the components of soap combine with the mineral salts found in hard water, a curd or scum is formed. This curd is most insoluble as it clings to the fibers and fabrics. The resultant laundry is boardlike, stiff, and grayed. Breaking down and removing this soap scum are difficult and further complicate home laundering.

A detergent is a synthetic, or manmade, cleansing agent. There are many varieties of detergent on the market today. Some are designed for specific purposes such as rug shampooing, dishwashing, or laundering, while others are made for general household tasks.

Basically, there are two types of detergents. Heavy-duty, also called all-purpose or "built," which contains an alkali for increased cleaning power. The heavy-duty detergent is for use with sturdy fabrics with medium to heavy soil. The second type of detergent is called mild, light-duty, or "unbuilt"; it does not contain alkali. The mild detergents are designed for use with more delicate fabrics such as silks and wools which are damaged by alkalis. Interestingly, packaging of these detergents helps identify their strength. Heavy-duty detergents are wrapped in bright, high-intensity colors, whereas pastels are used for the mild ones.

Either type may be high- or low-sudsing. This means the detergent may be formulized to give a large volume of suds or a small amount. Unfortunately, many women equate the cleansing ability of a detergent with its sudsing level. This is a completely misunderstood concept. Suds do not clean. It is the formula of the detergent that establishes the cleansing power.

One difficulty often encountered with the use of detergent in home laundering is a yellowing or graying of fabrics. This may be caused because an insufficient amount of detergent has been used for the amount of soil, water, or wash load. Hard water and inadequate rinsing of the clothes may also result in this discoloration. However, there are products on the market designed especially to recondition such damaged clothes.

The personal decision of whether to use soap or detergent as your cleansing agent is related directly to the quality of the water available to you. If the water supply is over three grains of hardness, the use of a detergent will be more satisfactory than soap. Water over eight-to-ten grains of hardness requires use of larger amounts of detergent. (A discussion of water conditions follows later in this chapter.)

ENZYME PRODUCTS

Enzyme cleaning agents are chemical protein products which have been developed to break down various types of soils and stains into simpler forms which are easily removed during washing. These products can be used on all washable fabrics. They remove body soils, grass stains, blood, egg, milk, gravy, chocolate, and some fruit and vegetable stains. They are not effective for stains from rust, ink, graphite, cooking oil, salad dressing, motor grease, coffee, tea, or mustard.[3]

Two types of enzyme products are the presoak formulas used before washing and the enzyme detergent used during washing. Directions should be followed carefully. If chlorine bleach is used with enzyme detergents, the bleach must be added during the last half of the washing cycle because chlorine bleach deactivates the enzymes in the enzyme detergent. Enzyme agents add to the pricing; their value must be considered in relation to this cost.

BLEACHES

Bleaching agents are used to remove color from stains and to make certain compounds of the natural soils soluble.[4] The type of bleach to be used will depend on the fiber and the finish of the fabric.

[3] Soap and Detergent Association, "Cleanliness Facts for Home Economists" (July–Aug. 1969), pp. 1–2, New York.
[4] "Fabrics, Fashions and Facilities," report of National Home Laundry Conference, Los Angeles, Nov. 1965 (Chicago: American Home Laundry Manufacturers' Association), p. 67.

Chlorine Bleach

Chlorine bleaches are the most effective. However, they cannot be used on all fabrics, especially on those fabrics with a wash-and-wear chlorine-retentive finish. The garment label will give this information. Do not use chlorine bleaches on silk, wool, some spandex, colors not fast to bleach, and some wash-and-wear finishes. Liquid chlorine bleach must always be diluted as directed before being added to the wash water. Bleach is added after the suds have had time to act, about five minutes. The optical brighteners used in detergents must be allowed to act for a few minutes as the bleach interferes with their performance. Once the optical brighteners have become attached to the fabrics, they will not be affected by the bleach. Avoid using chlorine bleach without a detergent or in cold water. The detergent acts as a buffer to protect fabrics.[5] In hard water chlorine bleaches intensify discoloration of fabrics.[6]

Oxygen Bleaches

Oxygen bleaches are safe for all washable fabrics including cotton, silk, wool, wash-and-wear, rayon, spandex, and resin-treated and colored fabrics. They do not perform as effectively for soil and stain removal as the chlorine bleaches. They will not restore whiteness, but they help to maintain whiteness when used consistently. Oxygen bleaches, found in granular form, are of two types: (1) perborate oxygen—most effective in very hot water and (2) potassium monopersulfate—used with lower temperatures with good results. This type is more effective than the perborate type.

FABRIC SOFTENERS

Fabric softeners are used in the final rinse water to make clothes fluffy, minimize wrinkling, and eliminate static electricity which causes clothes to cling. Overuse of the product coats the fibers of the cloth, which results in a lack of absorbency. This becomes a problem for towels, diapers, and other textile products that are used to absorb moisture. Fabric softeners should not be used in rinse water that contains any other laundry product, as a chemical reaction causes a curd to be deposited on fabrics. This curd is difficult to remove.

STARCHES

Starches are sizing agents used to give body to clothes and keep them

---

[5] "Lighten Your Laundry Load," HE–65, Iowa State University Cooperative Extension Service, Ames, Iowa (March 1965), p. 9.

[6] *The Maytag Encyclopedia of Home Laundry,* 2nd ed. (New York: Popular Library, 1969), p. 78.

clean longer. Clothes can be given a light starch for a little body or a heavy starch which will make them stiff. There are several types.

1. Dry—this product of cornstarch is mixed with cold water and then heated. It is the least expensive to use.
2. Precooked—pretreatment allows this starch to be prepared by just adding cold water. It is not boiled.
3. Liquid—addition of water is all that is needed in the preparation of this cornstarch product.
4. Plastic sizing—the concentrated liquid is diluted. Some plastic starches will remain on garments after several washings.

The above starches are used on clothes after they have been spun dried. Clothes may be starched in the washing machine on a rinse cycle. After clothes are starched and dried, they should be dampened with warm water and rolled up in a damp towel, or placed in a plastic bag, for about two hours so that the moisture is distributed. Ironing must be done at a high temperature to prevent the starch from sticking to the iron.

5. Spray—product comes in aerosol can and is the easiest to use but the most expensive. It can be used on either damp or dry articles, and clothes can be sprayed as they are ironed, or the entire garment can be sprayed, rolled in a towel for a few minutes, and then ironed.

FABRIC FINISHES

Fabric finishes come in aerosol cans. These impart less stiffness than starch, and their chief advantage is that they can be used at lower ironing temperatures, which many modern fabrics require.

laundry procedures

Clothes that are to be laundered need some attention prior to being put in the machine if satisfactory results are to be achieved. Remove all items from pockets; take off pins, detachable ornaments, detachable, and unwashable belts and buttons. Zip up zippers and turn dark clothing inside out to prevent lint from collecting on the outside. Inspect for needed repairs so that little rips will not become a major mending task during laundering.

SORTING

Laundering would be simplified if everything could be put into the machine together, but all clothes do not mix. Sorting is done in washing loads to keep similar fabrics together. Improper sorting causes lint to collect, color transfer, shrinkage, and graying. Sort as follows.

Dark colors—separate dark-colored clothing to keep them free of lint and to prevent any color transfer to light-colored garments.

White and light-colored synthetics—color pick-up from other garments is avoided if these garments are handled separately.

Fabrics to be bleached—white and light-colored synthetics and cottons to be bleached during washing are put together.

Colored clothes—brilliant colors should be washed separately to avoid color transference. These may require cold or warm water.

Terry and velvet cut towels—if these are dark, intense colors, they will be dulled by other colors, so should be washed separately.

Knits and delicate garments—these require gentle handling.

Durable-press—durable-press can be washed in the regular manner if an automatic dryer is to be used. If these garments are to be line dried, wrinkles caused by wear and washing will not be removed. In the latter case, the garments must instead be washed in warm water and given a cool rinse.

PRETREATMENT OF SPOTS AND STAINS

Spots, stains, and excessively soiled garments may need treatment before washing. Wash-and-wear, durable-press, and synthetics do not give up oil-borne stain readily. Those sections of the garment that are most readily soiled, such as the collar and cuff areas, should be treated with a concentrated liquid detergent and allowed to stand for fifteen minutes to an hour before washing.

Heavily soiled garments require presoaking. This can be done in the washing machine on a presoak cycle or in any machine on the rinse cycle. If the latter is used, turn the dial to rinse, let the machine fill, and turn it off. Detergent or an enzyme-acting laundry aid should be added to the water. Allow the clothes to soak for fifteen to twenty minutes, or follow the directions on the package.

Some stains require special preparation for their removal. Commercial products are available that remove stains safely and effectively. It is necessary to read and follow label instructions, know the fiber content of the garments, and know the nature of the soil in order to satisfactorily treat the stain. Always test the product on a hidden area of the garment to determine whether the fabric will be damaged by the product.

Oil spots can sometimes be removed by applying dry cornstarch directly to the spot. This absorbs the oil and can be brushed out easily without leaving a ring. Water spots on silks, rayons, and acetates may come out by rubbing or slightly scratching the area with your fingernail.

WASHING WATER

Hard water creates problems in the laundry, and the minerals present in the water will prevent the soap or detergent from cleaning effectively. Soap used in hard water causes a curd to form which adheres to the fabric, giving it a yellowish or gray appearance. When detergents are used, an increased amount of detergent should overcome the problem of water hardness unless the water is excessively hard.

Water hardness of zero-to-three grains is considered soft, and soap may be used satisfactorily. Between three to nineteen grains of hardness requires increased amount of detergent; over nineteen grains is so hard that increased detergent alone will not give satisfactory cleaning performance, and the use of a packaged water conditioner will be necessary.[7] Consult your city water department to learn the degree of water hardness in your community.

Water Temperature

The fiber, construction of the garment, fabric dyes, finishes, and the amount of soil will influence the degree of water temperature needed to clean clothes.

Hot water—140 degrees used for white cottons, white linens, and heavily soiled clothing.

Warm water—100–110 degrees used for colored cottons, delicates, spandex. Wash-and-wear, durable-press, and synthetics and blends which will be dryer dried can use this temperature.

Cold-water—wash-and-wear, durable-press, synthetics, and blends if no dryer is available. Washable woolens and knits used with gentle action. Bright colors or sensitive colors that have a tendency to fade.

Time During Washing Action

Overloading the washer causes wrinkles to form and does not result in effective cleaning. Use the correct cycle for the load.[8]

Washing times for a few types of fabric are as follows.

Handwash—two to three minutes

No-iron outerwear—five to ten minutes

Cotton and linen—eight to ten minutes

[7] *Ibid.,* pp. 76–77.
[8] *How to Read a Handtag* (Newton, Iowa: Maytag Company), p. 14.

RINSES

Wash-and-wear, synthetics, and durable-press require a cool rinse to prevent wrinkles from forming before they are spun. If these clothes are to be tumble-dried, this is not important because the heat of the dryer will remove the wrinkles. A warm rinse is preferred for most other fabrics, as a better job of soil removal occurs. Cottons, linens, and sheets treated with durable-press finishes can take a warm rinse. Thorough rinsing is necessary to remove loosened soil and detergent residue which can build up in clothes and cause grayness.

DRYING

Overloading the dryer causes wrinkles to form. Fabrics made of natural fibers should be removed when a little moisture remains to prevent a harsh feeling and a wrinkled appearance. Remove garments from dryer as soon as the cycle is finished and hang or fold to avoid wrinkling.

Dryer settings depend upon fiber and fabric finish.[9] A low setting should be used for manmade fibers and a medium setting for durable-press, wash-and-wear, and cottons. If a dryer has a wash-and-wear setting, the temperature will be raised sufficiently to release wrinkles, followed by a cooling period.

IRONING AND PRESSING

Modern textile technology has come a long way toward eliminating the need for ironing. Personal standards will influence the amount of smoothness expected of clothing. Many items need some "touching up" with the iron.

Equipment Needed

Ironing board—a well-padded, balanced board is necessary to obtain a good finish on fabrics. Insufficient padding results in an unsightly shine. A tight-fitting, lint-free cover is also essential.

Sleeve board or sleeve roll—these are long, narrow items that are used to press sleeves and small shaped areas so that a crease line is eliminated. A substitute can be made by rolling up a magazine, tying the ends with string, and covering with a small Turkish towel.

Iron—a steam iron is easier to use and more versatile than a dry iron. Some are equipped with spray; some with reversible cords for left-handed people. Sole plates with a nonstick finish are also a convenience. Some people prefer the weight of the standard dry iron. The choice is personal.

[9] *Ibid.*, p. 15.

Pressing mitt—this aids in pressing difficult areas such as sleeves and shoulders —rounded and shaped areas. It is also handy for small areas that need a "touch-up."

Press cloths—press cloths aid in preventing a shine when "touching up" is needed on the outside of the garment. These can be of a cotton drill or a large piece of wool.

Strips of heavy wrapping paper—paper placed in under the seam will prevent a seam impression from showing on the outside of heavy fabrics, particularly wool. Hems that are stitched with a running hem stitch slightly below the edge of the hem can accommodate the paper strip, thus preventing an unsightly line from forming.

Ironing Temperature

The ironing temperature is selected for the fiber of the fabric. Cotton and linen require a high temperature on dampened clothes unless a wrinkle-resistant finish has been used. Silks and wool need medium temperatures. Wool needs steam or a dampened press cloth. Blends and synthetics use low temperatures.

Techniques

Ironing is a sliding motion following the grain of the fabric. Items such as cotton garments, tablecloths, and men's shirts are ironed. Wools and better garments are always pressed. Pressing is a lifting motion, not a back and forth motion. Pressing technique eliminates shine.

Special Fabrics

Crepes—some crepes stretch or bubble with moisture. Try a hidden corner to determine whether moisture can be used.

Acrylics—some woven acrylics and acrylic blends do not respond well to moisture while ironing.

Wool—use a steam iron or a dampened press cloth, press on wrong side of fabric. Avoid using too much hand pressure on the iron as seam, hem, and facing imprints will show through to the outside. Should overpressing occur, causing a shine to form or a seam to show through, hold the steam iron (or dampened press cloth with the nonsteam iron) over the area and allow a little moisture to form, then press out the mark on the underside, under the seam or facing. Brush outside area lightly to raise the nap.

Dark-colored clothes—press on the wrong side to avoid shine.

Heat-sensitive fibers—these will glaze and melt when subjected to high ironing temperatures. Use low temperatures and a soft pressing pad which will permit seams and edges to sink into the pad to prevent glazing (flattening of the surface). Heat-sensitive fibers used in clothing are

Acetate
Nylon
Polyester
Acrylic
Modacrylic (extremely low temperatures)

disposable clothing

The demands on the time of the modern woman plus the scarcity of labor service and rising labor costs gave birth to the "throwaway." These garments, called disposables, are made of nonwoven fibers held together mechanically or chemically. These products have been a boon to hospitals, clinics, and industries which faced staggering laundry bills (Figure 19–2).

The disposable dresses (Figure 19–3) which appeared on the market could not compete with dresses that promised a longer life; however, disposable panties, bathing suits, diapers, and even graduation caps and gowns and bridal dresses have contributed sales of $500 million annually.[10] Vending machines located in air terminals are dispensing disposable white shirts for the traveling businessman. Other apparel items scheduled to follow are disposable socks and underwear.

Clothing care is eliminated by the use of disposables. However, until we can count on "throwaways" to take over the entire wardrobe, we are faced with the task of clothing care and maintenance.

summary

The practical and economic aspects of clothing care and repair are obvious to all that have given the subject the least amount of consideration. As our textile and clothing technology continues to expand, the knowledge needed to maintain the wardrobe must continue to grow. Understanding the information presented by the manufacturer on the hangtag of each garment is a key to keeping up with this scientific data. As some of this information is complicated or unique to the individual garment, a hangtag reference file is a recommended laundry accessory.

[10] Robert Dallos, "Disposables Boom: Wear It Once, Toss It Away," *Los Angeles Times,* March 30, 1969, Sec. H, p. 1.

Daily and periodic care will do much to expand the wearing life of the wardrobe items. Understanding the basic differences among the processes for dry or wet cleaning and knowing how to determine which is best for individual garments will add further longevity to them.

Proper selection of commercial products designed for specific cleaning problems is vital to obtaining the desired results. From the vast array of laundry and cleaning products available on the market today, educated choices must be made based on the understanding of the cleaning problems as related to garments, equipment, and local water supply.

Skills for handling various garments and fibers as they are cleaned must be developed. Understanding of temperatures, pressing, and ironing techniques must be exhibited for desired results. The modern laundress has a complicated task. No matter how advanced the cleaning equipment, it is the operator that makes the decisions that will result in fresh, wrinkle-free, new-looking clothing which can be worn with pride.

19–2 Institutions faced with high laundry costs solved the problem by the use of disposables. Now available for home consumption, these products are useful in the sickroom, for camping and travel. (Courtesy J. P. Stevens and Company)

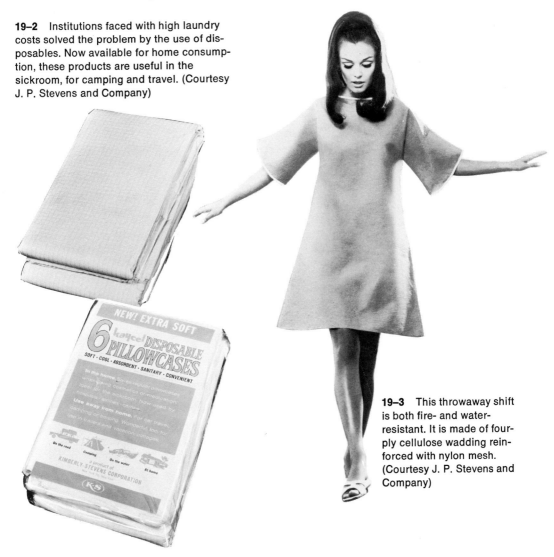

19–3 This throwaway shift is both fire- and water-resistant. It is made of four-ply cellulose wadding reinforced with nylon mesh. (Courtesy J. P. Stevens and Company)

FIBER AND FABRICS—CHARACTERISTICS AND CARE *

Fiber	Trademarks	Characteristics	Special Care Information
		Natural	
Cotton		Hand varies according to weave, texture, and type cotton plant used. Medium strength. Nonresilient unless special wrinkle-resistant finish applied. Shrinkage expected unless controlled by finish.	Some cottons may be labeled "Do not bleach"; never use chlorine bleach on these items.
Wool		Warm, resilient, medium strength, absorbent. Wiry, springy yet soft hand.	To avoid felting shrinkage, interpret care recommendations as follows: 1. Dry clean—send to reliable dry cleaner. 2. Even garments labeled "handwash" can be washed better in an automatic washer as follows: use full tub of cold water. Wash at gentle speed two minutes; soak in same water eight minutes. Allow washer to complete cycle. Use a cold-water laundry detergent. Block to original size on flat surface to air dry away from heat. 3. Machine wash and dry —wash three to eight minutes in warm water. Omit soak, tumble dry on Regular setting. Remove while item feels slightly damp, if dryer does not have electronic control.
Linen		Medium strength, nonresilient, very absorbent, poor wrinkle-resistance unless protected by finish.	Observe bleaching instructions if included on label.
Silk		Soft hand, highly drapable, resilient, luxurious.	Do not use chlorine bleaches. Usually drycleaned. If labeled "hand washable," machine wash in warm or cold water at gentle speed not more than three minutes.

*Courtesy Maytag Company.

Fiber	Trademarks	Characteristics	Special Care Information
Manmade (Cellulose Base)			
Acetate	Acele, Avicolor, Avisco, Celacloud, Celaire, Celaloft, Celanese, Celaperm, Chromspun, Estron, Fiber 25, Loftura, Quilticel	Luxury fiber at moderate cost. Drapes well. Luxurious hand. Usually used for satin, crepe, velvet as well as for suitings and sportswear.	Usually requires dry cleaning. If washing recommended, use gentle speed, three minute warm or cold wash. Iron while damp on wrong side at **coolest** setting. Use press-cloth for right-side pressing.
Triacetate	Arnel	Thermoplastic. Drapes well. Higher wet strength than acetate. Withstands higher ironing temperatures. Available in wide variety of woven textures. Often found in tricot or knit construction. Dresses and skirts often made with heatset pleats.	Air dry permanently pleated garments. If air or drip drying is necessary because of pleats, wash in cold water at gentle speed three to five minutes. Woven fabrics usually require ironing. Knit Arnel should be tumbled free of wrinkles in a dryer.
Rayon †	Avicolor, Avicron, Avisco, Avril, Avron, Bemberg, Bonacette, Coloray, Corval, Cupioni, Cupracolor, Cuprel, DyLok, Enka, Enkor, Fibro, Flaikona, Fortisan, Jetsun, Kolorbon, Lorella, Nub-lite, Nupron, Ondelette, Skybloom, Skyloft, Softglo, Suprenka, Topel, Zantrel, Zantrell 700	Absorbent, drapes well, may lose any original crispness after washing. Requires special finish to resist wrinkles. Various textures and hands available. Often blended with other fibers. Shrinkage expected unless controlled by special finish.	Iron to return maximum body of original texture. If wrinkle-resistant finish applied, no ironing is needed.
Chemical (Manmade Compounds with No Counterpart in Nature)			
Acrylic	Acrilan Creslan Glacé Orlon Orlon-Sayelle Zefkrome Zefran	Thermoplastic, medium strength. Takes color exceptionally well; great bulking power for soft, warm and lightweight fabrics. Resilient. Often made to look like wool. Orlon Sayelle—special fiber that expands when wet. Takes brilliant fast colors.	To retain shape, tumble dry (Sayelle) in a dryer.

† Newest rayons on the market have built-in wrinkle resistance and hold their shape due to the basic fiber being permanently altered by chemical recomposition.

Fiber	Trademarks	Characteristics	Special Care Information
Modacrylic	Dynel Verel	Heat sensitive. High pile or furlike textures (usually found in rugs, bath mats).	Air dry or tumble on the Air Fluff (no heat) setting on the dryer.
Polyester	Blue C Dacron Fortrel Kodel T-1700 Vycron	Thermoplastic, resilient, nonabsorbent, strong. Attracts oily soil; yellows with age.	Pretreat soiled areas before laundering by rubbing full strength detergent into stain. If tumbled dry, no ironing is required. Restore whiteness by use of hot water, a generous amount of detergent, and chlorine bleach. Never use chlorine bleach on colored items containing polyester.
Nylon	Antron, Beauknit nylon, Blue C, Cadon, Cantrece, Caprolan, Celanese nylon, Cumuloft, Enka, Enkaloft, Enkalure, Enkatron, 501 Nylon, Jetspun, Nylex, Nyloft, Nytelle	Strongest known fiber, thermoplastic, resilient, non-absorbent. Available in wide variety of textures, weights, hands. Scavenger for color.	Launder colors separately to avoid color transfer. Wash white nylon separate from other fabrics. Tumble dry to avoid ironing.
Spandex	Blue C, Glospan, Lycra, Numa, Spandelle, Vyrene	Exceptionally strong, lightweight elastic fiber. Yellows with age.	Never use a chlorine bleach. Tumble dry.
Olefin	Herculon, Marvess, Meraklon, Polycrest, Vectra	Lightweight, strong, thermoplastic, nonabsorbent, heat sensitive.	Air dry or tumble on the Air Fluff (no heat) setting. Do not iron.

Glass

Fiber	Trademarks	Characteristics	Special Care Information
Glass	Fiberglas PPG Fiber Glass Vitron	Medium strength. Fibers may break under constant stress or flexing.	Do not dry clean. Keep agitation at a minimum. Transferred broken glass fragments may lodge in other items causing skin irritation.
	Fiberglas Beta	Soft hand, more resistant to breaking under constant stress or flexing than other glass fibers.	Fiberglas Beta may be machine washed and dried. Wash alone in full tub of water.

Metallic

Fiber	Trademarks	Characteristics	Special Care Information
Metallic	Lamé Lurex Nylco	Nontarnishable.	When used in washable fabric, metallic yarns need no special care.

suggested readings

American Home Economics Association. *Textile Handbook.* Washington, D.C.: American Home Economics Association, 1966.

Blum, Madeline, and Jean McLean. *Shopper's Handbook.* Extension Bulletin No. 1093. Ithaca, New York: Cornell University, New York State College of Home Economics, 1969.

Consumers All; The Official Consumer's Guide. New York: Pocket Books, Inc., 1965.

Labarthe, Jules. *Textiles: Origins to Usage.* New York: The Macmillan Company, 1964.

"Lighten Your Laundry Load." HE–67. Iowa State University Cooperative Extension Service, Ames, Iowa (March 1965).

The Maytag Encyclopedia of Home Laundry. 2d ed. New York: Popular Library, Inc., 1969.

Patrick, Julia M. *Distinctive Dress.* New York: Charles Scribner's Sons, 1969.

20

dress of the future

ow will clothing be produced and procured and what will be the nature of dress thirty, fifty, or one hundred years from now? A glimpse into the crystal ball of the future is a guess at best. Speculation based on current trends and technology is possible, but the very basis on which our predictions are made is constantly changing. The basic psychological, physical, and sociological needs of clothing as they exist today will continue to be met, but new needs unknown at this time are sure to evolve. If we could envision with any degree of accuracy the social, economic, and cultural factors that will influence clothing, we would know more truly what the future will bring. Styles will continue to mirror the societies that create them.

production

Current research in clothing production gives some clues to the future. The computer has already been utilized in pattern grading, that is, the changing of the master pattern to all necessary sizes. The computer also keeps records in factory

415

416   production. The use of this equipment has resulted in improved quality, reduced costs, and speeded-up manufacturing time.

The cutting of garments by water jet has been reported by *The Clothing Institute Journal*.[1] A 2-inch thick stack of cotton and nylon fabric consisting of fifty-five layers can be cut at 105 inches per minute. The laser technique for cutting is also under experiment. The search for practical substitutes to eliminate needles, thread, and stitching as a means of joining garment sections is also underway. These include fusing, ultrasonic seam welding, adhesives, molecular bonding, and laser seam joining.[2]

fabrics

By the year 2000 it has been estimated that the population will increase to six billion. Land area will be limited; priority on ground space will be restricted for the housing of human beings and the growing of food until synthetic foods become common. Precious ground space will be severely limited for use in the raising of cotton and flax and the grazing of sheep for wool. The restricted supply of these natural fibers will result in their becoming "status" fabrics, and only the affluent will be able to buy them.

Synthetics will replicate all the desirable properties of the natural fibers; in addition, they will have advantageous qualities not currently found in existing fibers. One of these characteristics will be thermoreactivity: the fibers will react and adjust to differing temperatures thus enabling the wearer to have physical comfort irrespective of the weather. Fibers and fabrics will be colorfast to everything, water repellent, absorbent, germicidal, antistatic, and fire resistant. Further, they will be photosensitive, able to change color. This will be accomplished by a few seconds' exposure in a "chroma-radiation box," found in every home closet.

The current trend toward the increased use of knits indicates that this type of fabric construction will soon predominate for all wearing apparel. Men's suits, shirts, and coats and all women's and children's clothing will be knitted.

Another type of fabric construction, the nonwoven fibers, will gain importance. (See Figures 20–1, 20–2, and 20–3.) Although in limited use today, these fabrics already represent a $500 million per year industry. Technological research is now finding ways to give these fabrics high strength, drapability, and a softer hand. Wearing comfort is provided by tiny holes which make the fabric

---

[1] **16**:20 (Jan.–Feb. 1968).

[2] "Alternate Methods of Seaming; Ultrasonics," *Journal of Apparel Research Foundation*, **3**:2.

20–1 This open-minded fashion by custom designer Judith Brewer of Beverly Hills is made of Kaycel. (Courtesy J. P. Stevens and Company)

20–2 A disposable shift is priced low enough to permit the economy-minded to toss it away after several wearings. (Courtesy J. P. Stevens and Company)

20–3 Nonwoven fabric of 93 per cent cellulose wadding and 7 per cent nylon mesh is both fire- and water-resistant. A snip of a scissors will modify the design. (Courtesy J. P. Stevens and Company)

418

"breatheable." Nonwovens already simulate chiffon and velvet, and a polycoated nonwoven is made for rainwear. Some of these fabrics are fire resistant, washable, and non-iron, and, in general, have overcome many of their original shortcomings. Low production costs due to heat-sealed seams will enable these garments to be sold at fifty cents to a dollar. Disposable nonwovens will become more generally acceptable when people cease to equate "throwaway" with the concept of being wasteful.

Stretchable spray-on fabric is another method by which clothing will be produced. The substance will be sprayed on to a collapsible form and will result in a molded stretch garment without seams, darts, or tucks. The molded dress became a reality in 1968 when French designer Pierre Cardin made a three-dimensional molded dress of Dynel stretch.

procurement of garments

Shopping for garments in years to come will be relatively easy when compared to methods used at the present time. Today we must go from shop to shop in search of a desired style, color, fabric, fit, and price. A projection of future garment making illustrated in *Textile World*[3] shows the following procedure. A customer will stand between a laser camera and a hologram. Beyond the hologram is a scanner which transcribes in three dimensions the contours of the customer. A computer programs the style, color, and material desired. Next, the pattern is made by a three-dimensional plotter generator. Following this a garment molder forms the custom-contoured garment.

style

The fictional space-entertainment programs on television have already projected clothing styles of the future. A thermocontrolled stretch body sheath may replace separate hosiery, bras, girdles, and slips. Covering the body sheath may be a short, decorated, tuniclike garment which can serve to satisfy the aesthetic needs of the individual. Men and women alike may be dressed in this costume. Controlled diets will eliminate the chubbies and skinnies, so that the body sheath will be visually attractive on all people.

[3] (April 1968), p. 90.

clothing maintenance

Trips to the dry cleaner and laundromat will be eliminated. The home garment-storage module will contain equipment that will bombard apparel with electronic rays, thus making it clean overnight. No other maintenance will be necessary as there will be no seams which can pull out. Rips and tears, though rare, will be fixed by the simple application of a transparent, fusible fixative which seals the fabric invisibly and permanently.

This concluding chapter has been a brief flight into fantasy. The futuristic projections of Da Vinci and his flying machine, Jules Verne and underwater travel, and the exploits of Buck Rogers became realities. Today's projections of the future may become tomorrow's actualities.

index

___

a